The Post-1945 Internationalization of Economics

The Post-1945 Internationalization of Economics

Annual Supplement to Volume 28
History of Political Economy

Edited by A. W. Coats

Duke University Press
Durham and London 1996

Contents

Preface

This volume contains the proceedings of the History of Political Economy conference held in the R. David Thomas Center at Duke University, 7–9 April 1995. The topic, The Post-1945 Internationalization of Economics, differs somewhat in nature and scope from its predecessors in this annual series. It is less concerned with the history of economic ideas as conventionally conceived than with aspects of economic education (which largely determines the supply of economists), the economist's role in policymaking (a crucial component in the demand for his or her services), and the sociology and professionalization of the discipline. These matters have rarely been considered in international terms.

The list of participants reflects the distinctiveness of the topic, for while academic historians of economics constituted the largest single element, the roster also included two sociologists and several economists who have spent most or all of their careers working in international agencies, in government service, or in the practice of policymaking. One of the conference's most gratifying features was the vigor and effectiveness with which this diverse group of participants interacted and collaborated. The Report of Discussions below will, it is hoped, give some idea of the character of these interactions.

This project follows logically, albeit with a substantial time lag, from earlier studies of the role of economists in ten national governments and in five international organizations.[1] Against this background it was an obvious step to consider the international spread of economic ideas and professional expertise. Equally obvious was the impossibility of examining more than a limited proportion of this huge field. Attention was focused on the post-1945 period because of the major developments that have occurred in the past half century; but no one has seriously claimed that the internationalization of economics began only after World War II. An initial paper on major changes in postwar graduate education in economics in the United States was an obvious requirement, given that country's preponderant influence on the development of the discipline at all levels. But beyond that, the potential range and variety of relevant subjects was virtually endless, and hard choices were unavoidable. As a result, the volume includes a limited selection of "country" studies that is neither random nor systematic; papers on three international bodies (two of which, the International Monetary Fund and World Bank, were considered, somewhat differently, in the above mentioned international agencies volume); and a miscellaneous group of topics that reveal some aspects of the field and the opportunities for further research.

Partly by chance, partly by design, disproportionate attention is devoted to Latin America, but this restriction is readily defensible. Arguably, the post-1945 internationalization of economics has proceeded further, more dramatically, and with greater effect on that continent than in any other region of comparable size. Second, the geographical concentration made it possible to discuss certain specific cases in greater depth than if we had striven to cover the entire globe. And third, the Latin American experience raises in an especially intriguing form the question of the relationship, if any, between internationalization and Americanization, a question that recurs intermittently in the papers and in the discussions. Preparations for the conference included consultations with and advice from *HOPE* editorial colleagues and a variety of other experts, and also, more unusually, three preliminary sessions on the internationalization theme at successive annual History of Economics Society conferences: at George Mason University in 1992; in Philadelphia in 1993, under the auspices of Temple University; and at Babson College in 1994. These

---

1. Coats 1981. Also in *History of Political Economy* 13.3:1 341–404. The countries included were Australia, Brazil, Great Britain, Hungary, India, Israel, Italy, Japan, Norway, United States. Coats 1986. The organizations examined were the United Nations, the International Monetary Fund, the World Bank, the GATT Secretariat, and the Organization for Economic Cooperation and Development.

occasions provided opportunities to review the potential content and scope of the project; consider problems of comparison, for example, among educational institutions, national economics policies, and the status of the economics profession in certain countries; and to present draft papers, some of which are included, in a substantially revised form, in this volume.

Many people and several organizations have contributed to the success of this internationalization conference. Generous financial support was provided by the Calvin K. Kazanjian Economics Foundation, the Lynde and Harry Bradley Foundation, the Josiah C. Trent Memorial Foundation, and the International Studies Center at Duke University. The facilities at the R. David Thomas Conference Center were ideal, and the staff was unobtrusively helpful. Beth Eastlick, managing editor of *HOPE*, played a major part in the conference organizing process, especially after I left Duke in June 1994; and she has undertaken the essential work necessary to see the manuscript through the press. My former colleague, Crauford D. Goodwin, editor of *HOPE*, gave valuable advice, especially in the early stages, and subsequently provided essential service as co-organizer.

Most of the papers were prepared well in advance of the meeting, and many have since been revised. Special thanks are due to Margaret de Vries and John Williamson, whose comments went well beyond their concluding statements below. Special mention is also due to Richard Webb, who, though not required to give a paper, drew fruitfully in the discussions upon his great practical experience. And finally, I would like to thank my wife, Sonia E. Coats, who managed the tape recorder and has been extremely helpful in interpreting the resulting sounds!

A. W. Coats

References

Coats, A. W., ed. 1981. *Economists in Government: An International Comparative Study*. Durham, N.C.: Duke University Press.

———. 1986. *Economists in International Agencies: An Exploratory Study*. New York: Praeger Scientific.

Part 1

Introduction

A. W. Coats

The internationalization of economics is a complex, multifaceted process that has not hitherto been subjected to close scholarly scrutiny. This is hardly surprising, for the subject cannot readily be confined within conventional disciplinary boundaries and is therefore unlikely to appeal to economists specializing in international affairs, or to historians of economics primarily interested in the development of economic ideas and policy. Internationalization is a broad, amorphous theme rather than a well-defined subject, and its scope is so wide that the papers in this volume are necessarily selective rather than representative, and in some instances largely exploratory. In addition to economic ideas and policy as conventionally interpreted, they focus heavily on the role of institutions with educational, governmental, and policy-making functions and responsibilities. The remarkable post–World War II expansion of universities and postgraduate education in economics has been an essential enabling factor determining the supply of trained personnel, and this can be viewed not merely as an aspect of the sociology of a particular profession but also as an integral component of the culture of modernization. The supply-side expansion has been a response to the rising demand for economists and the concomitant growth in the number and variety of their employment opportunities, both within and beyond academia. This has been a worldwide phenomenon, though its timing and extent has varied markedly from country to country.

Given the United States' predominant influence on the expansion and internationalization of economics during the past half century, the volume begins with William Barber's synoptic survey of changes in the content and scale of postgraduate economic education in that country. A phase of Keynesian hegemony and enthusiastic support for the so-called econometric revolution was followed by a noticeable decline in professional self-confidence and public esteem. Internal disputes between proponents of rival doctrines and a rising groundswell of complaints about the overemphasis on techniques and the narrowing of the curriculum has been accompanied by a marked decline in the proportion of American students studying for the Ph.D. in economics. The significance of this trend has been partly obscured by the striking growth in the number of foreign students, which is both a reflection of increasing internationalization and a significant portent for the future.

As is apparent from the eight studies in part 2, the process of internationalization has by no means obliterated national differences in the character and scale of economic education and in the public role of professional economists. Although not strictly representative, the selected examples constitute a sufficiently wide variety to convey a clear general impression of the international forces in operation. Within the group, Sweden, as depicted by Bo Sandelin and Ann Veiderpass, is the most fully Americanized, notwithstanding that country's distinctive and distinguished achievements in economics from the 1930s through the early 1950s. Since that time, the use of the English language and American ideas, techniques, and research styles in textbooks, economic journals, and academic dissertations has become almost overwhelming, albeit somewhat less so in the discussion of public policy issues. In the British case too, as reported by Roger Backhouse, there is abundant evidence of growing American influence since 1945, for example, in the transatlantic movement of personnel, in the authorship of articles in some leading economic journals (at least up to the 1960s; thereafter the evidence is mixed), and in the structure and content of advanced instruction and research. More recently, however, there have been signs of a somewhat closer relationship with Europe. Backhouse's data on transatlantic airfares and Anglo-American salary differentials is limited but novel and fascinating. There are serious grounds for concern at the increasing role of central government in determining the number of university institutions, in controlling university budgets, assessing research performance, and exerting pressure toward intra- and interuniversity competition. This is in direct conflict with Britain's long and proud tradition of academic freedom.

Both Peter Groenewegen and Pier Luigi Porta emphasize the differences between internationalization and Americanization. After the early postwar decades, when British ideas and practices were predominant in Australia (as in India, in Canada, and, of course, in the United Kingdom itself) there was a steady growth of American influence. Nowadays Australian economists publish more on theoretical topics, often in mathematical form, in a wider range of international economic journals; and they are becoming increasingly involved in, and see themselves as part of, a worldwide economic culture. Indeed, Groenewegen even refers to the "cloning" of Australian economics from its American role model (a term Young Back Choi also applies to economics in Korea). Nevertheless, Groenewegen considers Australian economics to be more European than American in certain respects—for example, in the importance attached to undergraduate teaching, the slower development of postgraduate work, and the tendency to focus on economic problems of special interest to Australians. He makes the significant observation that in the early postwar years—at least through to the late 1950s, the dollar shortage imposed severe restrictions on the import of American textbooks. More recently there has been a shift from Australian to American authors. This was probably true also of many countries, though it is not mentioned in the other papers. The Italian experience has been very different, for although American influence has been limited, international forces have been dominant intellectually both before and since 1945. For example, as Porta observes, there has been a long-standing Italian tradition of pure science in economics, and the important postwar neoclassical synthesis was essentially a reexported version of Keynesianism, with few distinctively American characteristics. Also Marxist ideas have continued to be both strong and distinctive. The rapid university expansion, the sweeping national educational reform of 1969, and the additional government measures of the 1980s have not fundamentally changed university structures or brought dramatic innovations. Economics has been slow to gain recognition as an independent subject, hence specialization has been limited. Teaching has remained weak, whereas research, especially on public policy issues, has flourished with the aid of a number of distinguished private foundations.

S. Ambirajan paints a gloomy picture of economics in India, a country where there is a vast gulf in quality between the best institutions and performers and the general "sea of mediocrity." Many Indian universities have low standards owing to a combination of inadequate resources, poor facilities, periodic interruptions to teaching, a rigid examination system, and political interference. Consequently, leading economics professors discourage their best students from accepting academic appointments. There are numerous able economists in government, think tanks, and the few centers of academic excellence. Many Indian economists have studied in the United States and settled there, or they have returned home to form a professional elite. Yet economics is essentially an alien product. Fashionable mathematical analysis and econometrics is less characteristic than a broader Oxford Philosophy, Politics and Economics (PPE) approach. Nevertheless the American professional model is gaining adherents. During the earlier postwar decades the demand for economists was stimulated by the development of economic planning, a program supported by the American government and private foundations. However in more recent years, as elsewhere, there has been a shift toward a more market-oriented approach.

Since 1945, when the traditional links with Japan were broken, American influence and connections have been dominant in Korea. Choi argues that economists with American Ph.D.s have enjoyed the greatest professional prestige and the greatest employment opportunities in the nation's capital, Seoul. However, participation in President Park's interventionist administration necessitated compromises with their free trade and market-oriented ideology. In Korea, economics has been viewed as a technology of development and has served both as a means of legitimation and a lingua franca. Although competition for credentials in economics is compatible with the tradition of competition in Confucian scholarship, Western analysis and technique is incompatible with the Confucian ideal of general wisdom. Whatever the reasons, few Korean economists have produced significant original work conceptually or in mathematical analysis or econometrics. Discussion has often been merely a rehash of American debates. In recent years there has been a reaction against American influence and a rise in the number and status of Korean-trained Ph.D.s.

In Japan, as in Korea, prewar international links in Asia were severed, and Aiko Ikeo notes that despite American dominance during the occupation period, Marxist economists obtained a secure and continuing hold in academia, initially enjoying prestige because they had opposed the old regime. They were heterogenous, but they formed and maintained associations and publications separate from those of the non-Marxists. The latter cooperated actively with the Americans during the postwar recovery and expansion, making important contributions to Japanese statistics and econometrics, as well as doing outstanding, internationally recognized work in mathematical economics. There has, however, been great dissatisfaction with many Japanese undergraduate and graduate schools, the latter being accused of sectarianism, inbreeding, and schizophrenia. These defects have enhanced the value of foreign, especially American, training for civil servants as well as academics. Despite major cultural and linguistic barriers, the internationalization process, including the use of English, has continued to grow. International journals were established from the 1930s and are quite distinct from the numerous poor quality, unrefereed, in-house academic departmental periodicals. By international standards, modern economics developed late in Brazil where, as in Italy, there was a dramatic expansion and significant reform of the universities from the late 1960s. Maria Rita Loureiro demonstrates that postgraduate training abroad or at home with the aid of American professors funded by the Ford Foundation or various American government supported agencies created a clearcut polarization between the Americanized and non-Americanized sectors of the profession, as is evident in the course content, reading lists, and publication records of the different species of university departments. Resistance to American cultural imperialism has centered on structuralist doctrine and interventionist policy measures. The first generation of Brazilian economists emerged within government agencies, and economic studies in Brazil have had close connections with political agendas. This was attributable to the authoritarian regime, the fragility of the party system, and the successful institutional work of some groups. In government, there is a distinction between career "economist employees" and "economist policymakers" who come from universities but rarely return there when their official employment ends. There is now a professional elite of "economist scholars," most of whom have an international reputation and strong connections with foreign economists or official bodies.

Part 3 examines three leading examples among the innumerable organizations that have contributed to the development and international dissemination of economic knowledge. In his account of the International Monetary Fund (IMF), Jacques Polak emphasizes the continuities between the prewar and postwar eras, arguing that the League of Nations Economic and Financial organization was a direct forerunner of the IMF. The latter's role in the dissemination process was significant but not dominant by comparison with the activities of academic economists, yet Polak attaches greater importance to the Fund's innovations in economic analysis relevant to international economic problems. For a considerable period, its staff enjoyed a comparative advantage over academics, partly because of their superior access to relevant data and to policy makers in a range of countries. Latterly, however, this differential has diminished as the Fund has become increasingly involved in the provision of technical and financial assistance, leaving its staff less time for research, while academics have had increased opportunities to work in the Fund. The IMF has been an important influence on the development of an international community of economists through its highly selective recruitment policy and the training it has provided for officials from member countries. It is an agency of internationalization not Americanization.

Barend de Vries's essay on the World Bank is far too densely packed and wide ranging to be characterized briefly. Since the 1950s, the World Bank's activities have expanded and diversified, and they continue to change (in certain areas, such as environmental conditions, poverty, and human resource issues). The World Bank's influence is enhanced by its production and dissemination of a huge volume of reports and research studies, including general analyses of countries, project and sector studies, analyses of trade orientation and incentives, external debt problems, and cross-country analyses. Although its contribution to the creation of new ideas is limited, the Bank "absorbs ideas from many places, integrates them in its operational practices, tests their practicality and provides a forum for interchange among academics and government officials" (236). Its training and technical assistance programs, policy and projects discussions, and the training provided by its Economic Development Institute all contribute to the internationalization process. The Bank has sometimes been slow in entering new fields and in some areas has lagged behind academic discussion. Its work cannot be viewed merely as a species of Americanization.

As the European Community is unfamiliar to many economists, Ivo Maes sketches its historical development and institutional structures. The central economic objective is integration, and this presents considerable difficulties given the member states' varied policy outlooks and priorities. The commission's economists are more diverse in background and views than their counterparts in national governments or in the IMF and World Bank—though this is less true of the commission's central research department concerned with economic and financial affairs. These economists are somewhat more European than American in their approach to the discipline, though this is less true of the younger generation, and there have been continuing disagreements over economic policy strategies between the so-called monetarists and the economists in the commission. However they require essentially the same skills (for example, communication, persuasion, teamwork) as economists in other large organizations. The member states' differing policy aims create difficulties for the process of integration, and the commission's economists are often called on to provide justification for political decisions. Maes provides an outline of the main stages toward European Monetary Union and the obstacles it has encountered. Part 4 contains four interconnected essays on various aspects of the internationalization process. Verónica Montecinos's title is self-explanatory, and her paper adds a sociological dimension to Arnold Harberger's upbeat account of policy changes in Latin America. It also has links with William Ascher's synoptic analysis of development doctrines and A. W. Coats's review of recent economic policy reform literature. Although disproportionate attention is devoted to Latin American experience and problems, a wider geographical spread would have entailed some sacrifice in depth.

Montecinos interprets the developments in Latin America since the 1930s as a political process involving a strategy of professionalization that, after decades of intra-professional struggle, has led to a convergence of viewpoints and approaches within an internationalized profession. Up to the 1970s, the predominant outlook was statist, nationalistic, and protectionist, centering on the Economic Commission for Latin America (ECLA) structuralist school with its international staff, publications, training center, educational programs, and policy initiatives. From the mid-1950s, however, a rival orthodox North American–based countermovement emerged with a similar aim of utilizing economic ideas to modernize economic practices and institutions. Denying the validity of a Latin American economics, it employed a universal, purportedly ideology-free science to legitimize liberalization and the promotion of free enterprise and foreign capital, and to purge economics of leftist ideological bias. More recently a more pragmatic, less doctrinaire approach has developed among the neo-liberals, while the heterodox economists too have made efforts to incorporate themselves into the international community, for example by acquiring North American educational credentials.

According to Harberger, good economics in Latin America dates from 1955 when he and a group of colleagues inaugurated the famous "Chicago Boys" project in Chile. At that time, the region was experiencing severe economic problems resulting from the prevailing influence of interventionism, paternalism, nationalism, and socialism (see Montecinos, this volume). Successive phases of economic reform in the 1960s, 1970s, and 1980s brought major improvements in economic policies and conditions, although Harberger concedes that further progress is needed in the control of inflation, effective banking regulations, and capital controls. Reform was based on twin revolutions in economic training and economic policy. The structuralist approach lacked clear definition and rigorous analysis, and involved philosophical thinking and left-wing ideological bias rather than the technical Chicago-style analysis emphasizing the virtues of markets, trade liberalization, and privatization. There has been a gradual spread of North American–type economics training and the emergence of competent university departments in the region, so that Latin American economists are increasingly recognized as part of a world profession. Many examples of key thinkers and policy makers are cited; and the editor was especially interested in Harberger's brief reference to the role of economic teams (see Coats, this volume).

Ascher's review of postwar development doctrines argues that the structuralist and neoclassical approaches are not antithetical, as is often claimed. Indeed, over time they have been converging toward the neoclassical mainstream, and many economists could be classified under either label. As applied to developing countries, neoclassical economics has absorbed theoretical elements alien to its core principles, and the connections between economic theories, analytical approaches, and policy prescriptions are often very loose. Development economics has shifted from bold theories to an emphasis on techniques, as is evident in the dissertations produced by young recruits to the field. But calculations of rates of return can easily be manipulated, and decisions on project and policy selection are often governed by organizational and political judgments rather than technical considerations, and the same is true of the new antipoverty strategy. The direct association of neoclassical economics with income regressivity is an oversimplification. Some of the earlier failures of statist policies were due to political factors rather than to economists' ideas. However, neoclassical economists are methodological optimists but political and administrative pessimists. Development economists' policy advice is often split between doctrinaire exhortations that governments ought to eliminate policy distortions and practical work that takes these distortions as given. Economic policy reform is, or should be, the economics profession's *raison d'être*. Coats's review of the recent literature shows how the accumulated experience of economic policy experiments during the past two decades has inspired efforts to synthesize the results and generalize about the reasons for success or failure. John Williamson's concept of the Washington consensus (see Coats, appendix A) is a conspicuous example, one that has stimulated much discussion and critical examination. Recent research has been more particularistic, context dependent, empirically grounded, and historically sensitive than earlier work. Substantial efforts have been made to understand the respective roles of ideas, interests, and institutions as well as the interactions between economic and political factors. The part played by economic teams is of special interest to historians of economics. Simplistic public choice and other economistic interpretations have been discredited, and the multiple uses of the term political economy has been a source of confusion (see Coats, appendix B).

Postwar Changes in American Graduate Education in Economics

William J. Barber

One suspects that there would be little dissent from the general proposition that the center of gravity in the world community of economists in the past half-century has been located in the United States. It has not always been so. For the first century and a quarter of the nation's existence, the United States had been a net importer of economic ideas—primarily from Britain and, to a lesser extent, from France and Germany. It is at least arguable that this situation persisted, with British ideas again playing the lead role, until the end of World War II. Since then, however, the intellectual fertility of American economists has positioned the country to be a net exporter.

A useful barometer with respect to the more recent past is the success ratio of American economists with the Nobel Prize selectors. Twenty-six of the thirty-eight who have been accorded this distinction have pursued their profession in the United States. It should be noted, however, that the American position in this competition has been enhanced by the nation's hospitality to the talents of immigrants. Eight of the winners elected from the United States were born abroad. Even so, the American environment has contributed to their professional development. In all probability, the resources it could supply to support their scholarly endeavors were superior to those that would have been available to them in their countries of origin. By the same token, the United States has been the pacesetter in developing advanced programs of professional training and in opening opportunities to graduate students from abroad as well as at home. All of this would appear to testify to American supremacy in the discipline.[1]

Other evidence reinforces this conclusion. It has been pointed out, for example, that the 1986 edition of the *Who's Who in Economics* (edited by Mark Blaug and P. Sturges), in which inclusion is determined by frequency of citation counts, situated about two-thirds of the living economists deemed eminent by this measure in the United States (Portes 1987). American journals have also become the mainstays of professional communication. Citation count data for the period 1975–80, for example, indicated that American publications then overwhelmed the rest of the field in their impact (Liebowitz and Palmer 1984). This result was reaffirmed when a similar exercise on journal impacts was performed for the period 1970–90 (Laband and Piette 1994).

Even though various types of quantitative measures point to a common finding—namely, the postwar predominance of American economics on the world scene—it by no means follows that this phenomenon has been universally applauded. The measurable magnitudes, after all, do not capture the quality of professional contributions. It is not surprising that some Europeans should raise questions about the longer-term significance of the economics produced in postwar America. Nor should the indictment that American culture has tended to overvalue "marginal innovations" and to be excessively preoccupied with the trendy and the transient be dismissed out of hand. One European critic—who is certainly not alone in his views—has sharply criticized the intellectual perversity of the American academic incentive structure, which he perceives as "attach[ing] all the rewards of research—salary, fame, location—to producing fast within the received epistemological and ideological framework." In his judgment, "this system certainly induces work, but one which is conformist with respect to topic, method, aim, ideology, etc.; it is a disincentive for taking the time and effort of looking deeply, with the required culture and multidimensionality, into the basic causes, situation, and nature of economic questions. . . . Indeed, the fact that mathematical exercises are easier to classify and grade than philosophical developments or social insights probably accounts for the detrimental neglect of these latter tools as compared to the former one" (Kolm 1988, 210).

1. It is worth noting as well that only four of the non-American Nobel laureates made their major contributions after World War II; by contrast, all of the American winners were recognized for postwar achievements.

Before attempts are made to evaluate the significance of all of this for the fate of the discipline, it is appropriate to review the manner in which the professional preparation of economists has evolved in the United States in the second half of the twentieth century and the ways in which graduate programs have responded to the various challenges put before them. Along the way, there will be occasion to observe some of the more idiosyncratic features of a number of academic institutions. Reconfigurations in the "map" of American graduate education will also be noted, with data points taken at two-decade intervals. The moments selected roughly coincide with ones at which leaders in the nation's economics profession have deemed it timely to assess the "state of the art" and its prospects.

Challenges in the Early Postwar Years

Post-1945, the most immediate problem facing those responsible for the design of graduate education in economics concerned the treatment to be accorded to the Keynesian "revolution." Most of the standard academic programs had not been receptive to this analytic innovation in its early going. After 1937, Alvin Hansen's Fiscal Policy Seminar at Harvard was an exception, but it was atypical of mainstream academia. The bulk of the economists established in the academy were skeptical—if not actively hostile—to the claims of a "new economics." Keynesian-style thinking in the United States instead secured its first beachheads in the Washington bureaucracy. Its message was readily absorbed by a fair number of younger economists who were there either because the universities had no jobs to offer or because potential academic employers had no taste for their views. It is a telling comment on the climate of the late 1930s that none of the junior Harvard economists who participated in drafting one of the pioneering American statements of Keynesian doctrine—*An Economic Program for American Democracy*, published in 1938—achieved tenured status at Harvard.

The end of World War II gave a different twist to matters. Higher education was then experiencing a massive expansion in the demand for its services, fed in large measure by a population of veterans who were beneficiaries of government scholarships provided under the terms of the GI Bill. This produced a bull market for academic personnel. At the same time, Keynesian-type analysis was too visible to be ignored. The faculties mounting the leading graduate programs in economics were thus obliged to think hard about their intellectual identities.

Though various graduate departments confronted common problems, there was a considerable divergence in the ways they elected to deal with them. In a number of instances, the paths chosen bore the markings of an institutional style that had been defined earlier. Harvard, as had been the case when it modernized its curriculum in the late nineteenth century, moved with the times more readily than most. Hansen, whose credentials as a Keynesian "convert" were unimpeachable, was secure in his base there, and Arthur Smithies, a Bureau of the Budget veteran, was soon to be so as well. Harvard's reputation for a cosmopolitan eclecticism was damaged, however, when it allowed Paul Samuelson, whose textbook was to become a major vehicle for the transmission of Keynesian ideas, to escape to the Massachusetts Institute of Technology, where he put in place a formidable Ph.D. program. Nevertheless, the Harvard economics department had to endure a vociferous attack from a group of alumni (organized under the title of the Committee of One Hundred) who branded it a hotbed of radical Keynesianism that posed a threat to the tried-and-true virtues of the American free-enterprise system.

Yale proceeded cautiously, as it had in the late nineteenth century when under pressure to reform its traditional curriculum to make room for political economy. At the end of the war, its departmental power structure was dominated by the triumvirate of Fairchild, Furniss, and Buck, authors of a textbook that remained one of the more widely read statements of neoclassical orthodoxy. With Kent Healy (whose specialty was railway transportation) in its old guard, Yale also sustained a curricular commitment dating from Arthur T. Hadley's initiatives in the 1880s. But the academic year 1950–51 widened space for change when James Tobin's recruitment from Harvard ensured strong representation for the new macroeconomic perspective.

Stiff resistance to Keynesian ideas, however, characterized the positions of a number of institutions occupying important space on the Ph.D. production line. At the University of Chicago, Milton Friedman's arrival in 1946 (following wartime service in Washington) added a powerful anti-Keynesian voice that kept faith with the legacy of Henry C. Simons. Senior members of the University of Wisconsin's economics department were also disposed to distance themselves from the Keynesian "revolution," but for a different reason. As they saw matters, Wisconsin's primary mission should be to keep alive the flame of John R. Commons's institutionalism. And there were moments in the later 1940s and early 1950s when the competing claims for turf asserted by guardians of an older tradition on the one hand and by a younger breed of Keynesians on the other turned ugly. For example, the story of the University of Illinois's systematic purge of Keynesian sympathizers is not an attractive one.

Conditions such as these prompted a number of the profession's elders to encourage reflection on the direction in which graduate education ought to go. With this end in view, the executive committee of the American Economic Association commissioned a study, to be prepared by Howard R. Bowen (then at Williams College), which was launched in the academic year 1950–51.[2] Bowen's report stressed the importance of reaching for common ground in graduate programs, while recognizing simultaneously "the great virtue in diversity and in division of labor." He was well aware of the "substantial differences among the various graduate departments of economics, not only in their practices, but even in their objectives." But he did not recommend a standardized conformity: instead he sought to specify "the irreducible minimum in the program of education for persons who are to be entitled to call themselves 'economists'" (1953, iv-v). Bowen's conception of the objectives of professional training was as follows:

> [T]here is a substantial nucleus of subject matter which should be common to all economists regardless of their special interests. It is this common core which should bind the profession together and should enable economists of all types and persuasions to communicate with one another. This common core consists primarily of economic theory including value, distribution, money, employment, and at least a nodding acquaintance with some of the more esoteric subjects such as dynamics, theory of games, and mathematical economics. Other important parts of the core are economic history, history of economic thought, statistics, and research methods. No one has a claim to a Ph.D. in economics without a rigorous initiation into these fields.(42–43)

This proposal could certainly not be faulted for failure to think on a

2. Members of an advisory committee recommending that this project be undertaken included G. L. Bach (Carnegie Institute of Technology), Milton Friedman (University of Chicago), I. L. Sharfman (University of Michigan), and J. J. Spengler (Duke). D. Gale Johnson (University of Chicago) participated as an alternate to Friedman.

grand scale. Bowen himself was aware of impediments to its widespread adoption. His canvass of opinion on the content of the "common core," he reported, had led him to conclude that "economic theory is the only subject which all agree should be included." He suspected as well "that there was considerable difference of opinion also on the *kind* of economic theory that should be included" (105, 106; emphasis in original).

The vision of an ideal graduate program, as projected by Bowen, proved not to be a good predictor of the turn events were to take. Bowen was closer to the mark, however, in his views about the standard to be expected from a doctoral dissertation. In the immediate postwar years, it remained the case that most degree candidates were expected to deliver a scholarly project with the dimensions of a substantial monograph, if not a book, which purportedly advanced knowledge. In Bowen's view, this expectation was unrealistic: the dissertation should be reconceived as a modest exercise that demonstrated competence in research methods.[3]

Brief attention should also be paid to the operational scale of the economics doctoral industry nationally in the early postwar period. An impression of the general pattern can be conveyed through an inspection of table 1. By comparison with what was to come, several features of the scene at midcentury are noteworthy. Both the number of degrees awarded and the number of institutions awarding them were a fraction of the respective magnitudes to be reached in the decades ahead. The dominating position of a small number of producers was also arresting. In the immediate postwar years, four of them accounted for nearly 39 percent of the national output. By contrast, the small-scale operators— the 44 "firms" producing fewer than twenty doctorates over a five-year span—graduated collectively a total of only four more degree recipients than did the single largest operator.

Shifts in the Landscape in the 1950s and 1960s

A second revolution in the way professional economics was conceptualized gathered momentum in the 1950s. The foundations for an "econometric revolution" had been laid in the 1930s with the formation of the Econometrics Society and with the creation of the Cowles Commission,

3. In this connection, Bowen observed that "we cannot hope to make every Ph.D. into a Wesley Mitchell or a J. M. Keynes. We can, however, insist that they know something about the basic methods of research in economics and that they be able to apply these methods in relatively limited research situations" (1953, 48).

Table 1   Doctorates Awarded, 1945–46 to 1950–51

	Total (5 academic years)	Annual Average
Harvard	257	51.4
Columbia	132	26.4
Chicago	95	19.0
Wisconsin	92	18.4
Cornell	68	13.6
Illinois	66	13.2
Minnesota	48	9.6
Ohio State	47	9.4
New York University	46	9.2
Iowa	46	9.2
Pennsylvania	42	8.4
California (Berkeley)	40	8.0
Michigan	33	6.6
Texas	32	6.4
Iowa State	27	5.4
Purdue	25	5.0
Virginia	25	5.0
Yale	24	4.8
Northwestern	23	4.6
MIT	21	4.2
Radcliffe	21	4.2

"Four-firm Concentration Ratio" = .39.
Aggregate number awarded (5 academic years): 1,492.
Annual average: 298.4.
Total number of institutions conferring doctorates (5-year period): 65.
Number of institutions awarding <20 per 5-year period: 44.
Aggregate number of doctorates awarded by the 44 institutions: 260.
Source: Bowen 1953: 209–10. Degrees awarded by certain Canadian
institutions were reported in the *AER*, but are excluded from the
tabulations reported here.

which offered generous support for quantitative research. After World
War II, some members of the younger generation found it easy to meld
econometric techniques with the new macroeconomic perspective. But

the two "revolutions" did not necessarily move in tandem. Keynes's own tilts with Tinbergen's procedures in the late 1930s provide a reminder that champions of these respective causes need not be natural allies.

Over time, econometrics—and the mastery of sophisticated mathematical techniques that it required—was to play a more formidable and more durable role in transforming the shape of graduate studies in economics than did Keynesianism. But there were some uncertain moments along the way, as the story of the Cowles Commission in the 1950s attests. The Cowles commitment to fundamental mathematical and quantitative research was never in question. But, for a season, its institutional affiliations and its relationship to the profession at large were in need of some sorting out.

At the end of the war, the Cowles Commission was affiliated with the University of Chicago (an arrangement dating from 1939). A comfortable equilibrium in this relationship, however, had proved to be elusive. At Chicago, Frank Knight echoed Simon's skepticism toward the claims of the quantifiers. There was also a built-in friction between the aspirations of a number of Cowles's economists (among them, Jacob Marschak and Tjallings Koopmans) who hoped that econometrics would provide a "scientific" basis for policy intervention on the one hand and a Chicago point of view as articulated by Friedman et al. on the other.[4] The search for a new home for Cowles was accelerated when the University of Chicago's economics department refused to accept a dissertation submitted by a member of the Cowles staff, Harry M. Markowitz. In 1990, this treatise on portfolio theory contributed to the Swedish Academy's decision to confer a Nobel Prize on Markowitz. But in the judgment of Chicago's economics faculty nearly four decades earlier, it was not acceptable as economics, though it might be as mathematics. (A version of this dissertation was, however, allowed to qualify for the Ph.D. in economics in 1955, by which time the Cowles Commission had decamped from Chicago.)

From one point of view, Yale might have been regarded as an appropriate alternate site for the Cowles enterprise. The founding donor, Alfred Cowles, was a Yale graduate, indeed, he had proposed to locate the program in New Haven before he had positioned it at Chicago. Yale had not warmed to that proposition in 1939, but when the offer was renewed fifteen years later, the climate had changed. James Tobin, already on the scene, was named director and Koopmans, Marschak, and Gerard Debreu

4. Aspects of the history of the Cowles Commission are treated in Epstein 1987.

migrated east, where they were assimilated into the Yale faculty. Yale thus embraced disciplinary novelty with considerably greater alacrity than it had displayed in the late nineteenth century. Yet, in one respect, an aspect of its earlier institutional character remained intact. Change could be more readily accommodated when someone else picked up the tab: this was just as true in the mid-twentieth century as it had been in the late nineteenth century.[5]

In the later 1950s, the econometric "revolution" effectively snuffed out a tradition at one institution that had long spoken with a distinctive voice. As Wisconsin's departmental chair, Edwin Witte had continued to call for a reinvigoration of the local brand of institutionalism. But his efforts were undone by the revolt of his younger colleagues and by university administrators who were convinced that the department risked acquiring a reputation as an intellectual backwater unless it broke new ground on the quantitative frontier. Wisconsin, along with most other long-standing graduate programs, thus moved toward the mainstream with the emphasis on the "high technique."[6]

The drive toward pushing the discipline to ever higher levels of abstraction in these years was inspired in large measure by a desire to establish its standing as "science." In the 1950s, it is at least possible that another factor—and a less noble one—was at work: namely, an attempt to use the mantle of "scientific neutrality" as protective camouflage during the academic freedom and governmental loyalty scares of the McCarthy era. As Harry G. Johnson noted in an essay prepared on the occasion of the nation's bicentennial, this consideration had "been virtually ignored because of an academic conspiracy of silence." He was persuaded that something more than a dispassionate pursuit of knowledge affected professional practice in this period. During the witch-hunting days, in Johnson's view, American economists were made aware that it was

5. In the 1870s and 1880s, the Yale administration had vigorously resisted an opening of undergraduate curricular space to the teaching of such "modern" subjects as political economy. The official line then was that the traditional path toward a B.A., with its required classical courses, should not be compromised. By contrast, Harvard had already implemented the elective system. Yale still made nominal faculty appointments that gave political economy a presence in the university. This was initially allowed to happen when instruction was made available in the graduate school or in the Scientific School (and thus out of range of contaminating the core of the undergraduate college). Yale also preferred that funding for such initiatives not be a charge against the university's budget. A loyal alumnus who had stepped forward as a willing "angel" was instrumental in making this possible.

6. This episode is recounted in Lampman 1993.

"prudent . . . to confine their attention to 'scientific' problems and [to] steer clear of issues that might raise suspicions about loyalty" (1977, 25).

The early 1960s witnessed a revival of national self-confidence in the United States. And with it came a rejuvenated sense that expertise, guided by the insights of science, could solve the bulk of the world's problems. Economists in the Kennedy administration had managed to acquire greater leverage in the corridors of power than their predecessors in Washington had ever enjoyed and their initial success in macroeconomic management offered promise that "fine-tuning" could combine full-employment growth with price stability. With this turn of events, the prestige of the profession in the United States had never stood higher. Aspiring professionals entered the graduate school pipeline in record numbers at a time when public sector largesse—supplemented by major injections of private foundation funding—generated noteworthy expansion in the number of institutions mounting economics doctoral programs and in the number of student places they could offer. The "take-off" was dramatic in the mid-1960s. Data published by the Department of Education indicate that earned doctorates in economics, which had usually been in the range of 200 to 250 in the 1950s, reached 600 in the academic year 1967–68 and fell just short of 800 in 1969–70 (1992, table 281 and 294). Table 2, which captures some details of doctorate production in 1970–71, as reported by the American Economic Association, tells a similar story.

For the American academic community, these were vintage years. The expansionist optimism of the mid-1960s was reflected in a remark by a senior administrator in the University of California system, who then predicted that that state alone could absorb all of the Ph.D. output of the United States for the rest of the century! This projection was treated with the utmost seriousness at the time. It was in such an atmosphere that institutions that had not been substantial players in the Ph.D. business could leap to get on the bandwagon. By 1970–71, doctoral programs in economics that had been expanded and/or brought "on stream" during the euphoria of the mid-1960s left a considerable mark on the national scene. The increased weight of public sector institutions in the aggregate was particularly striking (see table 2).

As far as graduate education in economics was concerned, more than an enlargement in scale was involved here. Institutions aspiring to be on the cutting edge typically intensified the emphasis on mathematical techniques in their graduate programs. It was small wonder then that

Table 2   Doctorates Awarded, 1970–71

Harvard	64
Michigan State	62
California (Berkeley)	58
Purdue	43
Cornell	37
George Washington University	33
Pennsylvania	29
Minnesota	24
Alabama	23
Stanford	22
Columbia	19
Michigan	19
Wisconsin	19
Chicago	17
Duke	17
Yale	17
Florida	16
Washington State	16
Colorado	15
North Carolina	15
Iowa State	14
Illinois	14
Princeton	14
University of Southern California	14
Kansas State	13
Northwestern	13
Ohio State	13
Missouri	12
Oregon	12
Boston College	11
Indiana	11
Texas	10

"Four-firm Concentration Ratio" =. 26.

Aggregate number awarded: 889.

Total number of institutions conferring doctorates: 80.

Number of reporting institutions awarding <10 but >0 doctorates in 1970–71: 48.

Aggregate number of doctorates awarded by the 48 institutions: 173.

Source: "Sixty-Eighth List of Doctoral Dissertations in Political Economy in American Universities and Colleges"1971: 990–1064. Degrees awarded by certain Canadian institutions were reported in the *AER*, but are excluded from the tabulations reported here. No Yale Ph.D.s were reported in the *AER*'s listing for the academic year 1970–71. The data for Yale were obtained from the Registrar of Graduate Studies, Yale University.

instruction in this subject matter tended to displace what had once been held to be a standard part of the curricular menu, such as courses in the history of economic thought and in economic history. Revision was also under way in the type of scholarly exercise expected from doctoral candidates. The substantial treatise of an earlier day had generally yielded to shorter "essays" that demonstrated the candidate's technical sophistication. The language of Yale's Graduate School Bulletin for 1963–64 exemplified this trend: "The length and character of the dissertation will vary with the topic chosen. The student is advised, however, that an exhaustive treatise is in no sense required and that a short, sharply focused, and tightly organized study is preferred."[7]

An aspect of the temper of the 1960s is reflected in the manner in which members of the first team in American economics then chose to set new sights for the profession. The discipline's solid achievements seemed to be a matter of record and the payoff to society from economic research appeared to be established beyond peradventure. In that spirit, a study group operating in the later 1960s under the auspices of the National Academy of Sciences and the Social Science Research Council argued that a major expansion in doctoral programs in economics was in the national interest and projected an output of 1,700 doctorates by 1977 (up from an actual output of 680 in 1967) (Ruggles 1970, 15–16).[8] This panel recommended immediate action on the part of the federal government to develop a national economic database; governmental and foundation funding for large-scale social science research centers; and cooperative action by universities and government to provide computer facilities for economic research. With respect to the professional training of economists, the panel spoke as follows: "The panel recommends that departments of economics reorient graduate training toward providing more competence in research method and more research experience. Greater emphasis needs to be placed upon the tools—mathematics, statistics, econometrics, computer programming—required for research, and participation in research projects should occur at an earlier stage in the graduate program" (177). This was indeed a far cry from Bowen's "model" of an ideal doctoral program of the early 1950s.

7. The description of the requirements for the Ph.D. in economics contains these words. See *Bulletin of the Graduate School, Yale University, 1963–64.*

8. Other contributors to this volume were Robert M. Solow, James Tobin, Dale W. Jorgenson, Guy H. Orcutt, James N. Morgan, Henry Theil, Gardiner Ackley, Richard E. Caves, Joseph A. Pechman, Jerome Rothenberg, M. W. Reder, Vernon W. Rattan, Hollis B. Chenery, and Arnold C. Harberger.

Sea Changes in the 1970s and 1980s

The vision of the future—at least with respect to operational scale—projected by the economics panel serving the National Academy of Sciences and the Social Science Research Council was to bear little more relation to the subsequent realities than the one Bowen had sketched out earlier. Events in the 1970s suggested that dismalness may not, after all, have been banished from the "dismal science." Indeed the economics profession was to be bruised by turmoil in American society at large and by the "stagflationist" performance of the economy.

The generally "upbeat" mood that had prevailed in the academy in the middle 1960s was dealt a rude blow by the outbursts of campus protests against war in Southeast Asia and in support of the objectives of the civil rights movement. As depicted by the "New Left," established economists preferred rigor to relevance and thus had nothing constructive to contribute to discourse on the pressing social problems of the day. Still worse, mainstream economics was portrayed as offering little more than an apologia for the status quo: indeed, its critics in the student generation regarded it as an obstacle to radical reforms that were allegedly essential and one that should be removed. This cast of mind even disturbed the usual decorum of the American Economic Association: witness the association's annual business meetings, circa the early 1970s. In more ordinary times, these sessions struggled to get a quorum adequate to approve a series of pro forma reports. But these times were not ordinary. Unless the AEA's officers took pains to mobilize mainstream supporters, the business meetings could easily be taken over by younger members (and particularly by graduate students) urging the association to adopt an official position attacking U.S. foreign policy and denouncing manifestations of racism, sexism, and so on in American society. Few present at one of the business meetings in those years are likely to forget the plaintive observations of the AEA's secretary-treasurer. He had been instructed by the executive committee to introduce a motion calling for an increase in the association's annual dues while retaining the policy of offering membership to graduate students at half the standard rate. This ran counter to his personal preferences: given his druthers, he would have set the charge to graduate students at four times the standard rate!

The behavior of the economy in the 1970s also dimmed the profession's earlier luster. There were no policy successes to brag about when both the inflation rate and the unemployment rate rose simultaneously. In these years, a standard theme of presidential addresses to various professional organizations was a lament about the "state" of economics. Meanwhile the labor market for economists had softened, as belt-tightening had again become the order of the day in most colleges and universities. The boom years of ever-expanding budgets and enrollments had ended.

This reversal in climate left its imprint on what graduate programs in economics were to offer. The thrust toward emphasis on technique, which was then well nigh universal, did not diminish. But a sharpened differentiation in the intellectual orientations of various departments became a more significant part of their respective identities. Within the profession, a sometime Keynesian "consensus" was already extinct at the time when President Richard M. Nixon pronounced that "we are all Keynesians now." The distinction drawn in the early 1970s between "saltwater economics" and "freshwater economics" is worth recalling in this connection. The saltwater variety was presumed to be Keynesian—for example, at Harvard, MIT, Yale, and Stanford—whereas the freshwater variety was monetarist—the University of Chicago, the St. Louis Federal Reserve. Imperfect as these characterizations may have been, they still captured some of the flavor of the polemical warfare of the period, though they certainly did not capture it all. The late Murray Rothbard of the Von Mises Institute at the University of Nevada, Las Vegas, challenged the validity of such labeling. From the perspective of his brand of Austrianism, Keynesians and monetarists were fundamentally at one when tolerating a role for government: whatever its predispositions in other respects, the Chicago School accepts the existence of a central bank and assigns it some functions. Rothbard maintained that the real distinction was between "watered" economics and "no water" economics at UNLV. Meanwhile the turbulence of the 1970s heightened the prominence of two graduate programs—the New School for Social Research and the University of Massachusetts (Amherst)—that provided hospitality to critical perspectives from the vantage point of the New Left.

During the decades of the 1970s and 1980s, there was little change in the aggregate flow of graduate students through doctoral programs. Even in the peak years, the total doctoral output never got much more than halfway toward the target of 1,700 that the expansionists of the late 1960s had projected by 1977. Nevertheless, fundamental changes were underway in the composition of the graduate student population. Between the mid-1970s and the mid-1980s, the proportion of women in the doctoral graduating classes more than doubled (though women still accounted for slightly less than one-fifth of the aggregate in 1986). Even more arresting was the fall in the representation of U.S. citizens in the flow of economics doctorates: in 1977, about two-thirds of the doctorates were Americans, but by 1989 they represented less than half of the total (Hansen 1991, 1057–58). This shift in the "mix" toward a rising percentage of graduate students for whom English was not a first language can reasonably be presumed to have had some programmatic implications. As one informed observer has commented, "it is conceivable . . . that the content of graduate economics shifted somewhat to accommodate the changing mix of students by emphasizing quantitative rather than verbal skills and theoretical rather than institutional knowledge"(1058).

In the late 1980s, there was evidence of disquiet within the profession in the United States about the larger consequences of the priority assigned in graduate education to the mastery of techniques, as opposed to engagement with "real world" problems. This situation prompted officers of the American Economic Association to create a commission to investigate the existing state of affairs. The background studies conducted by W. Lee Hansen, who served as executive secretary of the AEA's Commission on Graduate Education in Economics, were particularly enlightening on two points. In the first instance, data gathered on what actually went on in graduate education pointed to the conclusion that there was a remarkable similarity in practice across institutions. This finding was based on surveys of requirements for degrees, on inspections of course syllabi, and on reviews of the content of examinations. But perhaps this tendency toward programmatic homogeneity should not have come altogether as a surprise. Structural change in the doctorate producing "industry" over the postwar years had been associated with expansion in the number of "firms" and with reduction in the "four-firm concentration ratio" (see table 3). With the market replicating competitive conditions more closely, a higher degree of product standardization might have been expected. A second finding drew attention to genuine differences between departments, notwithstanding homogeneity in the structure and content of their graduate programs. The differentiating features to which Hansen assigned important weight turned on indices of faculty quality (as evidenced by research productivity) and of student quality (as evidenced, for example, by scores on the Graduate Record Examination). Five "quality tiers" could thus be constructed. The contribution of institutions in tiers 1, 2, and 3 to the output of doctorates in 1990–91 is shown in table 4. If one takes these categories at face value, it would appear that the qualitatively inferior institutions then contributed nearly half of the national output.

Table 3   Doctorates Awarded, 1990–91

Harvard	57
Minnesota	37
Michigan	33
Stanford	31
Pennsylvania	30
California (Berkeley)	29
MIT	26
UCLA	25
Cornell	24
Chicago	23
Wisconsin	23
Ohio State	22
Purdue	21
South Carolina	19
Illinois	18
Colorado	15
Duke	15
New School for Social Research	15
Michigan State	14
Pittsburgh	14
Washington State	14
Boston University	13
Washington University (St. Louis)	13
Columbia	12
Iowa State	12
New York University	12
Florida State	11
Indiana	11
Princeton	11
Rutgers	10
SUNY (Buffalo)	10
Yale	10

"Four-firm Concentration Ratio" = .17.

Aggregate number awarded: 912.

Number of institutions conferring doctorates: 96.

Number of reporting institutions awarding <10 but >0 doctorates in 1990–91: 64.

Aggregate number of doctorates awarded by the 64 institutions: 282.

Source: "Doctoral Dissertations in Economics: Eighty-eighth Annual List" 1991:2076–2104. Degrees awarded by certain Canadian institutions were reported in the *JEL* but are excluded from the tabulations reported here.

Table 4   Doctorates Awarded, 1990–91, Distributed by "Quality Tiers"

Tier 1		
Chicago	23	
Harvard	57	
MIT	26	
Princeton	11	
Stanford	31	
Yale	10	
Total	158	(share of aggregate number of doctorates awarded: 17.3%)

Tier 2		
Columbia	12	
Michigan	33	
Minnesota	37	
Northwestern	5	
Pennsylvania	30	
Rochester	0	
California (Berkeley)	29	
UCLA	25	
Wisconsin	23	
Total	194	(share of aggregate number of doctorates awarded: 21.2%)

Tier 3		
Brown	6	
Cal. Tech	3	
Carnegie-Mellon	3	
Cornell	24	
Duke	15	
Illinois	18	
Johns Hopkins	6	
Maryland	11	
New York University	12	
North Carolina	3	
UC (San Diego)	6	
Virginia	8	
Virginia Polytech	0	
Washington (Seattle)	5	
Total	120	(share of aggregate number of doctorates awarded: 13.2%)

Share of aggregate number of doctorates awarded by 15 institutions in tier 4, 37 institutions in tier 5, and by 16 institutions regarded as not important enough to classify by tier: 48.3%.

Source: Doctoral Dissertations in Economics: Eighty-eight Annual List. 1991. "Quality Tiers" are those of Hansen (1991, 1055).

The "Report of the Commission on Graduate Education" (1991) offered some sobering reflections. Its authors expressed "fear . . . that graduate programs may be turning out a generation of too many *idiot savants*, skilled in technique but innocent of real economic issues" and recommended adjustments in the instructional balance to give greater weight to the "real world" (1044—45).[9] In the absence of such reforms, the commission indicated that promising potential recruits might turn their backs on the credentials expected for professionals—a doctorate in economics—and elect to pursue that degree in graduate schools of business or public policy. This line of argument suggests that further intensification in the high technique, the area in which the American component of the economics profession has enjoyed a competitive advantage in the past several decades, may thus be subject to diminishing returns, if not negative ones.

References

Bowen, Howard R. 1953. Graduate Education in Economics. *American Economic Review* 43, suppl: Part 2 (September): xv, 223.

Doctoral Dissertations in Economics: Eighty-Eighth Annual List. 1991. *Journal of Economic Literature* 29 (December): 2076–104.

Epstein, R. J. 1987. *A History of Econometrics*. Amsterdam: North Holland.

Hansen, W. Lee. 1991. The Education and Training of Economics Doctorates: Major Findings of the American Economic Association's Commission on Graduate Education in Economics. *Journal of Economic Literature* 29 (September): 1054–87.

Johnson, Harry G. 1977. The American Tradition in Economics. *Nebraska Journal of Economics and Business* 16:17–26.

Kolm, Serge-Christophe. 1988. Economics in Europe and in the U.S. *European Economic Review* 32:207–12.

Laband, David N., and Michael J. Piette. 1994. The Relative Impacts of Economics Journals: 1970–1990. *Journal of Economic Literature* 32 (June): 640–66.

Lampman, Robert J., ed. 1993. *Economists at Wisconsin: 1892–1992*. Milwaukee: The Board of Regents of the University of Wisconsin System.

Liebowitz, S. J., and J. P. Palmer. 1984. Assessing the Relative Impacts of Economics Journals. *Journal of Economic Literature* 22 (March): 77–88.

Portes, Richard. 1987. Economics in Europe. *European Economic Review* 31:1329–40.

9. Members of the commission were Anne O. Krueger (Duke), chair; Kenneth J. Arrow (Stanford); Olivier Jean Blanchard (MIT); Alan S. Blinder (Princeton); Claudia Golden (Harvard); Edward E. Leamer (UCLA); Robert Lucas (Chicago); John Panzar (Northwestern); Rudolph G. Penner (Urban Institute); T. Paul Schultz (Yale); Joseph E. Stiglitz (Stanford); and Laurence H. Summers (Harvard).

Report of the Commission on Graduate Education in Economics. 1991. *Journal of Economic Literature* 29 (September): 1035–53.

Ruggles, Nancy D., ed. 1970. *The Behavioral and Social Sciences Survey: Economics Panel.* Englewood Cliffs, N.J.: Prentice-Hall.

Sixty-Eighth List of Doctoral Dissertations in Political Economy in American Universities and Colleges. 1971. *American Economic Review* 61 (December): 990–1064.

United States. Department of Education. 1992. *Digest of Education Statistics.* Washington, D.C.: Government Printing Office.

Part 2

The Changing Character of British Economics

Roger E. Backhouse

1945–60

Though it retains many distinctive features, British economics is now undeniably international, exhibiting many of the features of what has been called American-style professional economics: students learn substantially the same theory as their counterparts in other countries, often using the same textbooks; graduate coursework is regarded as a necessary preparation for research; university teachers are expected to have doctorates; frequent publication is essential to professional advancement; the journals in which people publish are essentially international; and there is an emphasis on mathematical theory and econometric techniques. Links between Britain and various parts of the Commonwealth have remained strong, and in the past decade, as part of the process of European integration, there has been a dramatic increase in interaction with other economists in the European Community. The main connections, however, remain with the United States. A very large proportion of the staff in many universities have spent time in U.S. institutions, whether as graduate students or as visiting professors, and many U.S. visitors pass

I am indebted to many people for sharing their knowledge and insights with me. In particular I wish to thank Chris Archibald, Roy Bailey, Mark Blaug, Tony Brewer, Bob Coats, Bernard Corry, Frank Hahn, Geoff Harcourt, John Hutton, Jim Mirrlees, Denis O'Brien, Richard Portes, Peter Sinclair, Max Steuer, Keith Tribe, Ken Wallis, Basil Yamey, and other conference participants. None of them is to be held responsible for the use I have made of ideas they supplied. If inaccuracies have crept in, I alone am responsible.

through British universities. This situation has led one prominent British economist (of U.S. origin) to claim:

> It is perfectly reasonable to ask whether there is now any economics outside and independent of the United States. All the data confirm American leadership. . . . Moreover a significant proportion of the economics profession in Europe were trained as postgraduates in the United States. . . . Many take from the U.S. their professional standards, their views of what are interesting problems, and their approaches to them. (Portes 1987, 1330)

Whether one accepts this interpretation or places greater emphasis on the European contribution to contemporary economics (see Kolm 1988), this situation stands in sharp contrast to that prevailing in 1945.

In 1945, British economics was dominated by three institutions: Oxford, Cambridge, and the London School of Economics (LSE). There were other institutions, but they were small in size and provincial in more than the geographical sense. Of these LSE was perhaps the most open to international influences, notably from Europe, due to the presence of first Allyn Young (1927–29) and then Lionel Robbins (1928–61).[1] Robbins had an extremely cosmopolitan outlook, his awareness of European economic thought contrasting strongly with the Cambridge habit of focusing mainly on work by other Cambridge economists. His many overseas contacts included close links with several American economists, notably Jacob Viner. After the war both Viner and Frank Knight assisted with teaching at LSE (Robbins 1971, 219).

Wesley Clair Mitchell had made a significant impact on Oxford during a brief visit in 1931. His influence led to the establishment, with support from the Rockefeller Foundation, of the Institute of Economics and Statistics in 1935, with the aim of providing some of the conditions necessary for serious research to be undertaken. But though this was a significant step toward providing a greater central focus for Oxford economics, it was only a small one. Most economists in Oxford remained based in the colleges, isolated from other economists and with heavy burdens of elementary teaching in which they had to cover the entire range of economics, a situation that remains (to the detriment of Oxford's research) to this day.[2] Fellows would generally be appointed direct from

---

1. A lecturer from 1928–29 and, after a brief interlude in Oxford, a professor thereafter.

2. The main teaching was undertaken in one-to-one tutorials by college tutors who were judged by their success in getting their students through examinations of whose content they

taking a successful first degree (usually at Oxford or Cambridge) and were under little pressure to publish.

The most important institution, however, was Cambridge, dominated first by Marshall and later by Keynes. The situation there was bitingly described by Harry Johnson (1978), who arrived there as a student in 1945.[3] He pointed to the college system which, like Oxford's, isolated economists from each other, and criticized Cambridge's sense of intellectual superiority, with its view that there were only two universities worth taking seriously. The Department of Applied Economics, like the Oxford Institute, provided a partial focus for economists, but most economists were nonetheless relatively isolated from each other. Cambridge dominated the Royal Economic Society, the only national economic society, and the pages of the *Economic Journal*.[4] The *Review of Economic Studies* attracted an international range of contributors, but *Economica* was primarily an LSE journal and *Oxford Economic Papers* one for Oxford economists.

There were some developments in the 1950s. Hicks and Harrod began to develop Oxford's graduate school. Lawrence Klein headed the Oxford Institute of Economics and Statistics from 1954 to 1958, and Richard Stone fostered a wide range of econometric and other empirical work at the Department of Applied Economics in Cambridge. Outside the London-Oxford-Cambridge triangle a reputation for mathematical economics was established at Birmingham (Frank Hahn, Terence Gorman, and later Alan Walters), while important work in econometrics was being done at Manchester (Jack Johnston) and Leeds (Denis Sargan). But generally change was slow. Thus in 1963, J. R. Sargent could still write an article entitled "Are American Economists Better?" in which he argued that the answer was yes. American economists, he claimed, were more serious, more professional, and more willing to experiment

---

were not aware. Though lectures were given, they were not directly related to the examinations. This was different from the LSE, which had early on adopted the principle of examining what had been taught. A further difference was that, unlike Cambridge and LSE, Oxford offered no specialist undergraduate degree in economics; students wishing to read economics had to take philosophy, politics, and economics (PPE). On Oxford, see Young and Lee 1993.

3. In particular, chap. 7, "Cambridge as an Academic Environment in the Early 1930s: A Reconstruction from the Late 1940s," and chap. 10, "Cambridge in the 1950s." In view of his outright hostility to the place, it is worth pointing out that Johnson was, despite his being an outsider, accepted there.

4. Harrod took over from Keynes as editor in 1945. Prior to that Keynes had run the journal and the society (see Moggridge 1990, and Robinson 1990).

and to innovate. Though Sargent recognized that this might be taken too far, he saw the necessity of specialization within economics, criticizing the generalism that the Oxford and Cambridge systems produced. He even defended the American pressure to publish, arguing that it reflected a sense of public responsibility to disseminate expert knowledge. These criticisms were, he acknowledged, directed particularly at Oxford.

1960–76

In the 1960s and early 1970s the pace of change accelerated. Ely Devons, A. W. (Bill) Phillips, Richard Lipsey, and a number of their colleagues pushed the case for quantitative economics at LSE, a process accelerated with the arrival there of Harry Johnson in the mid-1960s (Hahn and Gorman were brought there). Johnson also exerted an influence, as an external assessor, on appointments in many provincial universities. At Oxford, Jim Mirrlees was also responsible for the appointment of a number of lecturers with strong technical skills who subsequently played an important role, alongside established lecturers, in developing the graduate program.[5] There were parallel developments in many other British universities, with expansion in the number of economists and in the technical level of what was taught. A particularly important role, however, was played by new universities, established in the mid-1960s. These included Essex, Warwick, and York, all of which went on to develop large and very successful economics departments. A substantial number of the professors in the new universities came from LSE, including Lipsey, Chris Archibald, and Jack Wiseman. In these institutions American influences were strong. At Warwick the founding head of the department was Sargent, the author of "Are American Economists Better?"[6] Lipsey and Archibald, at Essex, consciously set out to be "mid-Atlantic" in their approach to economics, this involving not so much common beliefs about economic doctrine but a common body of technique on which all economists could draw. As early as 1965, Lipsey went to the American Economic Association meeting to recruit staff. British economists

5. The industrial mathematics component of the engineering and economics degree was particularly important because lecturers on this were not constrained by the heavy teaching commitments of most college fellows. Fellowships at Nuffield involved no undergraduate teaching, an important factor in that college's performance.

6. See above. Prior to Sargent's appointment, the vice chancellor of Warwick, sponsored by the Ford Foundation, had toured U.S. universities to find out about developments there (Campbell 1966, 290).

who had experienced U.S. graduate education emphasized the serious-ness of American economists compared with their British counterparts, speaking of the dramatic culture shock provided by the stimulation of life in a top U.S. department. The organization of the graduate program involved a conscious attempt to follow the American model. American influence at Essex was strong due to a visiting professorship that, between 1965 and 1972, attracted people of the stature of Robert Clower, Carl Christ, Murray Kemp (Australian, but Ph.D. from Johns Hopkins), Arthur Goldberger, and Frank Brechling (Irish, but based at Northwestern).[7] In addition, there were people on the permanent staff who were trained in the United States (David Laidler) and several Americans who vis-ited Essex for short periods of time.[8] When Johnson, in the mid-1970s, penned a vitriolic attack on "What Passes for Economics in the British Establishment," he made exceptions of "the mathematical economists," "the econometricians," and "the competent economists at the provincial universities" (1978, 222).

1976 to the Present

In the mid-1970s the British university system moved from a period of rapid expansion to one of contraction. The major impetus was financial. The sterling crisis of 1976 was followed by enormous cuts in public spending, which included education. The 1980s saw further cuts as the government sought to reduce both taxation and the government deficit. There was also, in the late 1980s, a major change in ideology. Universi-ties were forced to become more competitive, market-driven institutions. Central funding was cut at the same time universities were encouraged dramatically to increase student numbers. When they were successful in this, the government, for financial reasons,[9] introduced quotas, limiting the expansion. Insofar as it has led to greater reliance on nongovernment sources of finance,[10] this may have increased the opportunities available

7. Not all the influential visitors had U.S. connections. Those with none included Michio Morishima and Rex Bergstrom.

8. The list includes James Tobin, Kenneth Arrow, Joseph Stiglitz, and William Brainard.

9. In the U.K., students who are accepted to a degree program are typically entitled to financial support from their local authority.

10. Some institutions have been very successful in raising private research funding. More sig-nificant, however, is recruitment of overseas (non-EU) students. Such students pay fees that are typically two or three times as high as those paid by EU students. As tight quotas have been intro-duced on EU student numbers, universities have actively increased numbers of non-EU students.

to universities. At the same time government intervention, both direct and indirect, increased. Research councils laid down conditions that had to be met if institutions' graduate students were to be eligible for research council support. These conditions covered both Ph.D. completion rates and aspects of what students were taught. More fundamentally, university funding was related to institutions' research output, as measured by publications.

This last point is very important. Though the pressure to publish frequently in the "best" places could be seen as an aspect of the American style, it has very different implications in Britain and the United States. In the United States, the pressure has arisen from competition within and between institutions, many of which are in the private sector. University league tables exist, but they are not produced by any central authority; in Britain, on the other hand, they are constructed by a central funding agency that links funding to research quality as assessed by this agency. Thus in Britain any resulting distortions in the nature of academic research (for example, in the direction of avoiding unfashionable themes) can be attributed to a central government initiative with all that implies.

The remainder of this paper seeks to document these changes. The starting point is the growth of British academic economics as measured by numbers and distribution of staff in British universities. The next stage is to consider, in turn, some of the main aspects of this process: changes in the nature of graduate programs; increases in the numbers of U.S. and U.S.-trained economists working in British universities; the internationalization of British economics journals; and changes in the character of British economics. These developments can be understood only against the background of massive changes in British higher education. Before that, however, there is a more general point that is worth making.

Increased International Travel

The internationalization of economics is part of a much wider phenomenon: the growth of international, and especially transatlantic, air travel. The extent of this is shown in figure 1, which provides measures of the real cost of airfares and the number of people traveling between the U.K. and the United States. They are clearly linked. There is no reason to believe that the increase in the numbers of economists crossing the Atlantic has been any less than the number of passengers in general. As contacts have increased, it is only natural that, as in so many other fields,

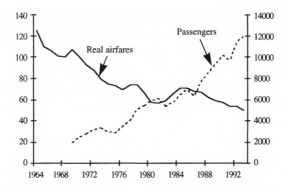

Figure 1   Transatlantic travel

Source: Real price of air travel is British Airways revenue per passenger kilometer, from BA Annual Report and Accounts, deflated by the U.K. consumer price index, from World Bank *World Tables*. "Passengers" is the number of passengers flying between the U.K. and the United States (thousands).

there has been a process of internationalization. The issue is not so much why economics has become internationalized, but what form the process has taken.

British Higher Education

Since 1945 there has been a substantial expansion of university education and a very significant change in its character. In the late 1940s there were few universities, and outside Cambridge, Oxford, and London economics departments were small and few in number. Higher education was, on the whole, available only to a small elite. In the 1960s, however, in response to the Robbins report, which established a policy of making higher education available to everyone considered capable of benefiting from it, several new universities were established, some as new institutions, others through changing the status of existing institutions. The Open University was established in 1969. Though colleges of advanced technology (such as Bath) were typically strong in science and engineering, several of the new universities (for example, East Anglia, Sussex, and Essex) emphasized arts and social science. There was thus a large increase in the number of university economics departments. In 1947 the number of teaching posts in economics was 166; by 1960 it was 367; by 1970 it was 853; and by 1974, 1,031 (Coats and Booth 1978, 480). The late 1970s saw the situation change. The 1973–74 oil crisis was followed by high inflation and a sterling crisis, in response to which large public spending cuts were introduced. Tight fiscal policy continued through the 1980s and early 1990s. Some departments continued to grow, but others shrank, the number of economists remaining fairly stable. In this sense the period of rapid university expansion was over.[11] There was a large rise in student numbers in the late 1980s and early 1990s, but without any corresponding increase in staff. In addition, in 1992 most polytechnics were granted university status, but though this meant the number of universities doubled within a year, it did not denote any real expansion. A survey in 1988 counted 1,116 economists working in university economics departments, with a further 1,044 working in research units, noneconomics departments, and in polytechnics (Blaug and Towse 1988, 51).[12] A very rough indication of the pattern of growth is provided in figure 2, which shows the number of staff employed in a sample of economics departments. This shows rapid growth to the mid-1970s and a slight decline thereafter.

At the same time, and partly as a consequence of such rapid growth, the character of the university system changed. In the late 1940s, Cambridge and LSE were clearly the leading economics departments, followed by Oxford and the provincial universities. In the years that followed, however, other departments grew rapidly, and established high reputations in terms of research. For example, of the new universities established during the 1960s, York employed 61 economists by 1988, Warwick 53, and Sussex 49, compared with 122, 80, and 60 for LSE, Oxford, and Cambridge, respectively (Blaug and Towse 1988, 52).

Financial pressures, the integration of universities and polytechnics into a unified funding arrangement, and ideology led to an important development during the 1980s: the attempt to link university funding

11. The University of Buckingham, the only fully privately funded university in Britain, was established in 1983, but remained small.

12. Problems of definition mean that these figures may not be directly comparable with Coats's. The significance of the distinction between universities and polytechnics lay primarily in their sources of funding. Though polytechnics were primarily teaching institutions, traditionally offering more vocational courses as well as "academic" ones, they undertook some research and offered courses leading to higher degrees. In the early 1990s the funding system was changed, bringing universities and polytechnics under a single funding body, and most polytechnics were allowed to change their status to that of universities. There was thus a doubling in the number of universities, most of which had economics departments, in 1992.

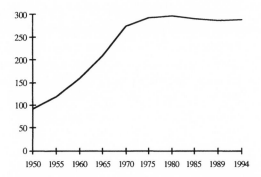

Figure 2 Number of economists in a sample of British universities

Source: *Commonwealth Universities Yearbook*. The sample (which is not random) includes Cambridge, Oxford, LSE, Birmingham, Bristol, Manchester, Essex, and Warwick.

to research output as measured in a series of research assessment exercises (RAEs) undertaken in 1986, 1989, and 1992.[13] These graded the research output of all U.K. economics departments that wished to be considered for research funding. Departments that received the top two grades ("outstanding" and "above average" in the 1986 exercise; 5 and 4 in the others) are listed in table 1.

Research assessment and internationalization are linked. Assessments of research quality are influenced, at least in part, by where research is published, and in economics many of the most prestigious journals are U.S. based.[14] Diamond's 1989 list of "core journals" was widely discussed in the context of the 1989 exercise.[15] Of the journals included in it, 14 are published in the United States, 8 in the Netherlands (North Holland/Elsevier), 4 in the U.K., and 1 in Canada. Judged by citation impact factor, of the top ten academic journals, only the *Review of Economic Studies*, very much an international journal, is published in the U.K. (Hodgson 1994).

13. The next is in 1996.
14. The procedure requires that universities submit statements about their research along with lists of staff and publications. In 1989 and 1992, universities had to submit quantitative information on publications (numbers of journal articles, books, discussion papers, etc.), plus two named publications per staff member. This information was then evaluated by a panel of economists appointed by the Funding Council.
15. In 1992 no list of core journals was used.

Table 1 Departments Receiving the Top Two Grades in Research Assessment Exercises

1986		1989		1992	
Outstanding	Above average	5	4	5	4
Bristol	Birkbeck	Birkbeck	Bristol	Birkbeck	Aberdeen
Cambridge	Birmingham	Essex	Cambridge	Bristol	Birmingham
LSE	Essex	LSE	Newcastle	Cambridge	East Anglia
Oxford	Glasgow	Oxford	Reading	Essex	Exeter
Warwick	Hull	Southampton	UCL	LSE	Glasgow
York	Newcastle	Warwick		UCL	Liverpool
	Reading	York		Oxford	QMW
	Southampton			Southampton	Newcastle
	Sussex			Warwick	Nottingham
	UCL			York	Reading
					Strathclyde
					Sussex
					Swansea

Source: UFC Circular 26/92; *Times Higher Education Supplement.*

Graduate Education

An important aspect of American-style professional economics is graduate education. This is in contrast with the "traditional" British model in which (a) the first degree is generally more specialized; (b) the Ph.D. involves simply submission of a thesis that may amount to a substantial monograph, possibly taking several years to complete; and (c) a Ph.D. is not a prerequisite for obtaining a university teaching position. Thus in Britain there were many instances in which the best graduates went straight into teaching posts, with the less good ones doing Ph.D.s. Some regarded the Ph.D. as continental nonsense, while others regarded postgraduate work as necessary only for slow learners and people with unfortunate histories.

Since the 1950s, however, there has been a movement away from the traditional model toward one in which postgraduate coursework is seen as an essential part of an economist's research training. This has been achieved primarily through the development of one-year master's programs containing compulsory courses in macro- and microeconomics and econometrics. Since the 1960s, successful completion of such a master's program has increasingly been regarded as a prerequisite for Ph.D. registration. The Ph.D. then typically requires two years of research toward a thesis (possibly with a limited amount of further coursework).[16] A few universities took steps in this direction in the 1950s, and many more did so in the 1960s. By the late 1980s the research councils (the Social Science Research Council, later renamed the Economic and Social Research Council, or ESRC) were putting pressure on departments to do this.

Oxford established a taught graduate program (the B.Phil., later renamed M.Phil.) soon after the war, in 1947. The main influence on the program came from Hicks and Harrod. However, it remained the case that bright undergraduates would, as late as the 1970s, go straight from their undergraduate course (PPE—philosophy, politics, and economics) to teaching positions. The doctorate, the D.Phil., was of minor importance; the criterion that the thesis be original was applied so tightly that for many years, while applied topics could get through, it was virtually impossible to pass with a theoretical topic.[17] The situation changed after

16. Some universities have also accepted the idea that a Ph.D. thesis may comprise three potential journal articles in a particular area, rather than the traditional monograph.

17. An exception was Ian Little. Distinguished economists who submitted theoretical theses

the arrival of Jim Mirrlees in 1968, and soon after a route was established from the M.Phil. (now a two-year course) to the D.Phil.: the dissertation required for the M.Phil. could be used as the starting point for a D.Phil. thesis.

One of the earliest universities to establish a one-year master's based primarily on coursework was Birmingham, which in 1952 started its M.Soc.Sc. program, the main component of which was four graduate courses, the dissertation comprising only a small part of the degree.[18] The Ph.D. remained by thesis. However, in 1963 the requirement was introduced that "Prospective candidates in the Faculty of Commerce and Social Science for the degree of PhD are normally required to register first for the degree of MSocSc and apply towards the end of the first year for permission to transfer" (University of Birmingham, *Syllabuses*, 1964–65, 83). In the following year, however, the situation was relaxed with the introduction of a number of routes into the Ph.D.: one was the traditional one involving a thesis based on at least three years' work; another was the American-style one made up of M.Soc.Sc. coursework followed by a thesis based on eighteen months' research. Though students did, from the 1960s, follow the American-style route, it was only around 1990 that it became the required one.[19] Birmingham's early lead thus was not sustained.

At LSE, Robbins had been persuaded of the case for American-style graduate programs by Jacob Viner. In his autobiography he wrote, "I shall never forget the day when Jacob Viner slyly remarked that the Chicago higher degrees, with their requirement of written papers and advanced study as well as a thesis, were of a severer standard than ours. I was shocked, and if it had not been Jack, I should have been slightly indignant. But on enquiry I found out that he was right; and in due course we improved our arrangements" (1971, 217).[20] This respect for the U.S. educational system extended further: "If we were starting *ab initio* there

that failed included Kenneth Boulding, Robert Clower, and Lionel McKenzie.

18. A further two papers could be substituted for the dissertation. A degree with a longer history was the M.Com., but this required only two courses to be taken, together with a dissertation.

19. There were two reasons for this. One was the view that serious research in economics required greater preparation than could be provided at the undergraduate level. The other was the need to control the quality of the intake into the Ph.D. program, given that by this time a large proportion of graduate students came from outside the European Community with widely varying educational backgrounds, making it difficult to judge their ability before they arrived.

20. The date for this is not given, but it is in the chapter covering the period 1946–61.

would be a strong case for modelling our system on transatlantic lines, regarding first degrees as being principally further general education and reserving specialisation for second degrees in special graduate schools" (Robbins 1955, 585).[21] However, he argued instead for an extension of British first degrees to four years, being much less "disturbing of existing arrangements" (593).[22]

In the 1960s there was pressure, notably from Devons and some of the younger economists associated with Lipsey, to shift LSE's graduate program in a more quantitative direction and to introduce a one-year program. Many economists at LSE were very impressed with the technical proficiency of U.S. visitors and even by the training received at some provincial British universities and wished to improve the training offered at LSE. Robbins was initially opposed to this development, regarding the existing two-year program, in which a thesis was prominent, as satisfactory. However, Phillips, to whom Robbins often turned for advice on quantitative matters, was strongly in favor of change and Robbins quickly accepted the idea. The one-year M.Sc. began in 1964. When he arrived at LSE Johnson introduced two important changes. He established the idea of starting the course in September (a month early) so that students could attend an intensive mathematics course before starting the main courses at the beginning of October. The other was introducing compulsory courses in both macro and micro theory, with only one option, rather than a single course in theory and two options.

In 1981 LSE introduced a new Ph.D. program. Students arrive without any thesis proposal (though having already done coursework at the master's level), but develop one in discussion with staff and other students during the first year. The core is a seminar in research strategy and a course, Topics in Economic Analysis, in which the emphasis is on why research is done the way it is. Though these and other aspects of the program are designed to ensure a more rigorous and consistent training than was provided under the old system, it is an attempt to develop a model for Ph.D. training that is significantly different from that followed by most U.S. universities. Some features have been copied by other British universities.

At some of the new universities, such master's programs were adopted from the start. Essex and Warwick, founded in the mid-1960s, offered

21. He also favored the American-style credit system (1980, 41).
22. His views on education are summarized and placed in the context of his other work in O'Brien 1988, especially 76–78.

master's courses similar to LSE's, and such a master's was a prerequisite for a Ph.D. In both universities, the master's coursework was always technical, oriented toward theory and econometrics. At Essex, Ph.D. candidates were required to complete a master's (usually though not necessarily at Essex) first, and usually took one or two courses after that. However, not all universities followed this pattern. An example is Bristol, which, despite a high reputation for research, remained primarily an undergraduate teaching department. Postgraduate coursework there became important only in the late 1980s, with the requirement that a master's precede a Ph.D. being introduced informally on the grounds that students required more rigorous training, particularly in econometrics, in order to do the work required for their thesis. A formal route to a Ph.D. involving a master's was introduced in order to meet requirements laid down by the ESRC.

Cambridge followed this pattern only a decade later with the establishment, in the mid-1970s, of its M.Phil. There was a compulsory theory paper right from the start, but divisions among the economists meant that there was no common core. Students might take neoclassical micro theory with Hahn, or they could opt for a less orthodox, left-wing alternative taught by an economist such as Bob Rowthorn. It is only recently that a master's by coursework has become a prerequisite for Ph.D. registration.

U.S. and U.S.-Trained Economists in Britain

In 1950, there were few American or U.S.-trained economists in British universities, but by the 1960s this had begun to change. As an indicator of the numbers of Americans employed in British universities, figure 3 shows, for a sample of universities, the proportion of economists with first degrees from U.S. universities. Several features stand out from this graph.

- The growth in the number of Americans dates from the mid-1960s, reaching a peak in the mid-1970s.
- Numbers declined in the late 1970s and early 1980s, recovering again in the late 1980s and early 1990s.
- Since the 1960s, LSE has had a much higher proportion of Americans than the other groups of institutions.

One possible explanation of this pattern is economic conditions, which worsened during the 1970s. There were extensive staff cuts and in many

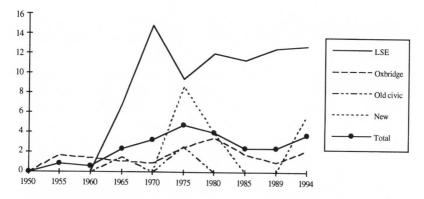

Figure 3   Percentage of Americans in a sample of British economics departments

Source: *Commonwealth Universities Yearbook.* "Americans" are defined as having a U.S. first degree. "Old civic" includes Birmingham, Bristol, and Manchester. "New" includes Essex and Warwick.

years salaries worsened relative to average earnings. A number of Americans returned to the United States. The recent rise in the proportion of Americans could be explained by a variety of factors, including the collapse of the U.S. academic job market in the early 1990s and a shortage of qualified British applicants.

In addition to British universities employing an increased number of Americans, British economists went to the United States to be trained. Figure 4 shows the proportion of academic economists, at the same sample of universities, with any U.S. degree. This includes Americans plus people with a master's or doctorate from a U.S. university but with a non-U.S. first degree. The presumption is that the latter are non-Americans who received training in the United States.

- The proportion of U.S.-educated economists grew steadily from the 1960s onward.
- LSE and the new universities employed higher than average proportions of U.S.-educated economists, while Oxbridge and the older provincial universities employed smaller than average proportions.
- The figure of 42 percent for new universities is of a very small number: 3 out of 7 staff had U.S. degrees. The universities concerned, Essex and Warwick, were in the process of being estab-

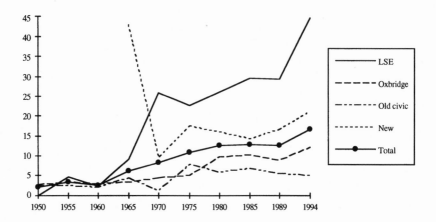

Figure 4   Percentage of U.S.-educated staff in a sample of British economics departments

Source: same as figure 1. "U.S.-educated" is defined as possessing a degree from a U.S. university.

lished. These staff were, however, in a very important position, being strongly placed to influence the direction in which the departments moved.

These statistics considerably underestimate the links between U.S. and British universities: (a) Canada, with its much closer links with the United States, is not included; (b) many economists have come to British universities after working in American departments, even though they did not obtain doctorates in the United States; (c) British economists frequently take leave to visit the United States; (d) U.S. visitors to British universities, if not on the payroll, will not appear in these statistics; (e) economists leave Britain to move to U.S. universities, some of them returning later. Though I have no firm evidence, all five types of contact are certainly much more frequent now than in the 1950s.

For an economist, the natural explanation for labor movements is changes in relative wages. Evaluated at market exchange rates, U.S. salaries have always been considerably higher than U.K. ones, as is shown in table 2.[23] Of more interest, however, is the relation between

23. U.K. grades are different from U.S. ones. The scales cited here are for roughly comparable positions. The U.K. senior lecturer scale, not listed here, runs approximately from the lecturer maximum to the professorial minimum.

Table 2   U.S. and U.K. salaries (in dollars)

	U.S. Assistant Professor (ave.)	U.K. Lecturer (min.)	U.S. Associate Professor (ave.)	U.K. Lecturer (max.)	U.S. Professor (ave.)	U.K. Professor (min.)
1970–71	11,176	3,393	13,563	9,732	17,958	11,803
1980–81	18,901	12,198	23,214	25,842	30,753	31,609
1990–91	34,420	22,680	41,388	41,867	55,527	50,163

Source: *Digest of Education Statistics* (U.S.); *AUT Bulletin* (U.K.). U.K. figures refer to the settlement made within each academic year. U.K. salaries have been converted to dollars using exchange rates taken from World Bank *World Tables*.

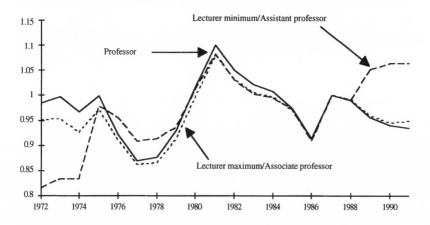

Figure 5   Relative real salaries in the U.S. and U.K., 1972–91

Source: same as table 1. The series show real U.K. salaries as ratios of the corresponding U.S. real salaries. Salaries are deflated using the respective countries' consumer price index. U.S. salaries are for academic years ending in the years indicated. U.K. salaries are for calendar years.

real salaries in the two countries, shown in figure 5. This shows that in real terms there has been no clear trend and possibly a narrowing of the gap. The fall in relative U.K. salaries in the late 1970s would be consistent with the decline in numbers of Americans in U.K. universities being due to economic factors. Though the U.K.'s relative salary position improved

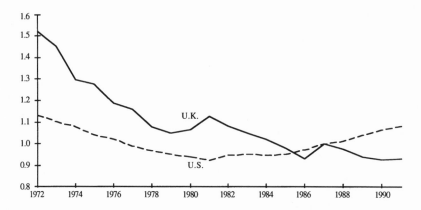

Figure 6   Ratio of real professorial salaries to average earnings in manufacturing, 1972–91

Source: same as figure 5. Real earnings in manufacturing are taken from World Bank *World Tables*.

in the early 1980s at the same time as more Americans came to Britain, there is no clear connection between numbers and changes in relative salaries for the rest of the 1980s.

These data, however, ignore the fact that real wages in the economy as a whole rose rapidly in the U.K. during the 1980s, whereas in the United States real wages did not grow. Thus if what matters is not absolute standards of living but standards of living relative to those in the rest of the economy, the position of U.K. academics relative to that of U.S. academics deteriorated during the 1980s. This is shown in figure 6, which shows that after 1981 the position of U.S. professors improved relative to manufacturing earnings, whereas that of U.K. professors continued to deteriorate.

The Internationalization of British Economics Journals

The Economic Journal and *Economica*

The geographical distribution of authors of articles in these two journals has changed dramatically since 1945. As Coats 1991 has documented, the proportion of British authors fell sharply from the 1940s to the 1960s (85 percent to 50 percent for *The Economic Journal*, and 79 percent to 53 percent for *Economica*). This was accompanied by an equally dra-

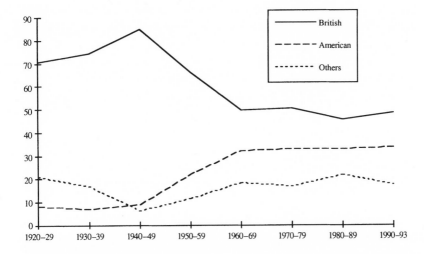

Figure 7   Percentage of British, American, and other authors in *The Economic Journal*, 1920–93

Source: Coats 1991 and author's calculations.

matic rise in the proportion of American authors (9 percent to 32 percent for *EJ*, and from 12 percent to 33 percent for *Economica*). Figures 7 and 8, which extend Coats's figures to the early 1990s, reveal that after the 1960s the pattern was very different for the two journals. The distribution of *Economic Journal* authors stabilized at close to 1960s levels, whereas American dominance of *Economica* increased even further, to the extent that American authors greatly outnumbered British in the early 1990s. This comes across very clearly in figures 9 and 10, which plot the distribution of articles by author on an annual basis.

   A further feature of figures 7 through 10 is the gradual rise in the proportion of authors from other parts of the world. By the late 1980s there were years when "Others" outnumbered British authors in *Economica*. The main reason for this was the increased number of articles by European authors, shown in figure 11.

   The stabilization in the shares of British and American authors in *The Economic Journal* and the gradual increase in the European input are reflected in figures on submissions, shown in figure 12. Compared with 1971–72 there has been a very small rise in the proportion of "Other" submissions (mainly Europeans). Insofar as there is a discernible trend

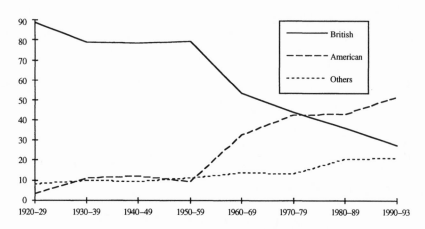

Figure 8   Percentage of British, American, and other authors in *Economica*, 1920–93

Source: Coats 1991 and author's calculations.

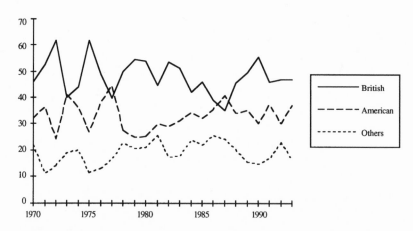

Figure 9   Percentage of British, American, and other authors in *The Economic Journal*, 1970–93

Source: Author's calculations.

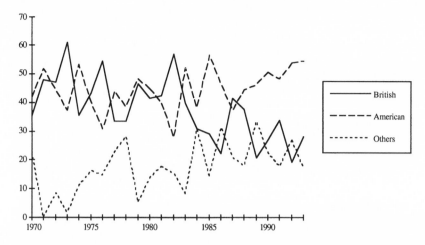

Figure 10   Percentage of British, American, and other authors in *Economica*, 1970–93

Source: Author's calculations.

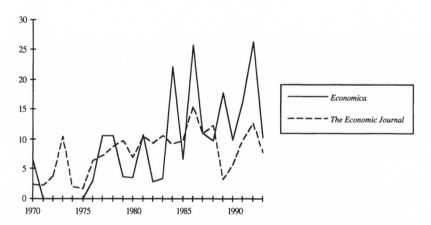

Figure 11   Percentage of European authors in *The Economic Journal* and *Economica*, 1970–93

Source: Author's calculations.

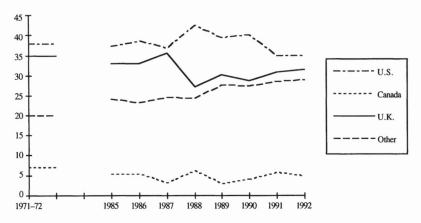

Figure 12   Distribution of *Economic Journal* submissions, 1970–92

Source: Champernowne, Deane, and Reddaway 1973, 502; and unpublished editors' reports to RES Council.

in U.S. and British submissions, the proportion of U.S. submissions is falling and that of British submissions rising. The ratio of submissions to articles published is higher for U.S. authors than for British. The editors' explanation of this is that many submissions by U.S. authors have already been rejected by other journals before they are sent to *EJ* and that British authors place *EJ* higher on the list of journals to which they submit papers.

At the same time as these journals became internationalized, the composition of British authors changed equally dramatically. Figures 13 and 14 extend Coats's data on the institutional affiliation of British authors to the early 1990s. Two features stand out.

- There was an enormous rise in the proportion of articles by economists from universities other than Oxford, Cambridge, and London. By the early 1990s more than half the British authors in both journals were from such universities.
- The proportion of authors from Cambridge contributing to *EJ* declined sharply in the 1980s, falling below that from Oxford. By the 1980s, *EJ* clearly was no longer identified with Cambridge in the way that it had been when it began.

It was in 1980 that the Managing Editorship of *EJ* moved after three years in Oxford (John Flemming) to a provincial university, York (Charles

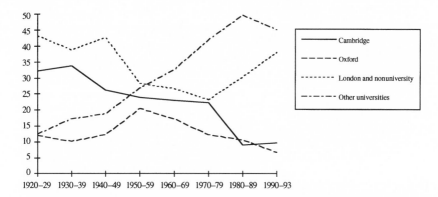

Figure 13   Distribution of British authors in *The Economic Journal*, 1920–93

Source: Same as figure 7.

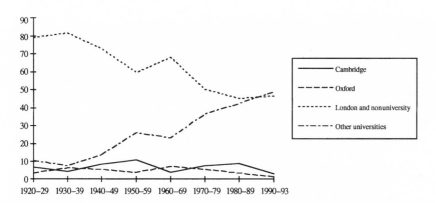

Figure 14   Distribution of British authors in *Economica*, 1920–93

Source: Same as figure 7.

Feinstein and John Hutton, 1980–86; John Hey, 1986–96). *Economica*, of course, remained at LSE.

Britain and Europe

Frey and Eichenberger (1993, 185) distinguish between European and American styles of doing economics:

1. Europeans consider participation in local and national affairs more important relative to the publication of journal articles than do Americans.
2. European research is "more concerned with practical issues and follow[s] a more steady course," whereas American research "tends to focus on abstract issues defined within the profession itself," with "academic fads" playing a considerable role.
3. European academics are engaged mostly in undergraduate teaching, in contrast with Americans, who are geared to postgraduate teaching.

They explain this situation, at least in part, in terms of the existence within Europe of many separate, not especially competitive, markets, divided from each other by language and institutional barriers. They concede, however, that within Europe there exists a group of internationally oriented economists who behave like American economists.

This picture fits British economics as it existed in 1945. There were internationally oriented economists, but Oxford and Cambridge were geared to producing generalists, and the small size of the profession and the dominance of three institutions meant that academic economists generally moved in the same circles as policymakers. There was little pressure to publish in the way accepted in the United States.[24] By the 1990s, however, British economics had, as this paper has shown, changed to such an extent that it was much better described in terms of the American model. Given the absence of a language barrier between Britain and the United States, it is hardly surprising that British economics has developed in this way. This explains the conclusion reached by Kirman (1994, based on Kirman and Dahl 1994) that, based on a count of articles in primarily English-language journals (those covered by the Social Sci-

24. I leave open the question of how far this situation was, as Frey and Eichenberger argue, desirable, and how far it implied, as Johnson 1978 claimed, second-rate economics. For a third perspective see Portes 1987.

ence Citation Index), among EC countries, the U.K. has a productivity rivaled only by the Netherlands and that it contains a large number of productive institutions.

Conclusions

The international spread of American-style professional economics has been accompanied by enormous changes in the relationships among U.K. universities. In the late 1940s LSE and Cambridge were without doubt the leading institutions. This situation has continued, though LSE has clearly emerged as the dominant institution. Oxford has risen from the clearly minor position it held in the 1940s to one where it might be seen as rivaling Cambridge. Cambridge is not the dominant force that it once was. At the same time, economics outside London, Oxford, and Cambridge has expanded to the point where it can no longer be neglected. There are important areas of economics where provincial universities have reputations that equal or exceed those of London, Oxford, and Cambridge.

The evidence presented in this paper shows clearly that the period when change accelerated was the 1960s. There was a dramatic increase in the number of economists working in Britain who had experience of U.S. universities, journals became more international, and a number of departments were started by people committed to undertaking research and providing training in a way that rivaled what was available in the leading U.S. universities. These changes continued throughout the 1970s and 1980s to the point where most universities had been affected.

Associated with these changes was a change in the nature of British economics. Economics became more technical and in many ways more like the economics that has come to dominate the United States. Despite this, the view is widely held that British economics has retained a distinct identity. Perhaps the best example to quote is macroeconomics; the new classical macroeconomics never caught on in the U.K. to the extent that it did in the United States (Patrick Minford is perhaps the only leading U.K. economist who could be described as new classical). Models of imperfect competition and bargaining are much more prominent than is the case in the United States (cf. Dixon 1992). During the 1970s the LSE became associated with a distinctive, empirically oriented approach to labor economics and inflation that differed from most U.S. work on the subject. In addition, open-economy issues have received much greater attention. The result is that, though students will have been trained in similar techniques, the style of macroeconomics found, for example in European-based textbooks, is very different from that found in U.S. ones.

This picture is reinforced by evidence from surveys of British and U.S. economists' opinions. Ricketts and Shoesmith (1992, 211–12) found that U.K. economists were more likely than U.S. economists to support the following propositions:

- In the short run unemployment can be reduced by accepting a higher inflation rate.
- The distribution of income in industrial nations should be more equal.
- Wage-price controls should be used to control inflation.

They were *less* likely than U.S. economists to support the following propositions:

- Cash payments are superior to transfers in kind.
- The level of government spending should be reduced.

Ricketts and Shoesmith drew the conclusion that "U.K. economists are more sympathetic with income-redistribution objectives and more willing to countenance government intervention to achieve them than are U.S. economists" (1992, 212). Thus the areas where British economists have made a major impact include the measurement of inequality (Tony Atkinson) and public economics (Ronald Coase, James Mirrlees, Richard Lipsey).

That British contributions to international economics have been particularly strong is hardly surprising (trade counts for a very high proportion of GDP, and the exchange rate is crucial to British economic performance). Other areas where British economists have been prominent, such as capital theory (Joan Robinson, Nicholas Kaldor, Piero Sraffa, Christopher Bliss), can perhaps be linked to the desire of most American economists to do work that is (ostensibly, at least) of more practical relevance. Similarly, in econometrics Britain has been strong in econometric theory (Denis Sargan, David Hendry, Peter Phillips[25]) but, at least until the establishment of the Center for Economic Policy Research, weaker in the type of applied, policy-oriented work associated with the Brookings Institution.

In some cases, the maintenance of a distinctive British tradition has

25. A New Zealander, but who trained and established his reputation in Britain.

been associated with opposition to the type of economics emanating from the United States. This is true of the capital controversy of the 1960s, when Joan Robinson and many of her followers saw themselves as putting forward arguments that undermined the whole of neoclassical economics. Indeed, it could be argued that this commitment to an unfashionable approach to economics, with the divisiveness it caused, was one of the reasons why Cambridge, though it produced a crop of brilliant students in the 1960s, failed to maintain its position relative to the LSE. But in most cases, a distinctive emphasis could be sustained without any such antagonism. A commitment to rigorous theorizing is, for example, quite compatible with a skeptical attitude toward U.S. educational methods. Thus many British economists feel that U.S. education relies too much on textbooks and inculcates overconfidence in the economics being learned at the expense of encouraging genuinely original thought. They would find evidence for this in the comparatively large number of British-trained economists in the leading U.S. economics departments, many of whom were trained before innovations such as graduate coursework were introduced into the British system.

References

Blaug, M., and R. Towse. 1988. *The Current State of the Economics Profession.* Unpublished report prepared for Royal Economic Society.

Campbell, M. B. 1966. *Nonspecialist Study in the Undergraduate Curricula of the New Universities and Colleges of Advanced Technology in England.* Comparative Education Dissertation Series, no. 10. Ann Arbor, Mich.: University of Michigan.

Champernowne, D. G., P. M. Deane, and W. B. Reddaway. 1973. *The Economic Journal*: Note by the Editors. *Economic Journal* 83:495–504.

Coats, A. W. 1991. The Learned Journals in the Development of Economics and the Economics Profession: The British Case. *Economic Notes by Monte dei Paschi di Siena* 20.1:89–116. Reprinted in Coats 1993.

———. 1993. *The Sociology and Professsionalization of Economics: British and American Economic Essays.* Vol. 2. London: Routledge.

Coats, A. W., and A. E. Booth. 1978. The Market for Economists in Britain, 1945–75: A Preliminary Survey. *Economic Journal* 88:474–95. Reprinted in Coats 1993.

Commonwealth Universities Yearbook. London: Association of Commonwealth Universities.

Diamond, A. M. 1989. The Core Journals of Economics. *Current Contents* 1 (January): 4–11.

Dixon, H. 1992. Review of *The New Keynesian Economics*, by N. G. Mankiw. *Economic Journal* 102:1272–75.

Frey, Bruno S., and Reiner Eichenberger. 1993. American and European Economics and Economists. *Journal of Economic Perspectives* 7.4:185–94.

Hey, J. D., and D. Winch, eds. 1990. *A Century of Economics: 100 Years of the Royal Economic Society and the Economic Journal.* Oxford: Basil Blackwell.

Hodgson, G. 1994. In Which Journals Should We Publish? *European Association for Evolutionary Political Economy Newsletter* 11 (January): 6–8.

Johnson, Harry G. 1978. *The Shadow of Keynes: Understanding Keynes, Cambridge and Keynesian Economics.* Oxford: Basil Blackwell.

Kirman, Alan P. 1994. Economic Research in Europe: Inputs and Outputs. *Royal Economic Society Newsletter* 85 (April): 11–13.

Kirman, Alan P., and M. Dahl. 1994. Economic Research in Europe. *European Economic Review* 38:505–22.

Kolm, Serge-Christophe. 1988. Economics in Europe and in the U.S. *European Economic Review* 32:207–12.

Moggridge, D. E. 1990. Keynes as Editor. In Hey and Winch 1990.

O'Brien, D. P. 1988. *Lionel Robbins.* London: Macmillan.

Portes, Richard. 1987. Economics in Europe. *European Economic Review* 31.6: 1329–40.

Ricketts, Martin, and Edward Shoesmith. 1992. British Economic Opinion: Positive Science or Normative Judgment. *American Economic Review* 80.2:210–15.

Robbins, L. C. 1955. The Teaching of Economics in Schools and Universities. *Economic Journal* 65:579–93.

———. 1971. *Autobiography of an Economist.* London: Macmillan/St Martin's.

———. 1980. *Higher Education Revisited.* London: Macmillan.

Robinson, E. A. G. 1990. Fifty-Five Years on the Royal Economic Society Council. In Hey and Winch 1990.

Sargent, J. R. 1963. Are American Economists Better? *Oxford Economic Papers* 15: 1–7.

Times Higher Education Supplement. London: Times Newspapers.

University of Birmingham. 1965. *Syllabuses 1964–5.* Birmingham, England: University of Birmingham.

World Bank. *World Tables.* Washington, D.C.: World Bank.

Young, Warren, and Frederic S. Lee. 1993. *Oxford Economics and Oxford Economists.* London: Macmillan.

The Australian Experience

Peter Groenewegen

Introduction and Background

Australia was settled in 1788 by British citizens, often involuntarily. During the nineteenth century, the continent was developed into six British colonies which, during the twentieth century as the Australian Federation (Commonwealth), first gained dominion status within the "Empire" and ultimately complete independence within the British Commonwealth of Nations. For much of its two centuries of history of white settlement, Australia's heritage was British even though, from the beginning, non-British people were also settling this new country. Australia is therefore a particularly interesting case study because the situation changed from one of British dominance to American dominance in economics.

The Second World War and postwar reconstruction started to change this significantly. The Curtin (Labor) war administration shocked British Empire loyalists by seeking closer ties with the United States in its conduct of the war in the Pacific, thereby placing Australian interests clearly ahead of former Empire ties and affections. Post-1945 adjustment implied further "breaks" with Britain.

Earlier versions of this paper were presented at Babson College (June 1994), Wollongong University and Victoria University of Technology (November 1994), and at Duke University (April 1995). Critical comments then received have helped to improve the final version of the paper. Research assistance from Mark Donoghue and Susan King, made possible through a grant from the Australian Research Council, is gratefully acknowledged. The usual caveats apply.

1. Postwar immigration drew heavily on non-British settlers, first
    from war-torn Europe, then from the Mediterranean region and,
    largely from the early 1980s, from all parts of the world, more
    especially Southeast Asia and the Pacific. With well over a third
    of its population non-British, Australia is now a consciously mul-
    ticultural society increasingly seeking its destiny in Asia.
2. A tendency to internationalize, visible in being a foundation mem-
    ber of the League of Nations and its agencies, was manifested
    more strongly post-1945. Australia was a foundation member of
    the UN, active in many of its agencies; involved with the World
    Bank, with GATT, and with the IMF from the outset; and a rel-
    atively early non-European member of the OECD. Such inter-
    national proclivities survive the current Asian-Pacific focus and
    supplement them.

Australia's economics and its universities reflect much of this history.
Its first six universities developed within the capital cities of the original colonies/states, their practice based on British universities (Scotland
and Oxbridge), initially hiring British staff and preparing for British-
style degrees. Economics entered Australian academe seriously from the
start of the twentieth century (Goodwin 1966; Groenewegen and McFarlane 1990, chap. 3). However, well before that Australia enjoyed much
vigorous, though not always rigorous, economic debate, and from the
beginning its economic writers often critically adapted imported thought
from the "mother country" (and, to a lesser extent, from elsewhere) to suit
the needs, institutions, and interests of this new, antipodean world. Following the example of the American Economic Association, Australians
formed their economic association some years before Britain took this
step, though this experiment, unlike its more solid British counterpart,
petered out after little more than a decade (Groenewegen and McFarlane
1990, chap. 4). By the 1920s, with economics taught at all six original universities, generally within a separate faculty, staff increasingly became
Australian born, though educationally finished in the United Kingdom
(London School of Economics, Cambridge) and oriented in its teaching
to Australian problems. The Economic Society of Australia (and New
Zealand until 1982), together with its journal, *The Economic Record*,
likewise concentrated on Australian applied issues, thereby generating a
distinctive Australian flavor to its economics, the reason why this period
has often been called "the golden age of Australian economics" (Scott

1990; Groenewegen and McFarlane 1990, 6–7, 10, chap. 6). Contact with Britain by young Australian academics as postgraduate students during the 1930s explains much of the rapid adoption of Keynesian economics. Post-1945 changes in economics and Australian academe must be seen in terms of two major developments and their consequences:

1. Rapid growth in the number of universities from the original six to nineteen by 1979, and to thirty-six by 1992 through the absorption of former Colleges of Advanced Education into the university sector after 1988. All teach economics (and/or business studies), so that the output of economics graduates has greatly increased.

2. This supply growth was largely induced by demand for economists within the public sector, in both secondary and tertiary education, and, especially from the early 1980s, in a deregulated financial sector and, more generally, the business sector. The 1980s probably constitute the peak of this phenomenon (enrollments in economics at secondary schools and tertiary institutions have started to decline during the 1990s).

Some implications of this growth in the number of economists for the transmission of economic ideas need to be noted. One is the increase in Australian economics journals. By the 1990s, these grew to over ten from the solitary *Economic Record* in 1945 (Groenewegen and McFarlane 1990, 176–78). Second, regular, large-scale economics conferences started in 1970, from 1977 on an annual basis (Scott 1990, appendix 10). These gradually replaced the monthly, semipublic lectures the Economic Society organized at the branch level (the Australian Capital Territory [ACT] branch remains a noted exception to this trend), the one-day symposia organized by the major branches (New South Wales Winter School, Victorian Autumn Forum), and the traditional economic segment of the Australian and New Zealand Association for the Advancement of Science (ANZAAS) congresses, which by the 1980s had greatly declined in importance. Annual economics conferences, combined with frequent and smaller specialist conferences, are also increasingly being confined to the practitioners of economics in university, government, finance, and industry who constitute the bulk of the Economic Society's membership. (Scott 1990, appendix 3, shows that for 1982, 17.8 percent of the membership were academics, and 59.1 percent were involved in other economic research and in business and management, of which 20.5 percent worked in the financial and 22.9 percent in the public sector.) The internationalization of Australian economics needs to be appreciated against this background of post-1945, and earlier, developments.

Internationalization or Americanization?
The Groenewegen- McFarlane Hypothesis
on the Australian Experience

Post-1945 Australian experience in economics has been depicted as its substantial Americanization (Groenewegen and McFarlane 1990, chaps. 8–10), a development not apparently confined to Australia (on Sweden, see Sandelin 1991, 214; and, for a variant, the picture of the absorption of Canadian economics "into an emerging, dominant, North American, if not global discourse" in Neill 1991, chap. 12, 204, for the quotation).

The Australian conjecture rested on varied pieces of evidence. It cited Gruen 1979 (230–32) on the strong American libertarian (public choice, Chicago, Virginia School) influence in public policy discussion from the late 1960s, its special importance among the younger economists at Monash and the Australian National University and, via their graduates, transmitted to the leading policy agencies of state and federal governments. This influence, particularly permeating treasury, finance, and industries commissions, was sharply contrasted with the immediate post-1945 policy objectives of the prewar-trained gurus such as Coombs, Crawford, Giblin, and Melville (Groenewegen and McFarlane 1990, chap. 9). In the portraits of the seven major post-1945 Australian economists identified in that study[1] (Arndt, Swan, Kemp, Corden, Salter, Harcourt, and Turnovsky, in order of birth), the two North American–trained economists rarely, if ever, dealt with applied Australian issues, and one, via his editorship of the *Economic Record*, appears to have exercised a strong influence on reducing the traditionally high content of applied issues in that journal.

The concluding chapter of the Australian story posed the Americanization issue starkly in terms of the end of an Australian economics via the "fatal embrace" of steady Americanization. This diagnosis was based on the extensive experience of its two authors in Australian economics education over nearly four decades. These concerned the practice of ap-

---

1. This selection was based on the economists included as Australian in Blaug and Sturgess 1983. Blaug and Sturgess 1986 includes five additional Australian economists, two of whom had taken their major postgraduate degree at North American universities, one at a British university, and two at Australian universities.

plying simplistic economic theory from the American texts, often without adapting it appropriately to Australian institutions and conditions; American-style graduate programs that paid insufficient attention to historical and institutional factors so essential for critical appreciation of the theory; an American research agenda that neglected important national issues or explicitly treated them as irrelevant; an American educational method symbolized by the drive toward semesterization and its greater emphasis on examination and assessment at the cost of introspection and reflection; and, last but not least, the growing dominance of American, as against British, undergraduate texts, partly because their Australian counterparts were generally not forthcoming. Some of this perhaps confused contemporary critiques of the dominant tendency in economic theory with the Americanization process and identified as American ideas and conceptions often imported from Europe by a Nazi-induced intellectual emigration. The account nevertheless contained much truth. American practice in economics appears to be differentiable from other styles, such as the traditional British (perhaps also an endangered species) and the European (Frey and Eichenberger 1993). Moreover, the discussion implied little more than a plea for careful adaptation to local conditions of imported theory. This is clearly stated in the closing paragraph of Groenewegen and McFarlane 1990 (238) and elsewhere. After all, the need for adaptation rather than crude imitation in absorbing dominant ideas from abroad in a small, peripheral country was a major theme in the book.

Some Evidence of the "Americanization" of Australian Economics

The evidence for an Americanization of Australian economics hypothesis is consistent with a dating of the phenomenon from the end of the 1960s. Given the many interacting factors, the evidence is often suggestive rather than conclusive. In combination, it presents an interesting picture of this aspect of the post-1945 process of internationalization in economics.

Major Postgraduate Qualification of Economics
Staff at Leading Australian Universities

Table 1 presents the data for five out of the six original universities by decade from the 1940s to the 1970s, inclusively. It shows a steady relative increase in the importance of North American qualifications for

Table 1 Major Postgraduate Qualification by Country (U.K. or U.S.) of Staff at Five Long-Established Australian Economics Departments: 1940–49 to 1970–79 (all staff for decade)

	1940–49			1950–59			1960–69			1970–79		
	U.K.	U.S.	Total	U.K.	U.S.	Total	U.K.	U.S.	Total	U.K.	U.S.	Total
Adelaide	2	—	8	1	1	13	7	5	35	7	4	29
Melbourne	4	2	15	8	—	24	10	—	26	7	4	34
Tasmania	1	—	7	1	—	7	2	—	8	4	—	12
Queensland	1	—	3	1	—	7	3	1	17	11	5	26
Sydney	3	—	8	4	1	13	4	1	18	10	9	36
TOTAL	11	2	41	15	2	64	26	7	104	39	22	137
Percent	25.3	4.9	100.0	23.4	3.1	100.0	25.0	7.9	100.0	28.5	16.1	100.0

Source: Compiled from data in university faculty handbooks.

Table 2 Major Postgraduate Qualification by Country (U.K. or U.S.)
of Economics Staff at Selected Major Economics Departments

		1983			1992	
	U.K.	U.S.	Total	U.K.	U.S.	Total
Adelaide	6	3	23	4	6	28
Australian National University*	10	7	37	5	9	44
Melbourne	9	4	23	6	6	29
Monash	7	11	24	3	10	31
New South Wales	9	5	24	6	11	41
Queensland	7	4	26	6	3	32
Sydney	9	5	26	9	6	26
Tasmania	2	1	10	4	7	21
Total	59	40	193	43	58	252
Percentage	30.6	20.7	100.0	17.1	23.0	100.0
Total { original five	33	17	141	29	28	136
Percentage { from table 1	23.4	12.1	100.0	21.3	20.5	100.0
ANU & Monash Total	17	18	61	8	19	85
Percentage	27.9	29.5	100.0	9.4	22.4	100.0

Source: *Commonwealth Universities Yearbook*, London, Association of Commonwealth Universities, 1984, 1993.
*Includes faculties and research schools of Pacific studies and social sciences.

the last of those two decades while the proportion of those with British qualifications remained remarkably steady. When the data of table 1 are combined with those of table 2 for the same five universities (with the caveat they are not fully comparable), this trend appears to have continued. This remains also the case when the overall position is compared. Given Gruen's (1979, 230–31) remarks on the growth of libertarian views among younger economic staff at Monash and the Australian National University, the high proportion of American-trained staff in these universities can be noted. Whether the data constitute evidence for a steady Americanization of Australian economics is more problematic.

The following should be noted when assessing the data. In table 1, staff turnover can affect the numerical outcomes, though with no bias in either direction. Intertemporal comparisons need to take into account that up to the end of the 1950s, the proportion of Ph.D.s in Australian economics departments was very small but that by the 1980s it was almost a condition of employment for lecturers and above. Availability of staff from abroad is a further factor: international hiring success for a country like Australia depends partly on relative salary scales and their effective purchasing power, partly on the relative state of the domestic market for academics in the exporting country, and partly on the capacity of domestic production (home-grown Ph.D.s) to supply the market. Only by the 1960s did Australian production of economics Ph.D.s begin seriously; evidence for the 1980s and 1990s (table 2) implies a rising proportion of Australian Ph.D.s among university economics staff.

The evidence of staff composition by origin of highest degree does nevertheless indicate a degree of Americanization that began during the 1960s and continued to accelerate thereafter. In Australia's case, this partly reflects a growing preference of Australian economics graduates to take their postgraduate studies in North America rather than Britain[2] if seeking an academic career. It also probably reflects (especially for 1992) the state of the American market for academics and the fact that a good economics department needs to have a significant proportion of young, North American Ph.D.s to connect with the frontiers of the mainstream. The last precisely encapsulates the Americanization hypothesis.

The Evidence from the Textbooks

A study of major texts set in first-year university economics studies at the five original universities (those in table 1) further supports a tendency of increased Americanization from the 1960s. This is less easy to tabu-late. In 1945, at four of the five universities, Benham's *Economics* was the major first-year text,[3] a situation that in three of these universities (Melbourne, Sydney, Tasmania) persisted until the mid-1950s. Tarshis's *Elements of Economics* was set at Adelaide (1949 to 1955) together with

2. Availability of scholarships was initially an important factor. In the early postwar years (up until the end of the 1960s), these were dominated by the British Commonwealth Scholarships and Rhodes Scholarships, directing graduate students to Britain (and in the case of the first, limited opportunities to study in Canada). American graduate studies were financially difficult for the small number of Australian students eligible for overseas postgraduate study at this time. When growing demand from increased student numbers for such study made the small pool of British scholarships increasingly competitive, this British financial advantage declined and North American studies became far more attractive.

3. The exception was Queensland, where Gifford's *Economics for Commerce* dominated the textbook list until 1964, the year of Gifford's effective retirement from the Queensland chair.

Hicks's *Social Framework* and Stigler's *Theory of Price*, a pattern partly followed by some of the other universities (Tasmania with respect to Tarshis, Sydney and Tasmania with respect to Stigler, and Sydney and Queensland with respect to Hicks). Boulding's *Economic Analysis* was briefly used at Sydney and Tasmania during the 1950s.[4] Samuelson's *Economics* tended to be used for preliminary reading at Australian universities, with some exceptions. Adelaide used it as a main text from 1955 to 1958, again in the 1960s for several years, and then (in its completely rewritten Australian version) during the 1970s; Queensland used Samuelson intermittently between 1957 and 1966 as a main first-year text.

North American texts began to dominate Australian first-year economics courses decisively from the 1960s. In Adelaide, Bain's *Price Theory* became a major text in 1963. In 1964 it was joined by Leftwich (which was retained until the early 1970s), by Lipsey's *Introduction to Positive Economics* (likewise retained through the 1970s), and by Brennan (*Theory of Economic Statics*) from 1966 to the late 1970s.[5] At Melbourne, Bach's *Economics* was the first major American economics text (in 1966); it was replaced by Lipsey from 1967 to 1979, initially with Stonier and Hague's *Principles* as a British alternative (until 1970). Supplementary texts to Lipsey were Dooley's *Price Theory* (1971 to 1972) together with Brennan, Leftwich, Mansfield, Bilas, and Cole successively through the 1970s. Australian texts supplemented: the Australian Samuelson in the early 1970s, Tisdell's *Economics of Markets* for some years from 1979, together with books on macroeconomics and money by Jim Perkins, a prominent Melbourne staff member. In 1964, Queensland broke the local Gifford monopoly by adopting Bach, replacing it in 1967 with Ferguson and Kreps (*Principles of Economics*). When separate first-year micro and macro modules were introduced from 1968 to 1972, Bain's *Price Theory* and McKenna's *Macroeconomics* were adopted ini-

---

4. Whether Tarshis's *Elements* and Boulding's *Economic Analysis* can be regarded as "normal" North American texts is somewhat debatable, even though both were working in the United States at the time their books were published. Tarshis was Canadian by birth but trained in Cambridge in the 1930s, and his text was at some stage almost branded "un-American" in certain circles (see Harcourt 1993, 79–80). Boulding was English by birth and by training (at Oxford) but spent his working life in North America, first in Canada and then in the United States. It was their Cambridge and Oxford connections that gave the books an entrée into Australia at the then Cambridge-dominated Adelaide, Sydney, and Tasmania.

5. In addition, as stated in the previous paragraph, Adelaide used the Australian edition of Samuelson produced by two Adelaide academics and another local product, the excellent *Economic Activity* by Harcourt, Karmel, and Wallace.

tially, with Bain replaced by Ferguson's *Microeconomic Theory* from 1971.

The story at the University of Sydney was very similar. Bach's *Economics* was the first-year text in 1964 and from then on American texts largely dominated. Ferguson and Kreps replaced Bach in 1965 until 1970, when Sydney introduced a complete microeconomics first-year, texts set included Bilas, Leftwich, Bain, Mansfield, Hirschleifer, and Hibden (*Price and Welfare Theory*). The return of a general "principles" first-year by the end of the 1970s was serviced first by Baumol and Blinder, followed by Dornbusch and Fisher and, apart from occasional experiments with Australian texts such as Tisdell's, American texts and their workbooks continued to dominate.

Tasmania reveals a similar story. Bach (together with Cairncross's *Economics* and Hicks's *Social Framework*) was the first American text (from 1961 to 1965), followed by Lipsey from 1965 to 1972 (supplemented by an Australian product by Tasmanian staff members Grant and Hagger) until a microeconomics first-year brought first Mansfield (1972 to 1976) and then Hirschleifer into prominence. There is little reason to doubt that this tale (with local variations) was replicated at Australia's other universities during the 1960s and after.

Other factors need to be mentioned in this account of how American texts came to dominate during the 1960s. First, the dollar shortage in the post-1945 "sterling area" (which in Australia effectively lasted well into the late 1950s) made adoption of American texts virtually impossible. Second, the international publishing agreement for the English-speaking world placed Australia firmly within the British zone, further stimulating adoption of British texts until competitive pressure from American texts simply became too great, facilitated as this was by the setting up of agencies and branches of American publishers within Australia. Third, there were few Australian texts, and when they existed, these tended to be set only within the university of their authors. Finally, although this account only relates to first-year texts, the same story can be told for later undergraduate years and for the postgraduate coursework degrees at the master's level that started to proliferate from the 1960s.

The Changing Content of the *Economic Record*

It is also instructive to examine Australia's first and continuing leading economic journal, the *Economic Record*, followed by *Australian*

Table 3   *Economic Record* 1945–94: Authorship of Articles and Notes by Place of Origin of Author (percentage)

	Australian	American	British	New Zealand[b]	Other
1945–49	77.2	1.0	—	18.7	4.0
1950–54	73.3	1.0	5.1	13.5	8.9
1955–59	72.9	3.4	3.7	13.8	1.0
1960–64	81.2	3.3	4.3	9.4	—
1965–69	79.0	8.4	3.9	5.5	—
1970–74	68.7	16.0[c]	3.9	4.9	—
1975–79	68.1	17.2[c]	5.6	2.4	—
1980–84	82.2	9.6	1.9	2.4	—
1985–89	69.4	21.3	2.7	3.1	—
1990–94[a]	70.0	20.4	2.1	1.9	—

a. Incomplete

b. New Zealand separated from *Economic Record* in 1982

c. Turnovsky editor of *Economic Record* 1973–77

Note.

	Australian	American
1945–69	76.7	3.4
1970–94	71.6	16.9

Economic Review and *Australian Economic Papers* (National Board of Employment, Education and Training 1994, 128, 145, 147, 152). Tables 3 to 5 present data on origin of authors, nature of articles, and books reviewed by place of origin in five yearly averages from 1945 to 1994.

Table 3 on authors by country of origin shows several clear trends. Most important is the dramatic increase in authors from North America, especially after 1970. This is partly explained by the fact that Steve Turnovsky, a North American–trained economist, held the editorial chair from 1973 to 1977. Equally striking is the drop in New Zealand authorship, encouraged by the creation of the *New Zealand Economic Papers* in 1966 and the formation of the New Zealand Association of Economists in 1973 (Scott 1990, 58–59). Australian contributors declined marginally over the decade, as did the relative (never substantial) number of British contributors and those from other (mainly Pacific) countries. In terms of the country of origin of contributors, *some* Americanization of the *Economic Record* is clearly visible.

Table 4   *Economic Record* 1945–94: Articles Classified by Contents (percentage)

	Australian Applied Topics	Overseas Topics	Theoretical
1945–49	47.8	30.5	17.0
1950–54	44.0	22.7	27.1
1955–59	42.0	21.4	33.7
1960–64	60.2[a]	15.6	34.2
1965–69	62.3	13.0	28.5
1970–74	32.2[b]	17.8	49.8[c]
1975–79	35.4	8.3	61.2[c]
1980–84	52.8	2.5[d]	44.7
1985–89	45.5	2.8	51.2[e]
1990–94[f]	48.6	2.6	48.9

a. Credit squeeze, unemployment, and policy debate generated many applied articles

b. *Australian Economic Review* commenced in 1968

c. Turnovsky editor of *Economic Record* 1973–77

d. New Zealand separated from *Economic Record* in 1982

e. 1988 Economists Conference and invited theory papers

f. Incomplete

Note.

Australian Applied Topics	Theory Articles
49.2% (1945–69)	28.1% (1945–69)
42.9% (1970–94)	51.1% (1970–94)*

*Turnovsky/*Australian Economic Review* factors.

Table 4 gives data on the type of article published in the *Economic Record*. These indicate the sharp increase in theoretical (internationalized?) articles relative to the Australian (and New Zealand) applied topics, for the discussion of which the journal had been founded originally. The Turnovsky-as-editor factor was once again significant in this switch, since this shift to theory articles began with his editorship. Other factors must be taken into account; these include changes in editorial policy following the establishment of *Australian Economic Review*, with its explicit Australian policy focus, and various attempts by the membership of the Economic Society to increase the "readability" of the *Economic Record* through publishing more policy-related and Australian applied articles. The support from table 4 for an Americanization hypothesis is considerably weaker. It may equally well be interpreted as a general internationalization hypothesis, that is, an editor's attempt to make content less parochial and hence more attractive to the international market.

Table 5 examines book reviews by place of origin of books reviewed. One unambiguous feature of the table is the rapid reduction in number of publications reviewed per issue of the *Economic Record*. Apart from the difficulties in unambiguously identifying place of origin of a book from place of publication, this makes the relative data more difficult to interpret. Other interpretation problems arise from the international publishing agreement, which places Australia in the British zone of influence. The strong showing of British books in the table may therefore disguise the extent of North American publications released under a British publisher's imprint. Fluctuations in Australian books reviewed are explained as follows: for the early post-1945 period, such books are relatively scarce; peaks (as in 1975–84) indicate conscious editorial policy to review the majority of key Australian publications. The data also show the steady decline in importance of other Commonwealth publications and, despite Australia's much heralded push into Asia, the almost total neglect of Asian/Pacific publications in the *Economic Record*'s diminishing review columns.

Some Implications of a Recent Australian Professors Survey

A survey of eighty-one Australian economics professors in late 1992 (Anderson and Blandy 1992) provides the strongest evidence of the degree of Americanization that has taken place in Australian economics. With a high response rate of 65 percent, the survey seems a good indication of what the majority of the leaders of the Australian academic economics profession think. Of greatest relevance for this paper is the degree of agreement among the respondents about a set of forty-four economic propositions classified into normative and positive, micro- and macroeconomics, with the normative microeconomic questions constituting nearly half (21) of the total. Questions were inspired by an earlier American survey (Kearl, Pope, Whiting, and Wimmer 1979), adapted for Australian conditions and the time shift. Apart from noting a substantial consensus in the responses and absence of any distinctive political bias among Australian professors, the survey also reported on some international comparative implications of the data, using results from an earlier comparative study (Frey, Pommerehne, Schneider, and Gilbert 1984). These are of

Table 5 *Economic Record* 1945–94: Book Reviews by Place of Origin of Books Reviewed (percentage), 5-year averages

	Total	Australia	England	North America	Commonwealth n.e.i.	Asia/Pacific
1945–49	323	10.2	22.9	34.7	10.2	1.9
1950–54	409	7.1	39.1	27.3	9.3	0.2
1955–59	169	19.5	37.2	31.3	4.1	0.5[c]
1960–64	157	19.1	43.3	27.4	2.5	0.6[c]
1965–69	193	31.6	31.6	19.2	3.6[b]	0.5[c]
1970–74	200	39.0	28.0	14.5	4.0[b]	2.0
1975–79	150	52.0	28.7	10.0	2.7	0.0
1980–84	120	46.7	40.0	4.1	2.5	0.8[c]
1985–89	210	30.9	43.8	10.9	1.0	0.0
1990–94[a]	182	21.4	47.8	16.1	1.0[b]	0.1

a. Incomplete

b. Largely New Zealand publications

c. 1 publication only

Note. Policy of preference for reviews of Australian books approximately 1965–84. International book publishers' arrangements make Australia part of British publishing zone. Steady decline of reviews: 36.6 reviews per issue 1945–54; 8.25 reviews per issue 1980–89. (Is this an Index of Americanization?)

interest for assessing an Americanization/internationalization hypothesis in Australia: "The Australian economists' responses are not significantly different from the U.S. economists' responses in 13 cases out of 20, from the German economists in 12 cases out of 20, from the Swiss economists in 10 cases out of 20, from the Austrian economists in 7 cases out of 20, and from the French economists in 6 cases out of 20. Clearly the Australian responses are most like those of U.S. and German economists and least like those of Austrian and French economists. . . . [W]e can conclude that, over a broad range of economic issues *Australian economics professors share a world economic culture with U.S. and European economists*" (Anderson and Blandy 1992, 27).[6] This conclusion loses much of its generality when it is realized that post-1945 German economics has been strongly Americanized, in sharp contrast to Austrian, French, and (on many issues) Swiss, and, for much of the period at least, that from Italy and other Mediterranean countries.

Second, the Australian survey tested specific views of their sample by Frey, Pommerehne, Schneider, and Gilbert 1984 on the "efficacy of market forces and competition" and, by implication, on the desirability of a relatively high degree of government intervention. To quote Anderson and Blandy (1992, 27) again: "The first point to notice is the *general* confirmation of Frey et al.'s five-country observation that there are indeed two distinct groups regarding attitude to the market economy. The United States and West Germany form a group as do France and Austria. The Swiss *just* fit into the former group rather than the latter."

Anecdotal evidence plus further findings on the differences between European and American economics and economists (Frey and Eichenberger 1993) confirm the importance of distinguishing Americanization from internationalization. Frey and Eichenberger (1993, 185) indicate three major differences between North American and European economic practice. First, North Americans publish more widely in the journal literature and gather more citations than their international colleagues. Second, North American economic research tends to be focused on more abstract issues (set within the profession itself) than on practical issues, which are less influenced by what is in vogue in economic research. Third, North American teaching is geared much more to postgraduate studies, while in Europe most teaching is directed at the undergraduate

6. The authors qualify the first paragraph of this quotation by stating: "On a binomial test of this pattern of differences, however, not even the French economists turn out to be statistically different at the 0.05 level of significance."

level. Although things are changing, "Australian" can still be substituted for "European" in these propositions without very great difficulty. Relative to population, Australians gather far fewer citations than their North American colleagues, if only because a still very substantial part of the content of Australian journals is devoted to Australian applied issues that only seldom appeal to overseas readers and hence do not get cited. The small number of Australian economists listed in *Who's Who in Economics*, plus earlier remarks on the contents of the *Economic Record*, bear this out. The latter also supports the validity of the second proposition, although, as indicated with respect to the *Economic Record*, this is rapidly changing with the sharp increase in (internationalized) theoretical content of the *Economic Record*. Last, Australian university teaching remains concentrated at the undergraduate level, with very large classes in the first and second years. Graduate teaching is small and, apart from the specialized research schools at the Australian National University, there are no major graduate schools in economics when business schools producing MBAs are neglected.

It may be noted that North American practices are increasingly being adopted in Australian economics graduate studies. Master's degrees by coursework, often preceded by a diploma course, have largely replaced the master's by research degree. The last was traditional at the older universities until the early 1960s when, for example at Sydney, it effectively constituted the only postgraduate degree in economics. At the Ph.D. level, coursework programs additional to a dissertation are increasingly replacing the traditional pure research degree. Following this American pattern ignores the high quality at Australian universities of undergraduate honors economics programs, which, together with a good master's coursework program, can achieve as much as if not more than the best Ph.D. coursework program in the United States. This change in Australian economics graduate education, ignoring as it does the highly selective and elitist honors undergraduate teaching tradition (borrowed from Scotland) is perhaps another case of uncritical Australian adoption of American practice in economics.

A fourth, anecdotal factor to the three propositions advanced by Frey and Eichenberger (1993) can be added. This concerns discrimination in the review columns of the *Journal of Economic Literature* in favor of North American books and against European books, particularly if they are published in languages other than English. Since this journal is (rightly) regarded as a major international journal and not just as the

American journal it *de jure* is as an organ of the American Economic Association, can this type of preference (justifiable though it is for members of the American Economic Association) be justified in its international role?

The last raises a number of important issues that more than justify academic research on Americanization and internationalization. These issues must be enumerated rather than discussed, given the space constraint. First, what are the international responsibilities of professional associations and journal editors in dominant countries in economics, especially toward the foreign section of their membership and their readers?[7] Second, how much of their international status is genuine when in many of these leading journals few foreign books are reviewed and few outside authors are invited to contribute to their pages? On the other side of the coin, to what extent should there be room for a national element in the economics of a small, peripheral country to preserve concerns about local institutions in the widest possible sense and perhaps also in matters of national interest? Dominant countries, all too often, present such national interests from their world position as equivalent to the world interest or, at least, the interest of their sphere of influence. In small countries, academic publishing incentives are against detailed empirical research in local applied topics, which cannot find an outlet in the leading journals. Finally, to what extent should genuine international action be *supranational*, in which case the associated question should be asked: Why are the International Economic Association and its publications not more esteemed than the American Economic Association and its journals?

Conclusions

What else can be learned from the Australian experience? As in the case of the United Kingdom, the growing importance of North American professional economics, and its practices, has altered the list of leading institutions at the university level. The Australian professors survey (Anderson and Blandy 1992, 31–33) listed the Australian National Uni-

---

7. This may be compared with the practice of early issues of the *Economic Journal* and *Quarterly Journal of Economics*. These reviewed a substantial proportion of foreign publications and contained reports by specially appointed foreign correspondents on national economic events that they believed had international economic significance. Is such practice now redundant given the flow of international comparative material from the international agencies (OECD, IMF, UNO) and the speed of communication that disseminates them?

versity, Melbourne, New South Wales, and Monash as the four major institutions for economics training; three of these, on the basis of the data in table 2, had a well-above-average presence of staff with North American postgraduate degrees, a position to which the other leading university, Melbourne, also seems to be moving. Is this a result of American consensus among the professors or something else?

Australian economics also produces internationally noted economists. The three years between the two editions of *Who's Who in Economics* almost doubled the number of prominent Australian economists based on international citations. However, two of the economists who featured in both editions (Corden and Harcourt) are no longer working in Australia. Unlike Britain, Australia has not produced a Nobel laureate in economics, nor can its economists be said to have frequently produced a major impact on a specific area; an exception is Trevor Swan (now deceased) in the theory of growth. There has also been important work about the development of small countries with open economies (by Arndt and Corden especially), starting from a perspective distinctly different from that produced on the subject in dominant countries (see Groenewegen and McFarlane 1990, chap. 8).

More importantly, and again different from the British experience as recorded by Backhouse, the development of Australian economics over the last decade has failed to maintain a distinctive Australian slant in specific topics. Moreover, where such slants formerly existed (as in the conception of equalization in fiscal federalism theory, and central wage determination in labor economics), they are now being demolished and/or savagely criticized by the young Turks with North American Ph.D.s, to the apparent applause of the majority of the Australian professoriate. In short, Australian experience appears to show that although internationalization of a profession like economics need not do so, it can nevertheless produce what is increasingly beginning to look like homogenization with, if not cloning from, its foreign role model. As a country with a small population, Australia is particularly prone to such effects. However, the North American economics being imitated, with its emphasis on abstraction and theory, leaves less room for the type of applied and policy-oriented work that made the 1920s and 1930s a "golden age" in Australian economics. In addition, when scoring in the leading journals is the name of the game, there is little kudos in doing patient, relevant, painstaking empirical work designed to highlight the economic problems of a small, open, peripheral country.

References

Anderson, M., and R. Blandy. 1992. What Australian Professors Think. *Australian Economic Review* 25.4:17–40.

Blaug, M., and P. Sturgess. 1983. *Who's Who in Economics*. Brighton: Harvester Press.

————. 1986. *Who's Who in Economics*. 2d ed. Brighton: Harvester Press.

Commonwealth Universities Yearbook. 1984. London: Association of Commonwealth Universities.

————. 1993. London: Association of Commonwealth Universities.

Frey, Bruno S., and R. Eichenberger. 1993. American and European Economics and Economists. *Journal of Economic Perspectives* 7.4:185–93.

Frey, B. S., W. W. Pommerehne, F. Schneider, and G. Gilbert. 1984. Consensus and Dissension among Economists: An Empirical Enquiry. *American Economic Review* 24.5:986–94.

Goodwin, C. D. W. 1966. *Economic Inquiry in Australia*. Durham, N.C.: Duke University Press.

Groenewegen, P., and B. McFarlane. 1990. *A History of Australian Economic Thought*. London: Routledge.

Gruen, F. H. G. 1979. Australian Economics 1968–78: A Survey of the Surveys. *Surveys of Australian Economics*. Edited by F. H. Gruen. Sydney: Allen and Unwin.

Harcourt, G. C. 1993. *Post-Keynesian Essays in Biography*. Basingstoke: Macmillan.

Kearl, J. R., C. L. Pope, G. C. Whiting, and L. T. Wimmer. 1979. A Confusion of Economists. *American Economic Review* 69.2:28–37.

National Board of Employment, Education and Training. 1994. *Quantitative Indications of Australian Academic Research*. Commissioned Report no. 27. Canberra: Australian Government Publishing Service.

Neill, Robert. 1991. *A History of Canadian Economic Thought*. London: Routledge.

Sandelin, Bo, ed. 1991. *The History of Swedish Economic Thought*. London: Routledge.

Scott, R. H. 1990. *The Economics Society of Australia: Its History 1925–1985*. Melbourne: Economic Society of Australia.

The Professionalization of Economics in India

S. Ambirajan

Introduction

That in the decades after 1945 there has taken place a process of inter-nationalization of American-inspired professional economics cannot be disputed easily. There is far too much evidence of the impact of the style, form, and even content of American higher education in many countries of the world. As long as the fires of the cold war were raging, the Second World resisted this Americanization, but since the late 1980s even those citadels have fallen. This impact, however, has not been uniform all over the world. A professional economist is engaged in a discipline that demands competency and awareness of current developments, qualities that depend upon his training and what is expected of him, as well as the institutional structure and cultural environment in which he works. All these differ from country to country. In view of this, it need not surprise anyone when the results of the process of professionalization are different in different countries. Technological, political, economic, and social developments in the world have made all nations susceptible to influences from outside as never before. But because of its peculiar historical and social circumstances, there are features that make the Indian case sufficiently different from other countries to merit attention.

I am grateful to A. W. Coats for helpful comments on an earlier draft of this paper.

Creating a Community of Economists

Economics as it is studied and practiced in India is not a native product of the soil, but an alien transplantation. The establishment of the British Empire in India in the nineteenth century saw the importation of many European institutions. Among these, the system of education established by the colonial rulers had the greatest impact on the intellectual life of the country. The new ideas that came along with the system of education totally transformed the way Indians understood the phenomena around them. The language in which education was imparted, the new institutional mode of learning, the social composition of the students, the secularization of education all contributed in no small measure to transform the intellectual content as well as the utilization of what was learned. In many respects the content and utilization of education resembled what was found in Britain.

Serious academic study of economics began only after the First World War as new universities came into being while the few existing universities expanded. A community of economists whose main interest was the study and teaching of economic problems began to form slowly during the interwar years. The main reason for the growth of the community of economists during the 1914–50 period was the expansion of university education in India. From the five largely affiliating universities in 1916[1] it had grown to twenty-five teaching, researching, and affiliating universities in 1950.

The economics they studied and taught was largely nonmathematical and only mildly statistical. It was allied more with politics and history. The basic degrees acquired by Indians were invariably of the Politics, Economics, Philosophy (PEP) type. A large number of those who went to England ended up in the London School of Economics and wrote doctoral dissertations in the areas of applied economics, economic history, or economic institutions. This was reflected in the subjects that were taught and the emphasis given to the research conducted at the Indian universities. Theory did not find much favor with professors who directed the way economics developed in India. The British economists in India were anxious to make students understand Marshall's statement that economics was "a study of mankind in the ordinary business of life," rather than go into the more speculative aspects of Marshall's thought.

1. Calcutta, Bombay, and Madras (1858), Punjab (1882), and Allahabad (1887).

Given the training received in Britain and the path charted by the early economists, academic economists' work was by and large limited to studying local Indian problems. Indian professors were content to follow the trend set by British academics, and even there, the significant theoretical developments either in the new welfare economics or Keynesian macroeconomics were not noticed much. The study of local Indian problems seemed adequate for their intellectual requirements.

If the interwar years witnessed the creation of an academic economic community, it was only in the years after the Second World War, as India approached total political independence, that economics began to be important both in academia and in the government. With political freedom imminent, powerful sectors in India—political as well as business— realized the importance of economic reorganization and development. The role of the professional economist in the process of achieving economic growth became obvious. The four major planning exercises undertaken during 1944–47 to prepare blueprints of the future economic policy had economists among its authors. After being in the academic wings, economists now took center stage.

Toward Professionalization

The study and practice of economics experienced a sea change after 1950. At first the change was not perceptible, but over the next four decades it had a cumulative effect, so that the scene in 1995 is very different from what it was in 1951. There was a transformation of what was studied, how it was studied, for what purpose it was studied, and how the practitioners fared in society. All this transformation took place in the context of a massive increase in numbers of students who chose to specialize in economics at the postsecondary-school level. In 1951 there were around 25 universities; the number rose to 82 in 1971, and twenty years later the number was 189, comprising affiliating, residential, open, and other kinds of institutions that produced more B.A.s, M.A.s, M.Phil.s, and Ph.D.s in economics than ever.

One can observe the professionalization of this discipline only in a particular sociohistorical context. In India numerous factors have contributed to this complex process of professionalization. Together these factors have transformed the discipline and have made it considerably more professional than it was in the decades before 1951.

Planning

The single most important factor that resulted not only in increasing the demand for economists but also in altering qualitatively the nature of economics practiced in India was planning for economic development, inaugurated in the early 1950s. The type of expertise required for participating in the actual process of planning was different from the more general (often bordering on the philosophical) understanding of economic forces needed for giving advice. From the Second Five Year Plan (1956–61) onward, preparation of the Plans in India became very sophisticated, requiring far more statistical and mathematical input than was the case earlier.

All this not only increased the demand for economists but also meant that the economists needed to have a strong background both in economic theory and modern quantitative techniques. In addition to the economic-statistical manpower needed by the planning organs, there was a great demand for a more rigorous kind of research about the Indian economy. Right from the beginning the Planning Commission sponsored numerous major and minor research projects. This type of support had a multiplier effect, for it spawned other inquiries funded by different agencies in the universities. These researches were aided by an expansion of the data-collecting organs of the government. The much larger volume of economic information that posed afresh many substantive issues of theory and policy stimulated both Indian and overseas economists to tackle them.

The urge to professionalize the subject was encouraged by this greater interaction between Indian and overseas economists made possible by the Planning Commission. P. C. Mahalanobis, in particular, invited to India many economists in the mid-1950s to interact with Indian economist-statistician-planners. American economists J. K. Galbraith and Paul Baran; American mathematical physicist and father of cybernetics Norbert Wiener; Polish economists Oskar Lange and Michał Kalecki; Dutch economists Jan Sandee and Jan Tinbergen; Norwegian econometrician Ragnar Frisch; British economists Nicholas Kaldor and Ian Little are only some of the great men who visited India in the mid-1950s. Most of them spent various periods of time either at the New Delhi Planning Commission or at Calcutta's Indian Statistical Institute. Similarly Indian economists visited the USSR, Poland, and other Eastern European countries and saw for themselves how planning techniques were being put to use. These visits are particularly important because it was in the mid-1950s that Soviet economic thinking itself was undergoing revolutionary changes as a result of the work of brilliant mathematical economists like L. V. Kantarovich, V. S. Nemchinov, and others. The professionalism of these economists rubbed off on the Indian economists who came into contact with them.

Economists in Government

Side by side with the Planning Commission, governments in India began to induct economists for their specific expertise because the largely laissez-faire policy was giving way to an active interventionist stance. A highly professional approach is expected of the economist in government, a professionalism different from that of an academic economist. The Indian Economic Service, as it is called, selected young economists after a grueling competitive examination, and they were provided with further training at one of the leading centers of economic research (Ambirajan 1981).

Centers of Excellence

With the enormous increase in student numbers and inadequate funding available from the state's resources, an inevitable dilution of quality occurred. In order to salvage the situation a new experiment was evolved to concentrate resources in certain specialized centers of excellence. Economics did quite well in this dispensation. The Delhi School of Economics, Institute of Economic Growth, Gokhale Institute of Politics and Economics, the economics departments of Delhi University, Jawaharlal Nehru University, Bombay University, Indian Institutes of Management, agricultural universities, the agro-economic centers, and the Population Studies centers, are only some of the teaching and research institutions that were liberally funded. Initial recruitment of well-trained faculty from leading overseas universities had a salutary effect in improving the quality of students who came out of these centers. The new faculty were able to encourage their students to move out of mere rote learning, to desire to enjoy the subject, and to compete with the best in the world.[2]

2. See "Epilogue: The New Generation" for an account of the improvement in the research quality of the Indian economics profession during the 1950–78 period (Datta 1978, chap. 16).

Think Tanks

The professionalization process of economics in India was aided by the establishment of numerous purely research institutes during the last four decades. At the time of independence, apart from the Gokhale Institute at Poona and the Indian Statistical Institute at Calcutta, there were no institutions solely devoted to research in socioeconomic conditions. At present there are more than a hundred such institutes—big and small—conducting inquiries into a wide variety of subjects. They engage in data gathering and policy studies as well as work in areas that only satisfy intellectual curiosity. A good deal of work is commissioned, but grants are also provided for research in areas that are not immediately aimed at any policy problems. The main funding comes from the central government (through the Indian Council of Social Science Research, University Grants Commission, and earlier from the Research Programmes Committee of the Planning Commission), and the state governments. The contribution of the private sector to social science research has so far been very minimal. However, foreign agencies such as UNDP, WHO, ILO, World Bank, IMF, and the Rockefeller and Ford Foundations have made substantial contributions to many of these centers of research. Some of the best and most promising economists are attracted to them because they are spared heavy teaching loads and dull administrative chores.

American Influence

Among the foreign influences since 1950 that shaped the study of economics in India, American influence was the greatest.[3] For historical reasons, as we have seen, Britain had great impact on the making of the Indian academic community, but during the postwar years the center of economic studies shifted to the United States. American universities had attracted many of the best minds in the profession since the 1930s, and by the late 1940s, the quality and quantity of American economics was unsurpassed. In addition to the quality of American economics, other factors too contributed to the American impact on the study of economics in India. There was first of all the expansion of

3. Britain could not match the resources America deployed in this area after 1950. There were British Council fellowships and Nuffield Foundation grants, but in the sheer reach and availability of funds, they could not match what the Americans were able to do through Fulbright Fellowships and Ford and Rockefeller Foundation grants.

graduate schools in America, flush with funds, that were interested in getting the best students from all over the world. This, coupled with the lack of resources experienced by the British universities, saw hundreds of young Indian graduates going to America for postgraduate study in the leading universities there. Those who returned to India to teach and research brought with them new ideas and instructional practices. Throughout the cold war period the American government poured vast sums of money into area studies in the United States, but also brought numerous academics through the Fulbright scheme to spend various periods in Indian universities. Under the Fulbright, Smith-Mundt, and other schemes, hundreds of Indian academics were able to visit American universities and experience the American system of higher learning first hand. During the period 1950–93, 3,925 Indian scholars visited the United States and 4,771 American academics spent time in India under the Education Exchange Scheme of the Fulbright Program.[4] When the PL480 funds accumulated with the U.S. authorities in India, they were spent in many ways, including publishing American textbooks at ridiculously low prices and conducting annual summer schools in India for Indian teachers of economics to bring them up-to-date in the study of economics. Invariably in these summer schools, two or three American university teachers participated. Thus this face-to-face meeting of American and Indian economists both on Indian and American soil over the long period has had considerable impact on the way economics is now practiced in India.[5]

The part played by leading American philanthropic foundations in encouraging economic studies in India also needs a mention.[6] While ideological reasons and the national interests of the United States were largely responsible for the massive efforts made to improve economic studies in India, that is not our immediate concern. The fact is that the efforts made by the foundations did have an effect in imparting a sense of professionalism to the Indian economic community.

A very perceptible conduit of American and, of course, other international influences and paradigms of economics is the increased involvement of international economic institutions in Indian economic af-

4. Information given by the United States Education Foundation of India, Madras.
5. There were also quite a few Indians who came back thoroughly radicalized by the student atmosphere in the United States that existed during the period when America was engrossed in the Vietnam imbroglio.
6. For an extended treatment of this subject, see Rosen 1985.

fairs. A position—even a temporary one—in the bureaucracies of the various international organizations has been highly prized by Indian economists from academia as well as from the government. There is a very large number of Indian economists in the different international organizations such as UNDP, WHO, ILO, FAO, IBRD, IMF, WIDER, and others. Many Indian government economists are seconded to these institutions and come back after serving a few years. There has hardly been a single senior economist in Indian government during the last two decades who has not had a few years in one of the above mentioned organizations. In the permanent roster of the international bureaucracy, there are scores of directly recruited economists who typically join the service after their studies and slowly move up the scale. With few exceptions these economists have either had their graduate school education in U.S. universities or have had some involvement with American higher education institutions. After a few years in a world organization many of them try to spend varying periods in senior positions within the Indian government. The present Finance Secretary, Montek Singh Ahluwalia, and the chief economic adviser, Shankar Acharya, did their postgraduate studies in the United States and served in the World Bank before occupying these positions in India. Similarly, Raja Chelliah, the founder of the Finance Ministry's think tank (the National Institute of Public Finance and Policy) and a consultant to the government on fiscal matters, received his doctorate in the United States under the Fulbright scheme and served his time in the IMF.[7] Other Indian-born American-educated economists residing outside India, with strong connections to world economic bodies, who have given effective policy advice to the Indian government in recent times, include Jagdish Bhagwati and T. N. Srinivasan. Certainly the shift in India's economic policy from its emphasis on dirigisme to market friendliness has been ascribed to these U.S.-educated[8] and IMF/WB-

7. Raja Chelliah's concern for professionalism in economic studies has resulted in the foundation of the Madras School of Economics this year to impart very high quality economics education at the graduate level. The first director of this new school is a Ph.D. from Wisconsin and a former student of Arnold Zellner.

8. Padma Desai and Jagdish Bhagwati point out that the economists in key government positions (e.g., I. G. Patel and V. K. Ramaswami, to name two) in the 1950s and 1960s were educated in Cambridge, England, where the "emphasis was typically on the inadequacy of the Invisible Hand with little attention to how the Visible Hand . . . would operate in practice." In contrast, American training continuously points out the "failures of actual intervention" and even goes to the extent of considering intervention to preserve the free market system as unnecessary (1975, 219). It is not without significance that in 1992, when the present government was replacing the old planning-socialist approach with a market-friendly policy, the chief economic

experienced professionals who had been inducted in the higher echelons of policymaking.

Coming of Age of the Economics Profession in India

What we have seen so far informs us that powerful forces have contributed to change the character of the study of economics in India. This has been made possible by the initial impact of European and American economists on the thinking of Indian economists. Quite apart from some of the most influential economists like Sukhmoy Chakravarthy and Ashok Mitra, who returned from universities in the Netherlands and occupied important academic/advisory positions, there were the ideas of Grigorii Feldman, Ragnar Frisch, Jan Sandee, and other quantitatively inclined European economists that left an imprint on the planning efforts. Similarly, American-trained economists like B. S. Minhas and T. N. Srinivasan, from their perches in the Indian Statistical Institute, exercised influence on the quantification of Indian economic studies. If professionalism means becoming more scientific, and scientific means studying measurable entities, economics in India certainly achieved a great increase in professionalism from the 1960s. An interesting sign of the coming of age of the discipline is the periodic professional pronouncements about the state of the economy by research-based public and quasi-public organizations. The predictive models of Indian macroeconomic performance issued by the Delhi School of Economics, the National Council of Applied Economic Research, the Reserve Bank of India, and the Centre for Monitoring Indian Economy are taken seriously and discussed by professional economists both within and outside the government. Similarly, the annual midyear review of the economy conducted by a group of economists from universities, research institutions, and journalism associated with the India International Centre in Delhi is given close attention.

The four decades since India won its freedom have had a major impact on the study of social sciences, in particular economics. As we have seen, economics in India has shown an increase in both quantity and quality. If we consider the achievement of self-sufficiency as an indicator of progress, it can be said that India has more or less achieved total import

---

adviser who was educated at Cambridge, England, was also replaced by one who had had his higher education in the United States.

substitution in the area of Ph.D.s in economics. The number of U.S.-trained economic faculty in Indian universities was around forty in 1968 and it is not much more than fifty at present, although the number of universities has doubled and the departments have expanded. The proportion of Indian Ph.D.s in the various teaching departments has gone up considerably. If individual Indian students still go overseas for doctoral work, it is more out of intellectual curiosity or because a foreign degree has better salability, rather than out of national necessity. From being purely local players, Indian economists educated during the fifties and sixties are playing a part not only in the development of the discipline but also in policymaking in India and in the international economic organizations.

Enemies of Professionalism

If we look at organizational structure and activities, the Indian academic community has all the characteristics of such communities in the United States, U.K., Canada, or Australia. Ultimately, of course, a test of professionalization is the competence of the individual professional vis-à-vis the rest. Unlike in certain disciplines like medicine, a minimum standard cannot be enforced from above in the economics profession: it must come from within, and the necessary conditions do not seem to be present in India. While there must be sufficient intellectual, psychological, and even spiritual resources for the individual to achieve a high degree of professionalism in the subject, ultimately the institutional milieu and incentive structure determine the professional quality of the community of economists. The professionalization of a discipline such as economics is a complex process because, unlike medicine or law, economics is not a practically oriented subject aimed at individual users for specific purposes. Economics has multiple but vague uses, and the users are of different categories. Hence we cannot give an unequivocal answer to the question, Has the Indian community of economists become fully professional? While we have seen an enormous expansion quantitatively, the qualitative improvement is confined to a fraction of the hundreds of thousands of B.A.s and M.A.s churned out by the Indian higher academic institutions year after year.

There are far too many obstacles that stand in the way of the community of Indian economists as a whole becoming fully professional.[9]

---

9. For an analysis—dated but still relevant—of why the Indian academic profession in general is not productive and important, see Edward Shils ([1969] 1974).

The forces that militate against the cultivation of modern scholarship in India are too many, and they range from the use of an alien language to the absence of a cultural climate conducive to the development of an academic meritocracy. This kind of an intellectual milieu is manifested in specific factors that in combination have had a ruinous impact on the academic profession's capacity to function effectively. First, the dictum "More means less" is very true for India. The hectic expansion of undergraduate, postgraduate, and doctoral studies in economics has been responsible for the decline in quality. Colleges and universities were (and still are) more often started for political reasons by governments without a preliminary analysis of needs and assessment of the available resources. Thus the sum available for education is spread very thin. Students decide to go for higher and higher levels of studies because the degrees are used as a filter by employers. The Ph.D. program in Indian universities has not undergone much change since it was introduced on a modest scale during the early decades of this century. While a number of features of the American higher academic system, such as semesters, grade-point averages, credits, and so on have been borrowed, the systematic organization of graduate schools to impart solid training in economics has not taken root in India.

Second, unlike the 1940s and 1950s, the best students prefer professions like engineering, management, and medicine rather than the social or physical sciences. Very few students opt for a teaching career because of its many disadvantages, such as low salaries, lack of social recognition, and bureaucratic running of the academies of higher learning. This is very hard on economics teaching because the few really bright economists tend to move toward research centers, business organizations, and government departments, and the teaching of economics is consequently often inferior.[10]

Third, an unfortunate fact is that India has lost hundreds of extremely bright economists to overseas universities. While one hears of the high fliers like Amartya Sen, Jagdish Bhagwati, T. N. Srinivasan, G. S. Maddala, and Meghnad Desai, there are a very large number of economists who had their initial education in India in American, British, Australian, and Canadian universities who could have helped to raise the standard of

10. Shils cites the economist Professor Shenoy: "Faculty vacancies are being filled, generally, by craven leftouts from other vocations"; he goes on to say: "except possibly for Presidency College, Calcutta, I know of no higher educational institution in India where teachers encourage their best pupils to enter the academic profession" (Shils [1969] 1974, 209).

economics education in India had they not migrated for good.[11] This is, in a sense, a result of the internationalization of the economics profession. An earlier generation of economists who went abroad for studies returned because their commitment to the country was more than their attachment to the discipline. But during the last four decades, economists have shown more anxiety to be recognized by peers spread all over the world than by their fellow countrymen. Consequently the economist/scholar moves to where he is able to pursue his academic discipline without distraction. There is, besides, the individual economist's yearning for international recognition, which is usually not forthcoming if he remains in the obscurity of an Indian university. The Indian-born Amartya Sen, working in the United States, has said: "One of the remarkable facts of Western academia is its open-minded catholicism in welcoming academics from abroad. There are few difficulties in the acceptance of scholars from the third world who choose to live in the West. Yet, at the same time, the neglect of attention to—and acknowledgement of—voices from a distance remains striking. . . . This contrast is of some significance in influencing the location choice of many promising academics from the third world . . . it is, I believe, a mistake to seek an explanation primarily in the high salaries in the West" (1994, 1150).

Fourth, the lack of adequate infrastructure (libraries, computing facilities, etc.) make it necessary for students to rely on one or two textbooks and classroom lectures. When there is a burgeoning growth in published research in books and journals and proliferation of other rapid modes of information flow elsewhere, the lack of access to these is bound to tell on the making of economists in India. Add to this the rigid and antiquated examination system, and you have a recipe for making a mockery of economics instruction. K. A. Narayanan of the economics department of the S. K. V. College, Trichur, confessed: "For all practical purposes, the working (i.e. instructional) period available is limited to about 100 days in a year due to several reasons like strikes, late conduct of examinations, late announcement of results, and the consequent late commencement of classes etc. Therefore, whatever the status of the syllabus, improved or not, the teacher is constrained to make adjustments, short-cuts and a selection of topics solely with the expected five essays in mind" (1987, 113).

11. B. S. Minhas, a leading economist-statistician and former member of the Planning Commission, complained as early as 1972 that "some of the think tanks and Western Universities had made a negative contribution [to the Indian economics profession] by sucking into their system some of the best scholars and economists from India" (1972, 184).

Fifth, one might have thought that the universities and institutes at the top rung would be free from such problems. But they have started experiencing some of the worst ills of the leading economics schools elsewhere. Due to the recent financial crunch, the faculty in previously well-funded institutions of excellence are encouraged to seek research grants from outside. Thus while the top professors are busy preparing research proposals and outside consulting, teaching is left to the raw recruits or the most junior faculty.

Finally, all the above are reflected in poor teaching. What is taught in most economics departments tends to be outdated and meaningless. The University Grants Commission lamented that "the existing course curriculum generally does not adequately acquaint the students with Indian reality and Indian ethos, nor does it equip them with the theoretical tools to analyse and solve Indian problems" (1989, 5). It is no doubt true that what is imparted in the classrooms is neoclassical economics of the type prevailing in the West at least a decade ago. A close examination of the economics syllabi at twenty-six leading Indian universities led Dr. Oommen to observe: "neo-classical economics, Keynesian economics and the so-called synthesis of the two dominate the curricula. Utility, consumer sovereignty, marginal productivity, production functions, isoquant-indifference curve analysis, cost-benefit analysis, general equilibrium etc. sing melodiously in the class room" (1987, 98). The University Grants Commission's guidelines for preparing economics syllabi in the various universities published in 1989 is clearly slanted toward neoclassical economics despite the committee's pious statement: "the contents of the courses should not be under the heavy dominance of particular models, approaches or ideologies. The courses devised . . . have kept this objective in constant view. They reflect all major internationally recognised professional schools of thinking" (1989, 60).

Much of the criticism about the economics taught is not only about the contents but also directed against the mechanical and meaningless mode of instruction. Even the few good departments are not immune to criticism on account of teaching. Imitating the top graduate schools of economics in the United States, they stress theory and technique so exclusively that the more interesting and relevant parts of the discipline as well as the imparting of knowledge about the economy as it exists are left out. A former student of the Delhi School of Economics, reminiscing about his university days, said: "there was too much fascination with theory to worry about the unfortunate and unruly drift in the Indian economy. About the actual predicament of people in India we were taught very little. . . . We mastered the equations of the Raj-Sen model without an inkling of the empathy these economists had for people in poverty. We were also ignorant about the National Sample Surveys . . . [we] did not . . . go out into the real world and seek to understand something about real people and their problems" (Sudarshan 1995, 187). The views of another former student of the Delhi School of Economics were very much like those of the Colander-Klamer subjects who talked about being "socialized" in the American graduate schools of economics into one particular mold: "this School was a club . . . one realises that a club closes itself mentally and physically to the environment. . . . What clubs stress is good behaviour, not ideas, not inventiveness. . . . The D. School is merely an intellectual plantation" (Visvanathan 1995, 202–3).[12] It is no wonder that the alumni of the Delhi School of Economics do so well in the top economics departments in the United States.

One could list many more reasons that militate against professionalism and obstruct the improvement in the study of economics. But it is enough to show that the factors listed above have cumulatively brought down economics studies in India to the present unfortunate condition. The disparity between the best and the rest within India, on the one hand, and between India and the more advanced countries in the West on the other is more likely to increase than otherwise.

Doctrinal Positions of the Academic Profession

It is necessary to emphasize that the Indian economists' ideological preferences have not stood in the way of developing a professional approach to the study and practice of economics. Not all American-trained economists in India hold the same views on economic matters. There are graduates from Stanford and Wisconsin teaching in Indian universities with pronounced leanings toward a strong Marxist position, but they are no less professional than other graduates from Chicago and Yale who profess variants of neoclassical economics.

Doctrinal divisions in the Indian academic profession are not nearly as sharp as elsewhere. During the pre-independence period, there were

12. On the emphasis on technique to the exclusion of all the rest in American graduate schools of economics, see Colander and Klamer 1987.

many different strands of thought, but they could be broadly classified
into three positions:

> a protectionist model that favored autarkic industrialization
> an orthodox Marshallian model that was against tariff protection but
> stressed the virtues of Victorian capitalism and an open economy
> a Gandhian model that envisioned an economic system based on the
> uplifting of rural societies

However, once India became independent and particularly in the decades following 1951, there developed a distinct consensus in the Indian
economics profession that was previously lacking. When, during the
mid-1950s, a pronounced shift in economic policy was initiated by Prime
Minister Jawaharlal Nehru, influenced by socialist ideals, and when Soviet economists inspired Mahalanobis, the majority of economists had
no difficulty in going along with it. The increased role of the state and
planning was accepted without any murmur as necessary and inevitable.
It is remarkable how quickly the profession took to Marxian sectoral
models of expanded reproduction that treated problems of capital accu-
mulation structurally. The Keynesian framework came in handy to justify
an interventionist stance due to the inadequacies of the capitalist system,
although Keynesian macroeconomic policy was found unsuitable because it was demand-centered. One has only to study the hundreds of
papers that have appeared in Indian learned periodicals as well as those
presented during the annual economics conference meetings to understand what a broad consensus Indian economists are capable of. Not that
disagreements were totally absent, but they were more within a paradigm
that could be called (for want of a better phrase) left-oriented development studies, for they revolved around such issues as the nature of Indian
capitalism, agrarian feudalism, the dependency thesis, and the nature of
the intermediate class. Industrial economics received some attention, but
the antimonopoly position was utilized not to encourage competitive
forces but to favor improved state control.

This broad consensus has shown significant strain since the early
1970s. A slow realization that the socialist-planning model has not been
able to solve the age-old problem of poverty, along with the emergence of
Thatcherism and Reaganomics and the miracle of the East Asian Tigers,
have had an impact on the doctrinal beliefs of the Indian economics
profession. The central role of the state, the idea of import substitution,
intersectoral planning of growth rates, institutional reforms as a tool for

better agricultural productivity, and many aspects of the earlier consensus are being critically analyzed with an increasingly major portion of the profession favoring higher growth rates and a freer play of the market mechanism as a better route to poverty elimination.

Conclusion

A gargantuan task faces Indian educational planners to enable a trickle down from the highly professional and qualitatively superior band of economists to the sea of mediocrity below. The only consolation is that even this fraction, that is, the superior types in the Indian context, is a substantial number. The professionalism of this elite group cannot be compared to the professionalism of the American economics community. It is more like the European-style professionalism as recently defined by Bruno Frey and Reiner Eichenberger (1992, 216–20; 1993). Notwithstanding the contributions to the stock of economic knowledge in economic theory and econometric methodology in recent times, leading Indian economists working in India tend to be, as Frey and Eichenberger say of European economists, "theoretically broad and institutionally specialized," besides being involved in policymaking and economic administration. This can be seen even in the basic approach toward economics practiced by active Indian economists during the last forty years. As Yoginder Alagh, an American-trained economist who has occupied senior positions in the Planning Commission and elsewhere in the government of India, has said: "the concern has been with the necessity of special approaches to analyse the Indian economy . . . [and hence] the emphasis . . . is not on the derivation of testable hypotheses, but on the construction of workable models with policy content" (1977, 72, 84). If we can dichotomize the Indian economic community into "resident Indian" and "nonresident Indian" (composed of the hundreds of highly proficient economists partly educated in India but working outside the country), it is the latter category that conforms to the American model of professionalism.

References

Alagh, Yoginder. 1977. Research Methodology in Economics. In *ICSSR, A Survey of Research in Economics*. Vol. 1. *Methods and Techniques*. Bombay: Allied Publishers.

Ambirajan, S. 1981. India: The Aftermath of Empire. In *Economists in Government: An International Comparative Study*. Edited by A. W. Coats. Durham, N.C.: Duke University Press.

Colander, David, and Arjo Klamer. 1987. The Making of an Economist. *The Journal of Economic Perspectives*. 1.1 (fall): 95–111.

Datta, Bhabatosh. 1978. *Indian Economic Thought: Twentieth Century Perspectives 1900–1950*. New Delhi: Tata McGraw-Hill.

Desai, Padma, and Jagdish Bhagwati. 1975. Socialism and Indian Economic Policy. *World Development*. 3.4 (April): 213–21.

Frey, Bruno, and Reiner Eichenberger. 1992. Economics and Economists: A European Perspective. *American Economic Review*. 82.2 (May): 216–20.

———. 1993. American and European Economics and Economists. *Journal of Economic Perspectives*. 7.4 (fall): 185–93.

Kumar, Dharma, and Dilip Mookherjee, eds. 1995. *D. School; Reflections on the Delhi School of Economics*. Delhi: Oxford University Press.

Minhas, B. S. 1972. Comments on Gustav Papanek's Paper on "Foreign Advisers and Planning Agencies." In *The Crisis in Planning*. Vol. 1, *Issues*. Edited by Mike Faber and Dudley Seers. London: Oxford University Press.

Narayanan, K. A. 1987. Comment. In Oommen 1987.

Oommen, M. A. 1987. Hidden Curricula in Social Sciences. In Oommen 1987.

———, ed. 1987. *Issues in Teaching of Economics in Indian Universities*. New Delhi: Oxford and IBH Publishing.

Rosen, George. 1985. *Western Economists and Eastern Societies: Aspects of Change in South Asia 1950–1970*. Delhi: Oxford University Press.

Sen, Amartya. 1994. Amiya Kumar Dasgupta 1903–1992.*Economic Journal* 104.426 (September): 1147–55.

Shils, Edward. 1969. The Academic Profession in India. *Minerva* 7 (spring). Reprinted in Amrik Singh and Philip G. Altbach, eds. 1974. *The Higher Learning in India*. Delhi: Vikas.

Sudarshan, R. 1995. Gold Strikes from KGF to the D. School. In Kumar and Mookherjee 1995.

University Grants Commission. 1989. *Report of the Curriculum Development Centre in Economics*. New Delhi: University Grants Commission.

Visvanathan, Shiv. 1995. De Schooling Myself. In Kumar and Mookherjee 1995.

The Americanization of Economics in Korea

Young Back Choi

Introduction

Like so many other things in Korea, economics as a profession has grown rapidly since the Korean War. In 1993 the Korean Economic Association boasted over 1800 members with the Ph.D. degree. The process of growth has one pronounced feature: the preponderance of graduate training in the United States, which may be called Americanization.[1] In a way, the economic profession in Korea has become an American clone.

The aim of this paper is threefold: (1) to establish this Americanization as a fact by describing the statistics compiled from *Hangook Kyungjehakhoe Hoewonrohk 1993* (hereinafter cited as *The List*);[2] (2)

1. I am using the terms "Americanization" and "American-trained" interchangeably. To the degree that there are doctrinal differences among economics departments in different universities in the United States, my usage of the terms hides the diversity in graduate economics training, and Koreans are not unaware of this diversity. For example, in recent years, left-leaning students at a university in Seoul have demanded that a graduate of the New School for Social Research be hired to teach labor economics, instead of one from a more orthodox economics department. Notwithstanding the recognized diversity, equating "Americanization" with "American-trained" is not a bad approximation, given the relative standardization of training in economics, that is, the dominance of neoclassical economics, in the United States. See Hansen: "the content and structure of graduate programs in economics are amazingly similar" (1991, 1085). To the degree that American-style training in economics has been spreading throughout the world, Americanization may also be called internationalization.

2. I thank Kyung Seop Shim for providing me with a copy of *The List* (1993) and Oh Hyun Chang for a copy of the *Hangook Kyungjehaagei Mohsaek* (1983; hereafter cited as *Introspections*). All translations from Korean texts are my own.

to speculate about the most important factors that generated the process, focusing especially on those factors influencing the demand for and the supply of economists; and (3) to describe some of the consequences of the process, for example, increasing professionalization, import substitution, and other local reactions such as nationalistic sentiments, attempts to diversify import sources, and doubts about the relevance of orthodox economics, among others. Let us first turn to facts.

Facts

Statistics compiled from *The List* 1993 reveal vividly the Americanization of the economics profession in Korea. Currently, the Korean Economics Society has 1,825 members with Ph.D.s. Of these, 1,001 are foreign trained (see table 1). This shows that the foreign-trained economists outnumber their Korean-trained counterparts.

By itself, however, this ratio is misleading. In a country such as Korea, there is an overwhelming concentration of political power and economic and cultural activities in the capital city, Seoul. Almost every South Korean wants to stay in Seoul, if possible. To get a better sense of the distribution of economists of different training backgrounds, therefore, the above ratio should be broken down based on the economist's place of employment, namely, within Seoul or outside Seoul (called the provinces in this paper). Of 1,065 economists with employment in Seoul—universities and colleges, government and research institutes—749 are foreign trained; that is, 70 percent of the economists working in Seoul are foreign trained. Of 760 economists working outside Seoul, only 252 are foreign trained; in the provinces, that is, only 32 percent are foreign trained. From this, one can get a better sense of the predominance of the foreign-trained economists in Seoul, the choice location in terms of desirability and influence. Domestically trained economists are largely left to find employment outside Seoul.

To see whether the idea of the Americanization of economics in Korea is valid, I have further divided the foreign-trained economists into two categories: U.S.-trained and non-U.S. foreign-trained. We find that an overwhelming majority, 79 percent, of all foreign-trained Korean economists

Table 1 Distribution of Korean Economists by Place of Employment and Educational Background

Employed in Seoul

		Type of Employment				
	Degrees from	Academic institutions	Business organizations	Government	Research institutions	Subtotal
DOMESTIC {	Seoul	199	17	11	72	299
	Provinces	7	0	0	10	17
FOREIGN {	U.S.	313	32	21	254	620
	Non-U.S.	66	7	7	49	129
	Total	585	56	39	385	1065

Employed in Provinces

		Type of Employment					
	Degrees from	Academic institutions	Business organizations	Government	Research institutions	Subtotal	Total
DOMESTIC {	Seoul	279	0	1	1	281	580
	Provinces	214	1	2	10	227	244
FOREIGN {	U.S.	156	3	0	17	176	796
	Non-U.S.	72	0	0	4	76	205
	Total	721	4	3	32	760	1825

were trained in the United States, as can be seen from the following ratio.[3]

U.S. : non-U.S. foreign = 796 : 205.[4]

If we consider only those with employment in Seoul, the balance tilts even more in favor of the American trained. In this case, we find that nearly 84 percent of the foreign-trained Korean economists working in Seoul were trained in the United States, as can be seen from the following ratio:

U.S. : non-U.S. foreign (Seoul) = 620 : 129.

Lately, however, the economists with a Ph.D. from domestic institutions seem to have done even better than the economists trained abroad, especially in the United States[5] (see table 3). That is, we observe a significant degree of "import substitution." Does the growing import substitution nullify the idea of Americanization? I do not think so. I think that import substitution means that locally trained economists are increasingly viewed as good substitutes in the market, especially in the provinces. But to the degree that domestic universities in Seoul have been staffed largely by U.S.-trained economists and their curricula fashioned after those in the United States,[6] and since we do not have any reason to believe that Korean economists are doing much to alter what they have imported, we may observe that the process of Americanization has become even more effective. Even those who are classified as domes-

---

3. Non-U.S. foreign countries where Korean economists obtained their degrees include, in descending order, Germany (64), Japan (56), France (31), U.K. (23), Philippines (14), Austria (8), Taiwan (4), Italy (2), Sweden (2), Belgium (2), Switzerland (1), and the Netherlands (1). Thus, of the economists trained in foreign countries other than the United States, more than half obtained their degrees from either Germany or Japan.

4. Fifty-five percent of the U.S.-trained economists have undergraduate training from the three most prestigious universities in Seoul, namely, Seoul National University, Yonsei University, and Korea University. Further, the most prestigious school, Seoul National University, outnumbers the other two combined. See table 2.

5. It is possible that many U.S.-trained Korean economists decided to sojourn in the United States at the end of their study, given the tightness of the job market for economists in Korea. The Korean American Economic Association, based in the United States, had about 250 members as of 1991. The KAEA members, who constitute only a small proportion of Korean economists in the United States, include naturalized U.S. citizens, permanent residents, sojourners, and graduate students.

6. Besides The List, the proportions of American-trained economists in the economics departments at the three top universities in Seoul—Seoul National University, Yonsei University, and Korea University—are 66 percent, 96 percent, and 82 percent, respectively. Pyun (1983a, 55) observes that there is no difference between studying economics in Korea and in the United States, as far as the content is concerned. The only significant difference is the language spoken.

Table 2 Distribution of Korean Economists by Place of Employment, Undergraduate Training, and Graduate Training

	Employed in Seoul				Employed in Provinces				Total
	Degrees from				Degrees from				
Undergraduate degree from	U.S.	Non-U.S. foreign	Domestic	Subtotal	U.S.	Non-U.S. foreign	Domestic	Subtotal	
Seoul University	297	30	45	372	60	16	62	138	510
Yonsei University	86	10	22	118	20	2	11	33	151
Korea University	58	13	25	96	29	7	30	66	162
Others	152	61	112	325	67	46	232	345	670
Total	593	114	204	911	176	71	335	582	1493

Table 3 Distribution of Korean Economists by Place of Employment, Educational Background, and Year of Ph.D.

Year of Ph.D.	Employed in Seoul					Employed in Provinces					
	Degrees from					Degrees from					
	U.S.	Non-U.S. foreign	Domestic: Seoul	Domestic: Provinces	Subtotal	U.S.	Non-U.S. foreign	Domestic: Seoul	Domestic: Provinces	Sub total	Total
1956	1	0	0	0	1	0	0	0	0	0	1
1957	0	0	0	0	0	0	0	0	0	0	0
1958	0	0	0	0	0	0	0	0	0	0	0
1959	0	1	0	0	1	0	0	0	0	0	1
1960	0	0	1	0	1	0	1	0	0	1	2
1961	1	0	0	0	1	0	0	0	0	0	1
1962	0	0	0	0	0	0	0	0	0	0	0
1963	2	0	0	0	2	0	0	0	0	0	2
1964	1	0	0	0	1	0	0	0	0	0	1
1965	0	0	0	0	0	0	0	0	0	0	0
1966	3	0	0	0	3	0	0	0	0	0	3
1967	2	0	0	0	2	0	1	0	1	2	4
1968	5	4	2	0	11	0	0	2	1	3	14
1969	2	1	3	0	6	0	0	1	2	3	9
1970	3	2	1	0	6	0	0	1	0	1	7
1971	10	1	2	0	13	0	0	0	1	1	14
1972	9	2	1	1	13	1	0	0	0	1	14
1973	9	0	0	0	9	1	0	1	5	7	16
1974	9	1	6	0	16	1	0	0	2	3	19

Table 3 Continued

Year of Ph.D.	Employed in Seoul					Employed in Provinces					
	Degrees from					Degrees from					
	U.S.	Non-U.S. foreign	Domestic: Seoul	Domestic: Provinces	Subtotal	U.S.	Non-U.S. foreign	Domestic: Seoul	Domestic: Provinces	Sub total	Total
1975	5	2	4	1	12	1	0	0	3	4	16
1976	13	2	1	0	16	2	1	0	2	5	21
1977	12	0	3	0	15	2	0	0	1	3	18
1978	14	3	4	1	22	0	1	1	0	2	24
1979	11	4	6	0	21	1	0	1	2	4	25
1980	11	3	8	0	22	0	2	2	4	8	30
1981	10	2	1	0	13	6	1	4	2	13	26
1982	12	3	5	1	21	4	2	2	3	11	32
1983	17	1	5	0	23	1	0	5	4	10	33
1984	24	4	8	1	37	6	3	8	3	20	57
1985	24	1	9	0	34	10	4	14	2	30	64
1986	28	7	10	0	45	8	3	16	10	37	82
1987	26	4	19	0	49	10	3	14	12	39	88
1988	34	4	8	3	49	22	2	31	1	56	105
1989	39	6	15	1	61	17	5	23	18	63	124
1990	46	8	15	2	71	13	6	20	17	56	127
1991	31	7	13	1	52	14	5	12	14	45	97
1992	20	10	7	0	37	4	2	14	8	28	65
1993	9	5	17	2	33	1	1	14	13	29	62
Total	443	88	174	14	719	125	43	186	131	485	1204

tically trained often have some exposure to foreign training—an M.A. or a visiting position in the United States.[7] What could be the reason for the Americanization of economics in Korea?

Possible Reasons for Americanization

One may observe that it is inevitable that South Korea should be influenced by the United States in economics as well as in other areas. The United States was the principal donor of military and economic aid to Korea since the end of WWII for over twenty years, and the United States remains the most important of her trading partners. It seems natural that ideas should follow trade routes.

Yet, on closer examination, the Americanization of economics in Korea is not as obvious as it might first appear. For example, Japan is almost as important a trading partner of Korea as the United States. In the last three decades, Korea has consistently imported more from Japan than from the United States (though Korea has consistently exported more to the United States than to Japan). Moreover, as the brutal Japanese colonial rule for almost forty years until 1945 forced the Japanese system on Koreans— forcing them to use the Japanese language and even to adopt Japanese names—generations of Koreans had near-native fluency in Japanese. For obvious reasons, Korean economists were largely trained in Japan until 1945.[8] Yet the influence of Japanese economics is minimal in the post-WWII era.[9] In fact, in *The List* the number of economists trained in Japan, fifty-four, is even less than those trained in Germany, sixty-four. Why?

The relative lack of Japanese influence on the Korean economics profession, despite the colonial past and the continued importance of trade with Japan, has much to do with the peculiarity of the economics profession in Japan and the division of Korea as frontiers on the opposite sides of the cold war. Before the surrender of Japan in 1945 (Shin 1983, 16) (and long after [Bronfenbrenner 1956, 390–95]), economics departments in Japanese universities were dominated by dogmatic Marxists. Though

7. There is a small hint of the diversification of import away from the United States, possibly because of the demand for economic information about the EC, which is increasingly important to Korea as a trading partner.

8. But they were few in number, as the Japanese discouraged the education of Koreans.

9. There has been renewed interest in studying economics in Japan since the late 1970s. Shin (1983, 21) thinks it is through the encouragement of the Japan Foundation. From what I know it also reflects a renewed interest in Marxism among radical students in the 1970s and 1980s.

there were Japanese universities such as Hitotsubashi University that had already established a tradition of modern economics by the 1930s, many Koreans under the Japanese colonial yoke were attracted to Marxism, as it was viewed as a liberating ideology (Shin 1983, 15; Kang 1983, 85–86; Pyun 1983a, 44, and 1983b, 262). Consequently, the majority of Korean economists were Marxists doing research on economic history with a particular slant. But most Marxist economists were no longer in South Korea by 1953. (They had either died or departed to North Korea.) At the conclusion of the Korean War, there was only a handful of non-Marxist economists in Korea who had been trained in Japan and elsewhere (Shin 1983, 17–19; Kang 1983, 93).[10] By the middle of the 1950s the situation in Korea was like that of Japan—without, however, her largely irrelevant academic economists[11] or her competent bureaucracy. The starting point for the growth of the economics profession in South Korea and its Americanization was, therefore, a virtual vacuum. Moreover, in the 1950s Japan did not look like an exporter of economics. If anything, Japan was in the position of importing economics from the United States.

If not trade, what then accounts for the overwhelming dominance of American economics in Korea? What are the concerns of Koreans who become economists, and American trained at that? Certainly, the relatively easier access for Koreans to higher education in the United States than in other foreign countries—in terms of accessibility of language,[12] the ease of admissions, lower net costs of education,[13] and so on—may

10. For nearly twenty years, between 1940 and 1960, institutions of higher learning existed only in name. This was due to the Japanese repression (which shut down most Korean-founded colleges and imprisoned Korean professors), the chaos under the American military rule, the mass destruction of the Korean War, and subsequent political instabilities leading up to the military coup in 1961.

11. Japanese academic economists have been largely excluded from the policymaking process because they are either doctrinaire Marxists or modern economists on the frontiers of mathematical economics, which is beyond the interest or comprehension of the majority of modern economists, let alone politicians or laymen. See Bronfenbrenner 1956; Y. Cho 1983, 153–54; and Komiya and Yamamoto 1981. U. Park (1983, 184–89) observes that Japan itself was beginning to import economics from the United States around 1958. According to Park, American-style economics in Japan is more frequently found in government bureaus and business firms.

12. It is not that English is widely spoken in Korea, but that English is widely taught in schools.

13. Higher education in the United States is nominally more costly than in European countries, where tuition is in general free. But if one considered such factors as the availability of slots in graduate schools, opportunities for scholarships, and other income-earning possibilities, the

explain why Koreans would prefer to acquire an economics Ph.D. in the United States rather than in other countries, if other things were equal. But other things have not been equal.

In what follows, I will first consider four factors that contributed to Americanization: (1) the demand for economics as a technology of development and administration; (2) the demand for the economist as a legitimizing device; (3) the demand for economics as a language necessary to communicate effectively with American officials and officials from international agencies; and (4) graduate training in economics as a signaling device. I will then consider some of the consequences.

Economics as a Technology

Economics, one may observe, is a technology of economic development,[14] and the preference for American training in economics reflects the desire to import what is believed to be the most advanced technology. The view that economics is a technology seems to have been prevalent in the United States until very recently (Coats 1989, 17; Nelson 1989, 7–10, and 1987, 64–71). More importantly, this was the impression imparted by the officials in charge of aid programs, and their expert consultants, in LDCs, including South Korea, since World War II (Y. Cho 1983, 154). If economics is the science of "the wealth of nations," then economics as taught in more prosperous industrialized nations seemed to have something to do with their prosperity. The people from poorer nations could, it seemed, benefit from learning economics as a contributing factor, if not *the* factor, to prosperity.

Viewed in this way, the preference for American economics seems natural. If a poor nation is to import technology, then, it should try to import the most advanced technology—which may be obtainable by studying in the United States, the most prosperous nation by a wide margin.[15] Moreover, in the 1960s the American economics profession

---

effective costs of graduate studies in the United States tend to be lower.

14. The term for economic science, *Kyungjehak*, which is used in all three Far Eastern countries though with different pronunciations, reveals the initial understanding of economics as a science of nation managing. See Kang 1983, 79–80.

15. Pyun (1983a, 47–49) observes that in the 1950s and early 1960s, even as American-style economics began to exert its influence on economics in Korea, people were skeptical about the value of studying economics in the United States, and an American Ph.D. was not highly regarded. I doubt the validity of this observation.

reached its peak in prestige, whereas Japanese academic economists appeared to be largely irrelevant: they were in the main either doctrinaire Marxists or pure theorists (Pyun 1983a, 56); the Japanese economy was managed by her able bureaucracy instead (Komiya and Yamamoto 1981, 262–89; Okita 1989, 188).

Indeed, in Korea most of the economists who have staffed the bureaucracy of development planning since the mid-1960s have been American trained.[16] If asked what the economic technology consisted of, they would have listed such things as macroeconomics, international trade and finance theories, the techniques of project analysis, theories of economic development, and the technique of developing indices to keep track of economic performance both at micro and macro levels (Pyun 1983b, 263–64). To many Koreans and other observers who feel that the American-trained economists have made important contributions to the rapid growth of the Korean economy (D. Kim 1983), the idea of economics as a technology may make perfect sense.[17]

Economics as a Means of Legitimization

But until the late 1970s, American-trained economists who staffed the economic planning bureaucracy carried out mercantilistic policies fashioned after those of Japan rather than those of the United States (S. Cho 1994, 14; Choi 1994, 237–39). How can we explain the demand for economics training in the United States?

While it is true that economists in Korea began to participate in economic policymaking from the 1960s, especially providing the technical service of keeping track of economic performance, it has been suggested that professional economists, especially academic economists, were used to bolster, or even to window-dress, the sometimes unpopular policies of the late President Park and his close associates (Pyun 1983a, 48; Y. Cho 1983, 155; Kang 1983, 100). Employing respected economists (Korea has over a thousand-year-old tradition of respecting teachers and professors), sometimes as cabinet members or key advisers (or more often

16. Some Koreans trained in Japanese banks later became important economic policymakers. But they were less economists than business managers or Japanese-style bureaucrats.

17. On the question of the nature of the economist's contribution in government, many people who served as high-level economists in the U.S. government observe that it is mainly basic economics, perhaps helping politicians avoid "doing something completely dumb" (Allen 1977, 81). See also Cairncross 1985 for confirmation from Britain.

giving them lucrative government-funded projects and using their "findings" to legitimize policies), was seen by some not only as an attempt to
purchase legitimacy for the unpopular government (Y. Cho 1983, 155;
Coats 1989, 19), but also to buy off potentially critical voices.

One may take a more charitable view and observe that the attempts
to legitimize constituted the beginning of an attempt to provide some
rational justification for government policies and to persuade people to
accept them, instead of forcing them upon people. Initially, the authoritarian government hired economists as cabinet members and key advisers
and handed out lucrative government-funded projects. Soon it began to
establish economic research institutes, in addition to staffing the economic bureaucracy with economists. The proliferation of government-
established research institutes has, since the early 1980s, been matched
by many privately established economic research institutes, in part to
gather intelligence and in part to better justify the demands of various
interest groups. By now, as a consequence, the policy debates appear
to be more reasoned. While a greater rationality in policy debates may
be largely in appearance only, or merely an increase in sophism, it is
still a vast improvement over the previous custom of resolving policy
disagreements by force.

The demand for economists for the purpose of legitimization may
not have been limited to internal politics. In a country such as Korea,
which had been on the receiving end of massive foreign aid and advice
over two decades since the end of WWII, the presence of competent
U.S.-trained local economists could be seen as lending some credence to
Korean governmental actions vis-à-vis U.S. agencies and international
organizations.[18] But in the case of Korea, the demand for American-
trained economists as a device of external legitimization has, in my view,
been relatively minor compared to the demand for effective communication with foreign entities.

Economics as a Lingua Franca

The preference for American training in economics also reflects a desire
to improve communication with Americans in the age of American domination. After the devastating Korean War (during which as many as two

18. Markoff and Montecinos (1993, 53–54) argue that this function is particularly strong in
Latin American countries. They suggest many interesting perspectives, such as the economist
as the manager of uncertainty, playing a role similar to that of the priest in earlier times.

million out of some thirty million Koreans are estimated to have died in a three-year period), South Korea became the recipient of massive foreign aid, both military and economic, largely from the United States (Woo 1991, 46; Parry 1988, 98). The American fears that South Korea was a "bottomless pit" where massive aid had no noticeable effects and that she had the potential to become a "permanent ward" prompted the American government to explore the possibility of weaning South Korea off aid and converting her into a viable economy (Woo 1991, 46). This concern had to involve South Koreans in various economic policy matters—for example, exchange rates, interest rates, government budgets, tariffs, tax collections, foreign loans, and economic planning in earlier stages—in addition to the administration of economic aid (Haggard, Copper, and Moon 1993, 298–324). Effective communication was needed.

Koreans who could effectively communicate with American officials, not only in terms of the English language but also comprehending their economic reasoning and concerns, were in great demand, with corresponding compensation and prestige. Under such circumstances it is easy to see how Koreans might wish to study economics at U.S. institutions as a means of acquiring greatly demanded communication skills.

The demand for American training in economics as a means of communication remained strong even after South Korea was weaned off U.S. aid. Insofar as access to the American market remains crucial to the economic well-being of South Koreans, effective communications with American trade representatives, who have increasingly toughened their stance in trade negotiations with Korea, have become even more crucial.[19] In dealing with U.S. threats of "a section 301 designation," or antidumping and countervailing duties, for example, Koreans realize that they need economists who command relevant facts and can effectively refute unsubstantiated charges of unfair trading practices (or expose double standards) and, at the same time, come up with believable excuses to delay opening their own markets to pacify nationalistic reactions. As Koreans have tried to diversify their exports away from the United States to deflect U.S. concerns, they have also come to face stiffened resistance from the European community (EC) or Association of South East Asian Nations (ASEAN). Whether negotiating with trading partners who are

19. Japan is South Korea's second largest trading partner, but trade negotiation has been less of a problem since South Korea has had chronic trade deficits. The Japanese ability to stonewall U.S. appeals to open her markets to foreigners is legendary. After nearly two decades of cajoling and threatening, and more, the United States has not had much success.

increasingly becoming protectionist or participating in protracted GATT negotiations, communication skills in economics have become absolutely essential.

I have considered four factors that seem to underlie the demand for a graduate training overseas, especially in the United States. Let us now turn to factors that have influenced the supply of economists.

The Ph.D. Degree as a Signaling Device

Michael Spence (1973) has observed that the desirability of education may lie less in the investment in human capital than in the acquisition of insignia to demonstrate native ability when it is not directly observable. That is, employers tend to favor a more (or better) educated worker knowing that, other things being equal, a more capable individual tends to acquire more (or better) education. Knowing this, the youth, or rather his or her parents, would try to acquire education as a means of signaling his or her native ability.

American training in economics has been especially valued as a signaling device. From the mid-1960s, when the reputation of economics as a profession reached its peak, President Park bestowed much prestige on economists when he placed all his political bets on economic development, which he meant to realize through planning and its effective (if sometimes ruthless) administration (Choi 1994, 245).[20] Evidently, the demand for economists rested on the assumption that some training in economics could make important contributions to the president's political objectives, as a technology of development, a language of effective communication, and a means of legitimization. But given President Park's mercantilistic designs in promoting exports as the vehicle of growth, it is not clear how an academic training in economics in the United States could prove to be useful in government, to which many Korean economists have been eager to render their service (Y. Cho 1983, 157; Pyun 1983a, 57).

More often than not, economists employed by President Park became "pragmatists" regardless of the place, or the content, of their graduate training (Y. Kim 1983, 247–54). The predicament of government economists everywhere appears to be similar. Asked to come up with an-

---

20. Pyun (1983a, 51) suggests that educational reform in the late 1960s, which abolished the "Ph.D. under the old system" and expanded graduate schools, might have provided incentives to study economics in the United States—to get a necessary diploma for university teaching.

swers on short notice, William Allen observes, a government economist in the United States "does much shooting from the hip"(1977, 51). And constantly asked to justify ideas they find repulsive, the staff members of the Council of Economic Advisors develop "a lot of waffling and weasel-wording" (1977, 60) into an art form. It is not too difficult to guess that Korean economists working for the authoritarian regime would have developed their art of weasel-wording to an even higher level. In fact, it was not uncommon for academic economists to propose policies that completely contradict the theses of their own books as soon as they were called upon to serve in government (Chu 1983, 123).

Moreover, government economists testify that the real value of their contributions in policymaking is the basic economic way of thinking, for example, the concepts of demand, supply, opportunity cost, the margin, and so on, and not much more (Allen 1977, 69–75; Cairncross 1985, 3; Nelson 1987, 83–85; Coats 1989, 7). What, then, is the use of graduate training in the United States, especially at prestigious U.S. institutions where a Ph.D. degree requires much endeavor to acquire esoteric techniques of no practical consequence? Isn't it like requiring several years of postbaccalaureate training to become an obstetrician only to do midwifery? While it is reasonable to observe that to acquire a solid understanding of basic economics one must keep at it,[21] the findings from a survey of graduate students in the most prestigious graduate schools in the United States suggest that graduate training at elite U.S. institutions these days may actually have the effect of dulling, not sharpening, economic understanding—producing *idiots savants* (Colander and Klamer 1987, 97; Grubel 1992, 250–57).[22]

21. Allen observes that "[There] are not many who have a thorough understanding of and . . . belief in the relevance of basic theory. Only a sophisticate is likely to make very productive use in a complex situation of elemental analytics" (1977, 74).

22. See Allen 1977 (80–81) for Gordon Tullock's remark on the failure on the part of the economics fraternity: "Economics is rapidly moving into . . . a highly escapist phase, in which the average economist works on some subject which either has no relevance to the real world at all—and therefore doesn't lead him into squabbles with his friends in the Department of English—or, if it has relevance to the real world, it is a very narrow area, and outside that very narrow area where he's working, he simply agrees with his friends in the Department of English as to what is good policy." Brenner (1992a, 30–31) takes Aumann's 1987 *Econometrica* article, "Correlated Equilibrium as an Expression of Bayesian Rationality," as an example of the use of mathematics as cosmetics while glossing over important issues. Quddus and Rashid (1994, 261) document "the concerns [about excessive formalism even] of a significant number of mathematical economists and econometricians of the highest rank," including Debreu, Allais, Hicks, Stone, Zellner, Leontief, Solow, Franklin Fisher, Haavelmo, Kantorovich, and Morishima. To this, Samuelson (1994) retorts "sour grapes" by once-pioneering mathematical

As the content of education seemed to matter little in their functioning as economists, and as the value of economists' service is difficult
to measure, American training came to serve as a means of signaling or
a screening device to discern innate abilities of job candidates, both in
government and in academia. That American training would be much
more difficult to obtain than domestic training, given costs and the language barrier, is clear. The prestige of American training compared to
training in some other foreign country derived mainly from the prestige
Americans commanded in international politics after World War II, in
general, and the U.S. domination in Korean politics, in particular. The
fact that many U.S.-trained economists did not return to Korea in the
1960s, given job opportunities in the United States, probably enhanced
the prestige, and price, of those who did return.

The argument is further supported by the tightening of the job market
for economists in Korea in the past ten years or so, caused by the rapid
increase in the supply of economists, intensifying the competition for
credentials (see table 3). During much of the 1960s and 1970s, a Ph.D.
in economics from any American university might have been sufficient
to land a professorial post in elite universities in Seoul. (A teaching post
in an elite university opened many opportunities in business and government, sometimes as a consultant, a cabinet member, or even a prime minister [Y. Cho 1983, 157].) The competition for the insignia of American
training gradually intensified, and soon the number of American-trained
economists began to outstrip the number of job openings in choice areas.
Having a Ph.D. from an American university was no longer sufficient;
additional insignia became necessary. From the late 1970s, only a Ph.D.
from the most elite American universities counted, while other PhD.s
had to settle for jobs in less desirable areas, for example, research institutes and universities in provincial towns. Then, from the early 1980s
on, even diplomas from the most elite American universities were no
longer sufficient.[23] One now has to show that one had some publications
in reputable journals and some teaching experience as well, preferably
in the United States.

---

economists who are fast becoming outmoded! B. Kim 1983 (191) expresses a similar view.

23. In *The List*, there are at least ten recent Ph.D.s from the top twenty or thirty graduate
programs in economics in the United States who have no entry under "current employment";
in all probability, they are unemployed. In addition, there are three recent German Ph.D.s and
eight recent domestic Ph.D.s with no entry for current employment.

Increasing Professionalization

The competition for an American training in economics as a signaling device is fully in keeping with a venerable Korean tradition: competition based on scholarship in Confucian classics and literature. Until the turn of this century, Korean governments for several centuries had relied on formal examinations, given at regular intervals, for the selection of the bulk of government officials, including the professorial posts in the institutions of higher learning. Under the system of state examinations, *Gwaguh*, those who successfully passed the exams were not only recognized as members of the social elite, but were also expected to impart *wisdom*, a Confucian ideal.

Surely modern learning has largely supplanted Confucian classics as the object of study in Korea, but traditions die hard. Given the scarcity of educated manpower in the 1950s and 1960s, people with graduate training used their diplomas as tickets to positions of power and wealth. Since a Ph.D. from an American university was accorded the highest degree of prestige, people with an American Ph.D. tended to secure jobs at the most prestigious universities, in powerful government bureaus, and as presidential advisers and ministers (Pyun 1983a, 57).

Initially, however, there was little emphasis on specialization or research in specialized areas. The reason is that those at prestigious posts were expected, in keeping with the centuries-old Confucian tradition, to be the repository of a general wisdom. No matter in which area one wrote the Ph.D. thesis, the university and government economist was expected to be a jack of all trades, dealing with social, political, and all sorts of economic issues.[24] Given the demands made upon his time, it left him with little time for study, even if he sought it.[25]

However, the intensification of competition for entry positions in Korea during the past decade and a half or so has changed the requisite insignia from simply a Ph.D. from an American university to a degree from an elite American university, and then to a degree from an elite American university and publications in prestigious journals. The change in the composition of economists in Korean universities, research institutes,

24. The Korean word for Ph.D., *Bahk-sa*, betrays the usage. *Bahk-sa* literally means "man of wide learning" (in what we would now call the humanities) and was a title of the professorial posts in government-established institutions of higher learning in Old Korea for over fifteen hundred years, until 1910. Today's Ph.D. in economics, of course, signifies no such thing.

25. Shin (1983, 23) confesses that at one time he undertook more than ten additional tasks, such as serving on a commission.

and government bureaus–from generalists who do a few things related to their specialization, to younger economists who publish in specialist journals—has brought important changes in the role of the economics profession in Korea. Fewer and fewer young professors pretend to have the answers to all questions, preferring to limit themselves to the area of their specialization and devote more of their time to research. And professors, in economics as well as in other fields, have increasingly come to be regarded as the repositories not so much of wisdom as of knowledge. The intense competition for insignia has also helped the process of professionalization of economics.

Other Consequences

The Americanization of economics in South Korea has had many other consequences, including (1) the overwhelming preference for mathematical economics and econometrics, (2) the rehashing of academic debates in the United States, and (3) reactions against the American influence.

The apparent preference for mathematical modeling and econometrics by Korean economists cannot be fully accounted for by the perceived demand for economics as a policy science or technology. It must be seen as a natural consequence of the attempts to acquire the necessary signals to secure employment back in Korea—that is, to get better and better credentials. Korean students have expressed a preference for elite graduate schools, which in turn emphasize mathematical and statistical methodologies (Kang 1983, 104–8; Colander and Klamer 1987, 108; Hansen 1991, 1086).[26] And as publication in prestigious journals is fast becoming another necessary credential for a desirable job in Korea, mathematical and statistical approaches have become even more imperative (Brenner 1992a, 36–42). At the same time, many Korean students, usually with excellent academic preparation but relatively limited command of English, have realized (as any prudent person should) that they have a comparative advantage in building mathematical models or in statistical manipulation, not in conceptual endeavors or other avenues that require much greater fluency in English, where the outcome is uncertain. Moreover, many discover that if they adopt a mathematical or

26. Krueger et al. (1991, 1039–40 and 1044–46) tend largely to defend the emphasis on mathematical tools in graduate training. See also Hansen 1991, 1073–75. Kang (1987, 547–48) observes that there is a prevalence of empirical studies, meaning statistical studies, among Koreans, neglecting completely institutions, history, or philosophical bases of economics.

statistical approach they can finish their graduate training much more quickly, which is another important strategic consideration in finding employment in Korea, where finishing quickly is commonly interpreted, as in a race, as a mark of ability.[27] Finally, given the practical bent of the majority of Korean economists—they tend to view economics as a policy "science"—they tend to value empirical studies, at least their appearance (Pyun 1983a, 56).[28]

Curiously, however, few pay attention to data collection, though the lack of data and the unreliability of available data make empirical studies very difficult in Korea. Moreover, the heavy emphasis on mathematical modeling and statistics has not led, as in some other countries, to the study of economics by mathematicians or engineers, who might excel in the game. The reason, I believe, is the importance of connections (established through undergraduate training in Korea) in securing a job in academia and government.[29] That is, a mathematician turned economist who does "high-powered" economics would have difficulty finding a job since he scarcely "knows" anyone who is in a position to hire him as an economist.

The Korean pragmatic approach to the study of economics—with its overwhelming concern for job implications back home and a labor market for economists that operates through informal networks or through cliques—has produced an army of economists (the majority of whom are American trained) extremely competent in importing techniques but seldom making original contributions or even undertaking fundamental research (S. Cho 1994, 182; Shin 1983, 22; Y. Cho 1983, 159).

In general, the process of competing for appropriate signals that drives the prospective economist in the direction of mathematical modeling

27. Since the early 1970s, the average age of Koreans earning the Ph.D. in the United States has been over thirty-four at the time of getting the degree (see table 4). Most of them had served three years in the Army before they started their graduate studies. In addition, many have worked or done some graduate training for a few years in Korea in order to save, to qualify for a scholarship offered by government or business firms, or to establish a contact at a university in Korea. This long prequalifying period may also explain many Koreans' desire to finish their studies as quickly as possible.

28. See Brenner 1992b for an interesting discussion of the problems of macro-index numbers and other data problems.

29. What Prof. Bronfenbrenner (1956, 395–96) calls "institutional inbreeding," describing economics departments in Japanese universities, is also largely applicable to Korea. The proportion of the economics departments in the top three universities in Seoul (Seoul National University, Yonsei University, and Korea University) staffed by their own baccalaureate graduates is 100 percent, 76 percent, and 53 percent, respectively. Also, the proportion of economics department faculty with economics undergraduate degrees is 93 percent, 96 percent, and 90 percent, respectively. See also Shin 1983, 23.

Table 4   Average Age of Korean Economists at the Time of Ph.D. Award by Year and Educational Background

Year of Ph.D.	Domestic Degrees		Foreign Degrees	
	Seoul	Provinces	U.S.	Non-U.S. foreign
1956	0	0	34	0
1957	0	0	0	0
1958	0	0	0	0
1959	0	0	0	30
1960	43	0	0	30
1961	0	0	37	0
1962	0	0	0	0
1963	0	0	33	0
1964	0	0	30	0
1965	0	0	0	0
1966	0	0	30	0
1967	37	44	37	38
1968	37	53	33	34
1969	45	39	32	30
1970	47	0	34	34
1971	46	38	35	37
1972	49	42	35	36
1973	63	43	33	0
1974	44	49	34	39
1975	45	44	35	41
1976	58	44	34	39
1977	36	35	33	0
1978	39	39	38	34
1979	45	41	34	38
1980	45	40	37	36
1981	45	46	34	31
1982	44	42	36	37
1983	39	45	34	37
1984	44	43	35	38
1985	42	39	35	38
1986	40	45	34	38
1987	43	41	33	37
1988	43	41	34	36
1989	41	43	34	35
1990	39	39	34	37
1991	39	38	34	36
1992	38	41	35	35
1993	38	42	34	35

and econometrics is well recognized.[30] The prospective economist may "do just enough" to get a degree that he hopes will get his foot in the door, with the help of the old-boy network. Given the tenure system in Korea, once a person with a Ph.D. is hired, it is understood that for all practical purposes he is tenured, right then and there. Since what he subsequently does as a scholar or teacher matters very little to job security, many subsequently undertake activities that will enhance their wealth: consulting (which often means doing government-funded research, often of dubious value), extra teaching, and cultivating connections that might lead to a high government post.

Anyone capable, especially the newly minted Ph.D., is eager to show off the newest wares acquired from, say, Stanford, MIT, or Chicago, as an attempt to "product differentiate," as if economics were an easily perishable good.[31] Thus it is not difficult to see how academic debates in the United States are repeatedly rehashed in South Korea, with some time lag (S. Cho 1994, 180). American-trained Korean economists tend to profess the tradition in which they are trained—monetarism, new classical economics, new Keynesianism, dependency theory, and so on—and when they interact with one another, they often reproduce the arguments that prevailed some time in the past in the United States when they studied there (Chu 1983, 123). But seldom are there serious doctrinal disputes.[32] More often, these doctrines are mentioned as marks of the economist's up-to-dateness. The manner of rehashing American academic debates is, unfortunately, not unlike the manner in which Parisian fashion is copied by people elsewhere.

The situation is not always improved when newly minted Ph.D.s become serious and try to put their newest, often half-baked, ideas into practice. Acting as true believers, as if their wares could make much difference, they try to implement them as soon as they gain some influence in the policymaking process (S. Cho 1983, 181). But such economists rarely survive the grueling process of policymaking, which reflects diverse interests, including those of the vast bureaucracy and powerful businesses.

30. It seems also to be the case in the United States (Brenner 1992a, 30–33).

31. B. Kim (1983, 188–89) speaks of the infantilism of ranking the superiority of an economist by the date of his or her Ph.D., the newest being the best.

32. U. Park (1983, 255) expresses his surprise at a foreign journal's report of heated debates in Korea between protectionists and free-traders. He implies that the journalist misperceived the situation in Korea.

Many Korean economists who do not take an active part in rehashing vintage American academic debates—mostly Korean-trained economists, economists trained in foreign countries other than the United States, or economists trained in the United States before the current fad—seem to wonder whether many of the imported economic doctrines have much relevance to the situations Koreans face, even if they seem valid in the American context.[33] Moreover, quite a few seem to have begun to have doubts about the scientific value of an American Ph.D. in economics and the value of the economics learned in the United States to the specific problems of Korea (B. Kim 1983, 185).[34] Alas, few have made any attempt to offer an alternative beyond the stage of making wish lists, including the diversification of import sources (geographically, e.g., studying in Europe and Japan, or doctrinally, e.g., studying Austrian economics or post-Keynesianism [Pyun 1983a, 56–57 and 62]) and the development of a "Korean economics."[35]

Finally, one of the interesting consequences of the internationalization of economics in Korea is the ascendency of the free-trade doctrine since the early 1980s. A number of factors have influenced this outcome, including (1) the increasing U.S. pressure to liberalize her markets as the trade volume between the two countries has exploded and as South Korea ran trade surpluses for a few years in the late 1980s and the early 1990s; (2) doubts about the efficacy of the heavy-handed approach by government in promoting industrialization after the failure of the late President Park's push for "heavy and chemical industries," resulting in a severe recession, widespread riots, and ultimately his assassination; and (3) the increasing confidence of Korean big business concerns, *chaebol* (which were carefully nurtured under the late President Park), in their ability to compete in the world market and the judgment that the government that did so much for them was becoming more a burden than a help.[36] But

33. See *Introspections*, which is a collection of essays on related issues written between 1973 and 1983.

34. Besides, there are simply too many American economics Ph.D.s out there relative to job openings.

35. Many of the essays in *Introspections* address this issue. See also W. Park 1983. One interesting reaction in the search for "Koreanness" has been in the history of economic ideas. For instance, some Koreans have rediscovered Yak-Yong Jung (1762–1836), an exiled intellectual, as an important precursor of economic thought in Korea. Motivated to relieve the plight of the masses, Jung proposed the encouragement of industry and agriculture. But I am yet to be persuaded as to what uniquely constituted Koreanness in his ideas. See Ra 1990. I thank Prof. Salim Rashid for drawing my attention to Ra's paper.

36. Like their counterparts elsewhere, Korean business interests do not see, or care about,

Korean economists have also played a major role in educating the public as well as rulers such as Presidents Chun, Roh, and now Kim about the desirability of an open economy.[37]

Concluding Remarks

While the idea that there may be a strong correlation between trade and the exchange of ideas, including economic ideas, is appealing, it is found wanting. As noted earlier, the influence of Japanese economics in Korea has been minimal even though Japan is for Korea as important a trading partner as the United States. In order to better understand the process of Americanization, the factors influencing the demand for and supply of economists in Korea must be considered. On the demand side, three sources of the demand for economics are identified: economics as a technology, as a means of legitimization, and as a lingua franca. Starting from a virtual vacuum, a steady increase in the demand for economists from the early 1960s resulted in prestige and generous compensations for economists, stimulating the supply in the long run.

As the quality, ability, and even the nature of an economist's contribution are difficult to measure, graduate training in economics has been used as a signaling device. This is supported by the fact that (1) American-trained economists administered mercantilistic policies in the 1960s and 1970s; (2) as the competition for jobs intensified, the necessary signal was continually upgraded from a Ph.D. from an American university, to a Ph.D. from an elite American university, and then to a Ph.D. from an elite American university plus publications in reputable journals, and so on; and (3) the great bulk of graduate training in economics in elite universities and published materials in prestigious journals are largely irrelevant to the workaday economist, a role to which many Korean economists aspire.

The increasing competition for insignia has brought a number of interesting consequences, including increasing professionalization, prevalence of mathematical and econometric methodologies, and the absence

---

the conflict between their desire to be free from government interference when cumbersome, and the desire to have special treatments when in need of protection.

37. It is most interesting to note that a rather abrupt shift in the economic policy orientation in Korea—from mercantilism to liberalism—was brought about by President Chun (who came to power through a military coup, restored order through brutal suppressions, and consequently remained unpopular), when he was persuaded by a few key economic advisers that only through liberalizing the Korean economy could it prosper, and he thereby gain legitimacy.

of genuine scientific disputes. These consequences have, in turn, produced some adverse reactions, including nationalistic reactions, skepticism about "American economics," and the call for a serious examination of heterodox doctrines, if only as a first step to develop a more satisfactory economic science.

The Korean experience in economics is not only intrinsically interesting, it should stimulate us to think about economics education in the United States and the nature of economists' contribution to society.

References

Allen, William R. 1977. Economics, Economists and Economic Policy: Modern American Experience. *HOPE* 9.1:48–88.

Brenner, Reuven. 1992a. Making Sense out of Nonsense. In *Educating Economists.* Edited by David Colander and Reuven Brenner. Ann Arbor, Mich.: University of Michigan Press.

———. 1992b. Macroeconomics: The Masks of Science and Myths of Good Policy. In *Educating Economists.* Edited by David Colander and Reuven Brenner. Ann Arbor, Mich.: University of Michigan Press: 123–51.

Bronfenbrenner, Martin. 1956. Economic Thought and Its Application and Methodology in the East: The State of Japanese Economics. *AER Papers and Proceedings* 46.2:389–98.

Cairncross, Alec. 1985. Economics in Theory and Practice. *AER Papers and Proceedings* 75.2:1–14.

Cho, Soon. 1983. The Nature of Korean Economics (in Korean). In *Introspections.* 178–84.

———. 1994. A Perspective on Economic Policy Direction During the Rest of the 20th Century. *KAEA Papers and Proceedings* 13–17.

Cho, Yong-Bum. 1983. Problems of Korean Economics (in Korean). In *Introspections.* 151–61.

Choi, Young Back. 1994. Industrial Policy as the Engine of Economic Growth in South Korea: Myth and Reality. In *The Collapse of Development Planning.* Edited by Peter Boettke. New York: New York University Press: 231–55.

Chu, Chong-Whan. 1983. Korean Economics in the Crisis of Contemporary Economics (in Korean). In *Introspections.* 121–44.

Coats, A. W., ed. 1989. *Economists in Government.* Durham, N.C.: Duke University Press.

Colander, David, and Arjo Klamer. 1987. The Making of an Economist. *Journal of Economic Perspective* 1.2:95–111.

Grubel, Herbert G. 1992. Educational Reforms Are Necessary but Not Sufficient. In *Educating Economists.* Edited by David Colander and Reuven Brenner. Ann Arbor, Mich.: University of Michigan Press: 249–62.

Haggard, Stephen, Richard Cooper, and Chung-In Moon. 1993. Policy Reform in Korea. In *Political and Economic Interactions in Economic Policy Reform.* Edited by Robert H. Bates and Anne O. Krueger. Cambridge, Mass.: Blackwell: 294–332.

Hangook Kyungjehaagei Mohsaek. [Introspections on Korean Economics]. 1983. Korean Economic Research Institute.

Hangook Kyungjehakhoe Hoewonrohk. [The List of Members of Korean Economic Association]. 1993. Korean Economic Association.

Hansen, W. Lee. 1991. The Education and Training of Economics Doctorates. *Journal of Economic Literature* 24.3:1054–87.

Introspections. [Hangook Kyungjehaagei Mohsaek]. 1983. Korean Economic Research Institute.

Kang, Myong-Kyu. 1983. Development Stages of Korean Economics (in Korean). In *Introspections.* 64–120.

———. 1987. The Structure of the Growth of Economics in Korea (in Korean). Seoul National University. *Economic Studies Series* 26.4:529–54.

Kasper, Hirscel, et al. 1991. The Education of Economists. *Journal of Economic Literature* 24.3:1088–109.

Kim, Byung-Joo. 1983. Economics in Korea: Present and Future (in Korean). In *Introspections.* 185–209.

Kim, Duk-Chung. 1983. Applications of Economic Theory in Developing Countries (in Korean). In *Introspections.* 232–43.

Kim, Yoon-Whan. 1983. Economists' Roles in Policy Formulation (in Korean). In *Introspections.* 247–54.

Komiya, Ryutaro, and Kozo Yamamoto. 1981. Japan: The Officer in Charge of Economic Affairs. In *Economists in Government.* Edited by A. W. Coats. Durham, N.C.: Duke University Press: 262–90.

Krueger, Anne O., et al. 1991. Report of the Commission on Graduate Education in Economics. *Journal of Economic Literature* 24.3:1035–53.

The List. [Hangook Kyungjehakhoe Hoewonrohk.] 1993.

Markoff, John, and Veronica Montecinos. 1993. The Ubiquitous Rise of Economists. *Journal of Public Policy* 13.1:37–68.

Nelson, Robert H. 1987. The Economics Profession and the Making of Public Policy. *Journal of Economic Literature* 25.1:49–91.

———. 1989. Introduction and Summary. In *The Role of Economists in Government.* Edited by J. Pechman. New York: New York University Press. 1–22.

Okita, Saburo. 1989. Japan. In *The Role of Economists in Government.* Edited by Joseph Pechman. New York: New York University Press: 173–91.

Park, Ung-Suh. 1983. Establishment of Korean Economics for Korean Economic Policy (in Korean). In *Introspections.* 255–58.

Park, Woo-Hee. 1993. *Economic Thought, Theory, and Reality in Korea* (in Korean). Seoul: Yupoong Publishing Co.

Parry, Thomas G. 1988. The Role of Foreign Capital in East Asian Industrialization, Growth, and Development. In *Achieving Industrialization in East Asia.* Edited by Helen Hughes. New York: Cambridge University Press: 95–128.

Pyun, Hyung-Yoon. 1983a. Development Stages in Korean Economics (in Korean). In *Introspections*. 39–63.

———. 1983b. Current Issues and Problems of Economics Education in Korea (in Korean). In *Introspections*. 261–69.

Quddus, Munir, and Salim Rashid. 1994. The Overuse of Mathematics in Economics: Nobel Resistance. *Eastern Economic Journal* 20.3:251–65.

Ra, Sung Sup. 1990. Sirhak (1681-1836), The Korean School: Economic Views of Yak Yong Chung, Che Ga Park, and Su Won Yu. Unpublished manuscript.

Samuelson, Paul A. 1994. The To-Be-Expected Angst Created for Economists by Mathematics. *Eastern Economic Journal* 20.3:267–73.

Shin, Tai-Whan. 1983. Annals of Korean Economics for 50 Years (in Korean). In *Introspections*. 13–23.

Spence, Michael. 1973. Job Market Signaling. *Quarterly Journal of Economics* 87: 355–74.

Woo, Jung-en. 1991. *Race to the Swift: State and Finance in Korean Industrialization*. New York: Columbia University Press.

The Internationalization of Economics in Japan

Aiko Ikeo

1. Introduction[1]

In the 1930s, a small group of Japanese economists started to read every issue of the internationally oriented journals of economics. They published academic papers in Japanese, which might have had an impact on the world economics community had they been written in English or German. Also, prior to World War II, Japan had closer contact with its neighboring countries, such as China and Korea, than with the United States and paid more serious attention to Russia's international strategy than to America's. In contrast, the American presence became very conspicuous in Japanese society after the Allied Powers, led by the United States, began their occupation of Japan in 1945. During the occupation period, the communists and Marxists enjoyed a favorable reputation because they were the only political groups who had opposed the war. The majority of economists in Japan were Marxists from 1945 until the mid-1960s. The balance of power in Japanese economics subsequently shifted

1. I thank the following people for their information and suggestions: Daisuke Arie, Kenneth J. Arrow, Martin Bronfenbrenner, A. W. Coats, Peter Groenewegen, Yukihiro Ikeda, Takutoshi Inoue, Shizuo Kakutani, Yo Nakanishi, Takashi Negishi, Michihiro Ohyama, Tetsuji Okazaki, Masahiro Okuno-Fujiwara, Paul Pecorino, Kiichiro Yagi, Richard Webb, E. Roy Weintraub, John Williamson, the participants in the annual meeting of the Society for the History of Japanese Economic Thought on 3–4 June 1995, Kyoko Arai and Chiduko Tsutsui. This paper is the result of joint research financed by the Grant in Aid of the Ministry of Education, Japan, 1995 (General Research A-07303003). Needless to say, remaining errors are mine.

from Marxist to neoclassical and Keynesian economists as Japanese economic life was enhanced by rapid economic growth.

2. The International Network for Economists in the Prewar Period

International journals of economics have been important for internationally oriented economists in Japan as well as in Europe and North America since around 1930. They played an important part in forming the international scientific community for economists. Japanese neoclassical economists were regular readers of three journals: *Zeitschrift für Nationalökonomie*, which began publication in Vienna in 1930, and *Econometrica* and *Review of Economic Studies*, which were both started in 1933. Japanese neoclassical economists regarded the *Zeitschrift* as the first truly international journal in the world (Ikeo 1993). Rather than remain limited to a single point of view, these journals were receptive to a variety of research traditions then coexisting in Europe and North America. For example, the Lausanne School was represented by Léon Walras and Vilfredo Pareto, the Austrian School by Carl Menger, Eugen von Böhm-Bawerk and Friedrich von Wieser, the Stockholm (Swedish) School by Knut Wicksell and Gustav Cassel, and the Cambridge School by Alfred Marshall and A. C. Pigou.

Ichiro Nakayama, one of the leading Japanese economists, reminisces about the 1930s:

Generally speaking, mathematical or theoretical economics rose up on a tidal wave around 1930, I think. One thing was the organization of the Econometric Society in 1930 and the establishment of their *Econometrica* in 1933. Speaking of journals, *Review of Economic Studies* was established in 1933, the same year as *Econometrica*. Four [Three] years before that, *Zeitschrift für Nationalökonomie* was started in Germany [Austria] in 1929 [1930]. These journals were issued quarterly for promoting theoretical economics. The studies by up-and-coming young economists flowed rapidly into Japan, too.[2] (1979, 61–62)

These journals provided Japanese economists with fresh economic insights from Europe and America and informed them of the current nature

2. When I met Takuma Yasui in 1990, he emphasized that he had read every issue of these three journals and that professional economists must read journal articles; it is not enough for them to read only books.

of economic research. They provided an international forum for theoretical economists and econometricians and helped unite economists in a common quest for economic knowledge. They extended the economics information network to Asia through the prompt distribution of each issue. Through their influence, young Japanese economists were encouraged to become involved in theoretical and mathematical economics rather than German historicism, Marxist economics, or war economics, which had claimed increased attention in Japan during the Great Depression.

It is noteworthy that a Japanese university started circulating a journal written in Western languages, including English and German, in order to help establish the Japanese Economics School in 1926.[3] The *Kyoto University Economic Review* has the longest tradition as an economics journal written in Western languages and published in Japan. The editor's foreword reflected their whole-hearted anticipation of intellectual cooperation with Western economists:

> Many of the studies in the natural and social sciences already published in our country have had far-reaching effects in the advancement of science and the enhancement of human happiness, but as the majority of them were written in the Japanese language they have not been accessible to Western scholars. Although studies in the natural sciences have been published by our scholars through books, university memoirs, reports of various associations and others all of which were written in Western languages, no similar attempts have, so far, been made as regards the studies in the social sciences, the results being that the real condition in the field of our economic science has been almost unknown to the Western countries. Realizing that such a condition is truly regrettable from the standpoint of intellectual cooperation which should be established by the scholars of all nations, the Economic Department of the Imperial University of Kyoto has decided to undertake the work of publishing a series of memoirs. (Editorial, 1926, ii)

They witnessed the power of the English language when Kei Shibata's

---

3. It is true that "The Japanese Economics School" sounds strange now. What they had in mind probably was to create a new school of economics differentiated from the Western economics tradition. Kyoto Imperial University, unlike other Japanese universities, included oriental economic thought in their curriculum in economics. It was not until 1950 that a similar attempt to publish journals written in European languages was made by Hitotsubashi University, the economics department of Osaka University, Kobe University, and other institutions.

"Marx's Analysis of Capitalism and the General Equilibrium Theory of the Lausanne School" (1933) in the journal was cited by Oskar Lange, a Polish economist. Lange referred to it in his "Marxian Economics and Modern Economic Theory" (1935) in the *Review of Economic Studies*, which was regularly read by Japanese theoretical economists. Shibata frequently contributed papers on current topics to the *Kyoto University Economic Review* in the 1930s. And this led Alfred Cowles to invite him to the Annual Research Conference of the Cowles Commission for Research in Economics, which was held in Colorado Springs from 1 July to 26 July 1940.[4] However, this channel to the international community of economists was shut down for Japan from 1941 until 1945.

3. The Direct Contact with America and the Influence of the Cold War after 1945

The Allied Forces, led by the American general Douglas MacArthur, occupied Japan from September 1945 until April 1952. The occupation period was longer than necessary for disarmament, economic relief, and the establishment of democracy in Japan because of the onset of the Cold War in 1947 (Hata 1976; Roberts 1994). The Americans or Allies destroyed facilities capable of making nuclear weapons and worked painstakingly to calculate how much effort and money they needed to allow Japan to stand on its own and to be incorporated into an international community based on free trade.[5] They also monitored the postwar settlements in East Asia (the Far East) and Southeast Asia, conducted a comparative study of the nations in these regions to get a better understanding of them, and tried to promote intra-regional trade (GHQ/SCAP 1945–52).

The Japanese yen became convertible into foreign currencies when the single exchange rate was fixed at $1 = ¥360 in April 1949. This was the first, important step forward to introduce foreign capital into a developing country like the Japan of the day. Japan became a member of the IMF and the World Bank in August 1952. In 1953, the World Bank lent money to Japan for the first time, to the Japan Development Bank (JDB), which was backed by the Japanese government, and JDB in turn lent the money

---

4. Cowles's letter to Shibata of 14 October 1939. According to the draft of his letter to Cowles, dated 9 December 1939, Shibata could not accept the invitation because the Japanese government would not fund his travel expenses.

5. More exactly, the American forces destroyed the cyclotrons in Tokyo. Cyclotrons are particle accelerators useful for basic research on nuclear weapons but not for their production.

to three private electric companies to import thermal power plants (Japan Development Bank 1976). JDB was the pro-economic growth faction in the Japanese government and its related sectors. It played an intermediary role when Japanese private companies in the electric, iron and steel, and machinery industries borrowed money from the World Bank. It also acted as a guarantor when Japanese electric and airplane companies borrowed money from foreign private banks. World Bank loans were also crucial to the construction of the Shinkansen bullet train line between Tokyo and Osaka, which was completed in 1964. Japan became a member of GATT in September 1955 and of the United Nations in December 1956.

It should be noted that World Bank loans and foreign capital played a decisive role in the construction of the Chiba plant of Kawasaki Steel from 1956 to 1960.[6] This case has been cited by a number of scholars interested in the post-1945 Japanese economy, because it was a significant example of cooperation between a private company, local governments, and the Japanese government in a huge project.[7] There was a complicated and time-consuming process of raising funds, since Kawasaki Steel's plan to build a new, integrated steel mill (pig iron to rolled steel; the world's most modern at the time) with the assistance of government-related funds became known to the Japanese government in 1950. The Chiba City Council and the Chiba Prefectual Council each promptly passed a resolution in support of the project. The Ministry of International Trade and Industry (MITI) approved only part of Kawasaki's plan, which had been already scaled down from the original in 1952. Then JDB started to negotiate seriously with the World Bank, both for Japan's steel industry as a whole and for Kawasaki in particular to get proposed loans. During the process of evaluation of their projects, they not only met in Japan with survey teams from the World Bank but also visited Washington, D.C. to directly lobby the Bank. First Yahata Steel secured World Bank loans in October 1955, and then Nippon Steel in March 1956. Finally in December 1956, the largest loan requested for the Chiba project by

6. Details of the Kawasaki case can be found in Calder 1993, 183–195 and Kawasaki Steel Corporation 1976, 66–120. I benefited from a conversation with Tetsuji Okazaki, who has been studying the history of the steel industry in Japan.

7. Kent E. Calder (1993) made the most detailed and careful study of the case. Chalmers Johnson (1982, 218) placed too much stress on the effectiveness of MITI's planning ability. Kyoko Sheridan (1993, 133) did not mention Kawasaki's six-year struggle to raise funds for the plan. This plan was also scaled down from the original in the process of the negotiations between Kawasaki and the Japanese government, and then between JDB and the World Bank.

Kawasaki Steel was approved. The World Bank loans made it easier for Kawasaki to introduce foreign private capital into the project.

The generous funds for the Government and Relief in Occupied Areas (GARIOA), and, later, the Fulbright scholarship program, brought Japanese youths to the United States and to other countries for advanced studies. Shin-ichi Ichimura, Tsunehiko Watababe, Tadao Uchida, and Ryutaro Komiya were fascinated by American empirical studies, such as the interindustry analysis originated by W. Leontief, and econometric modeling. Returning to Japan, they not only taught "American economics" to Japanese students but also conducted important econometric research, making economic plans and predictions in the 1960s. Hiroshi Furuya, who studied at Harvard during 1952–54, not only strongly advised economics students to study mathematics but also invited mathematics students such as Hirofumi Uzawa and Ken-ichi Inada to study economics. In addition, Michio Morishima studied at Oxford and attended the meetings organized by John Hicks during 1954–55.

In the 1950s, Japanese mathematical economists such as Hukukane Nikaido, Uzawa, Inada, Hajime Oniki, and Takashi Negishi joined Kenneth J. Arrow's project at Stanford backed by the Office of Naval Research (ONR).[8] They played active roles in the study of the existence and stability of general equilibrium in a competitive economy, two-sector growth models, and welfare economics (Ikeo 1994b; Tsuru 1984). David Gale, a mathematical economist, visited Osaka University, and studied with Nikaido, Ichimura, and Morishima in the mid-1950s. The Japanese dream of intellectual cooperation with Western economists had finally turned into reality.

4. The Societal Concerns of Japanese Economists

The first job of Japanese economists after 1945 was to work toward the recovery of the nation's ruined economy. Japan's top economists,

8. ONR was essentially acting as the office of national research from the postwar period until around 1957, the year in which the Soviet Union launched Sputnik, the first unmanned space satellite (Sapolsky 1990, 38). Kenneth J. Arrow recalled the project at Stanford as follows: "The title of the project was something like the Project on the Efficiency of Decision Making in the Economic System. It started in 1951 and continued though the 1960s. Scientific research in general has been promoted for defense purposes since World War II. It did not matter whether a project was directly related to defense or not. The role of promoting scientific research was gradually taken over by the National Science Foundation in the 1960s" (Personal communication with Kenneth J. Arrow in Tokyo on 12 September 1994).

including Marxist economists who had objected to armed hostilities, joined the Economic Stabilization Board, which was organized on the basis of instructions given by the Allied Occupation Force and later reorganized into the Economic Planning Agency (EPA). Hiromi Arisawa, a Marxist economist, played the leading role on the board. He proposed a recovery policy called the priority production system, that is, putting a priority on resource allocation for the two key industries of coal mining, and iron and steel production. The system broke through the bottleneck in the postwar Japanese economy. Arisawa was closely assisted by Saburo Okita, who graduated from the department of electronic engineering, got a job in the ministry of posts and telecommunications, and worked for the plan of mobilization during the war.

Shigeto Tsuru joined the board after he returned from Harvard by exchange ship in 1942.[9] He studied at Harvard from 1933 and received his Ph.D. in 1940. He brought back not only a cosmopolitan attitude but also imported American economic language into the community of Japanese economists. Tsuru and Okita coauthored the first White Paper on the Japanese economy, that is, the first official report published by the board in 1947. They analyzed current economic problems in non-Marxist, non-historical language. Okita and many other government officials were trained as economists while on the board. Okita was sent to the Economic Commission for Asia and the Far East, which was established by the United Nations to promote regional trade among Asian countries and the United States. He was the chief economic analyst for the Commission during 1952–53. He spoke English fluently and represented "the able Japanese bureaucracy" for a long time. He played the role of spokesman for Japan at international economic meetings and raised the status of Japan in the global community (Miyazaki 1993, 323).

The Marxists, including the communists, who were kept in prison during the wars against China and then against the Allies, were released and rehabilitated in Japanese society and at national universities. They declared themselves pacifists, democrats, and reformists, and they predicted that capitalism was just a necessary preparation for socialism. It seems that the wars, the establishment of socialist countries by newly

9. A few months after Japan opened the war against the United States in December 1941, both governments agreed that they would exchange the Americans who stayed in Japan and preferred to return home with their Japanese counterparts by ships. The people exchanged were mainly diplomats, businessmen, scholars, and students. The ships used for this purpose are commonly called exchange ships.

independent colonies, and the confrontation between the East and the West intensified Japanese Marxists' beliefs in socialism. The study of the historical development of Japanese capitalism was very important for them in the postwar period as well as in the 1920s and 1930s.

Marxists in Japan were a very diverse group and had separated into several sects since the interwar period. They included both revolutionary and nonrevolutionary elements: economists, economic historians, philosophers, and leaders of the labor movement. They usually criticized each other in their writings rather than exchanging direct criticism at meetings. However, the Marxists of the Uno School, such as Tomohiko (Thomas) Sekine and Makato Itoh were exceptions, as both had contact with their counterparts in the West after the 1970s (See Ikeo 1995).

Let us turn now to cooperation between the government and the non-Marxian economists. Japan returned to the international community on the basis of the San Francisco Peace Treaty in 1952, which marked the end of fifteen years of central control over the Japanese economy. Governmental agencies such as MITI, the Ministry of Finance (MOF), and the Ministry of Agriculture and Forestry (MAF) began to regulate the economy. For example, the electricity industry had been run by the government since 1939; nine private companies regained control of their businesses with the slogan of "democratization" or participation in 1951. They began to use a neoclassical-econometric analysis to make a report of the necessary increase in installed capital to MITI, based on estimates of economic growth and the increasing demand for electricity. Neoclassical and Keynesian economists, including Ichiro Nakayama, started to collaborate with MITI to rationalize the electricity industry more thoroughly in 1954.[10] MITI, MOF, and MAF made interindustry tables of the 1951 Japanese economy that were completed by 1956. They believed that the tables would be useful to regulate the economy and to mediate between consumers and producers after the end of the controlled economy. The MITI project was the biggest of the three and was led by Shin-ichi Ichimura, who received a Ph.D. in economics from M.I.T. around 1950. In

---

10. I. Nakayama was one of the top neoclassical and Keynesian economists in Japan from the 1930s until about 1970. He was mostly responsible for the spread of general equilibrium theory in Japan, was president of the Japan Association of Economics and Econometrics from April 1968 through March 1970, and joined numerous government committees. Kyoko Sheridan is wrong in saying that he was "a labor economist of Marxian orientation" (Sheridan 1993, 146). Nakayama understood deeply that the question of income distribution would not be solved by neoclassical economics when he was the chairman of the Central Labor Commission.

the process of creating the tables, the statistical data for national income and wealth were greatly improved in quality. The agencies decided to cooperate with one another to prepare the 1955 interindustry table. They asked neoclassical and Keynesian economists to discuss the economic issues in making policies and to teach economics to government officials in MITI and other ministries from around 1960 on.

The first econometric model of the Japanese economy was made by Isamu Yamada in 1948. After 1957, those who were trained in the United States began to build econometric models one after the other. In 1960, the Ikeda cabinet decided on the Income Doubling Plan, that is, the economic plan of doubling per capita national income in a decade. They asked econometricians to prepare the midterm plan after 1960. A variety of macroeconometric models of the Japanese economy were constructed for various purposes, such as long-term economic forecasts, business cycles explained by changes in investment, and the Klein-Goldberger-type model of the Japanese economy. Tadao Uchida, Tsuneo Watanabe, Masahiro Tatemoto, and Kei Mori played leading roles in simulating government policies with the use of the latest computer technology.

The Japanese enjoyed their new life equipped with an increasing number of durable consumer goods, which were the fruits of the economic development after 1950. Yet by 1970, when Japan had become one of the advanced countries, they found several negative external effects in the environment, such as mercury poisoning caused by sewage drainage, and air pollution and traffic jams in large cities. They also realized that they did not have a welfare system extensive enough for them to enjoy their retirement lives. Like other major countries, the Japanese economy suffered from stagflation and large government deficits in the 1970s and moved to a floating exchange rate in 1973. Japanese economists began studying a number of problems similar to those American and European economists had been interested in since the mid-1950s.

It is hard to determine the precise number of Marxist economists because there were several research affiliations, academic societies, and political factions that appeared and disappeared from 1945 through the 1950s. In 1961, the Society of Political Economy was established for the study of Marxist economics. Its membership numbered about 600 in 1961, 859 in 1970, and 1,031 in 1993. On the other hand, neoclassical or Keynesian economists join the Japan Association of Economics and Econometrics, which was formed by merging the Japan Association of Theoretical Economics, established in 1949, with the Japan Association of Econometrics, established in 1950; their members numbered 519 in 1961, 869 in 1970, and 2,155 in 1993.

With respect to international activities, the Econometric Society holds regional meetings in East Asia. The first Far Eastern meeting was held in Tokyo independent of the society in 1950, although its report appeared in *Econometrica* in 1951. Formal annual meetings were held in Japan from 1966 through 1970. After a long break, biennial meetings have been held in East Asia every other year since 1987. In July 1997, the fifth meeting is scheduled for Hong Kong, which will be returned to the People's Republic of China a few days earlier. In August 1995, the World Congress of the Econometric Society was held in Tokyo.

It is noteworthy that economic studies have also been promoted by a few private efforts. The Tokyo Center for Economic Research helped create macroeconometric models in the late 1950s and 1960s and has held an annual conference on current topics since 1963. According to the Tokyo Center for Economic Research (1994), it supports a wide variety of intercollegiate exchanges of research activities, including weekly meetings held in the Tokyo area. It has been eager to encourage international exchanges among economists. The center has published the *Journal of the Japanese and International Economy* since 1987 (see the next section). In cooperation with the National Bureau of Economic Research (NBER) in the United States and the Center for Economic Policy Research in England, it has organized annual international conferences since 1987. Since 1991, the center has held summer conferences for the purpose of exchanges among young economists both in Japan and abroad. It also supports a seminar on the East Asian economy, which was first promoted by NBER, and holds conferences on the economic connections between the United States, East Asia, and Japan under the auspices of NBER, the Korean Development Institute, and the Chung-Hua Institution for Economic Research in Taiwan. In addition, the Kansai Economic Research Center has supported annual meetings on econometric studies that have been held in the Kyoto-Osaka-Kobe area and has been eager to invite young economists into an open discussion of economics.

5. Economics Journals for Japanese Economists

In Japan, there are two kinds of academic journals published in the field of social sciences: those with the referee system and those without it. There are also some international refereed journals on economics that are headquartered in Japan or edited by Japanese economists (Ikeo 1994a, 21–22).

Kikan Riron-Keizaigaku was started in 1950 by the leading economists of the day, like Ichiro Nakayama and Seiichi Tobata. It became the journal of the Japan Association of Economics and Econometrics in 1959, and a referee system was introduced in 1960. Even prior to the name change to the *Economic Studies Quarterly* in 1986, it began to carry papers written in English. At the 1993 annual meeting it was decided that the journal would adopt English as the language of publication, change its title to the *Japanese Economic Review*, and be published by Basil Blackwell starting in 1995. They also issued an announcement bulletin in Japanese for business communication because English does not convey all the information needed for Japanese members. Translations always lose something from the original.

Keizai Kenkyu is a semi-open journal, whose English title is the *Economic Review*. It has been published by the Economic Research Institute of Hitotsubashi University since 1950. Shigeto Tsuru played an important role in starting the journal. Thanks to the intellectual connections cultivated in the United States, Paul M. Sweezy, Paul A. Samuelson, Martin Bronfenbrenner, and Maurice Dobb contributed articles in English to the journal in its first year.

The *International Economic Review* was first published by the Kansai Economic Federation in 1960. Their business offices are located at the University of Pennsylvania in the United States and at Osaka University Institute of Social and Economic Research Association in Japan. Their three major objectives in starting the journal were "(1) to provide a new truly international forum; (2) to facilitate, through such an international medium, the introduction of new national schools of thought (e.g., the newly developing Japanese school) to the world community of economists, and (3) to foster the development of quantitative economics" (Editorial note, 1960, i). The first chief editor was Lawrence K. Klein and the co-editor was Michio Morishima.

Two competing journals on the Japanese economy were established one after another by two groups of Japanese economists. The *Journal of the Japanese and International Economies* was founded in 1987 by M. Aoki, M. Ohyama, K. Hamada, and M. Okuno-Fujiwara, in cooperation with the Tokyo Center for Economic Research (see section 4 above). The next year, Ryuzo Sato started *Japan and the World Economy*, an international journal of theory and policy. These journals promote intensive discussion of the Japanese economy and help many economists around the world to understand the Japanese economy.

By contrast with these international ventures, each university or department has its own closed research journal, either without the use of anonymous referees or with the referee process being a mere formality. This kind of journal is called *Kiyo* and is regarded as an "in-house organ" in Bronfenbrenner 1956. Faculty members can freely contribute to their journal whenever they wish, although the door is usually closed to outside economists. Reprints of the papers in *Kiyo* are sent to those who might be interested in the topic. In addition, handwritten papers were circulated among a small group of economists before the rapid spread of Japanese word processors. Some neoclassical or Keynesian economists regard *Kiyo* as being close to a discussion paper series; the difference between them is that a paper in *Kiyo* is a publication evaluated for promotion, whereas a discussion paper is not. In fact, the spread of discussion paper series has occurred only recently in Japan.

According to the survey by the Science Council of Japan (1988, 113), other systems of evaluation of scientific works on economics are also used in Japan. They include personal recommendation, "amicable screening" by the editorial board of a journal, the evaluation of a presentation at a meeting by the chairperson, who is usually an influential older scholar called a *choro* or doyen, and an indirect referee system. In any case, the final decision is usually made by the *choro*, or his aides, and therefore the criteria of rejection are obscure and arbitrary (Ikeo 1990). Yet, since this survey was conducted, the use of a real referee system has been growing steadily, thanks to the trend of internationalization and the development of modern technology (such as less expensive computers and efficient word processors). It is difficult to read handwritten papers and make a valid judgment of the paper's merits.

After 1951, Japanese economists began to contribute their papers to the internationally oriented journals written in English, including the ones highly rated by econometricians and neoclassical economists such as *Econometrica*, *Review of Economic Studies*, and the *Journal of Economic Theory*. Kusumoto (1990) made a statistical study of a few sets of journal articles written in English by individual Japanese economists. The top ten Japanese economists publishing in the thirty journals (see the appendix for a full list) based on a page count during the 1960 to 1989 period were: Takeshi Amemiya, Ken-ichi Inada, Ryuzo Sato, Hirofumi Uzawa, Koichi Hamada, Takamitsu Sawa, Michio Morishima, Hiroki Tsurumi,

Masahisa Fujita, and Akira Takayama. They each published more than 140 pages in journals during that period.

6. The Making of Economists in Japan

The 1988 report by the Science Council of Japan maintains that economics graduate schools in Japan are neither efficient nor institutionalized enough to produce excellent economists. The graduate course has been a kind of appendage to the system of undergraduate education in universities since 1945, although it has been formally independent of undergraduate coursework in economics since the prewar period. There were three major turning points after 1945, that is, the postwar reform up to 1949, the period of student riots culminating in 1969, and the present, since around 1992.

First, education reform was conducted by the U.S. Education Mission from 1945 to 1949 (Tsuchimochi 1993). The old system of complex and rigid paths to specialization was replaced by a simpler path from the sixth year of elementary school through three years of junior high, three years of high school, four years of college and five years of graduate education. Before World War II, high school students had very limited opportunities to take entrance examinations to a particular course in a university.[11] Now they have more opportunities to study any subject at a university, yet they still must choose which department to enter before taking the university entrance examinations. In contrast to the United States, in Japan liberal arts education is given less weight and the systematic education in economics starts during students' undergraduate years.

Martin Bronfenbrenner reported on the state of Japanese economics in the 1950s as follows:

> Japanese economic thought . . . seems to suffer from three besetting ailments: sectarianism, inbreeding and schizophrenia. Sectarianism separates the different schools of economists unnecessarily from each other. Inbreeding characterizes nearly all the better-known economic

11. The old system was so hide-bound that high school students already had limited choices for their future course of study. For example, young Shizuo Kakutani was not allowed to take the entrance examination to the mathematics departments in the Imperial University of Tokyo or in Kyoto Imperial University. This was because he had not been on the science track in high school but in the literature course of Konan High School in Kobe. Fortunately, the mathematics department of Tohoku Imperial University was flexible enough to give him a chance to become a great mathematician.

faculties of the country. Schizophrenia separates the on-campus thinking from the off-campus thinking of many individual economists. On
the other hand, these ailments are common in Japanese intellectual life
and are probably less rampant today than they were a few years ago.
(1956, 390)

Sectarianism and inbreeding were interrelated within each closed community. Economists were raised in a kind of apprenticeship system, called
the seminar system, even at the graduate level. A professor wished to preserve the tradition that he had inherited from his own master and would
choose his successor from among his students. Mawatari (1988) con-
firms that this description is still valid. Yet, a neoclassical economist
would lead a double life: one was academic and the other was practical. Bronfenbrenner characterized such a Japanese economist, saying, "A
man with an outside job arranging dumping or price fixing for a sewing-
machine or shipbuilding cartel will preach in class the virtues of pure
competition and free trade" (1956, 396). It is also noteworthy that many
Japanese neoclassical and Keynesian economists have been trained in
the United States and Britain, thus counteracting the purely Japanese
influences.

An incident in 1968 in the department of medicine at the University of
Tokyo triggered nationwide student riots urging democracy, or individual freedom on campus, and fewer historical subjects in the curriculum.
Socialist and communist groups took this opportunity to try to direct
student power toward preventing the renewal of the U.S.-Japan Security
Treaty, scheduled in 1969. In that year, the University of Tokyo, which
had produced many of the Japanese top elite, especially in the government, could not give entrance examinations. The seminar system, which
bound students to their professors, was abolished, or at least its hold
was loosened in many universities, and graduate schools admitted only a
limited number of students. Graduate students gained freedom to choose
themes for their research and found that the prospects of getting a university job were improved. They lost discipline, or, in the neoclassical
terminology, they lost the incentive to study hard.

It is not surprising that the Japanese government has rarely relied on
graduate schools in Japan to produce the specialists in economics they
needed (Komiya and Yamamoto 1981). Many of the official economists
who work for MITI, EPA, BOJ, MOF, and other institutions have graduated from the department of jurisprudence or law school, especially

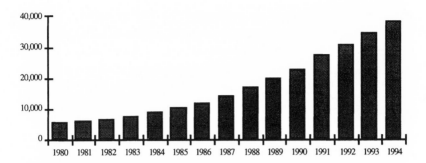

Figure 1   The Number of Students from Abroad in Japanese Universities

Source: Statistics Bureau, Management and Coordination Agency ed. (1980–95).

from the University of Tokyo. They have neither master's nor doctoral degrees in economics. Governmental organizations produce their own economists through on-the-job training and special intensive courses utilizing neoclassical or Keynesian professors. They send some young officials abroad, to America or Europe and recently to Japanese universities, for one or two years to study economics at the graduate level. They have recognized that the quality of advanced training in Japanese universities has improved. In addition, Japanese universities have admitted an increasing number of students from abroad, especially from Asia, at the average growth rate of 15% per year since 1980 (see figure 1 and table 1). This number was less than 5,700 until 1980 and increased to 38,251, 1.6% of the number of students enrolled, in 1994.

Considerable changes in economics education are currently underway. In the process of negotiation with the Ministry of Education, several universities have decided to place more weight on graduate rather than on undergraduate education. Graduate schools began to expand their student intake in 1994. They are screening candidates and producing more economics masters and doctorates. The major objective of this modification is explicitly stated in the outline of the doctoral program in socioeconomic planning of the University of Tsukuba:

Our program is . . . intended to train graduate students competent enough to possess international academic competitiveness. Researchers with international competitiveness are the ones who are capable of publishing articles in international academic journals which have highly

Table 1   The Number of Students from
Abroad Attending Japanese Universities

Year	Number of Students
1980	5,690
1981	6,246
1982	6,864
1983	7,806
1984	9,201
1985	10,300
1986	11,984
1987	14,449
1988	16,999
1989	19,673
1990	22,942
1991	27,435
1992	30,770
1993	34,441
1994	38,251

> selective screening processes. In our program, we strongly encourage
> students to send their research work to refereed academic journals for
> publication, particularly to international academic journals. (1994, 3;
> published both in Japanese and English)

Graduate students and young scholars in economics are still advised to
study abroad, preferably after they have studied for a couple of years in
Japan, otherwise many of them are likely to drop out due to the language
problem. The push to study abroad is partly because many Japanese
universities, unlike Tsukuba, do not have enough professors to give the
standard American courses in microeconomics, macroeconomics, and
econometrics to graduate students, as they have a heavy undergraduate
teaching load. Another reason is that it is hard to make international
contacts and to master the skill of writing academic papers in English
when one stays in Japan.

It seems that no one can stop the internationalization of economics
in Japan and the global use of the English language in academia. However, Japanese economists have many domestic problems to discuss and
historical topics to investigate, which are supposed to be discussed in
Japanese. Japan has recently developed domestic e-mail networks based

in Japanese. A good economist has to be able to communicate in both English and Japanese to be active in Japan.

Appendix

The thirty economics journals in English which Kusumoto (1990) chose were: *American Economic Review, Journal of Political Economy, Econometrica, Journal of Monetary Economics, Journal of Economic Theory, Review of Economic Studies, International Economic Review, Bell Journal of Economics, Journal of Econometrics, Scandinavian Journal of Economics, Brookings Papers on Economic Activity, Journal of Public Economics, Review of Economics and Statistics, Journal of the American Statistical Association, Quarterly Journal of Economics, Journal of Human Resources, Journal of Economic Literature, Economic Journal, Journal of Law and Economics, Canadian Journal of Economics, Economic Inquiry, Journal of Mathematical Economics, Journal of International Economics, Southern Economic Journal, Journal of Money, Credit and Banking, Economica, National Tax Journal, Journal of Regional Science, Journal of Urban Economics,* and *European Economic Review.*

References

Bronfenbrenner, Martin. 1956. Economic Thought and Its Application and Methodology in the East: The State of Japanese Economics. *American Economic Review* 46:389–98.

Calder, Kent E. 1993. *Strategic Capitalism: Private Business and Public Purpose in Japanese Industrial Finance.* Princeton: Princeton University Press.

Cowles, Alfred. 1939. Letter to K. Shibata, 14 October. In Shibata 1934–79.

Editorial. 1926. *Kyoto University Economic Review* 1.1:i–iii. Originally written in English.

Editorial note. 1960. *International Economic Review* 1:i–ii. Originally written in English.

GHQ/SCAP. 1945–52. The General Headquarter/Supreme Commander of Allied Powers Records. Economic and Scientific Section. Tokyo: National Diet Library. Microfiche.

Hata, Ikuhiko. 1976. *American Occupation Policy towards Japan* (in Japanese). Tokyo: Toyo-keizai shimposha.

Ikeo, Aiko. 1990. Japanese Economics from Another Sociological Perspective. *Kokugakuin Keizaigaku* 39:112–28.

———. 1993. Japanese Modern Economics, 1930–1945. In vol. 9 of *Perspectives on the History of Economic Thought*. Edited by R. F. Hébert. Cambridge: Edward Elgar.

———. 1994a. *The Network of Economists in the Twentieth Century: The Development of Economic Studies as Viewed from Japan* (in Japanese). Tokyo: Yuhikaku.

———. 1994b. When Economics Harmonized Mathematics in Japan: A History of Stability Analysis. *The European Journal of the History of Economic Thought* 1:577–99.

———. 1995. Marxist Economics in Japan. Paper presented at the first European Conferences on the History of Economics, Rotterdam. February 10–11.

Japan Development Bank. 1976. *A Twenty-Five-Year History of the Japan Development Bank* (in Japanese). Tokyo: Japan Development Bank.

Japan Statistical Yearbook. Edited by the Statistics Bureau, Management and Coordination Agency. 1980–95. Tokyo: Japan Statistical Association and the Mainichi Newspapers.

Johnson, Charmers. 1982. *MITI and the Japanese Miracle: The Growth of Industrial Policy, 1925–1975*. Stanford: Stanford University Press.

Kawasaki Steel Corporation. 1976. *A Twenty-Five-Year History of Kawasaki Steel* (in Japanese). Kobe: Kawasaki Steel Corporation.

Komiya, Ryutaro, and Kozo Yamamoto. 1981. Japan: The Officer in Charge of Economic Affairs. *Economists in Government: An International Comparative Study*. Edited by A. W. Coats. Durham: Duke University Press.

Kusumoto, Sho-Ichiro. 1990. Journal Publication Performance of Japanese Economists during 1960–1989. Institute of Socio-Economic Planning, Discussion Paper Series No. 441.

Lange, Oskar. 1935. Marxian Economics and Modern Economic Theory. *Review of Economic Studies* 2:189–201.

Mawatari, Shohken. 1988. Japanese Economics from a Sociological Perspective. *History of Economics Society Bulletin* 10:147–53.

Miyazaki, Isamu. 1993. Obituary Note on Saburo Okita: The Economist Who Carried the Post-War History (in Japanese). *Chuo-koron* 108.5:322–23.

Nakayama, Ichiro. 1979. *My Way: Economics* (in Japanese). Tokyo: Kodansha.

Roberts, Geoffrey. 1994. Moscow and the Marshall Plan: Politics, Ideology and the Onset of the Cold War, 1947. *Europe-Asia Studies* 46.8:1371–86.

Sapolsky, Harvey M. 1990. *Science and the Navy: The History of the Office of Naval Research*. Princeton: Princeton University Press.

Science Council of Japan. 1988. *A Survey of Scientific Research in Japan* (in Japanese). Tokyo: The Japan Science Support Foundation.

Sheridan, Kyoko. 1993. *Governing the Japanese Economy*. Cambridge: Polity.

Shibata, K. 1933. Marx's Analysis of Capitalism and the General Equilibrium Theory of the Lausanne School. *Kyoto University Economic Review* 8.1:107–36.

———. 1934–79. Correspondence. Department of Economics, Kyoto University.

Sugita, Hiroaki. 1989. *Economists in Showa* (in Japanese). Tokyo: Chuo-keizaisha.

Szenberg, Michael. 1992. *Eminent Economists: Their Life Philosophy.* Cambridge: Cambridge University Press.

Tokyo Center for Economic Research. 1994. *The Annual Research Plan of 1994 and the Report of 1993* (in Japanese).

Tsuchimochi, Gary H. 1993. *Education Reform in Postwar Japan: The 1946 U. S. Education Mission.* Tokyo: University of Tokyo Press.

Tsukuba, University of. 1994. *Doctoral Program in Socio-Economic Planning.*

Tsuru, Shigeto. 1964. Survey of Economic Research in Postwar Japan. *American Economic Review* 54.4, part 2, supp., 79–101.

The Dissolution of the Swedish Tradition

Bo Sandelin and Ann Veiderpass

The internationalization of science and scholarly work is not a new phenomenon—nor an always unchallenged phenomenon. The medieval European universities were highly internationalized.[1] Students and teachers came from many different countries and teaching was conducted in the same international language—Latin—everywhere.

The nineteenth century produced two contrasting trends. The rise of political nationalism had a parallel in the scholarly field. Patriotic emotions supported discoveries and inventions by explorers and scientists. The national language began to be used in teaching and writing; in economics, it had been used at Swedish universities since the inauguration of four chairs in the discipline during the period 1741 to 1759. There was, however, a countercurrent. From the middle of the nineteenth century the number of international scientific organizations began to grow rapidly. The evolution of the communications system made all kinds of cross-border contacts much easier than before. The modern form of scientific internationalism had begun (cf. Sörlin 1994, 191–208).

1. Financial support from the Swedish Council for Research in the Humanities and Social Sciences (HSFR) is gratefully acknowledged. Because territorial states in the modern sense hardly existed in the Middle Ages, Crawford, Shinn, and Sörlin (1993, 7) prefer talking about *translocal universalism* in their detailed discussion of different concepts within the field.

The first modern Swedish economist, David Davidson, was influenced mainly by German economists when he wrote his doctoral thesis. Knut Wicksell made study tours to England, France, Germany, and Austria at the end of the 1880s, and was especially influenced by the Austrians. He intended to go to America, too, but changed his mind. Gösta Bagge was a pioneer when in 1904–5 he studied at Johns Hopkins (Wadensjö 1990b). He was followed by Johan Åkerman and Bertil Ohlin, who in 1919–20 and 1922–23, respectively, studied at Harvard (Sörlin 1994, 203–9). Gunnar Myrdal's early stay in America in 1929–30 confirmed that the United States had become very important to Swedish economists. The version of internationalization that has been called Americanization had begun.

In this article, we shall discuss the internationalization of Swedish economics. By *internationalization* of Swedish economics we mean a process of integration of Swedish thought, techniques, behavior, and institutional solutions with foreign thought, techniques, behavior, and institutional solutions. Its mirror image is a *denationalization* of Swedish economics, implying that specific Swedish characteristics fade. *Americanization* of Swedish economics means that Swedish economic thought, techniques, behavior, and institutional solutions are being strongly influenced by, or even replaced by, American examples.

We will consider a selection of circumstances related to the process of internationalization of Swedish economics. We begin with the evolution of the postgraduate system, which in 1945 was characterized by two different degrees and hardly any courses. In 1969 it was replaced by an American-inspired system, which was fundamentally the same at all the (then) five universities that offered postgraduate training. We will discuss the postgraduate system at some length, as it has played a central role in Swedish economics. Under the former degree requirements, the grade of the thesis determined whether the doctor could hope for a university career, and the thesis often turned out to be the main scientific contribution even among professors.

To derive some bibliographic illustrations of the sources of influences, we will demonstrate the pattern of citations in Swedish doctoral dissertations and in the journals *Ekonomisk Tidskrift/Scandinavian Journal of Economics* and the *Ekonomisk Debatt*. Furthermore, we will study the flow of foreign books to Swedish university libraries. We will find that de-Germanization in favor of American influences started quite early in this century.

There are few specifically Swedish characteristics left, but we note that Swedish authors are overrepresented in the field of international economics and show less than average interest in nonmainstream thought. The so-called Stockholm School dissolved without its disciples transmitting a Swedish tradition that was accepted by the next generation. However, the replacement of national-specific thought by American-dominated international thought is a general, worldwide phenomenon. Therefore, the explanation must also be mainly at a general level. Myrdal's model of interrelated, cumulative causes may be usable in this context.

The Postgraduate System in 1945

The postgraduate system prevailing at Swedish universities in 1945 had remained largely the same since the nineteenth century. After undergraduate studies, ending with the first degree, the student usually had to take a *licentiate degree* before he (or, in a very few cases, she) was allowed to go on to the *doctoral degree*.

The licentiate degree required a written thesis and an oral examination. It was formally supposed to require two and a half or three years of full-time work after the first degree. Courses were seldom given, but different kinds of seminars took place. The student came to an agreement with the professor on a reading list for the oral examination.

Sometimes the licentiate thesis was extended to a doctoral thesis, but frequently the doctoral thesis had no connection with the licentiate thesis; after the licentiate degree, the student had to write a doctoral thesis to obtain the doctorate. However, most of those who had taken a licentiate degree did not go on to take a doctoral degree. During the period 1895 to 1974, 229 students took the old licentiate degree in economics while only 76 of them took the old doctoral degree (Wadensjö 1992).

After the licentiate degree, courses were rarely taken for the doctoral degree. The doctoral thesis was often very extensive, often the "lifework" of the author. It had to be printed and defended in public. Three official opponents were appointed, of whom the first, appointed by the faculty, was the most important. The second and the third were elected by the author; the third was supposed to crack jokes. Extra opponents often appeared from the audience. The grade of the thesis was important: it determined whether the author could hope for a university career or would have to be satisfied with a post at a senior high school or in public administration.

The system with two postgraduate degrees—a licentiate degree and a higher doctoral degree—was fairly similar to the system in several other European countries where two postgraduate degrees also existed or still exist; in Germany these were denoted Dr.Phil. and Dr.Habil, in France doctorat d'Université and doctorat d'État, and in the Soviet Union "candidate degree" and "doctoral degree." It differed from the systems in Britain and the United States.

Americanization: The New Postgraduate System

In the 1950s and 1960s, the question of postgraduate teaching and research was placed on the political agenda. In the opinion of influential circles, the old system had its shortcomings: there was too little postgraduate teaching—if any at all—and too little organized supervision for thesis writing; consequently, it took too long for a student to take the licentiate or doctoral degree. The median age of those receiving a licentiate or doctoral degree in 1960 was thirty-two and thirty-six years, respectively (*SOU 1966:67*, 30). Furthermore, the system with two different postgraduate degrees was called in question: one degree should be enough.

Therefore, in 1963 a government committee was appointed to provide recommendations for reform of postgraduate education and to scrutinize research careers and university appointments. The committee made a comparative study of the situation prevailing in certain countries. It stated in its main report, *SOU 1966:67, Forskarutbildning och forskarkarriär* (Postgraduate training and career): "Our more detailed investigation of postgraduate education outside Sweden is dominated by an account of the situation in the USA. The reason—in addition to what is said in the directives—is that the American doctoral degree, more than anywhere else, has become normative. Moreover, the training in the USA is more systematic and extensive than in most other places. Much that has been discussed elsewhere has been realized and tested in the USA" (28; authors' translation). The report of the committee implied that attention was being turned away from Europe toward the United States. The government bill 1969:31, presented by then Minister of Education Olof Palme, followed most of the propositions of the committee and resulted in an act that undoubtedly implied an Americanization of Swedish postgraduate training. The system that was introduced in July 1969 was quite similar to many American postgraduate programs.

The licentiate degree and the old doctoral degree were combined into a single doctoral degree.[2] This new doctoral degree would require four years of full-time work. The first two years would consist of a number of postgraduate courses and the last two years of thesis writing. More supervision than before was envisaged. The length of the doctoral thesis would be reduced. "The originality and comprehensiveness . . . that has traditionally been required of a doctoral thesis should, accordingly, be played down in the new system. . . . The most important scientific contributions to be made by the individual should be expected to come after the period of education rather than be made part of the education," says the minister in the bill (66).

Why did the reformers try to reproduce the typical American system? We could, of course, refer to general cultural influences from the United States, but more specific reasons can be put forward. The American system *was* conceived as more efficient than European programs: it evidently produced more doctors, faster, from a given stock of postgraduate students; at any rate this was the case at the best American universities. Furthermore, the traditional Swedish pattern of postgraduate training along a winding road, with perhaps no courses and hardly any supporting supervision, and reflections made largely in splendid isolation, was not in line with the ideology of the modern society where mass production, visible efficiency, and promptitude were the guiding lights.

Unfulfilled Goals

How did the new system succeed? Some important goals were not achieved. The age of new doctors decreased immediately after the reform, but then increased again. The average age of a new doctor at the end of the 1980s was 37.6 years, while the official goal was 28 years (Wadensjö 1990a).[3]

The continuing high average age is probably mainly explained by changes in student characteristics. In the old system, the student was aware that taking the doctoral degree was a job to be carried out single-

2. A "new" licentiate degree, not compulsory before a doctoral degree, was introduced in 1985.
3. The low number of obtained doctoral degrees in relation to admitted postgraduate students is not less conspicuous: during the 1970s and 1980s, the annual inflow of new postgraduate students was more than three times as large as the annual outflow of new doctors (Wadensjö 1992, 72–73). Many—perhaps most—of those who begin postgraduate studies never obtain the doctoral degree.

handedly. Those who began postgraduate studies were prepared to work alone. In the new system, many students begin postgraduate studies with the attitude that it is a matter of taking an additional number of courses—which most students are able to do—and then writing a thesis under the close guidance of a thesis adviser. In other words, many students are not prepared to work alone to the extent that had been required. The constant complaint from graduate students, at virtually all Swedish universities and in all disciplines, about deficient supervision indicates that there is a difference between what the students expected concerning the writing of a thesis and what the real world required.

An additional reason for the high average age of a new doctor is evidently that the length of the theses did not diminish as much as intended. While the old doctoral thesis ran on average to 341 pages, the average new thesis, up to the end of the 1980s, was 231 pages, although the upper limit according to the government committee should be 160 pages (Wadensjö 1990a).

The Commission for Evaluation of Swedish Economic Research

In the late 1980s, the Swedish Council for Research in the Humanities and Social Sciences initiated a comprehensive evaluation of economic research in Sweden. The result was published in a book edited by Engwall (1992), which included a number of background studies by Swedish economists and four concluding chapters by the evaluation commissioners: Avinash Dixit from Princeton, Robert Solow from MIT, and Seppo Honkapohja from the Academy of Finland. Some points are of interest to this study.

In the opening section, the commissioners maintain that "over the past three or four decades the literature of analytical economics has become almost completely homogeneous worldwide. Mainstream economists [others do not count in this book] in all countries now contribute to a single international literature as part of a single intellectual community" (1992, 129). Consequently, "over the past four decades Swedish economics has become successively more closely integrated into the broad international community of mainstream economics. In many areas of economics and in the most advanced departments and institutes, this process is now essentially complete" (130).

Nevertheless, the commissioners find several deficiencies in Swedish economics, especially in postgraduate training, and they "believe that the system requires some drastic reforms." Although "these should not consist of blind imitations of any other system" (1992, 180), the American system is clearly the norm against which the Swedish system is compared.

Thus, comparing the population and the number of departments providing postgraduate training in Sweden and in the United States and taking the American "numbers as rough guidelines, it would seem that Sweden has room for one large, or for the sake of competition, two smaller postgraduate departments of economics. In fact it has six," say the commissioners (1992, 161). They "recognize the practical impossibility of shutting down any of the existing departments" (180), but they do not question that the American ratio represents roughly the appropriate norm.

Another problem that should be taken care of, according to the commissioners, is "the astonishing degree of inbreeding and immobility in the Swedish university system. Most students and staff stay in the same department throughout their student years and their subsequent careers" (1992, 149).[4]

In a background chapter, Lars Jonung emphasizes, without disapproval, the traditional involvement of Swedish professors in public life, "a tradition going back to the founders of economics in Sweden, to Wicksell, Cassel and Heckscher" (1992, 179), and existing in the other Scandinavian countries, as well, as a consequence of their smallness (Sandmo 1988). For the commissioners such involvement implies "routine studies"; they "would like to register an opposing view" (179) to Jonung's, and seem to suggest that the traditional public concern of Swedish professors should be left to less qualified economists.

The analysis and the recommendations of the commissioners are clearly colored by American experiences and values. That is not surprising, in view of the commissioners' background. Some of their suggestions were already to some extent put into effect before they made them, for example postgraduate study overseas, which for a long time had been quite common. These studies do not usually make up the student's entire post-

---

4. The reader of the report may wonder what is the normal degree of inbreeding and immobility. The commissioners are evidently comparing the Swedish situation with that in the United States, but is the U.S. situation normal in an international perspective? From housing market studies, we know that the propensity to move is much higher in the United States than in, for instance, Europe, and the higher mobility among American economists is apparently a consequence of the higher general mobility in the country. Maybe the American mobility should be considered "astonishingly" high, and the Swedish more normal from an international point of view.

graduate program, but a semester or two of courses while the remaining part is accomplished in Sweden. The fact that only four out of about thirty full professors of economics in Sweden at the end of the 1980s had an American doctoral degree shows that the degree is usually registered in Sweden.[5] Other suggestions are difficult to reconcile with Swedish traditions and the Swedish way of living, for instance a considerably higher degree of mobility.

In one area, the proposal of the commissioners evidently has been taken *ad notam*. They point out that journal articles after the Second World War have become relatively more important within the profession at the expense of books. "Doctoral theses in the United States and in many other countries have quite properly followed this change, and consist of a number of essays that do not even have to be tied together by a common theme. In Sweden, too many theses continue to be written in the monograph or *magnum opus* form, despite an attempt made twenty years ago to change the system" (1992, 168). A normal thesis should consist of three essays of "publishable quality," according to the commissioners (169).

Not long after the committee had concluded its work the adherence to this principle was declared in a letter from the Department of Economics at Stockholm University to the other universities. Then the share of Swedish theses consisting of a few essays suddenly increased. If we take the words "essays," "papers," and "studies" in the title of a thesis as an indication that the thesis consists of a number of essays, we find that 26 percent of the theses in the period 1991–93 were of this kind, while only 6 percent had fallen into this category in 1988–90. We may interpret the fact that the average number of pages in a doctoral thesis decreased in the early 1990s as a result of the same spirit of change. For each of the six years, 1988 to 1993, the average length of a thesis was 208, 242, 211, 179, 167, and 166 pages.

The change in the formal character and the decrease in length of the thesis were, however, hardly combined with a clear decrease in the average age of the new doctors. The average age each year from 1988 to 1993 was 37, 39, 33, 38, 36, and 36 years.

---

5. During the period of the old doctoral degree in Sweden, there was in some circles a certain disdain for an American Ph.D., with its shorter thesis. One of our teachers once told the story of a Swedish doctor at Uppsala, who saw an acquaintance with an American Ph.D. at the other side of the street and shouted teasingly over the crowd: "Hi, you Ph.D."

The Direction of Citations

Although different kinds of bibliographic measures have different kinds of weaknesses, each provides some kind of information we should not neglect. Usually, they give some indication of the influences between different economists or groups of economists. Table 1 builds on the lists of references (or, in a few old theses, works mentioned in footnotes) in Swedish doctoral theses in economics from 1895 to 1993.[6] A cited work with its author constitutes a unit of observation; that is, authors who have published several cited works are counted several times. Only references where the cited author is included in Blaug's *Who's Who in Economics* are taken into account. The table is similar to an input-output table, but instead of input we have the country of birth of cited authors, and instead of output we have the country of employment of the same authors when the cited work was published. The country is denoted by the ISO norm. In table 1 cited works published before 1940 are the basis.

There are very low percentage numbers outside the diagonal in table 1. Thus, for books and articles published before 1940, there were very few authors working in a country other than their country of birth. Britain and Sweden account for about half the citations, although there are quite high total numbers for the United States and Germany, Austria, and Austro-Hungary, too.

Table 2 refers to cited works published between 1940 and 1992. We find two main changes in relation to table 1. First, the total figures for the United States have trebled to 50 percent or more. The percentages for the other countries (except "others") have diminished. The decline is particularly evident for the German-culture area and for Sweden.

The second main change is that in table 2 there are larger numbers outside the diagonal, and the total share for country of birth differs, in some cases considerably, from the total share for country of employment. Thus, there has been a net inflow to the United States; the cited authors were in 58 percent of cases employed there and in 50 percent of cases born there. The German-language countries and "others" have had a net outflow.

6. Eskil Wadensjö has published a list of theses in economics from 1895 to 1989 in appendix D in Engwall 1992, which has been used in this study. For the years 1990 to 1993 he has provided unpublished lists, for which we are grateful. We are also grateful to Ulla Mellgren for time-consuming assistance.

Table 1 Citations by Authors' Countries of Birth and Countries of Employment 1690–1939 (percentages)

Country of Birth	Country of Employment						Total by birth
	U.S.	G.B.	DE/AT/AT-HU	FR/IT/ES/PT	SE	Others	
U.S.	15.6	0.0	0.0	0.0	0.0	0.03	16.0
G.B.	0.14	25.7	0.0	0.0	0.0	0.14	26.0
DE/AT/ AT-HU	0.4	0.07	15.7	0.03	0.4	0.4	17.0
FR/IT/ ES/PT	0.03	0.2	0.07	5.9	0.0	0.17	6.0
SE	0.0	0.0	0.0	0.0	25.6	0.14	26.0
Others	0.8	1.2	0.24	0.17	0.0	6.8	9.0
Total by Employment	17.0	27.0	16.0	6.0	26.0	8.0	100.0

Note. DE = Germany, AT = Austria, AT-HU = Austro-Hungary, FR = France, IT = Italy,
ES = Spain, PT = Portugal, SE = Sweden.

Table 2 Citations by Authors' Countries of Birth and Countries of Employment 1940–1992 (percentages)

Country of Birth	Country of Employment						
	U.S.	G.B.	DE/AT/(AT-HU)	FR/IT/ES/PT	SE	Others	Total by birth
U.S.	49.0	0.2	0.02	0.0	0.02	0.3	50.0
G.B.	0.4	11.8	0.0	0.02	0.0	0.2	12.0
DE/AT/ AT-HU	1.8	0.4	3.4	0.0	0.07	0.3	6.0
FR/IT/ ES/PT	0.7	0.03	0.0	1.7	0.0	0.05	2.0
SE	0.02	0.0	0.0	0.0	5.8	0.07	6.0
Others	6.3	2.0	0.05	0.03	0.8	15.0	24.0
Total by Employment	58.0	14.0	3.0	2.0	7.0	16.0	100.0

Note. DE = Germany, AT = Austria, AT-HU = Austro-Hungary, FR = France, IT = Italy, ES = Spain, PT = Portugal, SE = Sweden.

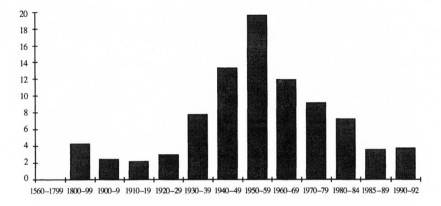

Figure 1   Proportion of cases in which country of birth is not equal to country of occupation (percentage)

If we look more closely behind tables 1 and 2, we find that the greater mobility between countries reflected in table 2 has not been a continuously growing phenomenon: in figure 1 we see that there is a peak for works published in the 1950s regarding the share of cited works for which the country of birth is not the same as the country of employment of the author when the publication was published. The 1950s' peak is a consequence of the political unrest in Europe in the 1930s and the Second World War, when many economists and budding economists, especially in Germany and Eastern Europe, had to leave their countries.[7]

It would have been an advantage if we could have based tables 1 and 2 and figure 1 on the authors of all cited publications, not only on authors included in *Who's Who in Economics*. However, the change is so manifest that there is no doubt about the main message: the United States has become the single most influential foreign country for thesis writers in Sweden.

The American dominance in foreign sources can be found in other material as well. In 1965 David Davidson's, Wicksell's, Cassel's, and the Stockholm School's forum *Ekonomisk Tidskrift* changed its name to *The Swedish Journal of Economics*[8] and published material only in English. Since the 1950s, its contents had changed in the direction of advanced

---

7. Hagemann and Krohn 1992 provide details on 314 German-language emigrants.
8. In 1976 it became *The Scandinavian Journal of Economics*.

Table 3   Citations in *Ekonomisk Debatt* by Country of Publication (percentages)

Country	Year				Total
	1973–79	1980–84	1985–89	1990–95	
U.S.	26	24	28	28	27
G.B.	13	10	19	13	15
DE/AT	1	2	2	1	1
FR/IT	1	2	1	1	1
SE	51	55	43	43	47
Others	8	7	7	14	9
Total	100	100	100	100	100

techniques and general theoretical problems. This meant that there was room for a new journal in Swedish, focusing on economic analysis of current problems and addressed to a wide audience of economists. It appeared under the name *Ekonomisk Debatt* in 1973, initiated by Assar Lindbeck and Nils Lundgren.

Table 3 shows the countries in which the publications cited in the *Ekonomisk Debatt* are published.[9] The high share of Swedish publications is hardly surprising taking into consideration the character of the journal. It is, however, lower during the last two periods than the first two. The United States has always been the most important foreign country, while Germany and Austria have played an insignificant role. The de-Germanization in favor of the Americanization of Swedish economics had essentially been carried out before the appearance of the journal.

An additional illustration of the fact that the de-Germanization took place quite early is found in table 4. It shows the distribution between countries of publication for foreign economic books acquired by Swedish research libraries (mainly university libraries).[10] We find that in 1903–7 more than 50 percent of the foreign books were of German or Austrian origin. This share was halved thirty years later, and almost halved once again in the mid-1950s. The emigration by intellectuals from Germany

9. The table is based on the first five issues out of eight in each annual volume.

10. The table has been constructed on the basis of the (almost) annual national Accessions Book.

Table 4 Foreign Economic Books Acquired by Swedish
Research Libraries (percentages)

Country of Publication	1903–7	1934–37	1954–55
U.S.	9	22	35
G.B.	16	26	17
DE/AT	51	26	15
Others	24	26	33
Total	100	100	100

in the 1930s and 1940s was not a starting point for the de-Germanization
of Swedish economics, but it reinforced an ongoing process.

Mathematics and Econometrics

There are two related aspects of mathematics in economic analysis. It is
a language in which economic relations (often) are expressed. But it is
also a science with theorems and lemmas that can be used in economic
analysis. The latter aspect is associated with what has sometimes been
interpreted as making science or engineering out of economics. Several
authors, for instance Johnson (1973), Portes (1987), and Kolm (1988),
perceive this as an American characteristic that has spread. For Johnson, the Second World War is the turning point in America, after which
the transition begins to "new techniques of mathematical analysis and
econometrics, as contrasted with the social wisdom and philosophizing
that characterized the older style of 'political economy' " (65).

For a comparison of the evolution in Sweden, we show in figure 2 the
proportion of pages in Swedish doctoral theses in economics that contain
at least one mathematical expression.[11] As early as the 1930s, the amount
of mathematics was almost as great as in the 1970s due to the work of
Tord Palander, Erik Lundberg, and others in the Stockholm School. (The
high proportion in 1895–99 is wholly a result of the mathematics in
Wicksell's thesis *Zur Lehre von der Steuerincidenz*, which was one out
of two theses in this period.) The sharp decline from the 1960s to the

11. The proportion has first been calculated for each thesis; after that, the average over theses
has been calculated.

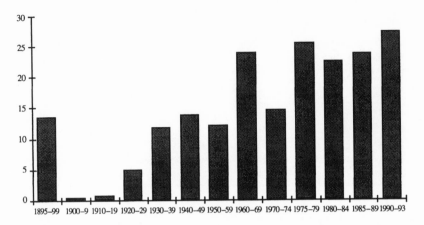

Figure 2   Proportion of Theses' Pages Containing Mathematics, 1895–1993 (percentage)

1970s is explained by the fact that during the 1960s, the last decade of theses solely of the old type, many theses had reached quite an advanced technical level. The first theses under the new, less demanding rules were published in the early 1970s. Several of them were not very sophisticated.

The fairly early use of mathematics makes it reasonable to question whether it is a result of American influence. We hold that it is not. This is not incompatible with the view that the American mainstream ideal has played an *amplifying* role for the use of mathematics after the Second World War.

When it comes to econometrics (figure 3), there is probably a more direct American influence since the early applications in Sweden.[12] That applies to the widespread introduction in the 1960s and 1970s, and to a large extent it applies to Johan Åkerman's solitary contribution in his thesis *Om det ekonomiska livets rytmik* (1928). Computerization also has been a contributing cause.

The Language

A common language facilitates the internationalization of economics. The dominance of the English language has now reached an extent where

12. We have included different kinds of statistical estimates performed by "nontrivial" methods. Correlation coefficients are included, but not simple averages. A few estimates of input-output tables are included as well.

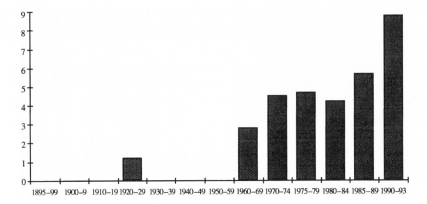

Figure 3 Proportion of Theses' Pages Containing Econometrics, 1895–1993 (percentage)

many Swedish economists need only two languages in their private and public life: Swedish and English. This evolution could be discerned long ago, when the situation was still different, thus, Johan Åkerman wrote forty years ago: "Swedish scholars, who are constantly stopped in their production by the language barrier, should in this context consider that the economic language is going to be American. Judging by the contents of English-language economic journals, publications in French and German are seldom read in the U.S., and even more seldom in Britain. The question is if not the same applies to Sweden. Therefore, it seems to be a justifiable objective in the field of social sciences to try to demolish part of the language barrier, which isolates new ideas and attitudes" (1955, 279).

A considerable part of that language barrier is now demolished by the almost general application of English in advanced economics. The changes in Sweden may be illustrated by different figures. Between 1895 and 1929, 74 percent of the doctoral theses in economics were written in Swedish, 22 percent in German, and 4 percent (i.e., Karin Kock's thesis in 1929) in English. In the 1970s, more than 50 percent were still in Swedish and the rest in English. In 1992 and 1993, all theses were written in English.

In the 1940s, 25 percent of the citations in the theses referred to English-language sources, in the 1970s 75 percent, and 1990–93 85 percent. Similarly, in 1940–44, 31 percent of the citations in the *Ekonomisk Tidskrift* referred to sources in English; in 1970–74, 91 percent (in the subsequent *Swedish Journal of Economics*); and in 1990–92, 97 percent (in the subsequent *Scandinavian Journal of Economics*). The last is, of course, also a result of the fact that Swedish authors had been reduced to a minority; in the early 1990s, the journal had almost twice as many American authors as Swedish (Ranki and Sandelin 1993).

The common use of English is advantageous not only for those whose native language it is, but also for those belonging to smaller language communities who otherwise wouldn't learn and use English. At the same time, it reinforces the American position in international scholarship. Those who use their native language in international communication are privileged.

What Remains?

The material presented in the previous sections suggests that country-specific characteristics of Swedish economics are not as distinct as half a century ago. However, with some effort, we can point to a few remaining, or new, characteristic properties. We may distinguish between characteristics related to economics proper (fields, theories, techniques) and institutional characteristics.

Economics Proper

In the sense that certain fields of research are overrepresented or under-represented, there are, of course, features that are characteristic of Sweden. Comparing Swedish publishing in different areas of economics with world publishing, Persson, Stern, and Gunnarson (1992, 124) classify more than 16 percent of the scientific articles by Swedish economists between 1973 and 1989 as articles in the field of "international economics," while the world figure is less than 9 percent. This is consistent with the widespread opinion that Sweden (and several other small countries) have their comparative advantage and their special interest in research on problems of small open economies. Sweden is also slightly overrepresented in "manpower, labour, and population," but has only about half the world percentage in "quantitative economics," "agriculture and natural resources," and "welfare programmes and regional economics."

Articles published by Swedish economists in different highly ranked journals do, of course, usually include theoretical or methodological contributions, but such contributions are seldom or never country specific.

On the other hand, it is a trivial fact that *applications* are often Swedish in the sense that the field of interest or the specific problem or data apply to Sweden, even if the method used doesn't have a Swedish origin. Thus, Dixit, Honkapohja, and Solow (1992, 139–40) state on the subject of Swedish econometric research: "In recent years Swedish economists, sometimes in collaboration with academic statisticians, have focused on the serious application of advanced methods rather than on the creation of new econometric techniques to deal with novel contexts of estimation or hypothesis-testing."

An extreme lack of interest in schools outside mainstream economics (and, consequently, more than average concentration on mainstream economics) may also be considered a Swedish feature. No economics departments are strongholds of institutional, Austrian, post-Keynesian, or Marxian thought. During the years of left-wing radicalism in the Western world around 1970, only one department (Göteborg) had a large Marxist group.

This extreme lack of concern for nonmainstream thought is reflected in a comparison of citations in economics articles from 1973 to 1989 to major schools of thought in macroeconomics. The relative citation rate[13] for Swedish authors to post-Keynesians is 0.30 and to neo-Ricardians 0.46, while the world rate is 1.00. On the other hand, the Swedish rate is clearly above the world rate for citations to monetarists, econometric approach, disequilibrium theory, and new classical economists (see Persson, Stern, and Gunnarson 1992, 118).

Institutional Characteristics

We have already mentioned the extensive involvement in public affairs as a traditional trait of Swedish economists. This seems to apply to several other small countries, too, and is evidently a consequence of the fact that the need for expertise in fiscal policy, central banking policy, social security systems, and so on is almost as great for small countries as for large. The involvement can take the form of activity in political parties and parliament, as in the case of Ohlin, Myrdal, and, in recent years, Hegeland and Södersten. More frequent, however, is the involvement in government and other committees that result in different reports. Such

---

13. The relative citation rate is defined as the percentage of a country's citations that refer to a certain school divided by the corresponding percentage for the world as a whole.

involvement has probably not diminished; at any one time, one can find a number of well-known economists engaged in such work.

However, in one respect there has been a change in recent decades. Formerly, it was not unusual for the author of a government report to present it as a doctoral thesis. Probably the last thesis of this kind was presented in 1975 and concerned international conglomerates in industrialized countries. The disappearance of such dissertations seems to be a consequence of several factors. One is the mathematization of scientific economic texts; the mathematical language cannot be used by an author who writes for a larger audience of politicians and government officials. A closely related cause, which seems to have emerged in the 1960s and 1970s and which to some extent may reflect a generation gap, is a low esteem or even slight contempt for applied research on local problems.[14] The fact that there are now a sufficient number of doctors able to write government economic reports—so that less qualified, junior experts are seldom needed—may be a third reason.

The Swedish system of appointments is another interesting institutional feature that only recently began to change. Normally, nobody is appointed as, for instance, a professor or lecturer unless there is a vacant post and applications have been processed by strict formal rules. Tenure is usually permanent for those who have received their post in such a way. (Of course, less formally appointed substitutes and temporary teachers exist.) Creating a professorship has been a fairly complicated affair. Consequently, there have been relatively few full professors at Swedish universities. In 1945 there were 9 in economics in the entire country; in 1980 there were 19 out of a total population of 8.3 million people.

However, during the 1980s these strict principles began to dissolve. The universities themselves became able to appoint professors, not only the government as before. Chairs could be financed by external donations. During the early 1970s that would have been politically difficult; it would have been considered an undue opportunity for private interests to control research. Chairs of subfields of economics were established, sometimes determined by the wishes of the donor, sometimes in order to obtain a more adequate staffing structure or to promote a special individual by

14. The then young Bo Södersten's (1969) polemic with Bertil Ohlin is illustrative. Södersten, alluding to Ohlin, criticized the course that implied we would "continue the tradition of the 1930s in Swedish economics, turn up our noses at more abstract theory, keep the banner of provincialism flying, and bury the wisdom that we may possess in Government Reports" (345).

the exclusion of able competitors.[15] With new rules introduced in 1993, the nonsocialist government, which was in power during 1991–94, left the appointments entirely to the universities. The contents of the national university code were reduced and to a large extent replaced by local rules decided upon by the universities themselves. Furthermore, as one of its last actions in this field, the government changed the formal status of two small universities from being subject to government authority to being more independent.

Since 1980, the number of professorships has doubled in the country. There are currently (1995) about forty. To a large extent, this is a consequence of institutional changes.

Why So Little Left?

Taking account of the strong Swedish tradition, especially the success of the well-known Stockholm School economists in the 1930s, we may ask why there is now, according to many observers, so little specifically Swedish in Swedish economics. One trivial answer is that it is not only Swedish economics that has lost most of its national features; it is something that has occurred in other countries as well. Nevertheless, the alleged Swedish early excellence might have been expected to be an antidote against such an evolution.

As part of the answer, the characteristics of the Stockholm School and its members cannot be neglected. First, we may question whether there really was a vivid, coherent school from which disciples could be expected to emerge. Ohlin tried to describe the Stockholm School by specifying a number of attributes in his famous 1937 *Economic Journal* article where the name was coined. However, that has been challenged by others. For instance, Erik Lundberg (1987), who preferred to call himself a Keynesian, wrote in his last article: "It is generally accepted, I think, that the Stockholm School was and is a *myth*. As early as in 1937, when Ohlin launched the concept in the *Economic Journal*, many of us economists in Stockholm protested and thought it was a curious idea. But the language dominates the thought. The concept was accepted and used (sparsely) even by ourselves. Even a myth has a real background; the myth can become at least a real as the reality" (280).

---

15. Sometimes those chairs are very narrowly defined, for instance, a chair at Uppsala in "economics, especially corporate taxation."

Second, several of the Stockholm economists soon left "the School," either for research within other traditions or for public commissions. Ohlin wrote very little within "the School"; he made his most important economic contributions at an early date within neoclassical trade theory and then turned to politics. Similarly, Myrdal made his most important contributions as an institutionalist and also devoted several years to public commissions. Dag Hammarskjöld started an official career in his early thirties and ended up as secretary-general of the UN. Alf Johansson, one of the most gifted, wrote a number of government reports on housing policy after his thesis and set his mark on Swedish housing policy during several decades; some years before his retirement, he was given the title of professor. Karin Kock, too, made a career mainly in the public service. The rigid Swedish appointment system, described above, was surely one of the reasons that Hammarskjöld, Johansson, and Kock made careers mainly outside the university.

Third, the habit of giving professors credit for their ability to collect and train successful disciples is quite new in Sweden. Thus it is difficult to point to a direct disciple of Wicksell, although at a general level, he clearly influenced subsequent thought. The Stockholm School economists had very few, if any, immediate disciples. Until the 1970s writing a doctoral thesis was considered a matter only for the author; the professor was neither blamed for nor credited with failure or success. In the case of Lundberg, this attitude was combined with an inclination to destructive censure when a student dared present a draft at a seminar.

At a more general level—as these developments are not unique to Sweden—it may be fruitful to look at the process in a way similar to Myrdal's scheme for the evolution of a system of interrelated "cumulative causes" (or groups of causes), used in his analysis of poverty. The most important cumulative causes in our system are: (1) research training, (2) university code and other formal rules, (3) read and written publications, (4) language, and (5) political and economic power.

If for some reason there is a shift in one of those causes, there will subsequently be changes in the others as well, with repercussions from the first change, which will influence the others in a second round, and so on. The pattern of causes and effects becomes so complicated that we are only able to hint at one possible thread in the net: Suppose that American political and economic power increases. Commercial and other relations with America would increase. The need for better knowledge of English would be apparent in other countries, and more English teaching would be introduced into schools. This would increase the ability to read and write texts in English, which would give American and British authors a stronger position in graduate training. This could in turn inspire university reformers to look at the American university system, which may influence a new University Code. The major American influences would now indicate that there is a need for even better knowledge of English, and so on. The beginning (and the possible end) of the process is largely wrapped in mystery, but in order to express one element of this complicated course of events in words, one has to start somewhere arbitrarily.

References

Åkerman, Johan. 1928. *Om det ekonomiska livets rytmik*. Stockholm: Nordiska Bokhandeln.

―――. 1955. Komparativ metodanalys. *Ekonomisk Tidskrift* 57:274–79.

Crawford, Elisabeth, Terry Shinn, and Sverker Sörlin, eds. 1993. *Denationalizing Science*. Dordrecht: Kluwer Academic Publishers.

Dixit, A. K., S. Honkapohja, and R. M. Solow. 1992. Swedish Economics in the 1980s. In *Economics in Sweden: An Evaluation of Swedish Research in Economics*. Edited by Lars Engwall. London: Routledge.

Engwall, Lars, ed. 1992. *Economics in Sweden: An Evaluation of Swedish Research in Economics*. London: Routledge.

Hagemann, H., and C-D. Krohn. 1992. *Die Emigration deutschsprachiger Wirtschaftswissenschaftler nach 1933*. 2d ed. Stuttgart: Institut für Volkswirtschaftslehre, Universität Hohenheim.

Johnson, Harry G. 1973. National Styles in Economic Research: The United States, the United Kingdom, Canada, and Various European Countries. *Dædalus* (Spring): 65–74.

Jonung, Lars. 1992. Economics the Swedish Way 1889–1989. In *Economics in Sweden: An Evaluation of Swedish Research in Economics*. Edited by Lars Engwall. London: Routledge.

Kolm, Serge-Christophe. 1988. Economics in Europe and in the U.S. *European Economic Review* 32:207–12.

Lundberg, Erik. 1987. Minnen kring Stockholmsskolan. *Ekonomisk Debatt* 15.4:280–86.

Ohlin, Bertil. 1937. Some Notes on the Stockholm Theory of Savings and Investments. I-II. *Economic Journal* 47:53–69, 221-40.

Persson, O., P. Stern, and E. Gunnarsson. 1992. Swedish Economics on the International Scene. In *Economics in Sweden: An Evaluation of Swedish Research in Economics*. Edited by Lars Engwall. London: Routledge.

164   Bo Sandelin and Ann Veiderpass

Portes, Richard. 1987. Economics in Europe. *European Economic Review* 31:1329–40.

Ranki, S., and Bo Sandelin. 1993. Internationalisering eller amerikanisering av den svenska nationalekonomin? *Ekonomisk Debatt* 21.4:335–46.

Sandmo, R. 1988. Introductory Remarks. *European Economic Review* 32.2/3:491–94.

Södersten, Bo. 27 October 1969. Allmän jämvikt och utrikeshandel. *Sydsvenska Dagbladet*. Reprinted in B. Södersten. 1975. *Den svenska sköldpaddan*. Stockholm: Rabén and Sjögren.

Sörlin, Sverker. 1994. *De lärdas republik. Om vetenskapens internationella tendenser*. Malmö: Liber-Hermods.

Statens Offentlinga Utredningar (SOU) 1966:67. *Forskarutbildning och forskarkarriär*. Betänkande avgivet av 1963 års forskarutredning.

Swedish Government Bill 1969:31.

Wadensjö, E. 1990a. Nya forskargenerationer. *Ekonomisk Debatt* 18.4:381–90.

———. 1990b. Gösta Bagge. In *Ekonomporträtt. Svenska ekonomer under 300 år*. Edited by Christina Jonung and Ann-Charlotte Ståhlberg. Stockholm: SNS Förlag.

———. 1992. Recruiting a New Generation. In *Economics in Sweden: An Evaluation of Swedish Research in Economics*. Edited by Lars Engwall. London: Routledge.

Italian Economics through the Postwar Years

Pier Luigi Porta

Introduction

The relationship between national and international characteristics in the development of a discipline such as economics is a fascinating issue in intellectual history. It can probably be said that, in the general opinion, the case of Italy stands out as an intriguing one. Curiosity, or even enthusiasm, however, is not enough to produce practical results. That is why a retrospective analysis on the production of economics in Italy during the last fifty years must be built almost from scratch.

Let us begin with a general observation on the terminology adopted in the present book. The twin ideas of "internationalization" and "Americanization" are often used interchangeably; in a number of instances, particularly with the post-1945 period in mind, admittedly they do overlap to some degree. However, it seems appropriate—and particularly so, as will be apparent, in dealing with the Italian case—to *distinguish* the two concepts, for they in fact refer to *different* phenomena to a much greater extent than is commonly supposed.

We find a useful definition of "Americanization" in J. A. Schumpeter's *History of Economic Analysis* (1954, chaps. 1 and 3, esp. 1154–55 and 1146). Schumpeter points out two features of Americanization. The first is the "inexorable progress of specialization," both in research and in teaching; the other is the multiplication, both inside and outside government departments, of research institutes concerned with economic problems and the analysis of the economy. To these elements we may add the oft-noted increasing mathematization of economic studies in every subfield (Coats 1992, 5).[1]

These considerations emphasize relevant *methodological* aspects of the issue of Americanization in economic research and teaching throughout the postwar years. Equally important, however, is the substantive side of the issue, which pertains to the specific content of postwar economic analysis. The thrust of Americanization, in fact, becomes felt historically through the spread of neoclassical synthesis, almost to the point of being identified with it.[2] Schumpeter, in discussing the impact of the Keynesian message, describes the excitement provoked by the idea of "a novel view of the capitalist process . . . a novel view that was as attractive to some as it was repellent to others." There is little doubt that this has to do with America and her worldwide influence, much more than with Britain. It is one of the interesting facets of our recent intellectual history (even before being an issue in the history of economic thought and analysis) that Keynesianism was reexported worldwide from the United States under the label neoclassical synthesis (Schumpeter 1954, 1180).[3] Of course, other intellectual feats could be discussed in the same fashion and thus come under the umbrella of Americanization. For example, the recent revival of monetarism together with the rise of new classical economics certainly might be described as an "American" phenomenon. However, I shall not enter that discussion, for in this paper I am only concerned with the first appearance of "Americanism."[4]

Almost every current discussion of Americanization in any particular context is meant to convey the idea of a causal link from external factors and from the environment. The term "internationalization," on the contrary, happens to be neutral with respect to causes; it merely indicates a *process* without further implications. This distinction is useful for the

1. Further elements of the relationship between producing economics and a specific environment are discussed in "Is There a European Economics?" 1995.

2. Coats 1985; also 1992, esp. p. 7 (on "Keynesian hegemony" harboring the seeds of its own ruin).

3. On Keynesian hegemony, see Hall 1989 (introduction, 3–26); on the neoclassical synthesis see, in particular, Hall's conclusions (364–65). An intriguing narrative on the formative years of American Keynesianism, largely through unpublished materials, is offered in Asso 1990.

4. Hirschman (1989, 348) observes: "Increasingly, the theoretical predominance Keynesianism had long exercised was contested by neomonetarists and supply-side doctrines that largely originated in the very country—the United States—that had originally been spreading the Keynesian message."

discussion of the Italian case. The history of postwar economic thought and analysis in Italy appears to be one of continuing and intensifying internationalization. Americanization, on the contrary, occurred only in the limited sense of a gradual acquisition of its methodological aspects. As a result, the Italian case is dominated by a lack of uniformity in ideas and research lines, and by predominantly internal factors pushing in the direction of intensified internationalization. It is important to note that the process was stimulated by a generational rift caused by the insufficient space and scope for articulation in the development of the profession within the country. The oft-mentioned issue of the urge to escape linguistic isolation is, in the present context, only part (probably a small part) of the problem.

To substantiate these claims I first provide a brief overview of the Italian university system as a whole and then proceed to examine economic studies, research, and teaching in particular. Given the present lack of a more comprehensive analysis, I shall only hint at a few significant examples of the internationalization of Italian economics.

Universities in Italy

Three features of the Italian system need to be briefly outlined: access to university, students' curricula, and recruitment of research and teaching staff. The general picture through the postwar years is of an explosion in numbers; the recent introduction of "American" ingredients (for example, a sequence of degrees patterned on the progression B.A.-Master's-Ph.D., careers modeled after the sequence lecturer-associate-professor, and so on) appear to be belated attempts to control the situation rather than the outcome of convincing reforms.

Access to University

Table 1 summarizes a few data.[5] We have gathered data on a time span of thirty years, which show the number of students to have multiplied by about five times while the total population increased only marginally. The turning point occurred on the "day after" 1968. The problem is that, while formerly only the *liceo* (covering 20 to 25 percent of the pupils) gave access to universities, from 1969 onward all university faculties, at

5. Data are taken from Istat's *Statistics of Higher Education* unless otherwise stated.

Table 1 Students, Degrees, Professors

Years	Total Students	Fuoricorsos	Degrees Awarded	Number of Professors	Number of Universities	Total Number of Faculties in the University System
1962–63	312,344	86,548	23,019	6574	29	207
1967–68	500,215	130,139	31,243	7867	36	231
1972–73	802,603	144,987	64,570	16,301	44	282
1977–78	996,162	233,337	76,015	24,195	44	288
1982–83	1,022,282	304,914	74,456	26,814	45	302
1987–88	1,153,298	349,821	77,869	30,016	47	326
1992–93	1,564,569	490,239	96,153	33,600	52	348

Table 2   Students by Group of Subjects (percentages)

Years	1966–67	1976–77	1986–87	1992–93
Science	13.87	13.46	12.06	11.17
Medicine	8.13	18.43	10.54	5.16
Engineering	13.23	15.24	14.99	17.11
Agrarian studies	1.42	2.99	3.09	2.02
Economics	18.84	7.39	14.89	16.87
Political and Social Studies	2.94	6.23	6.58	8.26
Law	9.36	12.52	15.75	16.75
Classical and Modern				
Languages	29.90	22.10	20.12	19.75
Diplomas	2.30	1.61	1.97	2.92
Total numbers	456,476	981,348	1,085,900	1,564,569

a stroke, were made accessible on demand to any kind of high school graduates. Numbers blew up. Apart from total numbers, the breakdown by groups of subjects (table 2) also deserves some immediate comment. Soon after the open access law of 1969, faculties of economics and business suffered a setback in terms of their relative ability to attract students. The last decade or so has witnessed a growing percentage of students in economic studies, when economics and especially business studies became fashionable.

Other significant general traits of the Italian system can be gauged from tables 3 and 4. From table 3 it can be inferred that about one freshman out of four reaches the *laurea* in Italy at present. Table 4 shows that students' fees cover, on average, less than 10 percent of the costs of higher education. On the one hand, this shows that education is viewed as a public investment good, the cost of which should be borne by the community; this practice probably involves a transfer of resources to the middle classes.[6] On the other hand, it is still conventional wisdom that every single high school graduate is entitled to be a *dottore* in life. But, on both accounts, the view is gaining currency that behind a facade of fairness the system favors irresponsibility rather than equality of opportunity.

6. For a recent brief survey on the Italian case, together with Ministero del Tesoro 1992a and 1992b see Monteduro 1994.

Table 3   Matriculations and Degrees by Groups of Subjects

	Entering Freshmen/Women	Degrees Awarded	Ratio of Degrees Awarded to Matriculations
Science	39,669	12,055	30.39
Medicine	9300	9349	100.01
Engineering	54,185	12,498	23.06
Agrarian studies	6513	2737	42.02
Economics	58,119	15,260	26.25
Political and Social Studies	37,260	5242	14.07
Law	64,372	14,253	22.14
Classics and Modern Languages	74,590	18,719	47.24
Total numbers	344,008	90,113	26.19

Table 4   Financing the Italian System of Higher Education, 1990 (Billion current lire)

	State	%	Private	%	Other	%	Total	%
Public funds	8,091	91.20	147	35.70	532	77.20	8,770	88.0
Students	473	5.30	135	32.70	149	21.60	757	7.60
Private contributions	89	.01	20	4.80	1	0.14	110	1.10
Own sources	216	2.40	110	26.70	7	1.07	333	3.30
Total	8,869		411		690		9,970	

Source: Ministero del Tesoro, 1992a (table 7.1, p. 147).

Curricula

Parallel with the described changes in admission requirements, the 1969 open access law marked a turning point in students' curricula. As a general rule, curricula are fixed centrally, by law, and are the same throughout the country in terms of courses and corresponding exams, leading to the final *laurea* exam where a thesis is discussed and the title of *dottore* is awarded. In 1969 the big change occurred: one morning students were told they can propose *any* curriculum they choose; with the approval of the faculty board, the student's choice replaces the official curriculum. This has been (I am afraid) a typical Italian way of introducing change: from complete rigidity to complete flexibility. Of course, the discussion of intermediate positions would be a standard way of preventing *any* change from getting through. It is unnecessary here to describe the countless embarrassing cases to which the 1969 law gave rise. Now, after a quarter of a century, in retrospect, one can see that, by a decentralized process, faculties have regained control of curricula: more choice both of individual subjects and curricula has been introduced.

Recruitment

The Italian system was based traditionally on two tenured positions: the assistant and the professor. From 1980 the professorship category has been split in two: *ordinario* and *associato*, with the assistant being changed into *researcher*. Recruitment works through nationwide competitions. In practice, when a tenured position becomes vacant, the faculty board either decides to fill the vacancy by inviting applications from people already holding the same position at another university, or asks for a competition to be announced for that particular position. Competitions are announced by the minister for higher education and research and are decided by specially elected national committees of professors.

The transition from a two-tier to a three-tier career system was introduced by the 1980 law and deserves a brief explanation. Toward the end of the sixties, Italy had come under the pervasive power of large trade unions, which expressed themselves in a lofty, bombastic, "progressive" style. The unions insisted on the view that all university competitions should stop in order to give way to a full-scale reform of the system, designed to break the power of the "barons," a cant name for full professors. Favorite ideas envisaged the decline of the power of the faculty boards and the creation in every research field of departments governed on an egalitarian basis by anyone qualifying as "doing research." In a representative democracy, however, reforms must of course be voted on by parliament, and it soon became clear that parliament would be unable to agree on any reform. Increasing student numbers thus led to the proliferation of the administrative practice by which faculties could make appointments on a provisional yearly basis to teach a course for which no tenured position existed, by nominating a *professore incaricato*. The procedure had been authorized by the ministry as a measure to face urgent needs, usually in the expectation that a new chair could be established later. Until the end of the sixties this phenomenon was limited; subsequently, however, the situation exploded and for a few years the ministry was unable to exer-

Table 5   Graduates by Groups of Subjects (percentages)

Years	1966–67	1976	1986	1992
Science	15.41	15.75	13.34	12.54
Medicine	8.65	13.89	17.83	9.72
Engineering	11.87	14.99	13.58	12.99
Agrarian studies	1.70	1.81	3.98	2.85
Economics	11.58	5.53	10.74	15.87
Political and Social Studies	3.53	5.48	4.55	5.45
Law	13.92	8.35	12.34	14.82
Classics and Modern Languages	28.31	31.29	19.90	19.47
Diplomas	5.01	2.90	3.75	6.28
Total numbers	29,054	72,076	75,810	96,153

cise adequate control: in a single year, from 1970–71 to 1971–72, the total number of professors, including temporary positions or *incaricati*, increased by 58 percent. Given the freeze on competitions for tenured professorships, the whole of the increase consisted of *incaricati*. It is hardly surprising that the army of temporary professors, thus created, turned into a lobby exercising political pressure to change temporary posts into tenures. The creation anew of the *associate professorships*, as an intermediate tenured position, came to the rescue.

To summarize, through the 30 years from 1962 to 1992 the overall number of students increased by a factor of 5 while the number of official professors increased by a factor of 5.1. This may be taken as proof that the system has not gotten out of control as it had seemed to be doing in the early seventies. Of course, one can argue that the ratio of degrees to students has somewhat declined; accordingly, the number of degrees (*lauree*) awarded has increased by a factor of only 4.1; the number of degrees per professor has declined from an average of 3.5 to 2.86. The phenomenon has affected groups of subjects differently, as is indicated by a comparison of the breakdown by groups of students's subjects on one side and graduates on the other (tables 1 and 5). Faculty life has changed considerably in a system where faculties have a unique governing body, namely the faculty board. In a large university, the typical faculty board, which used to consist of, say, five to ten members, would nowadays perhaps include 30 to 50 if the same membership rules had been retained. In fact, under the present system, including associate professors and representatives of researchers it can easily total 70 to 120 members. Faculties are governed, in almost every detail of their life, by large assemblies.

How far, one may ask, have the peculiar characteristics of the Italian system—caught in stalemate between revolutionary unrest and defensive positions—served to insulate it from international competition? Further analysis should be made by faculties and subjects and should include such recent developments as exchanges of professors, researchers, and students under the Erasmus service in the EEC or under bilateral agreements between universities.

In what follows, we can only try to give some indications concerning the field of economics. In general terms, Italian universities appear as large, rather static structures. Since the 1980s there have been attempts to introduce change. Opinions, however, are still strongly divided: some argue in favor of a more thorough Americanization, in the sense of largely dismantling state controls and transforming individual universities into autonomous bodies. Others emphasize the need to increase power sharing within the existing framework as more important than updating the structure and facing competition. At the same time financial constraints do seem to bite; but again in practice little is done about raising students' fees. Private institutions (the Bocconi and the Catholic University in particular) are struggling to distinguish themselves from the state system. They have been successful in increasing students' fees, introducing admission tests, creating dynamic and diversified research structures with strong external links, and achieving a pronounced internationalization in research and also in teaching (seminars and special courses). This is not to say, however, that an ideal model has emerged: despite its apparent success, the private model is not free from weakness or compromise. The emerging overall picture is one of an uneasy state of the system as a whole. Tables 6 and 7 offer a quick glance at data from Milan where the main private institutions are based.

Teaching and Research in Economics:
The Italian Case

The development of the kind of economic training in Italian universities as we know it today derives from the latter part of the nineteenth century. The teaching of economics took place largely in the law faculties; however, a significant role was played by the foundation of the *scuole superiori di commercio*. In their curricula, accounting and business economics

Table 6 Comparison of Private Universities in Milan and the State System: Increase in Student Population 1951–52 to 1992–93

	Factor Increase
State University	10.79
Politecnico	11.08
Catholic University	4.24
Bocconi University	2.39

Table 7 Comparison of Private Universities in Milan and the State System: Number of Matriculations and Degrees 1992–93

	Matriculations	Degrees Awarded	Ratio of Degrees Awarded to Matriculations
State University	19,334	5857	30.29
Politecnico	7590	2754	36.28
Catholic University	5565	2201	39.55*
Bocconi University	1869	1564	83.68

* 52 percent for the faculty of economics

were largely dominant. A number of such institutions were founded, in Venice, Bari, Genoa, and later in Rome, Turin, and elsewhere.

The *scuole*, rather than the law faculties, are the real forefathers of the contemporary faculties of economics and business. Originally the *scuole* were placed under the supervision of the Ministry of Agriculture, Industry, and Commerce. A number of steps then led to the *scuole's* being incorporated into the universities of their respective towns. This set the stage for the *scuole* to be turned into proper faculties within each university under the supervision of the Ministry of Education. This happened at a time (1925–35 approximately) when university curricula were subjected to increasingly rigid centralized rules. The consequence was that the curricula of the *scuole* largely dictated the environment of the future faculties. Turin is a typical example.

With a decree in 1906 the Scuola Superiore di Studi Applicati al Commercio was founded, which was the ancestor of the present faculty of economics and business. The law faculty already hosted the famous Laboratorio di Economia Politica, founded by Salvatore Cognetti de Martiis, an influential institution supporting the fundamental role of economics proper as a scientific discipline in higher education. It is interesting to observe that the Laboratorio was the father of the present *dipartimento di economia politica*, which has little connection with the faculty of economics and is attached to the faculties of law and of political sciences in the University of Turin. In sum: the Laboratorio has had little influence on the formative steps of the economics faculty. Its influence is confined to the noneconomic faculties, where the scope for economics proper is, however, bound to be limited. This explains the Italian peculiarity that, in spite of a strong school of *research* in economics, the *teaching* of the discipline has been confined to a relatively minor role even within the faculties of economics. The teaching of economics has generally served as an *auxiliary discipline*, albeit an important one, with respect to other fields, notably jurisprudence, business studies, and political and social studies.[7]

The Laboratorio in Turin had an influence—mainly through Luigi Einaudi, who had been a pupil of Cognetti—on the early stages of the Bocconi University, founded in Milan in 1902. This famous institution had been keen from its beginning to emphasize its difference from the *scuole*. The very name of *università* was indicative of a program of studies explicitly putting scientific economics at center stage: again, however, it is interesting to observe that a thriving Italian school of economists was unable to seize the occasion and acquire a leading role even in that institution. A similar story could be told about the Catholic University, which was founded in Milan in 1921, where the prevailing neo-Thomist ideology assigned an important place to economics as a social and political science. Giuseppe Toniolo, one of the main founders of the Catholic University, who died in 1918, had been an economist.

The important conclusion to be drawn on the teaching of economics down to the present day is that there is *not a single example* within the Italian system where a real primacy of the study of political economy can be said to have been established. The interpretation put forward here implies that Italian economics suffered, not so much or not only from political events or lack of continuity of any kind. A large research potential did not acquire a correspondingly large place and audience in the curricula of higher education, compared to what was happening abroad. An insufficient development of the profession fostered defensive attitudes. The stage was then set for the explosion of xenophilia in the

---

7. Some information on the developments described above can be found in the volume by the Comitato per lo studio 1967, esp. 129–200. On the Laboratorio, see Faucci 1993.

post-1945 years. That explains also why xenophilia did not coincide with outright Americanization. In Italy, the internal factors or forces were more important than the external ones. Xenophilia—and the drift to internationalization attached to it—has been one way to reverse the situation described, or at least an attempt to do so.

The difficulties encountered in the spread of Samuelson's textbook result, in the Italian case, from this situation. The vision put forward by Samuelson's *Economics*, that is, the neoclassical synthesis, has always aroused a curious mixture of attraction and repulsion. It is not simply a fluke that in Italy Samuelson's *Economics* only very recently became a popular textbook for students in the Italian translation, when its ideological message, as a symbol of the neoclassical synthesis, had already lost its appeal and influence. This can be taken to reflect the uneasy life of Americanization in Italy.

Economic Research in Italy

The process of expansion of Italian universities has been going on in parallel with changes in attitudes toward teaching and research. The resulting situation exhibits different characteristics in different disciplines. It would probably be interesting to extend the analysis, along with economics, to the social and political sciences and possibly to jurisprudence, to highlight some relationships, and also some of their idiosyncrasies, with respect to economics in research and teaching. Here, however, the exposition will be confined to economics.

A Generational Rift

In economics the generational rift took the form of a series of attacks, from different positions and in different ways, against that original blend of neoclassicism that had been developed by the Italian school at the turn of the century and was later continued and improved by distinguished epigones in the interwar period. Even a scholar of Pareto, for example, could never have imagined coming as a visitor to Italy during this postwar period. If such a scholar had happened to choose Italy for research purposes, he would certainly have found very little interest in Pareto among Italian economists. Such a situation captures a feature of the intellectual climate in which a whole generation of Italian economists has been brought up. For a long time there was some kind of embargo on the Italian tradition. It is no exaggeration to say that the Italian tradition in economic studies—much like fascism or similar issues—was something simply *not* to be talked about. Although the process is bound to be painful, one can note that the advantages of memory are coming to be much better appreciated today.

A phenomenon of this kind belongs, in the first place, to the intellectual history of a country. In economics, as in general culture, the generational rift was combined with the revival of Marxism and took shape within a left-wing cultural hegemony. Isolated but authoritative, independent voices of protest were raised from time to time, even during the most obscure years, before the situation gradually began to change.[8]

Keynes

The introduction of Keynes into Italy has been widely discussed in the literature.[9] The problem, often raised, of a belated introduction of Keynes's thought in Italy can be readily dismissed as a false problem. The works of Keynes were amply known, discussed, and criticized in Italy in the interwar years.[10] The idea, sometimes cherished (notably perhaps in philosophy), of Italy as a culturally insulated country is false. Concerning economic analysis Schumpeter's judgment on the interwar period is substantially correct: "Purely scientific work was not interfered with at all . . . scientific economics continued to move at . . . a high level, both within and without the Pareto school, until the war" (1954, 1156–57).

The critical attitude of a number of major economists certainly contributed to create delays and difficulties for Keynesian ideas in their spread into courses and teaching and—more particularly, a few years later—for the spread of the neoclassical synthesis as a vision in analysis

8. Federico Caffé (1975) vigorously protested against the intellectual ban then current in Italy against the ideas and works of the Italian school. We have come today—Caffé wrote in his *Frammenti*—to the paradox of reimporting under foreign names arguments and results substantially due to the Italian School. Among pioneering contributions, providing a reappraisal of the Italian School, we may mention Finoia 1980. For original highlights on the Italian School, see also the volumes edited by Quadrio Curzio and Scazzieri (1977–82). On the Italians and Pareto, we refer the reader to Morishima 1994.

9. See *Keynes in Italia* 1984 (this volume prints the proceedings of a conference organized in Florence, June 1983, on the initiative of Piero Barucci).

10. See *Keynes in Italia: Catalogo Bibliografico* 1983.

and research. Thus it was really Samuelson, rather than Keynes, who encountered obstruction.

The shift to the macroeconomic perspective met with difficulties due to a tradition largely skeptical of the advantages and of the scientific acceptability of abandoning a microeconomic approach. The Italian school remained largely faithful to principles of methodological individualism. However, admittedly to a significant extent, Americanization became an issue. To some extent, Keynesianism did become a vehicle of Americanization, with strong emotional overtones, although this has to be balanced against the strong influence of Cambridge, England. Italian exiles did have a role in fostering attitudes of innovation and a break with tradition. Concerning Keynesianism, we should mention the work of Franco Modigliani, not only his own scientific work, but more particularly his theoretical and practical contribution to the postgraduate education of a generation of economists who were then to exercise their influence both in universities and in other key institutions, such as the Bank of Italy.

Marx

It is perhaps the greatest achievement, and also the greatest paradox, of communism in Italy to have been pivotal in establishing and supporting the idea, among the intelligentsia at large, that Marxism meant unqualified novelty and avant-gardism in culture. This was so for many years after the late war, and it spread to economics too. Again, emotional overtones became dominant against the tradition of Italian economics, charged with being basically limited to abstract modeling and concerned about matters of interest to bourgeois political parties. Paolo Sylos Labini has recently written that he "never was a Marxist." He acknowledges, however, that his Marxian sympathies were for some considerable time rather strong. He prefers to describe himself as a Schumpeterian today. Having studied in both Cambridges, he has excellent credentials for both the Marxian and the Schumpeterian affiliation. His experience is, in a way, typical. His strong good sense led him to some degree of uneasiness and even impatience with the tradition of the Italian school and their academic aloofness. Marxism evidently meant to him a critical attitude to the workings of the Western capitalist system and was an expression of a longing for political engagement.[11] Here were, probably, two forces

11. See Sylos Labini 1994a, esp. 3–4, and 1994b.

pushing in the direction of Cambridge, England. It is not surprising that Marxism in Italy, at least as far as economists are concerned, cannot be discussed without mentioning Cambridge, England, where another well-known Italian exile is at center stage: Piero Sraffa.

Particularly during the sixties and early seventies the idea had gained currency in Italy that a Marxist coalition would fairly soon take over and replace the corrupt and inept Catholic ruling class. The cultural primacy, which Italian Marxists have always sported as their distinctive look, was felt to be close to yielding its fruits also in terms of power. In that climate of opinion new "pioneer" faculties were created that seemed to accomplish the old dream in which political economy would have the lion's share in curricula and research, with business studies accordingly duly subordinated. That has in fact been one meaning of the drift to internationalization in Italy. Characteristically, it all got mixed up with ideology at a time of Marxian revival worldwide. Ideology proved a powerful attractor of intellectual talents. In some cases, in fact, it succeeded in stamping on higher education a solid anti-neoclassical bias and securing a place for Marxism. The two instances of the faculty of economics at Siena and the faculty of economics at Modena provide good illustrations of that process although they cannot be discussed here in detail. These facts help to explain the limited role of Americanization in economic research in Italy. The Marxist nouvelle vague was even more opposed to Samuelson than to the tradition of the Italian school. Thus opposing the tradition did not produce a paradigm shift or a scientific revolution because the opposition was divided.

Conclusions

The idea among economists that the intellectual tradition in Italy was weakened by abstractedness, academic aloofness, and detachment from the real world is nowadays less frequently heard. On the contrary, it is increasingly recognized that the Italian liberal tradition in economic thought and analysis was constructed and upheld by scholars singularly conscious of their political responsibilities and playing their part in full in the political struggle. The examples of Pareto and Pantaleoni, among others, are cases in point.[12]

12. On the reappraisal of the Italian tradition, see the recent book edited by Ciocca and Bocciarelli (1994).

After years of "creative destruction," a substantial reappraisal of the tradition goes in parallel with reassessing and strengthening the place of economic studies in higher education and research. This in turn emerges in parallel with the pervasive process of internationalization experienced by the profession. The Bocconi University of Milan appears now to have curbed the hegemony of business studies by introducing a wide range of curricula in which the emerging complementary role of business studies and economics is emphasized, particularly in the applied subjects. The Catholic University has perhaps been unique in the country for its conspicuous tradition in economic theory and analysis throughout the postwar years.

It is proper to end with a brief mention of some of the institutions—without any possible pretence either of doing justice to their important role and activity or of any degree of completeness—that have most contributed to the process of continued and increased internationalization of Italian economics during the postwar years. What follows simply constitute examples and suggestions of sources available to the interested reader.

The best known of those institutions is the Bank of Italy. Its economic research unit has displayed an impressive activity, creating strong ties between Italian and foreign economists. The reader can consult in particular Baffi 1985 for the immediate postwar period and, for the later period and the increasing support given to economic research within the Bank of Italy, the recent book by Carli (1993) along with the even more recent treatment by Fazio (1995). Friedrich and Vera Lutz, during the former period, and Franco Modigliani, during the latter period, emerge as outstanding international connections. Valuable information, with special reference to the construction of the econometric model of the Bank of Italy, is provided by Nardozzi's (1994) survey and extended bibliography.

On industrial development and planning remarkable research was sponsored at Svimez, the association for the development of the Mezzogiorno established in 1946. A considerable part of the activity of Svimez was in fact research activity with important international connections, among which the name of P. N. Rosenstein-Rodan is conspicuous. Negri Zamagni and Sanfilippo (1988) offer a reconstruction; Cafiero (1975) deals particularly with international connections, emphasized also in Saraceno 1982. The activity of the Centre for Economic and Agrarian Research for the Mezzogiorno, at Portici, near Naples, is summarized in

Graziani 1990 and in Marenco 1990. The intense activity of postgraduate education and research promotion are connected with the personality of the founder, the agrarian economist Manlio Rossi-Doria. Important international connections, in particular with the University of California at Berkeley and with the Giannini Foundation, are also recalled.

Two other institutions deserve a mention particularly for their pioneering activity in postgraduate education in economics: the Einaudi Foundation in Turin and the Istao of Ancona.

The Einaudi Foundation was established in 1964, and its teaching and research activities are described in the first section of the yearly volumes of *Annali*. The *Annali* also publish some of the most significant papers of scholars doing their research at the foundation. Some idea about the foundation can also be gained from the illustrated book on the Palazzo D'Azeglio (1991), the seat of the foundation. Since 1960, in Ancona, in connection with a new faculty of economics, a group of scholars has gathered around Giorgio Fuà, the economist. With the financial assistance of the Olivetti Foundation, the U.S. Social Science Research Council, and the Italian National Research Council, the Istituto Superiore di Studi Economici Adriano Olivetti (Istao) was established. A retrospect of the activities, involving a number of Italian and some foreign economists, is presented in Istao 1993.

All these institutions and initiatives, along with others that should be included in a more thorough account, have powerfully contributed to the internationalization of economic studies in Italy and have done so by consolidating the space and scope for education and research in economics per se and also by discovering the emerging connections of economics to other social and political disciplines.

References

Asso, Pier Francesco. 1990. *The Economist Behind the Model: The Keynesian Revolution in Historical Perspective*. Rome: Ente Einaudi.

Baffi, Paolo. 1985. Via Nazionale e gli economisti stranieri, 1944–53. *Rivista di storia economica*, n.s.:2. Reprinted in Baffi 1990. *Testimonianze e ricordi*. Milano: Scheiwiller. 93–152.

Caffé, Federico. 1975. *Frammenti per lo studio del pensiero economico italiano*. Milano: Giuffrè.

Cafiero, Salvatore. 1975. La nascita della "Cassa." In *Studi in onore di Pasquale Saraceno*. Milano: Giuffré. 177–92.

Carli, Guido. 1993. *Cinquant'anni di vita italiana*. Bari: Laterza.

Ciocca, Pierluigi, and Rosanna Bocciarelli. 1994. *Scrittori italiani di economia*. Bari: Laterza.

Coats, A. W. 1985. The American Economic Association and the Economics Profession. *Journal of Economic Literature* 23.4 (December): 1697–727.

———. 1992. The Post-1945 Global Internationalization (Americanization?) of Economics. Duplication.

Comitato per lo studio dei problemi dell'Università italiana. 1967. *Le Facoltà Umanistiche*. Bologna: Mulino.

Faucci, Riccardo. 1993. Economia, storia, positivismo: Cognetti de Martiis e le origini del Laboratorio di economia politica di Torino. Paper read in Turin on 4 December 1993 to celebrate the hundredth anniversary of the Laboratorio.

Fazio, Antonio. 1995. Ricordo di Ezio Tarantelli. In *L'attualità del pensiero di Tarantelli*. Banca d'Italia: Documenti n. 479 (March).

Finoia, Massimo, ed. 1980. *Il Pensiero Economico Italiano 1850/1950*. Bologna: Cappelli.

Graziani, Augusto. 1990. L'economia del Mezzogiorno nel pensiero di Manlio Rossi-Doria. In *Manlio Rossi-Doria e il Mezzogiorno*. Napoli: Edizioni Scientifiche Italiane. 47–70.

Hall, Peter A., ed. 1989. *The Political Power of Economic Ideas: Keynesianism across Nations*. Princeton, N.J.: Princeton University Press.

Hirschman, Albert O. 1989. How the Keynesian Revolution Was Exported from the United States, and Other Comments. In Hall 1989. 347–60.

ISTAO. 1993. *Struttura e attività 1967–1993*. Ancona: Istao.

"Is There a European Economics?" 1995. *Kyklos*, special issue, 48:4.

Keynes in Italia. 1983. Catalogo bibliografico a cura della Facolta' di Economia di Firenze. Prefazione di Piero Barucci. Firenze: Banca Toscana.

Keynes in Italia. 1984. Milano: Ipsoa.

Marenco, Gaetano. 1990. Il Centro di Portici: Attualità di un'esperienza trentennale. In *Manlio Rossi-Doria e il Mezzogiorno*. Napoli: Edizioni Scientifiche Italiane. 71–88.

Ministero del Tesoro. Commissione tecnica per la spesa pubblica. 1992a. *Il finanziamento del sistema universitario italiano*, a c. di G. Catalano e P. Silvestri. Rome (June).

———. 1992b. *Il governo delle risorse nel sistema universitario italiano*. 2 vols. Rome (October).

Monteduro, Maria Pia. 1994. Gli effetti redistributivi della spesa pubblica universitaria. *Econpubblica* 27 (November).

Morishima, Michio. 1994. Foreword to *Vilfredo Pareto: Neoclassical Synthesis of Economics and Sociology*. By Alfonso de Pietri-Tonelli and George Bousquet. London: Macmillan.

Nardozzi, Giangiacomo. 1994. Money and Credit: Twenty Years of Debate in Italy (1970–1990). *Banca Nazionale del Lavoro Quarterly Review* 188 (March): 3–51.

Negri Zamagni, Vera, and Mario Sanfilippo, eds. 1988. *Nuovo meridionalismo e intervento straordinario*. La Svimez dal 1946 al 1950. Bologna: Mulino.

Palazzo D'Azeglio in Torino: L'edificio e le istituzioni culturali. 1991. Milano: Gruppo editoriale Fabbri.

Quadrio Curzio, Alberto, and Roberto Scazzieri, eds. 1977–82. *Protagonisti del pensiero economico.* 4 vols. Bologna: Mulino.

Saraceno, Pasquale. 1982. Premessa. In *Gli anni dello schema Vanoni.* Edited by Piero Barucci. Milano: Giuffrè. 59–84.

Schumpeter, Joseph A. 1954. *History of Economic Analysis.* London: Allen and Unwin.

Sylos Labini, Paolo. 1994a. *Carlo Marx: È tempo di un bilancio.* Bari: Laterza.

———. 1994b. Una certa idea dell'economia. *Meridiana* 20.

The Professional and Political Impacts of the Internationalization of Economics in Brazil

Maria Rita Loureiro

Introduction

If the increasing intervention of the state in the economic sphere in Brazil since the 1930s and the adoption of a Keynesian model of action, even in embryonic fashion, from the 1940s and 1950s on, had implied the presence of a great number of "technicians" (as economists were called in that period) in the Brazilian government, this process was consolidated with the military regime (1964–84).[1] The intensification of the process of political centralization, the hypertrophy of the executive power and of its control over the economy, and the need to provide legitimacy for an authoritarian government on the grounds of economic efficiency, brought about an increase in the number of governmental positions that were practically monopolized by economists. From 1964 on, ten of sixteen finance ministers were economists; in the Ministry of Planning from

1. In the 1930s, a political movement broke down the power of the agrarian oligarchies that had dominated the country during the period known as the First Republic (1889–1930) and unleashed an important process of political and administrative centralization. A central agency was then set up for the coordination of the civil administration and for control, by the federal government, of several policies adopted by the various states. Most important, a broad and complex institutional system was established for control over strategic spheres of the economy by the federal government. Thus it was that the leader of that revolutionary movement, Getulio Vargas, who governed the country for fifteen years (1930–45), was then able to start the formation of the so-called developmentalist state which, in the 1950s, carried out the process of industrialization and modernization of Brazil. Detailed analyses of this process can be found in Wirth 1970, Leff 1968, and Lowenstein 1944, to quote only books written in English.

1963 when it was created and headed by Celso Furtado, nine of eleven ministers were economists. These professionals also almost exclusively held the positions of president and director of the Central Bank and of the National Economic and Social Development Bank (BNDES).

The aim of this article is to link the internationalization of economics in Brazil with the process of consolidation within the academic system for the training and qualification of economists and with their participation in government.

The main features of the process of modernization and internationalization of economics that have taken place in Brazil since the 1960s were analyzed in an earlier paper (Loureiro and Lima 1995). It was defined as the systematic incorporation, on the part of Brazilian research and teaching institutions, of the theoretical and methodological patterns prevailing in the most advanced countries, particularly in the United States. As a result, academic production in economics started taking a more theoretical shape, expressed mainly in formal models and in accordance with scientific standards that characterize international academic publications.

Here, this discussion is resumed and improved with the study of professional and political impacts. By professional impact or effects of internationalization, I mean the reinforcement of the polarization of the schools of economics around two divergent positions: at one pole, the schools that are completely integrated into the international or North American scientific patterns; and, at the other pole, the schools that resist this process for theoretical and ideological reasons; and also the different academic practices and professional strategies generated by this polarization.

Because the scientific field of economics in Brazil is closely connected with the governmental agencies of economic policymaking, the process of internationalization also generates political impact due to the way economists provide their specific legitimation as ruling elites. The more an economist is integrated into the international scientific network, the more recognized he is in the government and more credible his decisions.

The present paper is organized as follows: section 1 presents the consolidation of the academic system that took place in Brazil from the 1960s on and links this process with the internationalization of economics. Section 2 analyzes how the internationalization process reinforced the polarization existing in the scientific field of economics in Brazil and generated differentiation in terms of professional strategies on the part of the members of each pole. Finally, section 3 shows that some assets provided by participation in the international scientific network bring prestige to certain economists and give them legitimacy for high positions in the government.

1. The Internationalization of Economics and the Consolidation of the University System

Parallel to the increased availability of positions in government agencies, important modifications have taken place in the system of training and qualification of economists in the last few decades in Brazil. Until the 1950s and 1960s the preparation of personnel for economic management occurred mostly outside the university system, for instance in international agencies such as ECLA (the Economic Commission for Latin America, an agency of the United Nations created in 1948, with headquarters in Santiago, Chile); in applied economics research centers such as the IBRE (Brazilian Institute of Economics) of the FGV (Getulio Vargas Foundation); and within organs of government, the so-called practical schools of economic knowledge such as the Superintendency of Money and Credit, created in 1945, inside the Banco do Brasil, with an important function in the monetary area and in exchange; the BNDE (National Economic and Social Development Bank), and the CFCE (Federal Council for Foreign Trade) (Loureiro 1992).

Since the 1970s, university courses, in particular graduate programs, have become the principal mechanism for training specialists in the area of economics and the privileged path that gives access to high positions in governmental agencies of economic policymaking.

With the University Reform of 1968, the system of higher education in Brazil experienced substantial modifications. The French model of faculty organization in public universities, based on chairs held for life, was replaced by North American style teaching departments. There was also an enormous expansion in the overall number of schools of higher education (above all, of private establishments) and a corresponding increase in the numbers of enrollments, from fewer than 100,000 in 1960 to over 1,500,000 in the 1990s. According to statistics provided by the Ministry of Education, in 1968 there were 84 schools, and 17,000 enrolled students in undergraduate courses in Brazil in the area of economics; in 1980, the figure reached 129 schools with more than 62,000 enrolled students. Another significant element of the Reform of 1968 was the establishment of graduate programs in all areas, which received systematic support from federal government agencies in the form of funding and institutional support for improvement in the academic qualifications of their faculty. The institutional setup of graduate programs was a considerable step forward in terms of the consolidation of scientific competence as a whole in Brazil. Between 1969 and 1982, the numbers of graduate courses in Brazil increased from 125 to 1,324, and by 1989, in the area of humanities alone, there were about 290 graduate programs.

Partly because of the participation of economists in the government, the area of economics was particularly privileged by governmental funds for graduate programs. Besides the regular funds allocated to all graduate programs in the country, the specific area of economics was provided with additional financial resources from agencies such as BNDES and IPEA (Institute for Applied Economic Research, associated with the Ministry of Planning). BNDES has been giving annual awards to the authors of the best theses in economics (master's and doctoral levels), and IPEA provides complementary funds to the annual conferences of ANPEC (National Association for Graduates in Economics) and its publications. And, as will be shown later, economics received privileged benefits in the international exchange programs sponsored by North American agencies such as USAID (U.S. Agency for International Development) and the Ford Foundation in the 1960s and 1970s.

Since 1966 fourteen graduate programs have been created in different parts of the country in the area of economics. About five hundred candidates apply every year for the national selection competition, coordinated by ANPEC. Those who achieve the highest overall grades have preferential choice of program, and thus get accepted to those programs considered the most selective. Among these graduate programs, five stand out as the most selective: the graduate school in economics of the Getulio Vargas Foundation, set up in Rio de Janeiro in 1964;[2] the Depart-

2. This school arose from a former program for further studies in economics created at the Getulio Vargas Foundation at Rio de Janeiro in the early 1960s. One of its aims was to make up for undergraduate-level deficiencies in candidates who were applying for doctoral degrees in economics in the United States. Indeed, the Getulio Vargas Foundation is a pioneer institution in the formation of technicians and high-level staff for the state bureaucracy. Founded in 1944, its principal area of activity has been the production of studies and applied economic research. Since the late 1940s, it has produced a great deal of statistical data based upon Keynesian variables, for example, national accounts and price indexes (in 1986 the official inflation index was calculated by the Getulio Vargas Foundation). Moreover, some directors of the Brazilian Institute of Economics, the branch of the Getulio Vargas Foundation that carries on those statistical activities, were members of economic councils in the federal government as well as

ment of Economics of the Catholic University of Rio de Janeiro (PUC), which opened in 1977; the Institute of Economic Research (IPE/USP) in São Paulo, which was created in 1964 by the faculty of economics and business of the University of São Paulo, today considered the most important university in the country; the graduate program in economics of the Federal University of Rio de Janeiro (IEI/UFRJ), which replaced the first National School of Economics, established in Rio de Janeiro in 1946; and the Institute of Economics of the State University of Campinas (IE/UNICAMP), which is a more recently created university, also in the state of São Paulo, and which is currently considered the second most important university in the country.

As far as the expansion of the academic market is concerned, studies carried out by ANPEC show that between 1967 and 1985, 564 professors taught in these fourteen programs and supervised 688 theses in economics, 92 at the doctoral level. It is also estimated that between 1978 and 1987, some 906 articles were published in the country's leading journals of economics (Agarez 1986).

The establishment of graduate programs, together with the other changes that occurred in university teaching of economics (the increase in numbers of both students and courses, the growth of academic production, the development of a system of institutional research, the publication of new journals, etc.), should be seen within the broader context of the modernization of economics in Brazil. These transformations are part of a process of internationalization or North Americanization of economics. As previously mentioned in Loureiro and Lima 1995, this process occurred from the 1960s on through two basic mechanisms.

The first and most important step toward the integration of Brazilian economics into the mainstream of international economics was pursuit of young Brazilian students, on a systematic basis, of doctoral studies abroad, particularly in the United States. The data in table 1 indicate that 60 percent of those professors now teaching graduate courses in Brazil in economics qualified outside Brazil. Of these, 46 percent (158 professors) went to American universities, 7.5 percent studied in France, and 5.5 percent in England. Of the American universities that trained Brazilian economists, seven have played an important role: Vanderbilt, where 18 Brazilian professors completed their graduate studies thanks to

---

of international economic committees, including Bretton Woods, where they met Keynes himself. This was before some of them became ministers of finance in the 1950s and 1960s.

Table 1 Faculty Members Affiliated with Graduate Programs in Economics in Brazil: National Origin of Master's and/or Ph.D. Degree, 1991

Graduate Program*	Total**	U.S.A.	%	France	%	U.K.	%	Brazil	%	Others	%
CEDEPLAR	35	15	43.0	3	8.5	3	8.5	14	40.0		
EPGE/FGV	30	24	80.0					4	13.3	2	6.7
IEPE	27	17	63.0	2	7.4	1	3.6	7	2.6		
IPE/USP	55	21	38.2	3	5.4			31	56.4		
NAEA	24	5	21.0	5	21.0	1	4.0	13	54.0		
PIMES	27	13	48.0	1	4.0	5	18.0	8	30.0		
PUC/RJ	17	14	82.3			2	11.9	1	5.8		
UFBA	17	7	41.1	3	17.8			7	41.1		
IEI/UFRJ	20	5	25.0	1	5.0	4	20.0	10	50.0		
UNB	32	14	43.8	8	25.0	2	6.2	6	18.8	2	6.2
IE/UNICAMP	28	2	7.2					26	92.8		
CAEN	18	13	72.2					5	27.8		
FGV/SP	14	8	57.1			1	7.1	5	35.7		
TOTALS	344	158	46.0	26	7.5	19	5.5	137	40.0	4	1.0

Source: Catalogues from graduate programs associated with ANPEC. Does not include the newly created program at Fluminense Federal University.

*CEDEPLAR - Federal University of Minas Gerais; EPGE/FGV - Getulio Vargas Foundation at Rio de Janeiro; IEPE - Federal University of Rio Grande do Sul; IPE/USP- University of São Paulo; NAEA - Federal University of Para; PIMES - Federal University of Pernambuco; PUC/RJ - Catholic University of Rio de Janeiro; UFBA - Federal University of Bahia; IEI/UFRJ - Federal University of Rio de Janeiro; UNB - Federal University of Brasilia; IE/UNICAMP - State University of Campinas; CAEN - Federal University of Ceara; FGV/SP - Getulio Vargas Foundation at São Paulo

**Includes both full- and part-time faculty members.

agreements with universities in Brazil; the University of Chicago, where 16 economists received their Ph.D.s, 13 from EPGE and 3 from USP; Berkeley, with 12 doctorates; and Harvard with 11. Yale University has graduated 8 Brazilian economists, and the Universities of Michigan and Illinois 7 each. This process was greatly facilitated by the agreements mentioned below.

The second mechanism was the arrival of American professors to teach in the newly created graduate programs. This process was subsidized by USAID (U.S. Agency for International Development) and by the Ford Foundation, which signed cooperative agreements with several schools in Brazil. The faculty of economics of the University of São Paulo (FEA/USP) was one of the academic programs that benefited from those agreements. Through agreements with USAID as well as with the Council for Technical Cooperation of the Alliance for Progress, its graduate program was set up in 1964. USAID assumed responsibility for the travel, board, and lodging expenses of some North American professors by means of a contract with Vanderbilt University, which in turn undertook "the duty to advise the creation of the program, the development of its curriculum, the planning for research, and student grading" (FEA/USP, 1981, 229–30).

The Ford Foundation also took part in that cooperative agreement by providing several faculty members associated with FEA/USP with grants for graduate studies in Brazil and abroad, resources for the purchase of equipment and books, and financial support for visiting professors to teach graduate courses in the newly created programs.[3] Indeed, the Ford Foundation can be conceived as having played a quite decisive role in the internationalization process discussed here. According to a Brazilian sociologist who has done extensive research on the history of social sciences in Brazil:

> the amount of resources granted by Ford Foundation to Latin American countries, and particularly to Brazil, was the largest and most important inflow of external finance for educational purposes, so that it exerted decisive money influence over the process of consolidation of the social sciences in Brazil. . . . In the early 60s, most of the resources

---

3. The professors who taught there were W. O. Thweatt (who was responsible for the management of the cooperative agreement) from Vanderbilt University, Warner Baer, Gian Sahota, Samuel Levy, and Andrea Maneschi.

granted by Ford Foundation to social sciences in Latin America were for economics and business which were conceived as being more in conformity with the Ford Foundation's concerns with development issues. (Miceli 1990, 17–22)

As far as government agencies are concerned, the University of California at Berkeley sent some professors to advise economists at IPEA, an agency associated with the Ministry of Planning. Outstanding in the Berkeley group was Albert Fishlow, in particular for his extensive work on Brazilian income distribution, a topic of great controversy in the 1970s.

According to a Brazilian professor who was involved with the cooperative process, the North American economists were more concerned with the transmission of a model of organization of teaching and research than with actual knowledge of advanced economic theory. In his view, Brazilian academia was already endowed with professional economists who had considerable theoretical background, so that "what was really missing at the time was the spread, on a reasonable scale, of attitudes and positions which might characterize a solid scientific community. And it was here that the North American economists really came in" (Ekerman 1989, 127).

2. Professional Impacts: The Polarization of Economics in Brazil

The internationalization of economics, with its implications of bringing into Brazil the theoretical and methodological practices prevailing in developed countries, particularly in the United States, had acquired the concrete meaning of North Americanization; to a certain extent, one can indeed refer to it as a process of neoclassicalization. Such a process was not, however, uniform in all the various Brazilian institutions, some of them seeing it as just another form of cultural colonialism carried out by North American imperialists. There was strong resistance, in particular from groups lying further to the left politically, so that not all graduate programs in economics adhered with the same intensity to the international academic patterns. As shown in table 1, the Institute of Economics of UNICAMP (IE) has the lowest percentage of professors with doctorates from abroad. Only two have American Ph.D.s, as compared with twenty-six doctorates at UNICAMP itself or at the University of São Paulo. On the other hand, the largest numbers of professors with North American doctorates are to be found at PUC-RJ, with more than 82 percent and EPGE/FGV, with 80 percent.

Indeed, these figures indicate a quite complex process of polarization on the part of the local schools of economics around theoretically divergent positions. To a certain extent, such a polarization dates back to the antagonism within the Brazilian political field in the 1950s and 1960s, when economics as a separate discipline was taking shape. During that period, economic development was the key issue that led to manifest conflicts in both intellectual and political circles. On the one side were the members of a liberal group that strongly opposed any proposal of state intervention in the economic system, thus accepting only corrective measures for market deficiencies and/or conventional monetary and fiscal policies; given their rejection of any protectionist policies for the infant national industry, they were often identified as representatives of the interests of foreign capital. On the other side was a variety of nationalist groups on the left of the political spectrum, which strongly stressed the necessity of state intervention to promote the industrialization process; in their view, this would involve a great deal of state intervention and the protection of local industry against external competition. Associated with some of these groups were economists affiliated with ECLA. As is well known, this agency of the United Nations played an active role in shaping both Brazilian and Latin American economic thought during the 1950s and 1960s, in particular with regard to the chronic inflation experienced by most Latin American countries.[4] Briefly, ECLA economists developed theories that explained the backwardness of the continent through factors related to the structure of the terms of trade between developed and underdeveloped countries, and so they became known as structuralists.

Not surprisingly, the Brazilian economists associated with ECLA were opposed to the economists affiliated with the Getulio Vargas Foundation in Rio de Janeiro, who were frequently identified with groups

4. The principal Brazilian representative to ECLA, Celso Furtado, was the minister of planning in the last civilian government before the military coup of 1964, which resulted in his exile. Furtado was one of the best known and most widely read economists in the 1960s in Brazil. His classic book, *The Economic Formation of Brazil*, written while he was still working for ECLA and published in 1959, can be considered "the cornerstone of Brazilian political economy" (Mantega 1985).

on the right of the political spectrum due both to their close professional links with foreign enterprises and to their theoretical adherence to monetarism.[5]

To a certain extent, those antagonisms still persist today, though transformed by new and more complex elements in that ideological and theoretical conflict. Notwithstanding the more solid university qualification that currently prevails, the growth of academic production (in the form of theses, articles, and books), and the creation of several research institutions, it is reasonable to argue that the current polarization goes back to the old opposition between structuralists and monetarists. Thus, one way to classify the most representative local graduate programs in economics is as follows.

On the one hand, there is the EPGE/FGV school in Rio de Janeiro, which is considered the home of the most orthodox strand of neoclassical thought in Brazil and whose faculty attribute a great deal of importance to mathematical modeling and the tools of econometrics; it is not just by chance that 72 percent of its members majored in engineering and mathematics. On the same side is the PUC-RJ, made up of ex-students and dissident professors from the EPGE/FGV and other universities. Most of these professors are qualified in engineering and mathematics; thus their programs also place emphasis on mathematical modeling. These two schools constitute the most internationalized pole, that most fully integrated with the mainstream of the profession. It is worth recalling that 80 percent and 82 percent, respectively, of their faculties hold Ph.D.s from North American universities.

On the opposite side stand the graduate programs in economics offered by UNICAMP and the UFRJ, most of whose faculty members

5. The leaders and founders of the group of professional economists associated with the Getulio Vargas Foundation were Eugenio Gudin and Octavio Bulhões. The former was an engineer and a director of English firms connected with the construction of public works and railways in Brazil. An intellectual and self-taught in economics, Gudin became a professional economist not only through his activities as a professor and author of textbooks, but mainly through his membership on several economic councils during the Getulio Vargas government (1930–45) and his role at the Bretton Woods conference. Bulhões was a lawyer who became known as an economist through his activities as an economic adviser to the Ministry of Finance in the Vargas government, through his teaching, and as Brazilian representative to several international technical councils and committees. It is worth mentioning that in the 1950s and 1960s, though some schools of economics already existed, the education of those economists who were appointed to high office occurred not through university education but mainly through their participation in government agencies (Loureiro 1992).

are former disciples of ECLA and are concerned with issues that can be broadly defined as structural. This group comprises a considerable number of professors trained in law and the social sciences; their work, especially at UNICAMP, is carried on in language with little mathematical formalization and emphasizes a historical and sociopolitical approach to economic processes. Somewhere in between these two extremes lies the graduate program offered by the University of São Paulo, the largest in terms of number of professors. Although most of them (thirty-one professors) hold doctorates from USP itself, quite a significant number also studied in the United States (twenty-one professors). Only EPGE has a higher number of faculty members with doctorates from the United States (twenty-four professors).

The figures in table 2 reveal other aspects of the heterogeneous intensity with which the internationalization process occurred in the graduate programs as well as the degree of resistance that process has had to face in others. While 90 percent and 78 percent respectively of the bibliographical references used in EPGE/FGV and PUC/RJ graduate courses are written in English, less than 10 percent of the references used in UNICAMP graduate program are written in English. Almost 70 percent of the ones used in the latter are written in Portuguese (or edited in Brazil), 22 percent are written in Spanish, most by ECLA authors, and some are written in French. As far as the theoretical and methodological approach is concerned, EPGE and PUC present high percentages of references in the area of theory and quantitative methods: 98 percent and 95 percent respectively. By contrast, UNICAMP presents only 55 percent of the references in this area and 45 percent in the area of economic history, history of economic thought, and political economy.

In addition, table 3 shows the weight given by each graduate program to the various sections of the national examination for admission of candidates. Whereas the weights given to microeconomics and macroeconomics are relatively similar for all programs, the orientation toward the section on quantitative methods and the Brazilian economy, which is essentially historical, are quite another matter; the degree of dispersion thus reinforces the polarity outlined above. At one extreme, EPGE/FGV attributes greater weight to the sections on economic theory (macro- and microeconomics) and quantitative methods, and proportionately less to that in the Brazilian economy; at the other extreme, IE/UNICAMP gives the greatest weight to the section on the Brazilian economy, as well as

Table 2 Quantitative Balance of Bibliographic References Used in Selected Disciplines from Some Brazilian Graduate Programs in Economics

Part A *National Origins of Books and Articles*

Selected graduate programs	A		B	C		D	
	Works written in Portuguese	Works translated to	% of A over the total	Works in English	%	Works in other languages*	%
Getulio Vargas Foundation at Rio de Janeiro	18	0	8	208	90	4	2
Catholic University of Rio de Janeiro	39	9	16	233	78	19	6
State University of Campinas	280	53	69	45	9	108	22

*Spanish and French

Table 2 Continued

Part B *Theoretical and Methodological Approach*

Selected Graduate Programs	Theory and Quantitative Methods*	%	Econ. History/ History Econ. Thought/ Political Economy**	%
Getulio Vargas Foundation at Rio de Janeiro	226	98	5	2
Catholic University of Rio de Janeiro	286	95	14	5
State University of Campinas	266	55	220	45

*Includes disciplines such as macroeconomic and microeconomic theory (game theory), monetary theory, international trade theory, industrial organization theory, agricultural economic theory, labor market economic theory (the two latter as applied microeconomic theory), economic development theory, mathematics, statistics, econometrics.

**Includes general economic history, history of economic thought, Brazilian economy, philosophy of sciences, methodology, sociology, political science, Marxist theory.

Source: Franco 1992, using information from ANPEC catalogues. As each program was asked to send to ANPEC not all the disciplines they offer to the students but only ones more representative of the program profile, these data are very expressive of the polarization stressed in the present paper.

Table 3 National Competitive Selection Examination for ANPEC: Weighting of Exams, 1993 (percentages)

Graduate program	Micro	Macro	Mathematics	Statistics	Brazilian Economy
Federal University of Minas Gerais	20	20	15	15	30
Getulio Vargas Foundation at Rio de Janeiro	22.5	22.5	22.5	22.5	10
Federal University of Rio Grande do Sul	20	20	20	20	20
University of São Paulo	20	20	15	20	25
Federal University of Para	20	20	10	10	40
Federal University of Pernambuco	20	20	20	20	20
Catholic University of Rio de Janeiro	20	20	20	20	20
Federal University of Bahia	20	20	15	15	30
Federal University of Rio de Janeiro	20	20	15	15	30
Federal University of Brasilia	20	20	20	20	20
State University of Campinas	17.5	17.5	12.5	12.5	40
Federal University of Ceara	25	25	15	15	20
Getulio Vargas Foundation at São Paulo	20	20	15	15	30
Flumineuse Federal University	20	20	20	20	20

Source: National Association of Graduate Programs in Economics (ANPEC).

assigning the least weight to mathematics and statistics among all graduate programs.[6]

Another important professional effect of the process of internationalization of economics in Brazil is the internal differentiation within the academic field in terms of career strategies on the part of the members of each pole. Thus, the members of EPGE/FGV and PUC/Rio have more intense participation than others in the international scientific network (as members of scientific societies, and through their presence in international congresses or conferences and publication of articles in journals or in books abroad, especially in the United States)[7] and in international agencies such as the International Monetary Fund or the World Bank. Tables 4 and 5 show that the professors of these two schools published the most in U.S. scientific journals or in others in English. On the basis of table 4, while 60 percent of the PUC/RJ professors' publications mentioned in the ANPEC catalogue refer to articles and books issued in English, only 6 percent of the publications from UNICAMP professors are in English. In general, the UNICAMP professors' publications abroad are restricted to Latin American issues. They published predominantly articles in Brazilian journals and books: 56 percent and 38 percent respectively of the total references mentioned in the ANPEC catalogue.[8]

Yet in terms of the differentiation of professional strategies, the pole constituted by EPGE/FGV and PUC/Rio might be called *privatizing* due

6. Loureiro and Lima (1995) have already analyzed other aspects of the process of internationalization of economics in Brazil, such as the curricula and syllabi of the local graduate programs as well as the quantitative balance of bibliographic references contained in the articles published in the main Brazilian journals of economics.

7. Six professors from PUC/RJ and three from FGV are mentioned as members of the American Economic Review and as fellows of the Econometric Society (see the survey of the members of *American Economic Review* and *Econometrica*, respectively, in 1989 and 1993). Three other professors from USP are also on this list. According to the present analysis, it is not necessary to say that no professor from UNICAMP is mentioned.

8. According to Whitley 1991 the features of each scientific field determine the importance given to books or articles in journals as privileged channels for communication of the research outputs to peers. Distinguishing three types of scientific field, "fragmented adhocracies," "polycentric oligarchies," and " partitioned bureaucracies," this author states: "In fragmented adhocracies, for instance, the relatively low degree of skill and concept standardisation, limited autonomy from lay elites and ordinary discursive language and variety of legitimate audiences for intellectual contributions, limit the ability of particular groups to dominate the reputational system and establish their goals and standards . . . . The lack of technical standardisation means that research outputs are not easily communicated through brief journal articles. . . . [In fields such as management studies, sociology, etc.] journals do not dominate the formal communication system . . . but monographs, general books and semi-popular articles are still legitimate means of communicating research outputs" (1991:24–25).

Table 4 Scientific Publication by Brazilian Professors from Selected Graduate Programs

Graduate Program	Articles in English		Books in English		Articles in Portuguese		Books in Portuguese		Total	
	N.	%	N.	%	N.	%	N.	%	N.	%
Getulio Vargas Foundation at Rio de Janeiro (20 profs.)	11	22	3	6	21	41	16	31	51	100
Catholic University of Rio de Janeiro (7 profs.)	9	45	3	15	4	20	4	20	20	100
University of São Paulo (33 profs.)	9	10	4	4	43	48	34	38	90	100
Federal University of Rio de Janeiro (24 profs.)	3	6	2	4	34	73	8	17	47	100
State University of Campinas (18 profs.)	1	3	1	3	15	38	22	56	39	100

Source: Catalogue from graduate programs in economics in Brazil published by ANPCEC/IPEA, 1992. Percentages are approximate.

Table 5   Publications in International Journals by Brazilian Professors from Selected Graduate Programs in Economics: Quantitative Balance of Articles

English-language journals	Getulio Vargas Foundation at Rio de Janeiro	Catholic University of Rio de Janeiro	State University of Campinas
		Graduate Programs	
J. Math. Economics	3	–	–
J. Econometrics	1	–	–
Econometrica	4	–	–
J. Econ. Theory	6	–	–
Quarterly J. Economics	4	2	–
The Bell J. Economics	–	1	–
The Economic Journal	–	1	–
World Development	–	8	–
Economic Hist. Review	–	1	–
Subtotal	18	13	–
Number of professors	30	17	28
Rate of English articles/professor	0.6	0.7	0
Spanish-language journals			
El Trimestre Economico	4	13*	6
Revista de la CEPAL	1	3	5
Total	23	29	11

Source: Data collected in the most important international economic journals, from the 1970s on. The journals in the list above are the ones where there are articles from Brazilian professors.
*Only one professor from Catholic University, Edmar Bacha, wrote seven articles published in *Trimestre Economico* in the period from 1984–92. This professor also wrote two articles in *Trimestre Economico* when he was at the Getulio Vargas Foundation (1970–71) and another three when he was at Brasilia National University (1974–77).

not only to the theoretical value they place on the role of the market in the economic system (it is not by chance that most of the professors affiliated with EPGE/FGV got their doctorates at the University of Chicago) but mainly because its faculty members have close relationships with the private sector, in particular with financial institutions, for which several of them work as consultants.

On the other hand, the less internationalized pole constituted by UNI-CAMP and UFRJ might be called the *public* pole: their studies stress the political aspect of the economy, the work of their members is carried out in public universities, and in general they offer consultancy to government agencies and public sector enterprises. Finally, the intermediate position between these two poles represented by the faculty of economics of USP also is manifested in a wide variety of professional careers and consultancy practices, in private or public organizations attended by its members.

3. Political Impacts: Careers and Legitimation of Economists in Government

Two principal types of career may be identified for economists in government. The first is a career as *economist-employee*, that is, a governmental employee qualified in economics. Young economists enter, by competitive examination or on direct contract, certain governmental agencies for the management of the economy; there they carry out the most important part of their professional activity. Most of the economists who follow this career path remain at the intermediate level of government agencies.[9]

The second career type, and more important from the viewpoint of the present paper, is that of *economist-policymaker*. It is filled by scholars who are appointed to positions in the government not only as advisers but also as ministers or presidents and directors of federal banks. They are in general "brilliant" professors (some of them still young) who, on finishing their theses, are eager to put into practice the theories and models they have just learned. Indeed, the very subjects of the theses tend to express the more immediate needs of the political economy.[10]

9. Coats 1981 shows that in those countries where he carried out his comparative study of economists in government, these professionals were predominantly active at middle levels.

10. A bibliographic investigation of three Brazilian journals in the 1970s, the *Revista Brasileira de Economia*, *Estudos Econômicos*, and *Pesquisa e Planejamento Econômico*, shows that one of the principal subjects of articles published was "the foreign sector." The authors of the study explained this thematic concentration by the opening up, at that time, of the Brazilian economy to the outside market and to the growing difficulties faced by the government in keeping control of the balance of payments (see Gonçalves and David 1982). Also, associated with economic development as the main issue on the political agenda from the 1940s to the 1960s, Brazilian economic thought at that period was centered around this subject (see Bielchowsky 1988).

To be invited to participate in government demonstrates recognition of the academic competence of an economist. These scholars used to be recruited by co-optation among colleagues from the university or from the international agencies network.[11]

Each of the two profiles already mentioned for the careers of economists in government implies specific links between their members and the public positions occupied. While the economist-employees carry on in government posts the most extensive part of their professional careers, the scholars "pass through" government. The time, longer or shorter, spent there does not matter; their relationship with their posts is transitory, a stage in a broader career, usually organized from university to government to private consulting. Although they do not necessarily exclude each other, each new stage is considered more important than the one it replaced.

The different types of relationship between economists and government produce behaviors and attitudes that deserve emphasis. Leaving their universities to take up government office, scholars are filled with a mission: to resolve the problems of the economy. They put into practice the theories they have brought from their university of origin; in general, their action in government involves high-impact measures, shock tactics, economic plans intended, for example, "to do away once and for all with inflation." They are less concerned with the machinery of government or with the need to construct a career therein, and are more involved with projects to change the economic order they criticize. Soon disillusioned by the impossibility of change and compelled to leave government, they are usually replaced by politicians or, sometimes, by economist-employees. These, driven by the characteristics of their own careers, carry out a specific type of economic policy, which is based only on the reorganization and maintenance of the bureaucratic machinery, with no great intention of change. Such was the case, for example, of Mailson da Nóbrega, who followed the scholar Bresser Pereira, with his so-called rice and beans (i.e., ordinary) economic policy.

After spending time in government posts, most scholars do not return to their universities. Instead, they choose a career in consulting for private or even public enterprise, where they have the chance to make a profit

11. There is no formal mechanism for appointing high-level officials to the Brazilian government, and informal patterns and personal relationships are the most frequent at those levels, therefore scholars' recruitment can be explained by features of the broader Brazilian political system (see Schneider 1991).

on their accumulated capital of information and knowledge acquired in the course of their experience in government.

To sum up, the increasing participation of economists in the government and the consolidation of a modern and international academic system for their training and qualification created a new ruling elite in Brazil: the economist-scholars. This elite has inaugurated a new path of access to power: the academic notoriety sustained by strong links with the international scientific network and with international economic agencies, such as the IMF and World Bank, as well as visibility in the local press and strategic relationships with political and entrepreneurial leaders.

The words below are very expressive of this process. They are quoted from a journalist's description of the work done by two Brazilian economists in order to obtain international approval (and consequently local political approval) for their inertial inflation theory, which was transformed some time later into an economic plan for inflation control.

September 1984, IMF meeting. Persio Arida was here with his proposal of monetary reform, written in English. André Lara Resende arrived with his Brazilian article, not yet published. The papers were distributed among the authorities. One copy was sent to Alexandre Kafka, the IMF Brazilian representative, who did not make any comments as it was convenient. Another copy was sent to Peter Knight from the World Bank, who said to the authors that their idea was splendid. Lara Resende explained the proposal to the Federal Reserve officials, who were reasonably receptive to his ideas. Persio Arida was invited to speak at a seminar at the Woodrow Wilson Institute, where he is working at the moment. The paper discussed in the meeting was his article, written in English, "Economic Stabilization in Brazil." The meeting was held in a large and classically decorated library and the audience was composed of World Bank, State Department, and IMF officials, people interested in Brazil for academic or professional reasons. Ana Maria Jul was present from IMF; she is a very well-known person, who had already participated in several missions in Brazil and who has become a symbol of that institution. She listened to Persio Arida's proposal in silence and did not take part in the discussion. As Arida had watched her reactions during the lecture, he was convinced that she did not like it at all.

But the proposals resonated and the papers eventually fell into John Williamson's hands. He had been a professor at PUC-RJ and was working at the International Economic Institute in Washington at that moment. He met Lara Resende and Persio Arida and they decided to organize an international seminar about the experience of inflation control in Europe and countries such as Brazil, Argentina, and Israel. Arida and Lara Resende promised to write a more detailed paper about monetary reform. The seminar happened in December 1984 and put together several economists who would lead, some time later, successive reforms in Israel, Argentina, and Brazil. The international connection was being shaped. . . . After the IMF's meeting, Arida stayed in the United States and Lara Resende came back to Rio de Janeiro. He arrived to find a tumultuous and even hostile climate [on the part of some orthodox economists]. . . . His articles had been published and gained the explicit approval of Professor Mario Henrique Simonsen [from EPGE/FGV]. This changed the nature of the controversy, at least for the greater public. Lara Resende, Arida, and Franciso Lopes [another professor from PUC-RJ involved with inertial inflation theory] were respected academic professors but not great public personalities as Simonsen was. The latter had been minister twice and his name was respected not only in the international academic community, but also in the entrepreneurial and financial ones. He was a frontline public man. [Following Simonsen's acceptance of inertial inflation theory] the press became excited: the news was in the headlines, with TV networks and the weekly magazines connected as well. (Sardenberg 1987, 42–43)

Both Persio Arida and Andre Lara Resende were at that time economists from PUC-RJ and both had studied in the United States, where they had the opportunity to establish contacts with the international scientific network as well as with agencies such as the IMF and World Bank. When they were appointed to high positions in the Ministry of Finance and Central Bank in Brazil during the Cruzado Plan (February 1986), they put into practice their inertial inflation theory through the mechanism of heterodox shock by freezing of wages and prices.[12] With them on the economic team of the Ministry of Finance and Ministry of Planning

12. As already mentioned, the theory of inertial inflation directly followed from the structuralist tradition of considering Latin American inflationary regimes as very specific in nature. Rejecting several orthodox approaches that saw the cure for Brazilian inflation exclusively in budget tightening and monetary restraint, the proponents of inertial theory explained that inflation perpetuated itself largely as an inevitable and perverse consequence of past inflation, transmitted through both formal and informal indexing of wages, public sector prices, and the exchange rate (see Loureiro and Lima 1995).

were several other economists from IE/UNICAMP who participated in the implementation of this plan as PMBD's economists (the government political party).

It is worth mentioning that the Cruzado Plan's failure produced not only economic and political effects, but also a professional impact on economists in terms of a relative decline in the social recognition of their professional competence. That this impact was greater on the professors from UNICAMP than the ones from PUC can be explained by two factors: first, while the economists from UNICAMP appeared in the economic policymaking arena through their relationships with PMBD's leaders, the economists from PUC-RJ participated in their professional capacity. Second, the latter knew when to leave their government positions, that is, before the press completely realized the plan's failure, and they could create political explanations for that failure that were accepted by academia.

According to frequent explanations at the time, "the Cruzado Plan was a good plan in terms of its theoretical coherence or technical correctness; its failure was due to the political constraints and to the populism of President Sarney and his party" (Pereira 1992; Sardenberg 1987).

Thus it is not by chance that the current Real Plan has been conducted by economists from Catholic University—the same ones who prepared the Cruzado Plan. In the present government, Persio Arida is president of the Central Bank; Edmar Bacha holds the post of president of BNDES; Pedro Malan, a professor from PUC-RJ after coming from the World Bank became Minister of Finance; and Gustavo Franco, another professor from PUC, is one of the most important directors of the Central Bank. As the Real Plan has been implemented with great autonomy from political parties' constraints and is considered a success, at least at the present time, the economic team claims that now they are putting into practice all the technical conditions they intended to in 1986, during the Cruzado Plan, but which the electoral interests of PMBD's politicians did not allow. Thus, the actions of the scholar-economists in the government are considered "the correct application of the adequate theory, unless the politicians hinder them," as the well-known technocratic viewpoint claims.

4. Concluding Remarks

In this paper, I have attempted to show that the internationalization of economics in Brazil is not only a process of modernization of economics, that is, a process of integration in an area of knowledge from a developing country into the international or North American scientific patterns. More than that, it implies professional and political effects.

The internationalization of economics in Brazil has both reinforced the theoretical and ideological polarization existing between schools and research centers of economics in Brazil and generated different career paths on the part of the members of each pole, such as types of studies or research done, structures of graduate programs organized, vehicles privileged for publishing scientific outcomes, areas chosen to develop external professional consulting, whether private (financial institutions) or public agencies, and more.

As far as the political aspects are concerned, this paper recalls that the education of the first generations of economists in Brazil took place inside government agencies and economic studies in Brazil arose in close connection with the political agenda. It is worth mentioning as well that this feature did not change with the emergence of a modern and internationalized scientific field of economics. The links between academic circles and government are still very strong.

It is not within the context of this paper to analyze the historical and political factors that explain the presence of scholars in high positions in government (as economic policymakers) in Brazil. It is enough to indicate some dimensions, such as the authoritarian regime, the fragility of the party system, and the successful institutional work done by several groups from the 1940s on to set up new governmental agencies for economic management (attributed almost exclusively to the economists), as well as the use of economic schools as a path to power (see Loureiro 1992). What is stressed here is the role played by academic prestige, associated with the participation of professional economists in the international scientific network, in legitimating their presence in government posts.

References

Agarez, Isis Carneiro. 1986. A produção de teses em economia nos centros da AN-PEC. *Literatura Econômica* 8.2 (June): 215–41.

Bielchowsky, R. 1988. *O pensamento economico brasileiro (o ciclo ideológico do desenvolvimentismo*. Rio de Janeiro: IPEA/INPS.

Coats, A. W. 1981. *Economists in Government: An International Comparative Study*, Durham, N.C.: Duke University Press.

Ekerman, R. 1989. A comunidade de economistas do Brazil: dos anos 50 aos dias de hoje. *Revista Brasileira de Economia* 43.2:113–38.

Faculty of Economics, University of São Paulo. 1981. História da Faculdade de

Economia e Administração (FEA/USP) da Universidade de São Paulo (1956–1981). 2 vols. São Paulo.

Franco, G. 1992. *Cursos de Economia*. ANPEC.

Gonçalves, R. C., and M. Dias David. 1982. A Produção Acadêmica nas principais revistas de economia: balanço de uma década. *Literatura Econômica* 4.3 (May/June): 283–307.

Leff, N. 1968. *Economic Policy-Making and Development in Brazil 1947–1964*. New York: John Wiley and Sons.

Loureiro, M. R. 1992. Economistas e Elites Dirigentes no Brasil. *Revista Brasileira de Ciências Sociais, Relumé/ Dumará* 20.7:47–69.

Loureiro, M. R., and G. T. Lima. 1995. Searching for the Modern Times: The Internationalization of Economics in Brazil. In *Research in the History of Economic Thought and Methodology*. Greenwich, Conn.:JAI.

Lowenstein, K. 1944. *Brazil under Vargas*. New York: Macmillan.

Mantega, G. 1985. *A economia política brasileira*. São Paulo: Polis/Vozes.

Miceli, S. 1990. *A Desilusão americana*. São Paulo: CNPQ/IDESP/Editora Sumaré.

Pereira, L. C. B. 1992. Problematizando uma experiênica da governo: contra a corrente no Ministério da Fazenda. *Revista Brasileira de Ciências Sociais* 7:19 (June): 5–30.

Sardenberg, C. A. 1987. *Aventura e Agonia, Nos Bastidores do Cruado*. São Paulo: Companhia das Letras.

Schneider, B. R. 1991. Politics Within the State, Elite Bureaucrats and Industrial Policy in Authoritarian Brazil. Pittsburgh, Pa.: University of Pittsburgh Press.

Whitley, R. 1991. The Organisation and Role of Journals in Economics and Other Scientific Fields. *Economic Notes by Monte dei Peschi di Siena* 20.1:6–32.

Wirth, J. D. 1970. *The Politics of Brazilian Development (1930–1954)*. Stanford, Calif: Stanford University Press.

Part 3

The Contribution of the International Monetary Fund

Jacques J. Polak

Introduction

The immediate postwar years saw the emergence of a large number of international organizations whose activities were entirely or to an important extent devoted to economic matters. These included the United Nations and its early regional economic commissions, in particular those for Europe (ECC) and Latin America (ECLA); the International Monetary Fund (IMF) and the World Bank; the General Agreement on Tariffs and Trade (GATT, not technically an international organization but performing comparable functions and operating on comparable lines); the International Labour Office (ILO, the only holdover from the interwar period), and the Food and Agriculture Organization, to mention only the most important ones of that period. Others followed, such as the Organization for European Economic Cooperation (later transformed into the OECD) and United Nations Conference of Trade and Development (UNCTAD)—the list of organizations qualifying to send observers to the annual meetings of the IMF and the World Bank runs to sixty-five.

All these organizations engage in a variety of activities that contribute something to the dissemination of economics throughout the world: they assemble international staffs, hold meetings attended by national delegations or international experts, organize training activities, offer technical assistance to their member countries, and much more. But the contribution that most of these organizations make to the internationalization of economics is, I think, marginal compared to the spread of economics that comes about through the more normal academic channels: the welcome mat to foreign students in major universities, national and international economics journals (now overwhelmingly published in English), economic congresses, guest lectureships, and so on.

In the early postwar years, the IMF stands out as the international organization that made the most noticeable contributions not only to the dissemination of existing ideas, but also to the development of new economic thinking, making it a major actor in the internationalization of economics. By contrast, the development of the World Bank as the premier source of development economics, it should be recalled, came only some twenty years later.[1]

But it would be wrong to see the role of international organizations in the internationalization of economics as an entirely novel, post-1945 development. On the contrary, there was a clear precedent in the interwar period. Starting as early as 1920 and carrying on until it was absorbed by the United Nations in 1946, the economic section of the League of Nations contributed importantly to both the development and the dissemination of economics. Before we analyze the role of the IMF it is useful, therefore, to give a brief overview of the League's activities in this area as well as the various ways in which these spilled over, so to say, into similar activities of the IMF.

The Role Played by the League of Nations in the Internationalization of Economics

The Versailles Peace Conference created the League of Nations as a political association of states; international action in the economic field seemed to be required only "to secure and maintain . . . equitable treatment for the commerce of all Members of the League" (Hill 1946, 18–20). The same laissez-faire attitude explains why the organizers of the League did not surround it with a set of specialized agencies in the economic field, with the exception of the ILO. But the extreme disruption of the markets for goods and finance in the immediate postwar period demonstrated almost at once the need for international cooper-

---

1. Mason and Asher 1973 (467–68): "at least until the mid-1960s, [the Bank's] Economics [Department] was a small undermanned department" and members of its staff "were rarely employed in research of basic significance for an understanding of development processes."

ation in the economic and financial fields. The League responded to this need by calling an international financial conference in Brussels in early 1920. This initial step was followed in the next few years by the creation of what became known as "the Economic and Financial Organization of the League of Nations."[2] This "Organization," as it was called for short, was not an independent or separate body but a kind of proto-specialized agency within the League, through which it was able to address any economic or financial issue that it believed required its attention.

The preponderance of financial subjects pursued by the Organization made it, in many respects, the forerunner of the International Monetary Fund.[3] Thus, for example, it concerned itself with the working of the international monetary system and the question of the adequacy of international reserves—as in the Brussels conference in 1920, the 1922 Genoa conference, which recommended worldwide use of the gold exchange standard, and the studies of the Gold Delegation in 1930–31 on the adequacy of the supply of gold. In the 1920s it arranged financial stabilization loans (with resources borrowed from the market under guarantees from the major powers) for a number of countries in Central Europe, with strict supervision of the budgetary policies of the receiving countries. When the world economy started to crumble in the early 1930s the League began a series of annual reports that it kept up until 1944. These *World Economic Surveys* are comparable in scope to the IMF's *World Economic Outlook* papers. Conscious of the profound damage that depressions and their propagation from country to country could do to the world economy and indeed to world peace, the League commissioned two major studies on the subject, the first by Gottfried Haberler and the

2. According to Hill the term connoted the Assembly and the Council (in so far as they dealt with economic and financial questions), various committees and subcommittees of the Council, including the Economic, Financial and Fiscal Committees and the Delegation on Economic Depressions, as well as the relevant department of the secretariat (1946, 3–4).

3. In terms of organizational structure, the League had to make do with the organs it had. From today's vantage point, one can see rough parallels between the Assembly and the IMF's annual meeting, the Council and the Interim Committee, the Financial Committee and the executive board, and the secretariat and the staff of the IMF. All this would hold for the financial activities of the Organization, perhaps most clearly in the case of the financial reconstruction work in Central Europe. But in some other activities, such as the 1927 World Economic Conference, the League could be seen as anticipating the GATT; and in the 1930s the Organization became stretched over a wide field of interests including migration, population movements, nutrition, housing, and conditions of rural life.

second by Jan Tinbergen—studies that had their reverberations after the war in the work of the Fund.[4]

This range of activities made the League an important contributor to the spread of economics among participants in many countries. With a much smaller staff than the postwar organizations, it relied heavily on memoranda by outstanding contemporary economists from many countries to provide the basis for discussions in its many conferences. The membership of its major committees was also drawn from the best available international experts (including Americans, although the United States was not a member of the League). It attached outstanding experts to its staff through temporary appointments, including in the late 1930s Gottfried Haberler, Jan Tinbergen, and James Meade. At that time Geneva, which was also the home of the Graduate Institute of International Studies, was one of the leading centers (perhaps *the* leading center) of applied economics in Europe. The Rockefeller Foundation, which had financed the League's business cycle research since 1933, called an international conference at Annecy near Geneva in 1936 to consider establishing an international coordinating center for business cycle research in either the economic organization of the League or the Graduate Institute (De Marchi 1991, 149). Further evidence of the League's catalytic role in the internationalization of economics just before and during the war is provided by the two lengthy reports of its Delegation on Economic Depressions.[5] These reports (League of Nations 1943 and 1945) contain a detailed presentation of the prevailing informed opinion ("the general trend of social-economic thought in the United Nations today," as it was put in League of Nations 1943, 8) of the economic and financial policies that would be appropriate to the postwar period. With reference to the first report it was claimed in 1946 that "no other League document in recent years has . . . so much influenced the thinking of statesmen and officials concerned with economic policies" (Hill 1946, 132). The second report embraces the full-employment policies incorporated in the

4. This linkage between the economic work of the League and that of the IMF has been highlighted by Neil De Marchi (1991).

5. This "delegation" was created in 1938 as an eight-member subcommittee of the Economic and Financial Committees (two members from each) with a representative from the ILO and three outside experts, originally Oskar Morgenstern, Jacques Rueff, and Bertil Ohlin. It was to report on measures "for preventing or mitigating economic depressions" (League of Nations 1943, 5). There were some changes in membership during the war, but the international character of the membership of the delegation was maintained (see League of Nations 1943, 4, and 1945, 14).

charter of the United Nations, the need for orderly exchange rate arrangements reflected in the Articles of Agreement of the IMF—this part of the report based on Ragnar Nurkse's *International Currency Experience* (League of Nations 1944)—and the importance of international policy coordination to smooth business cycles: in brief, the international consensus that underlay the broad burst of international and intergovernmental policy action of the first decade after World War II. In both scope and depth, though not in its substance, this consensus reminds one of the "Washington Consensus" half a century later, to which I shall turn below.[6]

The Role Played by the IMF in the Internationalization of Economics

The IMF is unique as an international organization in that its life blood is made up almost entirely of economic corpuscles. With few exceptions, those crowding around its cradle at Bretton Woods were economists, and prominent economists at that. The design of the institution came out of a debate among economists. Its initial staff consisted almost entirely of economists, assembled in a single major department, the Research Department. There was some delay until this department was put formally under Edward M. Bernstein, very much an economists' economist, but this delay was related only to some infighting in the U.S. Treasury (Black 1991, 56–57).[7] There was never any question in those early days (nor for quite some period afterward) that the Research Department was the heart of the Fund, or, disregarding legal niceties, *was* the Fund.

   In this setting it was only natural that the Fund provided a considerable impetus to the internationalization of those branches of economics in which its staff operated, which included both a wide range of domestic economic policies and international economics. But it seems important to distinguish two strands of this process—one related to the dissemination of existing knowledge, the other to the creation of new knowledge.

6. It seems to me that John Ikenberry underestimates the breadth of the consensus on postwar policies that had been built up in the late 1930s and the early 1940s when he credits this consensus almost entirely to the British and American negotiators of the postwar financial arrangements (Ikenberry 1992).

7. A story I heard at the time, but of which I have never seen any written record, was that some European executive directors had proposed Ragnar Nurkse as an alternative candidate to head the Research department.

The IMF and the Dissemination of Economics

From the very early days of the Fund, a rather large number of economists, drawn from many countries around the world, had to acquire a set of reasonably consistent views on many economic and financial issues that were to be reflected in papers to the board on general or country matters and, increasingly, in missions to member countries. This involved a major educational task as well as a strict supervisory system before papers saw the light of day. Bernstein's role in this process of what might perhaps be called the "homogenization" of the staff of the Research Department was crucial. During the first year or so, Friday afternoons were devoted to seminars for chiefs of the various divisions. The main course on the menu for these sessions was lectures by Bernstein against the background of recent policy issues in the Fund or in member countries. Bernstein also went carefully over papers written by staff members and himself wrote the most important papers for the board, speeches delivered by the first managing director (Camille Gutt, a Belgian ex-minister of finance), and crucial passages of the first few annual reports. Some of the Fund's major approaches of this period—for example, on the subject of "latent inflation" or the proper choice of an exchange rate in a period of scarcity of supply—originated with Bernstein.

At the same time, Bernstein's highly selective hiring policy brought together a stable of economists with sufficient background and training to need only a modicum of indoctrination to become productive in the new institution. For example, of the dozen or so "division chiefs" in the original Research Department (there was no further refinement of titles under the director at that time), four had attended the Bretton Woods Conference and had helped shape their countries' attitude toward the Fund (Allan Fisher of New Zealand, Walter Gardner of the United States, Felipe Pazos of Cuba, and Jacques Polak of the Netherlands). A good many of the younger economists, whatever their nationalities, came to the IMF from the two Cambridges (England and Massachusetts) on the recommendation of two professors, Dennis Robertson and Gottfried Haberler, equipped with the latest fashions in economic thought.

Later, the Fund started an institute to conduct on a systematic basis training courses for officials from member countries, and these of course contributed to a broader understanding of the economic approaches that were common among the Fund staff. At least equally important to the same end were "consultation" visits to countries by staff missions (which became annual events from about the mid-1950s) and negotiating discussions on standby arrangements. In terms of the dissemination of economic ideas, these were two-way streets, with the staff widening its understanding of economic processes from their exposure to a broad spectrum of institutional arrangements and special situations. To cite an example, the Fund staff, while it can take some credit for developing the monetary approach to the balance of payments (more about this below), was both stimulated and supported in the development of its ideas by the fact that this same approach had a strong intuitive appeal to some of the most thoughtful governors of central banks, such as Marius Holtrop of the Netherlands and Don Rodrigo Gomez of Mexico.

The cumulative effect of these discussions over the years was in many cases to bring about a certain parallelism in economic thinking that greatly facilitated agreement on the conditions governing the extension of Fund credit when the need for a Fund arrangement presented itself (Polak 1991, 64). More generally, these various channels of communication on economic policy between the Fund and officials in its member countries were among the factors contributing to the emergence of what has been called "the Washington Consensus," a most welcome convergence in thinking about economic policy that began to unfold in the late 1980s (Williamson 1990).

But although this was the broadest postwar consensus (or at least became the broadest consensus when the countries of Central and Eastern Europe joined it), it is questionable to what extent it should be interpreted as the culmination of the internationalization of economics. We noted above the wide consensus on a policy program existing at the end of the war. Nor should we overlook the very substantial consensus of the 1950s and the 1960s among ministers and senior officials in many countries in anglophone Africa and Asia, often graduates of British universities, who were in charge of dirigiste economic policies similar to those that were then popular in the industrial countries. The process of conversion from one consensus to another in large areas of the world owed less, it would seem, to the growing force of internationalization than to the accumulating evidence of success of neoclassical policies, in particular in East Asia, contrasting with the dismal results of previous policies in so many other countries.

In sum, therefore, it would seem cautious not to overemphasize the role of the Fund as a disseminator of economic knowledge. The widening and deepening of economic understanding in the postwar years was a worldwide process in which the Fund played a respectable but in no sense a dominating part. The Fund's contribution to the development of economics was, in my view, fundamentally more important; it certainly was more exciting. Moreover, since the Fund was (and is) recognized as a place where the staff is encouraged to do original economic thinking, its credibility as a disseminator of economic ideas was enhanced.

The IMF and the Development of Economics

The interwar period had been one of almost continuous economic and financial upheaval, which had spawned an extensive literature on a wide range of policy issues: inflation and hyperinflation, trade and payments discrimination, business cycles and their international consequences, fluctuations in international trade and capital movements, gold and reserve currencies, exchange rates and exchange rate regimes, and many others. As mentioned earlier, studies commissioned by the League of Nations or performed by its staff had been an important source for the development of some of the new understandings of the 1920s, the 1930s, and the early part of the 1940s.

And yet, when the Fund staff started its work, it found almost at once that the existing books and articles on the newly installed shelves in 1818 H Street N.W. in Washington did not contain nearly enough applied or applicable economics for the situations it faced. In 1918, at the end of World War I, the answers had appeared simple: return to the tried verities of the prewar period—balance the budget, abolish trade restrictions, get the government out of the foreign exchange business; and the task of the early postwar conferences (Brussels 1920, Genoa 1922) was mostly to persuade weak or interventionist governments to heed these verities. At the end of World War II—as so clearly foreseen in 1939 by Alexander Loveday, the imaginative director of the economic work of the League—there would be nothing that anyone wanted to go back to.[8]

Faced with new problems—or more often new versions of old problems—the staff of the Fund was under continuous pressure to refine existing economic concepts, to devise new concepts, or to discover "new" theories. Some of these theories might have had an earlier existence in the dim past (something like the monetary approach to the balance of payments can be found in the writings of David Hume); but they did not

8. Cited in De Marchi 1991, 173.

reenter current textbooks on international economics until rediscovered in the Fund.

Most of the theoretical work performed at the Fund can be found in successive issues of *International Monetary Fund Staff Papers*, a professional economics journal published since 1950.[9] But not everything could wait that long. The analytical presentation of each country's monetary statistics in a "monetary survey" (inspired by Robert Triffin's distinction of "money of internal and external origin"), which in turn provided the jumping-off point for the Fund's operational monetary programming and the monetary interpretation of the balance of payments, has appeared in *International Financial Statistics* from the very first issue (January 1948). The Fund view on the proper criteria for a par value for a country struggling with immediate postwar shortages—an exchange rate sufficiently depreciated to encourage exports but not so low as to restrain imports without the support of restrictions—was set out in early annual reports. Much of the staff's thinking on a variety of aspects of the Special Drawing Right (SDR) was published in a conference volume (IMF 1970) and in three Fund pamphlets (see Polak 1994, vii). The extensive, and in many respects original, work of the staff in coming to numerical judgments on appropriate changes in par values for major currencies (sterling in 1967, the French franc in 1968, and the dollar and other currencies between August 1971 and the Smithsonian conference) has for obvious reasons never seen the light of day. On a more purely theoretical question, only the Fleming half of the Mundell-Fleming model—perhaps the most important theorem in international economics originating at the Fund— appeared in *Staff Papers*, while Mundell's contribution is dispersed over a number of papers in other journals (Frenkel and Razin 1987). In spite of these qualifications, *Staff Papers* was, at least until about 1980, the main source from which to get an impression of the scope and quality of the contributions to economics that were hatched in the Research Department of the Fund, especially in the early years.

In drawing from this source, I shall limit myself in this section of the paper to the period 1950 to 1980. This was roughly the period of my association with the Research Department, when I was familiar with

9. The Fund undertook the publication of this journal in response to a suggestion by Dennis Robertson. In recommending yet another of his brilliant students (this time it was T. C. Chang) for the Research Department he expressed concern that the Fund's recruitment might submerge too many of the new generation of bright young economists into "an anonymous international bureaucracy."

many of the papers as they were being written; it also happens to be the only period for which an analytical index is available. Other reasons for stopping well before the latest issue of the journal include the relative decline of the role of *Staff Papers* among the Fund's publications and the change in the relationship between economists on the Fund staff and those in the academic community that took place gradually over the last decade or so; I shall return to these changes in the final section of this paper.

It is not an easy task to infer, from the roughly five hundred papers that make up the contents of the first thirty years of *Staff Papers*, the contributions to international economics that specifically emanated from the Fund during that period. The task is made even more intractable by the fact that, as I have described elsewhere, the Research Department in its early years operated to some extent as an intellectual commune where the property rights to particular ideas were not solidly established and one staff member's ideas might first show up in another's paper (Polak 1994, xxv and xix). For reasons such as these I shall limit myself to a brief discussion, in the list below, of a number of principal topics without presenting a supporting bibliography and thus without singling out authors.[10]

1. Probably of greatest interest are two contributions to the economics of balance of payments adjustment. Curiously enough, each of these can be traced back to a devaluation of the Mexican peso, in 1948 and 1954, respectively, each of which set off a great deal of discussion among Fund staff.[11] The first, the "absorption theory of the balance of payments," arose out of dissatisfaction with the partial-equilibrium answers provided by the then common elasticities approach. Devaluation, the absorption theory argued, could improve the balance of payments only in so far as it brought about the required net reduction in domes-

10. I am not sure that there is any statistic that would be indicative of the professional standing of the Fund staff members who wrote in *Staff Papers*, but I cite the following number as of some possible interest: of about 250 authors and coauthors in the first seventeen volumes of the journal, 11 are listed in Blaugh's 1986 *Who's Who in Economics*. Listings in this source are based on frequency of attributed quotations, which may have something to do with the fact that two authors prominent enough to be often referred to in terms of their contribution rather than by a source reference (Fleming and Tanzi) are not among these eleven.

11. An excellent discussion, with bibliographical references, of these and many other instances of Fund staff responses to challenges encountered in member countries is given by Margaret de Vries (1987).

tic absorption (consumption plus investment), and this depended on many factors other than relative prices and trade elasticities, including changes in income distribution, taxation measures and changes in the real money supply. The second theory, going under the name of the "monetary approach to the balance of payments," focused attention on the crucial (and at the time often overlooked) role played by credit creation by the banking system as a source of additional demand and hence domestic absorption and, ultimately, an increase in the current account deficit.[12] Another demonstration of staff concern with questions of balance of payments adjustment, as well as of the growth performance of the world economy, is found in the successive generations, from the 1940s until today, of "world trade models"—in fact, increasingly sophisticated models of the world economy. Since the 1980s, the Fund's latest model (MULTIMOD, which forms the background of the half-yearly *World Economic Outlook* papers) has acquired a leading place in the efforts among international economists to construct a world model that would be serviceable for purposes of international policymaking.

2. Many papers originated in the need to develop new concepts in connection with the research and operational activities of the Fund, such as "latent inflation," "competitive depreciation" and "fundamental equilibrium," the "basic balance of payments," "effective exchange rates," "multiple exchange rates" and "dual exchange markets," and "objective indicators" as a guide to exchange rate changes.

3. The policy implications of alternative monetary systems, including fixed versus floating exchange rates, and their significance for domestic financial policies gained increasing importance as the chances for survival (or revival) of the par value system declined.

4. There were very few years in the Fund when the subject of international liquidity was not on the agenda. As early as 1949 South Africa proposed that the Fund use its statutory power (under Article IV, section 7 of the original Articles of Agreement) to increase liquidity by a "uniform change in par values."[13] After an acrimonious discussion, the executive board voted down this

12. Ten papers written by Fund staff members on the "monetary approach to the balance of payments" between 1957 and 1976 were republished in International Monetary Fund 1977.
13. Horsefield 1969, vol. 2, 192–94.

proposal, but the broader issue of international liquidity would not go away and has continued to absorb a great deal of staff thinking ever since. Contributions in *Staff Papers* and elsewhere have dealt with the theory of the adequacy of international liquidity in terms of the performance of the world economy; its effect on world inflation; the dynamics of its various components (both traditional, such as gold and reserve currencies, and those created by the Fund, such as the "reserve tranche" and SDRs); and the nature and the design of the SDR.

5. Only exceptionally does one find a scientific paper on the rationale for the Fund's financial policies, but *Staff Papers* was the place where the theory underlying compensatory financing of export fluctuations was developed.

6. After the fiscal division of the Research Department was split off as a separate department (in 1965), *Staff Papers* also began to contain a rich stream of articles dealing with fiscal questions, among which the "Tanzi principle" on the effect of inflation on tax revenues and the "operational budget balance" (though not originating in the Fund but made widely known through its publications) deserve to be mentioned here.

The ability of economists on the staff of the Fund to make original contributions to these and other subjects often ahead of the work done in the leading universities was indicative of a clear comparative advantage. Initially, the Fund staff had far better access to data and to the policymakers in a wide range of countries. The problems of these countries demanded the attention of the economists in the Fund; those in the universities would have had to make special efforts to become acquainted with these problems.

The IMF and the Internationalization of Economics: Recent Developments

In more recent years however—say, since 1970 or 1980—this comparative advantage has tended to disappear. Both data and travel funds have become much more generally available. Also, the increasing workload on the staff of all departments occasioned by the great demands on the Fund for technical and financial assistance has cut into the time available for research, even in the Research Department; in retrospect, it may not have been an accident that some of the most interesting research activities of the institution date from the years when Fund transactions were limited to a few a year. Perhaps most important of all, relative salaries have changed. In the earlier years Fund officials earned substantially more than they could have made in the top American universities. That difference has eroded over time and has probably disappeared by now.

To some extent the impact of this last change on the quality of economics conducted in the IMF has been offset by the introduction of a wide-open invitation to academics to spend from one to six months as visitors in the Research Department, a policy inaugurated when Jacob Frenkel became head of the department in 1986. Papers written (or started to be written) during these visits can now also be published in *Staff Papers*, in which "outsiders" now account for about 25 percent of the contents. As a result the quality of that journal may, for all one knows, have improved, but its character has changed: it has lost some of its specialty as a Fund publication and now primarily competes in the league of academic economics journals. Still, papers offering contributions on subjects close to the heart of the Fund stand out, for example on the debt crisis of the 1980s or the new wave of capital flows to developing countries of the 1990s.

At the same time, as the Fund has grown and has felt the need to reach a wider variety of audiences, *Staff Papers* has lost its unique character as *the* vehicle for the publication of economic thinking in the institution. On the one side, that of the dissemination of somewhat more popular or applied ideas, *Staff Papers* has been complemented by *Finance and Development* (published jointly with the World Bank) and a series called *Occasional Papers*. On the more theoretical side, only a fraction—about 20 percent—of research papers written at the Fund and approved for circulation eventually ends up being printed in *Staff Papers*, but all now enter the supply of "published" literature, either as *IMF Working Papers* (since 1989) or as *IMF Papers on Policy Analysis and Assessment* (since 1993).

In response to the needs of the new member countries in Central and Eastern Europe and elsewhere, the Fund has stepped up its technical assistance and other activities through which it contributes to the dissemination of economics throughout the world. But as regards the advance of the science of international economics, the economics staff of the Fund has increasingly become a capable but no longer clearly distinguishable part of the large body of economists that populate the universities, governments, and businesses of the world.

References

Black, Stanley W. 1991. *A Levite Among the Priests: Edward M. Bernstein and the Origins of the Bretton Woods System*. Boulder, Colo.: Westview Press.

Blaugh, Mark. 1986. *Who's Who in Economics*. Cambridge, Mass.: MIT Press.

de Marchi, Neil. 1991. League of Nations Economists and the Ideal of Peaceful Change in the Decade of the "Thirties." In *Economics and National Security*, By Craufurd D. Goodwin. Durham, N.C.: Duke University Press.

de Vries, Margaret G. 1987. *Balance of Payments Adjustment, 1945 to 1986: The IMF Experience*. Washington, D.C.: International Monetary Fund.

Frenkel, Jacob A., and Assaf Razin. December 1987. The Mundell-Fleming Model a Quarter Century Later: A Unified Exposition. *IMF Staff Papers*. 567–620.

Hill, Martin. 1946. *The Economic and Financial Organization of the League of Nations*, Washington, D.C.: Carnegie Endowment for International Peace.

Horsefield, J. Keith. 1969. *The International Monetary Fund, 1945–1965*. Washington, D.C.: International Monetary Fund.

Ikenberry, G. John. 1992. A World Economy Restored: Expert Consensus and the Anglo-American Postwar Settlement. *International Organization* 46.1 (winter): 289–321.

IMF. [International Monetary Fund.] 1970. *International Reserves: Needs and Availability*. Washington, D.C.: International Monetary Fund.

———. 1977. *The Monetary Approach to the Balance of Payments*. Washington, D.C.: International Monetary Fund.

League of Nations. 1943. *The Transition from War to Peace Economy: Report of the Delegation of Economic Depressions*. Part 1. Geneva.

———. 1944. *International Currency Experience*. Geneva.

———. 1945. *Economic Stability in the Post-War World: The Conditions of Prosperity after the Transition from War to Peace. Report of the Delegation on Economic Depressions*. Part 2. Geneva.

Mason, Edward S., and Robert E. Asher. 1973. *The World Bank since Bretton Woods*. Washington, D.C.: The Brookings Institution.

Polak, Jacques J. 1991. *The Changing Nature of IMF Conditionality*. Essays in International Finance no. 184. Princeton, N.J.: Princeton University Press.

———. 1994. *Economic Theory and Financial Policy: The Selected Essays of Jacques J. Polak*. Aldershot, England: Edward Elgar.

Williamson, John. 1990. *Latin American Adjustment: How Much Has Happened?* Washington, D.C.: Institute for International Economics.

The World Bank as an International Player in Economic Analysis

Barend A. de Vries

This paper first gives an overview of the World Bank's history with emphasis on the development of its analytical work. Next it discusses major aspects of the Bank's economics, both research and what is directly related to operations. The third part reviews the various ways in which economic work and research are disseminated around the world. The paper ends with some concluding observations and questions for further thought.

Historical Overview

Who would have expected when it opened its doors in 1946 that the World Bank would become a major player in international economics and development research? The Bank's early loans were for the reconstruction of Western Europe. After the start of the Marshall Plan the Bank turned to infrastructure projects in developing countries. During the presidency of Eugene Black (1949–62) the Bank had to establish its own credibility and creditworthiness in the bond markets, where it had to raise funds for making loans. The Bank had to demonstrate that its projects were well defined and financially viable. For their part the recipient countries had to convince the lender that they were responsible borrowers, both in honoring existing obligations and in being able to service new loans.[1]

Along with this project-specific approach the Bank, from its early years on, had to have an economywide view of the borrowing countries. It would initiate or continue lending only where it was satisfied with the country's economic policies and the use it made of resources. It had to establish the priority and the justification of the projects selected for finance, and it had to assess the country's debt-bearing capacity. Inside the Bank the determination of the bankability of projects made for an often lively interchange between different disciplines on the staff, especially among economists, engineers, and regional experts. The Bank also had to have an understanding of trends in the international economy that could vitally affect the countries' repayment capacity. Bank economists had to keep abreast of several commodities traded on international markets (see, for example, Grilli and Yang 1988).

The sixties were very exciting years in the Bank. By 1960 the Bank had undertaken comprehensive economywide studies of a large number of countries. It was operating the India and Pakistan Aid Consortia, which required in-depth work on both external and domestic financing needs. It started coordination of external lending to additional countries in the framework of "Consultative Groups." The first such group was the one for Colombia, which began formal operations in 1963. The Bank had accumulated considerable experience in major infrastructure sectors and was getting ready to broaden into new fields of lending. Under the innovative presidency of George D. Woods (1963–68) the Bank began lending for education, waterworks, and sanitation and strengthened its economic analysis and research staff. At the same time economic research as well as country work (notably on Brazil) helped it gain a better understanding of the debt-bearing capacity of developing countries and their ability to pursue development in an inflationary environment.

Robert S. McNamara (1968–81) was a strong leader who greatly increased the level and scope of Bank lending, emphasized poverty alleviation, and continued Woods's efforts to strengthen economic research. His annual speeches to the Bank's board of governors demanded a major input from the Bank's research staff. He made the preparatory work for Bank lending more systematic and personally led the preparation and

---

1. Many countries, particularly in Latin America, had defaulted on their bonds. As a condition of initiating operations the Bank required that borrowers make a settlement with their creditors.

discussion of country programs that took account of economic, technical, and sociopolitical factors. He started major operations in Indonesia and toward the end of his tenure laid the basis for a large program in China.

McNamara's leadership was missed badly when the developing countries had to face the debt crisis of the eighties. The three presidents who succeeded him (Clausen, Conable, and Preston) all stayed for only one five-year term or less, after coming to the Bank at the end of their careers. Conable induced the Bank to give more attention to the environment and to women in development. Preston started the process of improving the quality of Bank lending, shedding excess staff, and turning an increasing portion of Bank operations to the private sector. Throughout the 1980s and early 1990s economic analysis and research continued to play an important role in the Bank's work, with an increasing share devoted to issues in the environment and human resource development. By the early 1990s the Bank also began making a greater effort to attract local participation in the preparation and execution of its projects.

Scope and Focus of the Bank's Economic Work

Over the years economic work in the World Bank has become more diverse and its emphasis on individual topics has evolved. Throughout the period the Bank has pursued economic work that was necessary for country relations and the conduct of lending operations. But from the very start the Bank also undertook more general economic analyses that eventually developed into a full-scale research program.

This research is part of a broader range of analytical activities that in all make up about one-fourth of the Bank's total administrative expenses.[2] Country and sector studies account for two-thirds of analytical work and policy studies for one-fifth. The latter include special studies of African development and cover such areas as primary and technical education, food security, and urban development. Research accounts for 13 percent of analytical work, 120 staff years in all, and costs about $25 million in staff, travel, and support costs.

Most of the Bank's senior staff and managers are primarily interested in operations and have always tended to look at research with a critical

---

2. Mr. Gregory K. Ingram, administrator of the Bank's research program, provided useful information on the program. Stern 1993 gives an overview of the Bank's research program over the last twenty-five years. He gives little coverage of the Bank's research on industry, to which this paper pays special attention.

eye. Over the years research has been one of the most closely monitored programs of the Bank. Each project is reviewed by a research committee composed of senior economists. Special assessments of the program were conducted by Sir Arthur Lewis (1979) and Assar Lindbeck (1982). The Bank's executive directors are kept informed with occasional detailed reports on the status and direction of the program.[3]

Perhaps the most important components of the Bank's economic work are economywide country studies and project and sector reports. These reports are directly related to operations. Bank research contributes both staff and ideas to work directly related to operations. Research on price incentives and trade orientation has had an impact on project design and selection as well as the nature of policy conditions attached to the Bank's loans. Analysis of country indebtedness and trade prospects likewise contributes to Bank lending decisions. Currently the Bank emphasizes poverty and human resource development. In the words of the 1994 annual report: "The major objectives of the Bank's current programs are poverty reduction and human resource development, enhancement of the role of women in development, private sector development, environmentally sustainable development, and economic management. Bank research is focused on those areas where critical policy questions remain unanswered" (158).

Bank Country Studies

Bank country studies are unique in that they combine macro- and microeconomic analysis, incorporate project and sector knowledge, and reflect familiarity with the countries' social conditions. They lay the basis for operating programs, lending strategy, and dialogue with countries.

Starting in the 1950s the Bank's survey missions, often composed of outside experts, drew up plans and priorities for countries' development. Many of the published reports contributed to the economic thinking in the countries concerned. For example, the Bank's first survey mission, to Colombia in 1951, was headed by Laughlin Currie, a well-known North American economist. He stayed on in Colombia for over forty years, helped organize the country's planning office, and was as an adviser to

---

3. See, for example, World Bank, 10 January 1994.

many presidents. One of these presidents, Virgilio Barco, told me that in Colombia there were only two kinds of economics, B.C. and A.C., that is, before and after Currie.

In-depth economywide studies are typically organized to meet a special need. The 1964 Brazil economic mission, composed of twenty economists and sector experts, covered the country's economic and financial situation and such key sectors as steel, transport, agriculture, and education. At the start of his presidency George D. Woods wanted to take a new look at Brazil, which had been in the Bank's "deep freeze"; that is, the Bank had stopped new lending because it was dissatisfied with the country's economic policies. The 1964 report studied the impact of financial and economic policies on Brazil's development, reassessed the country's creditworthiness and reviewed critical sector policy issues. It laid the basis for what became the Bank's largest lending program during the Brazilian miracle of moderate inflation and rapid growth in the sixties.

Another example of a comprehensive mission was the Bell mission to India in the mid-sixties. It was of special interest because of the Bank's role as chair of the India Aid Consortium. Its report was not published, but was an important document in the dialogue between India and the Bank. One of the results of this dialogue was the 1967 devaluation of the Indian rupee.

An important part of economic work is the review of the priority and viability of countries' public investment plans, plans that usually stretch over three to five years. These reviews draw on the Bank's macro and micro as well as project and sector knowledge. They are often organized in special situations, for example, the start of a new administration. They may also be carried out as part of the regular work of a resident mission with support from headquarters staff, as, for example, the work undertaken by the resident mission in Indonesia in the seventies and the present resident mission in Russia.

Country studies also lay the basis for meetings of consultative groups, chaired by the Bank, to mobilize and coordinate external finance to selected countries. In addition, they were important in the preparation and discussion of structural adjustment loans which made up one-fourth of Bank lending in the 1980s. The scope of these reports was circumscribed by the areas selected for special attention, for example, trade incentives, agricultural pricing, or public investment planning.

Project and Sector Studies

Project and sector studies are essential for most of the Bank's lending. As is clear from Baum and Tolbert 1985, cost-benefit analysis is only one of the elements of project studies. Others are the assessment of the borrowing institution; legal arrangements; local finance, including user fees, engineering design, and feasibility; and the impact of the project on local conditions (including the environment).

Principles of cost-benefit analysis have been presented by well-known economists working for institutions other than the Bank (Little and Mirlees 1969 [OECD] and Dasgupta, Marglin, and Sen 1972 [UNIDO]). The Bank has tested and refined the methodology for determining the economic return of projects in the context of hundreds of real-life situations. Bank economists Squire and van der Tak (1975) discuss project economics in the broader setting of social analysis. Andarup Ray (1984) and Leff (1985) took further in-depth looks at issues in cost-benefit analysis.

In practice the Bank calculates a financial rate of return, based on market prices of inputs and outputs, and an economic rate of return (ERR) that uses international ("border") prices. But it makes limited use of shadow prices for nontraded inputs and wages. Shadow wages are of course especially important in labor surplus situations. Social analysis, including equity and income distribution considerations, is seldom used in the formal calculation of the ERR, but is nevertheless an important ingredient in the selection of projects for Bank lending and in the new crop of poverty assessments beginning about 1990.

The Bank's sector work combines knowledge of specific projects with the study of policies such as pricing, the setting of priorities, and the provision of finance. The priority of projects, their sequencing and sectorwide policies must be addressed in directly productive activities such as agriculture and industry as well as the social sector (education, health, etc.).

Apart from numerous technical and institutional factors, economic analysis does not change markedly from sector to sector. Consideration of intersector differences is outside the scope of this paper. Analysis of health, education, and the environment gain special importance as greater attention is given to poverty eradication.[4]

Industrial sector work is of special interest because of the macroeco-

---

4. See Baum and Tolbert 1985. For poverty analysis and the environment, see *World Development Report* 1990 and 1992. The 1995 World Bank *Index of Publications* lists Bank studies on various topics in agriculture.

nomic policy issues it addresses and the differences between large and small industry. It has made the Bank face up to many critical issues like the wisdom of starting large capital-intensive industry in relatively small developing economies; sponsoring large-scale industries in enclaves that are, in effect, isolated from the rest of the economy; rehabilitating or privatizing state-owned industries, as well as finding ways of supporting small industries and promoting export-oriented industries. A comprehensive review of the Bank's industrial sector work was undertaken in de Vries 1980b. Industrial policy issues have been studied in the context of research projects as well as operational work (For work on the textile industry, see de Vries 1984).

The Bank makes loans for large capital-intensive as well as smaller labor-intensive industrial projects. Large-scale projects to which the Bank lent directly were usually in import-substitution industries (e.g., steel, fertilizer, chemicals), although some produced mainly for export (e.g., mining and cement). Economic analysis is especially important to make sure that an import-substitution project does not embody uneconomic use of the country's resources.

Smaller projects are usually assisted by loans to financial intermediaries, including development finance companies (DFCs). From the 1950s to the 1980s the Bank made a considerable effort to build up local development banks or DFCs. One objective was to have a channel for the disbursement of loan funds to different industrial projects. The intermediaries had to become familiar with project appraisal methods that they applied to their "subprojects." Operations with DFCs, as well as macroeconomic work, gave the Bank an entrance into the entire financial sector to which it started to give more focused attention in the 1980s. Financial sector studies concentrated on financial policy issues such as the achievement of positive real interest rates, overcoming the effects of government direction of commercial credit, and the rehabilitation of banks that had come under stress as a result of a combination of government interventions, negative real interest rates, and rapid inflation.

Trade Research

Research in trade orientation and incentives has been closely related to the Bank's operations in both manufacturing and agriculture as well as structural adjustment lending (SAL), which often has conditions on incentive policy. The Bank has long had an interest in outward orientation.

This is evident from the publication in the 1960s of occasional papers by Baranson (1969), Ciringiroglu (1969), and de Vries (1967). The Bank's Economics Department took a strong interest in the OECD-sponsored research by Little, Scitovsky, and Scott (1970). Bela Balassa's oeuvre, mostly accomplished while at the Bank, was crucial to wider recognition of the role of markets and the need for and feasibility of lowering effective protection.[5]

The Bank country study "Industrial Strategy and Policy in the Philippines" (World Bank 1980 and de Vries 1980a) went beyond Balassa's type of analysis in that it linked reduction of effective protection with reform in a number of specific industries (steel, machinery, textiles, clothing and footwear, food processing, etc.). The report recommended a phased reduction in tariffs, reform of investment incentive policies, liberalization of import restrictions, combined with rehabilitation of specific industries. The report and subsequent policy understanding with the government laid the basis for the Bank's first SAL.

External Debt Analysis

External debt analysis has always been important in deciding how much to lend to a country. In the 1950s, when most developing countries had rather low debt burdens, the bank typically considered a country creditworthy when its debt service ratio (DSR, debt service as a percentage of export earnings) was below 10 percent. But as the debt service of many countries began a steady climb in the 1960s the Bank needed a more adequate analytical framework.

The study orchestrated by Avramovic (1965) showed the interrelation between growth, the need for foreign resources (the foreign resource gap), and the debt service. It envisaged that as growth proceeded and accelerated over time, the resource gap would rise and form part of the increasing gap financed by external borrowing. Toward the end of the sequence the resource gap would start declining and eventually turn into a surplus. However, debt would first continue to go up to finance interest on outstanding debt obligations. The surplus would, however, continue to increase and progressively pay off the outstanding debt. Even in a well-managed and orderly sequence the DSR could rise well above 50

5. See, for example, Balassa 1971 and 1982. Additional contributions were made by de Vries 1980; Michaely 1977; Papagiorgiou, Michaely, and Choksi 1991; Rhee 1984; and Tyler 1981.

percent. The process stretches out over a period of years and is particularly sensitive to the rate of the country's growth, especially of its exports, its savings rate, the quality and viability of its investments, and the terms on which external debt are contracted. The conceptual stages of development and growth have been applied in a cross-country analysis in de Vries 1971.

Two conditions are critical to ensure that the buildup of debt is accompanied by an even more rapid improvement in countries' ability to service debt:

1. The rate of return on investment must be higher than the interest cost of the external loans used to finance it. If capital is not employed effectively for high-yielding investments, the project's or country's ability to service the debt is threatened.
2. The growth of the borrowing economy, and particularly of exports, must exceed the interest rate on new external debt. If the interest on new debt exceeds the borrowing country's export growth rate, the country's debt will rise beyond bearable bounds. It will rise to excessive levels, at which point the debt servicing process breaks down, the country experiences debt servicing difficulties and must ask for some kind of debt rearrangement.

The study envisaged that each country had a critical interest rate, determined mostly by its growth performance. If it borrowed externally at an interest rate exceeding its critical rate, it would soon experience debt servicing problems. This consideration governed the case for some countries, notably at the time India and today Africa, borrowing on concessionary terms, that is, at interest rates of zero or in any case below those set in the market.

Moreover, when after a period of heavy borrowing (e.g., the 1970s) countries simultaneously face a sharp rise in interest rates on their outstanding loans (they borrowed at rates varying with the market) and a decline in export growth, the second condition breaks down. This was the immediate cause of the debt crisis starting in 1982.

Debt Upheaval in the Eighties

The 1982 debt crisis, and the accompanying unwillingness of banks to provide new funds, set the stage for drastic internal adjustment measures in the heavily indebted countries, many with dire consequences for the poor. It also raised difficult questions of how to deal with the debt overhang. The World Bank initially stood on the sidelines in this debate. Yet, well ahead of the debt crisis, the Bank had in hand detailed information and analyses of the external financing problems countries were facing.

In the late 1970s the Bank in fact considered the debt problem manageable.[6] After the second oil shock in 1979 the Bank recognized that countries needed increasing levels of external finance to sustain their adjustment to the changed external conditions. In fact the 1981 *World Development Report* (WDR) projected high levels of external finance, for example, private capital flows of $30 to $43 billion to the oil-importing developing countries in 1985, and increasing at a 5 to 10 percent growth rate in 1980–90.[7] As it turned out, capital flows would become strongly negative[8] in the mid-eighties and onward.[9]

Against the Bank's lack of leadership in the debt crisis, however, it did contribute to alleviating countries' problems through rapidly disbursing loans to the highly indebted countries and by providing its share of lending under the plans put forth by U.S. Treasury Secretaries Baker and Brady (Diwan and Husain 1989).

World Development Reports in 1981–86 put strong emphasis on the need for internal measures. These included restructuring of public expenditures and improvements in supply incentives, measures to be put in place without substantial external help and often at the expense of the poorer strata of society. But by the end of the 1980s the Bank again stressed the need for an increase in external financing in the interest of more effective adjustment that would also make allowance for the poor. WDR 1988 advocated that the resource outflow from the developing countries be cut and that ways be found to reduce the debt overhang. The report's recommendations preceded the proposal of U.S. Treasury

6. Cf. McNamara 1981, 297 and 456; Stern 1993, 61.

7. See *World Development Report* 1981, 62, table 5.3.

8. Net lending by commercial banks to developing countries was a *negative $178 billion in 1984–90*. Net transfers from commercial banks to developing countries (i.e., the total net payments after repayment of principal and interest) turned around from a positive inflow of $18 billion in 1981 to an outflow of $9 billion in 1984. The outward transfer stayed above $20 billion after 1985, and with a renewed increase in interest rates rose above $30 billion in 1988. In 1990 the developing countries suffered outward transfers of $21.6 billion, of which $10.4 billion was from Latin America alone (World Bank, *World Debt Tables* 1991–92).

9. See, for example, Conable's statement in Corbo 1987, 5. The role of external finance in the adjustment process is described on page 472 and throughout.

Secretary Brady that various steps be taken to reduce outstanding indebtedness.

World Development Reports

Since the late 1970s, WDRs have been a vehicle for focusing attention on crucial development issues. Several WDRs have already been mentioned, including those dealing with debt and adjustment. They are written to be understood by a large lay audience and are widely distributed. They draw on outside as well as inside experts who work under the overall direction of the chief economist. Over the years the content and approaches have tended to vary with changes in the external policy environment.

McNamara's interest in poverty reduction and his emphasis on human resource development was reflected in WDR 1980. After a shift toward greater stress on efficiency in resource allocation during 1981–86 the Bank once again returned to its emphasis on poverty reduction and presented a new in-depth treatment on poverty issues in WDR 1990. This report was accompanied by other publications on poverty reduction, such as the policy paper "Assistance Strategies to Reduce Poverty" and the *Poverty Reduction Handbook.*

Environmental policies were the central concern of WDR 1992. The report anticipated the 1992 Earth Summit in Rio de Janeiro (UN Conference on Environment and Development). It concluded that growth can be compatible with protection of the environment, but care had to be taken that policies took account of their environmental implications.

In addition to analysis and background of selected issues the WDRs present an analysis of the global economy based on the Bank's models. A 1991 review confirmed that global projections tend to be on the optimistic side. The statistical annex presents data on both economic and social topics.

Cross-Country Analysis

Cross-country analysis utilizing the Bank's database has proven to be a fruitful area for research. In the 1970s Hollis B. Chenery (1979, 1986) published a number of studies on the patterns and sources of growth. The analysis of data in these studies could be used as input into the introduction of Bank country economic reports. But they lacked an analysis of causality. (In the language of Trygve Haavelmo and Tjalling Koopmans, they lacked "indentification.") They had little relation to Bank operational issues. However, the economics profession regarded these studies as an important contribution to development economics.

Another research area of considerable interest to the Bank was the study by Kravis, Summers, and Heston of the University of Pennsylvania on purchasing power parity comparisons based on the real value of family consumption and other elements (Summers and Heston 1988). These comparisons are of direct interest to the per capita income calculations that underlie the determination of whether or not a country can receive credits from the International Development Association, the lending arm of the World Bank that makes loans on concessionary terms. The Bank has collaborated with this study since the days of the Economics Department in the 1960s.

Statistical Publications

The statistical publications of the Bank also contribute to the development dialogue and to improvements in development analysis. In addition to the WDR tables already mentioned, the Bank publishes annually its *World Debt Tables*, a presentation of both public and private external debt. For each country this publication presents statistical details derived in part from the Bank's debt-reporting system which has been in operation since the 1940s. The main volume is accompanied by a summary volume that discusses major debt developments of interest to the economics profession and the financial community.

Perhaps the most popular statistical publication is the *World Bank Atlas*, which presents in attractive form data on GNP, population, demographics, and school enrollment for close to two hundred countries.

The Bank also publishes regularly a comprehensive volume of *World Tables* giving economic and social data on individual countries, based on the Bank's data files. On particular occasions it publishes specialized volumes such as the *World Population Projections* (1994), presented in connection with the 1994 UN International Conference on Population and Development in Cairo. The Bank maintains a database of twelve hundred projects on which cost-benefit calculations have been performed over the past twenty years.

The Bank's analytical work extends *well beyond* economics. Work is steadily proceeding on agricultural research in the context of the Consultative Group for International Agricultural Research (CGIAR). Application of medical research comes into play in the sub-Saharan project to fight river blindness. Problems of resettling people displaced by big dams and other large-scale projects raise issues that deserve the attention of anthropologists (now at work in the Environment Department).

Spreading the Word: Dissemination and Dialogue

The Bank's economic thinking and the results of its research are made known throughout the world through two main channels: dialogue with borrowers and associated contacts with co-lenders, and publication. In addition, the Bank's conferences and training courses enhance familiarity with its studies and publications. Officials of industrial countries who supervise Bank policy and operations must necessarily acquaint themselves with its analyses and methodology. Academic development courses throughout the world use World Bank material.[10]

Discussion of Bank economic, sector, and project reports is a major ongoing function of the Bank's methodologies and the results of research. Their discussion in various contexts cannot help but spread understanding of the analytical work underlying the Bank's economic and project work.

Quantifying this staff input is beyond the scope of this paper. It is probably gauged in the Bank's internal budgeting process. A very substantial effort, it covers each year over two hundred new projects and a hundred or so countries. Staff continues to be engaged in many ongoing projects. In many situations the Bank provides technical assistance for project preparation, which also helps countries become familiar with the Bank's methods. The discussions for each project and country involve numerous local experts and officials, many of whom become participants in the preparation of projects and programs and their subsequent execution.

Bank reports are also read and reviewed by bilateral aid agencies in the industrial countries. Many of these agencies do not have the staff to prepare their own reports and consequently rely on Bank reports for many of their operational decisions.

Against the very large staff input for preparation and discussion of Bank reports, the resources (about $7.5 million per year) devoted to publication are relatively modest. Yet by any comparison the Bank's

10. James Feather, director of World Bank Publications, provided helpful information on this topic.

publication effort is substantial. Each year the Bank distributes *one million books and papers*. Its publications catalogue lists *five hundred titles*. The Bank's program is the equivalent of the operation of a publishing house with a sales volume of $10 to $30 million. A sizable proportion is distributed by outside publishers (like Oxford University Press) that pay the Bank a royalty for each book sold. Commercial distribution of publications actually makes them available on a wider geographical scale (World Bank Annual Report 1994, 156).

The scope of the Bank's dissemination can also be told from the volume of distribution of some publications. For example, 120,000 copies of the WDR and 5,000 copies of the *World Debt Tables* are distributed each year; 21,500 copies of the Baum and Tolbert volume *Investing in Development* 1985 have been sold. The joint Fund-Bank quarterly *Finance and Development* has a circulation of more than a quarter of a million; more than half of the articles are written by Bank staff.

The Bank makes a special effort to bring its work to the attention of audiences in the developing countries. The bimonthly *Research Bulletin* has a distribution of 22,000 copies, of which 14,000 are sent to developing countries. The *World Bank Economic Review* and the *World Bank Research Observer* each has a distribution of over 15,000, of which 13,000 are distributed freely to developing countries. The Bank maintains 150 depository libraries in developing countries, containing all its publications.

The Bank's Annual Conference on Development Economics has, since the late 1980s, been another means of dissemination and interchange. The conference deals with one or two topics of current interest. Presentation and discussion of papers by outside experts and Bank staff make for effective interaction. In 1994 the conference focused on the transition in socialist economies and had participants from Eastern Europe and China as well as from development institutions and universities in both industrial and developing countries. The Bank also conducts conferences on special topics like those on the debt crisis in the 1980s.

No discussion of dissemination would be complete without mentioning the Economic Development Institute (EDI). It influences the nature and quality of policy discussions and administration in developing countries. In 1994 the Institute taught close to five thousand participants in 140 training programs around the world. The courses present general as well as project and sector economics. Most of them are based on studies prepared in the Bank or by outside experts on selected topics. Started in 1956, the Institute first dealt with questions of overall development and plan preparation. In the 1960s it began placing greater emphasis on general project planning and in the 1970s on particular sectors (education, transport, and urban development). After 1984 its general courses gained new importance. A number of EDI studies have been published and given wide circulation.[11]

Hence the Bank has, from its earliest days on, applied and taught its methodologies and approaches in its economic studies in many different ways. Many were directly related to operations and only indirectly motivated by dissemination. In the 1950s it started to publish its comprehensive country studies and opened its staff college, the EDI, to train officials in both general and project-specific methodologies. As the Bank's research and other analytical work became more diverse, its dissemination also expanded. Much of the Bank's publication is aimed at the developing countries. Its activities have now been expanded to the former socialist countries in Eastern Europe and Asia. It has significant interchange with experts in both industrial and relatively more advanced developing countries. In all, the Bank's dissemination matches the wide scope of its analytical work and development research.

Concluding Observations

The World Bank is an important center for development research and economics. While a large number of development economists are concentrated in the Bank many development experts are employed outside. Development research is undertaken in several industrial countries as well as some of the larger and relatively more advanced developing countries. But the Bank's influence is enhanced by its dissemination, training and technical assistance, its policy and projects discussions, and the distribution of its studies to centers of development research elsewhere and to universities and aid agencies.

It has spearheaded the use of price incentives in resource allocation while at the same time using (and building) government agencies for

---

11. Publications sponsored by the EDI include, for example, Economic Development Institute 1961; J. Price Gittinger, *Economic Analysis of Projects*, 1982 (15,600 copies printed); R. Dornbusch and F. L. Helmers, *The Open Economy: Tools for Policy Makers in Developing Countries*, 1988 (9,300 copies); and Gerald Meier, *Pricing Policy for Development Management*, 1983 (6,700 copies). (See Stern, table 6b; and *World Bank Research Program on Research*, December 1991.)

the preparation and execution of development plans and projects. Hence while the Bank is now committed to privatization it is decidedly not antigovernment, and while it has long practiced what came to be called supply-side economics it has done so in a balanced way without practicing the extremes of the latter-day converts in the eighties.

Nevertheless one can say that the Bank is only to a limited extent a creator of new ideas. It absorbs ideas from many places, integrates them in its operational practices, tests their practicality, and provides a forum for interchange among academics and government officials.

The Bank has shown considerable flexibility in its economic work. Thus in the early sixties the economic mission to Brazil concluded that, contrary to earlier thinking, effective investment was feasible in a moderately inflationary environment, and Bank research showed the conditions under which countries could tolerate relatively high levels of debt service without impairing their balance of payments management and growth. In the 1980s the Bank sought a better understanding of rural and urban development. At present the Bank is engaged in rewriting development economics to make explicit allowance for environmental considerations.

The focus of Bank research has shifted over time in response to the politics of its major shareholders, changes in general economic thinking, and experience in the execution of its programs and projects. In the first half of the 1980s research and WDRs emphasized efficient resource allocation to a greater extent than poverty alleviation. But by 1990 the Bank had returned to its roots by reemphasizing the fight against poverty. These shifting trends are not always clearly noticeable in the Bank's research publications at any one time. In practice the lag between new research and subsequent publication can be large. Moreover economic and project work, as well as research, must necessarily deal continuously with the basics of determining what constitutes sound investment and development policy.

The Bank has sometimes been rather slow in entering new fields. This was particularly true for environmental degradation. But the Bank now appears to be committed to environmental policy issues and finance. Environmental problems require a thorough rethinking of conventional economics. One can expect that the Bank will muster the resources required for this complex task. It should be a major new area for Bank research and applied economics work.

In other areas the Bank has tended to lag behind academic discussion. This occurred, for example, with the consideration of solutions to the debt crisis of the eighties. More than likely this hesitancy of the Bank was influenced by outside political factors such as the conviction of the Reagan administration that the debt crisis would be resolved through the free play of markets without intervention by the Bank. The Bank had, however, the knowledge to deal with the crisis. In fact, it organized two conferences on debt and continues to publish the most authoritative annual volume of debt analysis and data.

A considerable amount of research is proceeding in the relatively more advanced developing countries, for example India, Korea, the Philippines, and the Latin American countries. A major question is whether the Bank makes sufficient use of research in these countries. Some have argued that the Bank employs a disproportionate share of development research resources. On its part the Bank has made a substantial effort to disseminate the results of its economic analyses and research and sought to have an effective interchange with outside academicians. Yet Bank research makes only limited use of the resources of universities in developing countries and their scholars in the field. This is because in practice it has proven difficult to incorporate local talent of developing countries in projects directed from headquarters in Washington and to concentrate research on these projects in the developing countries themselves.

Anyone concerned with individual sectors can ask why more research is not undertaken in a particular field. Thus an institution like the Bank, dedicated to fighting poverty, that has been operating for fifty years should by now have a well-articulated position on how to reduce poverty in different circumstances and what kind of progress can reasonably be expected. Likewise the Bank's experience with restructuring capital-intensive industries, largely in the public sector, remains to be published. Nor has the Bank published its guidelines on what industries can be most competitive in small and relatively less developed countries. These and other questions deserve attention in the reshaping of research that will undoubtedly follow in the wake of the current emphasis on privatization and the experience with the transition from socialism to free markets.

The size and complexity of the Bank's research program and its application to project and country situations does not permit this paper to give a complete coverage of its economic output. For practical reasons this paper has given more emphasis to work on incentives, protection, and industrial development than the equally important fields of agriculture, rural and urban development, and transportation. This selectivity does not affect the nature of the above observations about the Bank's overall program.

The Bank has developed a highly diverse program of research and other analytical work. Its work covers many types of sectors and countries and has adapted to changing circumstances over time. It now extends to both developing countries and countries in transition from socialism. Development economics holds important lessons for both poor and rich countries alike. The Bank's dissemination, dialogue, training and technical assistance, and interchange with the academic profession have expanded with the scope of its analytical work. From the evidence presented here it is clear that the Bank is indeed a major player in the spread of development and international economics around the world.

References

Avramovic, D., et al. 1965. *Economic Growth and External Debt*. Baltimore, Md.: Johns Hopkins University Press.

Balassa, B., et al. 1971. *The Structure of Protection in Developing Countries*. Baltimore, Md.: Johns Hopkins University Press.

———. 1982. *Development Strategies in Semi-Industrial Countries*. Baltimore, Md.: Johns Hopkins University Press.

Baranson, Jack. 1969. *Automotive Industries in Developing Countries*. World Bank Staff Occasional Papers no. 8. Baltimore, Md.: Johns Hopkins University Press.

Baum, Warren C., and Stokes M. Tolbert. 1985. *Investing in Development: Lessons of World Bank Experience*. New York: Oxford University Press.

Chenery, H. B. 1979. *Structural Change and Development Policy*. New York: Oxford University Press.

———, with S. Robinson and M. Syrquin. 1986. *Industrialization and Growth: A Comparative Study*. Washington, D.C.: The World Bank.

Ciringiroglu, Ayhan. 1969. *Manufacture of Heavy Electrical Equipment in Developing Countries*. World Bank Staff Occasional Papers no. 9. Baltimore, Md.: Johns Hopkins University Press.

Corbo, Vittorio, with Morris Goldstein and Mohsin Kahn. 1987. *Growth-Oriented Adjustment Programs*. Washington, D.C.: International Monetary Fund and The World Bank.

Dasgupta, Partha S., S. Marglin, and A. Sen. 1972. *Guidelines for Project Evaluation*. New York: United Nations.

de Vries, Barend A. 1967. *The Export Experience of Developing Countries*. World Bank Staff Occasional Papers no. 3. Baltimore, Md.: Johns Hopkins University Press. (Also available in French from Dunod in Paris, and in Spanish from Editorial Tecnos in Madrid.)

———. 1971. *The Debt Bearing Capacity of Developing Countries: A Comparative*

Analysis. Rome: Banca Nazionale de Lavoro.

———. 1980a. *Transition Towards More Rapid and Labor Intensive Industrial Development: The Case of the Philippines*. New York: United Nations, Industry and Development.

———. 1980b. *Review of Industrial Sector Work*. 2 vols. *The Main Report* and *Country Summaries*. Washington, D.C.: The World Bank, Industrial Development and Finance Department.

———. 1983. International Ramifications of the External Debt Situation. *The AMEX Bank Review*, special paper no. 8.

———. 1984. Restructuring of Manufacturing Industry: The Case of the Textile Industry. *International Journal of Development Banking*.

Diwan, I., and I. Husain. 1989. *Dealing with the Debt Crisis*. Washington, D.C.: The World Bank.

Economic Development Institute. 1961. *Investment Criteria and Project Appraisal*. Washington, D.C.: The World Bank.

Grilli, E. R., and M. C. Yang. 1988. Primary Commodity Prices, Manufactured Goods Prices and the Terms of Trade of Developing Countries. What the Long Run Shows. *World Bank Economic Review* 2:1–47.

Leff, Nathaniel H. 1985. The Use of Policy Science Tools in Public-Sector Decision Making: Social Benefit-Cost Analysis in the World Bank. *Kyklos* 38:60–75.

Little, I. M. D., and J. A. Mirrlees. 1969. *Manual of Industrial Project Analysis in Developing Countries*. Paris: OECD Development Centre.

Little, I. M. D., Tibor Scitovsky, and Maurice Scott. 1970. *Industry and Trade in Some Developing Countries*. London: Oxford University Press.

McNamara, Robert S. 1981. *The McNamara Years at the World Bank*. Baltimore, Md.: Johns Hopkins University Press.

Michaely, Michael. 1977. Export and Growth: An Empirical Investigation. *Journal of Development Economics* 4. 1 (March): .

Papagiorgiou, Demetris, Michael Michaely, and Armeane M. Choksi, eds. 1991. *Liberalizing Foreign Trade*. Oxford: Blackwell.

Ray, A. 1984. *Cost-Benefit Analysis: Issues and Methodologies*. Baltimore, Md.: Johns Hopkins University Press.

Rhee, Yung Whee, et al. 1984. *Korea's Competitive Edge: Managing the Entry into World Markets*. Baltimore, Md.: Johns Hopkins University Press.

Squire, L., and H. G. van der Tak. 1975. *Economic Analysis of Projects*. Baltimore, Md.: Johns Hopkins University Press.

Stern, Nicholas, with Francisco Ferreira. Forthcoming. The World Bank as Intellectual Actor. Draft chapter for the World Bank history.

Summers, R., and A. Heston. 1988. A New Set of International Comparisons of Real Product and Price Levels, Estimates for 130 Countries. *Review of Income and Wealth*, series 26, 1:19–66.

Tyler, William. 1981. Growth and Export Expansion in Developing Countries. *Journal of Development Economics*. 9. 1 (August): 121–30.

World Bank. 1977. *Manufacturing Export Industries in Portugal*. Report no. 1695a.

————. 1980. *Philippines: Industrial Development Strategy and Policies*. A World Bank Country Study.

————. 1990. *Setting Research Priorities at the World Bank: An Historical Review*. Report SecM 90-1215.

————. 10 January 1994. *Report on the World Bank Research Program*. R94-2, IDA R94-2.

————. 1994. *The World Bank Research Program, 1994, Abstract of Current Studies*.

————. 1995. *Index of Publications*.

————. Various years. *World Development Report*. [WDR.] New York: Oxford University Press.

The Development of Economic Thought at the European Community Institutions

Ivo Maes

Introduction

This paper is an attempt at a "rational reconstruction" of the development of economic thought at the European Community institutions.[1] A basic problem that one encounters is that the European Community is a very special construction, an entity sui generis, as lawyers like to say. It is neither a federation nor an intergovernmental organization, but rather something between the two.

It is an intergovernmental organization to the degree that changes in the treaties governing the EC have to be approved by all countries after an intergovernmental conference. However, within the areas designated in the treaties, it can exercise sovereign powers and, through time, the influence of the commission (its executive) has been growing.

Delineating the development of economic thought at the EC institutions then is not easy. It should certainly comprise the development of ideas at the commission. However, this will not suffice. National initiatives and study groups with representatives of the different countries have

I would like to thank F. Abraham, A. W. Coats, S. Deroose, M. Fase, F. Ilzkovitz, A. Italianer, M. Mors, J. Mortensen, A. Saether, P. Van der Haegen, and J. Vanginderachter for comments on previous drafts. The usual disclaimers apply.

1. In this paper the term "European Community" is used. The Maastricht Treaty institutes the "European Union," which not only comprises the "Community" but also the intergovernmental cooperation on foreign and defense policy and justice and interior policy. Here the term "European Community" is preferred, as the focus of this paper is on economic matters.

Table 1   Institutions of the European Community and Staff Numbers, Budget 1995

Parliament	3,827
Council	2,379
Economic and Social Committee and Committee of the Regions	661
Commission	19,667
Court of Justice	837
Court of Auditors	458

Source: *Official Journal of the European Communities* 369.37. 31 December 1994, p. 153.

played an important role in the development of the EC and the thinking at its institutions. In this paper, a more encompassing approach, taking into account the work of important study groups, is taken.

The paper starts with an overview of the institutions of the EC, with a special focus on the role of economists in the commission, in sections 1 and 2. Economic thought at the EC institutions is, to an important extent, centered around the notion of integration, which is the topic of the third section. Then the development of economic thought at the EC institutions, in relation to the actual process of integration, is presented. This is followed by an overview of elements of continuity and change and an assessment of international influences.

1. The Institutions of the European Community

The major institutions of the European Community are the parliament, the council, the commission, and the Court of Justice[2] (see table 1). The European Parliament consists of the representatives of the people of the member states; since 1979, they have been elected by direct universal suffrage. The parliament has advisory and supervisory powers; however, its supervisory powers are limited to the commission, and not to the council. The parliament has to approve the budget of the EC. It has certain legislative powers, which were extended with the Maastricht Treaty. The council is made up of representatives of the governments of the mem-

2. Smaller institutions are the Economic and Social Committee and the Court of Auditors. With the Maastricht Treaty, a Committee of Regions was created. For an overview, see Noël 1993.

ber states. It is the main decision-making institution of the EC. Since 1974 there have also been regular meetings of the heads of state or government (the "European Council") where the general guidelines for the development of the EC are set out. The commission consists of twenty members, appointed by agreement between the member governments. They have to act in complete independence and in the general interest of the EC. It has three main functions: (a) guardian of the treaties, to ensure that the provisions of the treaties and the decisions of the institutions are properly implemented; (b) executive arm of the EC; (c) initiator of EC policy. The commission has the sole right to present proposals and drafts for EC legislation. The Court of Justice ensures that the implementation of the treaties is in accordance with the rule of law.

As the commission is the largest EC institution and as it has a crucial role in the initiation and execution of EC policy, the functioning of the commission and the role of economists therein will be analyzed in greater detail in the next section.

2. The Functioning of the Commission and the Role of Economists

The term "commission" is used both for the College of the Commission, the body of twenty commissioners, and for the services of the commission, the administration.

While the College of the Commission is a collegiate body, each member has a special responsibility for some part of the institution's work and for the services dealing with these areas. Each commissioner has a personal staff, called a cabinet, which works directly with him.[3]

The services of the commission consist of the Secretariat-General, twenty-two Directorate-Generals, and some specific services (see appendix 1 for an overview of the organigram). Important posts in the administration (director-general, deputy director-general, and director) are allocated according to a quota system by nationality. There is a remarkable continuity in the occupation of senior positions by nationality. Thus the director-general of DG VI (Agriculture) has typically been a Frenchman, the director-general of DG IV (Competition) a German, and so on. The higher the position, the greater the possibility that a vacancy will be filled by somebody from outside the commission, with the appropriate nationality. The lower the position, the less important these

---

3. For an insight in the functioning of the Delors cabinet, see Ross 1994.

influences. However, even at junior positions, there is very great concern for "equilibria," so that the different countries of the EC should be represented.

The commission administration is certainly more heterogeneous than national administrations, as diversity is one of the main characteristics of the EC. This diversity, in terms of nationality, language, political opinion, trade union membership, and so on, is naturally reflected in the commission and contributes to a more complex and heterogeneous informal structure and "enterprise culture." Generally, personnel are often together with people of the same nationality or language. There are also different "networks." One of the most famous was certainly the Delors network. As Grant (1994, 104) remarked: "Any official who is French, socialist and competent, with a useful area of expertise, is almost certain to be invited into the Delors network. Anyone with a couple of those qualities would be seriously considered, as long as one of them is competence." Another network, of a very different nature, is the so-called Brugge network of the graduates of the College of Europe, a famous graduate school in European studies in the Belgian town of Bruges, who keep excellent contacts with each other.

An economist in the commission can fulfill a job as a general administrator or as a "professional economist." The need for specialist economic expertise by the commission is clearly recognized, as there are special recruitment competitions for economists. However, economists in the commission seem, qua methodology and worldview, to be a more heterogeneous group than economists at international institutions like the IMF or the World Bank, where many graduated from American universities. This compares with a still more important diversity among European universities qua economic methodology and Weltanschauung. So, as a general rule, British economists are more free-market oriented and Frenchmen more activist; Germans are typically more concerned with questions of economic order and policies necessary for the functioning of a free-market economy (e.g., competition policy).

A prime place for professional economists is DG II, Economic and Financial Affairs (see appendix 2), which can be considered the economic research department of the commission. In DG II, attention is given to both macroeconomic issues (mainly directorates A, National economies; C, surveillance of the EC economy; D, monetary matters; and F, international economic and financial matters), as well as to sectoral aspects of EC policy (mainly directorates B, economic service, and E, financial instruments and capital movements). An important outlet for the results of their analysis is *European Economy*, a publication of the services of the commission. Inside the commission administration, the economists of DG II have the reputation of being a relatively homogeneous group, free-market oriented and fairly conservative.

To get a better idea of economists at DG II and their educational background, I organized a short survey. Of the 130 A staff (university graduates) 74 replied.[4] As far as I can judge the sample seems representative. A few important features of the survey are (cf. table 2):

- 47 out of 74 economists studied abroad (64 percent); this is an indication of the existence of a kind of mutual attraction beween people who studied abroad and international institutions
- 28 economists had a Ph.D. (38 percent), while a few others were still working on it; 21 of them had studied abroad, not necessarily for their Ph.D.s
- the Belgians are very well represented, 11 out of 74; elements of explanation are the relatively high commission salaries and the location of DG II in Brussels
- economists from the southern countries (Italy, Spain, and Greece) are fairly well represented and have mostly studied abroad; this could be an indication of a lack of well-qualified positions for persons with an advanced education in these countries

To obtain a better insight into the internationalization and Americanization process, a classification according to age group, distinguishing between European and American universities, is presented (table 3). A few remarks:

- one clearly notes the internationalization process: younger economists were more likely to have studied abroad than older economists
- DG II economists had a clear preference for studying in a "foreign" European country rather than in America; however, the American share is slightly higher among younger economists
- among the European countries, Belgium was the most popular (13), due to the attractiveness of the College of Europe in Brugge

4. Not all the A staff at DG II are economists. However, the number of noneconomists is rather limited.

Table 2   Economists at DG II: Educational Background According to Nationality

	Economists	Studied abroad*	Ph.D.
Belgium	11	4	1
Denmark	4	1	0
France	6	4	4
Germany	17	13	10
Greece	5	5	1
Ireland	3	1	1
Italy	8	7	2
Netherlands	5	3	3
Portugal	2	1	0
Spain	8	7	4
United Kingdom	5	1	2
Total	74	47	28

Source. Based on a survey of the A staff of DG II; 74 out of 130 replied.

*Studied abroad—a European country different from the country of origin, or the United States or Canada; not always leading to a degree.

Table 3   Economists at DG II: Educational Background According to Age Group

	Total	Studied abroad	Studied in America*	Studied in a "foreign" European country	Ph.D.
50 and above	16	9	3	6	9
40–49	19	9	3	7	5
below 40	39	29	12	20	14
Total	74	47**	18	33	28

Source. Based on a survey of the A staff of DG II; 74 out of 130 replied.

*America = United States and Canada.

**The total number of economists who studied abroad is lower than the sum of America and "foreign" European countries, as there are four people who studied both in America and in a "foreign" European country.

(8 graduates); then followed the United Kingdom (10), France (9), and Italy and Germany (4 each)
- among the American universities, the University of Chicago was the most popular, with 3 graduates in the sample

Other services that, to different degrees, use specialist economic expertise are the Statistical Office, DG I (External Relations), DG III (Industry), DG IV (Competition), DG V (Employment, Industrial Relationships, and Social Affairs), DG VI (Agriculture), DG VII (Transport), DG VIII (Development), DG XIII (Telecommunications, Information Industries, and Innovation), DG XV (Internal Market and Financial Institutions), DG XVI (Regional Policies), DG XVII (Energy), and DG XXIII (Enterprises' Policy, Distributive Trades, Tourism, and Social Economy).[5]

In general, however, the commission services are administrative and legally oriented. Typical is that, until recently, there were only a few economists in DG IV (Competition), which was dominated by lawyers. During recent years there has been a tendency to use more economists, especially in services related to the internal market and external relations. The commissioners Cockfield and Brittan, both British, played a stimulating role in this. The growing use of economic expertise is also reflected in a greater economic input in policy preparation in these areas.

A not atypical career for an economist in the commission is to start in DG II. After some years, there comes a move to another DG or a cabinet, where he will become the economic specialist. Later, he will move further to a more administrative job, higher up in the hierarchy, if his career goes well.[6] However, even for so-called professional economists there are some important differences between economics at the commission and academic economics.[7] The reason is that the commission is a policy-oriented institution, where certain qualities of academic economics are less useful. Instead, other characteristics are at a premium:

- being a good team member, also with noneconomists. There are limits to "independent originality": as remarked by one observer, "Economists working in government service have a vested interest

5. I have the impression that, in comparison to other international organizations (cf. Coats 1986), relatively more economists in the EC work as general administrators than as economic experts.

6. A not atypical phenomenon in a government service (cf. Coats 1981, 10).

7. I draw here largely on the comparison that George Baldwin makes between academic economics and economics in the World Bank (in Coats 1986, 116).

in promoting consensus on basic issues of economic analysis. Academics, on the other hand, while they must ride with the tide, have a vested interest in differentiating their product" (Marris 1986, 109)

- quick judgment, as there is less time for in-depth analysis of problems
- good communication skills: writing clear and accessible papers and achieving consensus in meetings; this can be different from "academic brilliance"
- emphasis on empirical work, with special attention to the method-ology of the statistics

Hereby, one should stress that "skills in communication and the art of persuasion are generally at a premium in international agencies, given their limited powers" (Coats 1986, 167). However, also to have an impact inside a multinational (and multilingual) organization, communication and negotiation skills are more important than in national organizations.[8] Marris's remarks about the OECD apply equally well to the European Commission: " 'good economics' merges almost imperceptibly into the art of persuasion" (1986, 113).

Economists at the commission can really work as economists, and some have been offered certain positions because of their specialist eco-nomic expertise. However, it was mostly stressed that decisions were political compromises. A not unimportant function of economists, then, is to produce arguments that justify political decisions. This primacy of politics leads sometimes to frustrations among economists.[9]

Recently economists have been taking a more important role in the preparation of EC policy in certain areas. Examples are competition pol-icy and environmental policy, where, under the influence of economists, there is a greater concern for the costs and benefits of alternative instru-ments to attain certain objectives.

3. Some Remarks on the Notion of Integration

As expressed in the preamble to the Maastricht Treaty, the purpose of the European Community is to stimulate the process of European integration. However, the notion of integration is difficult to define.

8. As also remarked by Delors (cf. Hay 1989, 17).
9. An example is certainly the Common Agricultural Policy.

As Tinbergen remarked, economic integration concerns the regulation of international relations. As such it is in essence a question of the organization of economic policy: "Integration may be said to be the creation of the most desirable structure of international economy, removing artificial hindrances to the optimal operation and introducing deliberately all desirable elements of co-ordination or unification. The problem of integration therefore forms part of a more general problem, namely that of the *optimum economic policy*" (1954, 95; original italics).

A crucial question in the organization of economic policy is the degree of centralization. This is intimately connected with the question of economic integration: "Which functions in international economic life should be subject to central control and which should be left to individual countries, enterprises or persons?" (Tinbergen 1954, 98).

The appropriate degree of centralization of instruments of economic policy (containing both elements of coordination and harmonization) depends on the spillover effects they provoke, "their effect on the well-being of each of the countries concerned" (Tinbergen 1954, 98). In general, Tinbergen argues, there is a strong case for decentralization, as it gives more freedom to the economic agents. The strongest arguments for centralization apply to instruments with important spillover effects.

This corresponds to the "subsidiarity principle," which is actually a fundamental criterion by which to judge the appropriateness of EC action. It is enshrined in the Maastricht Treaty. This subsidiarity principle states that "functions should be allocated to the lowest level of government, unless welfare gains can be reaped by assigning it to the next higher level" (cf. Van Rompuy et al. 1991, 111).

European integration is a very important political decision, as it implies a transfer of sovereignty from the member state to a supranational authority. This means that there is a transfer of decision making to common institutions and a corresponding limitation of the areas of decision making remaining with the individual state (cf. Louis 1990, 11).

With the formation of the European Community the emphasis is on a concept of sovereignty consistent with sovereignty being divisible. Transfers of sovereignty are not to be seen in quantitative terms, like surrendering territory. Rather, the focus is on partial transfers of jurisdiction: power and responsibility for certain broad areas are transferred from the member state to the EC (cf. Louis 1990, 13).

The integration process can have two dimensions: deepening and widening. Deepening implies a more thoroughgoing integration, bringing more areas into the sphere of the EC and strengthening its institutions. Widening entails opening the EC to new members (cf. Maes 1991). In this paper, the widening of the European Community will not be analyzed. However, one should remark that different rounds of enlargements have made the European Community more heterogeneous, both from an economic and social point of view and from a more political view. With respect to the deepening of economic integration, different phases can be distinguished (cf. Balassa 1961). They are characterized by an increasing transfer of sovereignty from the national state to the supranational authority:

1. Free-trade area: tariffs and quotas are abolished among the participants; there is no common external trade policy
2. Customs union: conditions of a free-trade area plus a common external trade policy
3. Common market: not only free movement of goods and services (customs union) but also free movement of factors of production (labor and capital)
4. Economic union: characteristics of a common market and also a harmonization of economic policy
5. Economic and monetary union: not only an economic union, but also fixed exchange rates and a coordination of monetary policy, and eventually a common currency

4. A Brief Historical Overview

Toward a European Economic Community[10]

The Second World War marked a turning point in European history. It was a catastrophe that led to an almost complete collapse of Europe. It also discredited the previous international order, based on the nation-state.

In this atmosphere, initiatives at European integration flourished. Crucial was the Schuman Declaration, which laid the basis for the European Coal and Steel Community. The gist of the proposal was explained in these terms: "the French Government proposes to take action immediately on one limited but decisive point . . . to place Franco-German production of coal and steel under a common High Authority, within the framework of an organization open to the participation of the other

10. For a succinct chronology of European integration, see appendix 1.

countries of Europe. . . . The solidarity in production thus established will make it plain that any war between France and Germany becomes not merely unthinkable, but materially impossible . . . this proposal will build the first concrete foundation of a European federation which is indispensable to the preservation of peace. . . . " In 1951 France, Germany, Italy, Belgium, Luxembourg, and the Netherlands signed the Treaty of Paris that established the European Coal and Steel Community.

The next step was the formation of the European Economic Community and the European Atomic Energy Community (EAEC) in 1958. The European Economic Community provided for the creation of a common market (with free movement of goods, services, labor, and capital), several common policies, the coordination of economic policy and the establishment of institutions to improve social and regional cohesion. The objective of the EAEC was to strengthen cooperation in the nuclear industry. However, with the coming to power of de Gaulle in France in 1958, it was increasingly marginalized as it came too close to the heart of France's national sovereignty: the nuclear "force de frappe" (cf. Pinder 1991, 10).[11]

For a better understanding of the philosophy behind the Community and the treaties it may be useful to give a short overview of the major differences in economic paradigms and national interests in France and Germany, the two crucial countries. Economic policies in France and Germany in the first decades following the war were based on quite different conceptual frameworks, even if both were embedded in a social market economy. France followed a more dirigiste economic policy (cf. Schor 1993, 6). Key elements were the nationalization of crucial sectors of the economy and a policy of indicative planning. In 1945 firms in the credit, energy, and transport sectors were nationalized. In 1947 the first plan was launched, under the instigation of Jean Monnet. It determined the main orientations of the economy and, while providing incentives, remained indicative. While it can be situated in the French tradition of *colbertisme*, the French planning office was also a spearhead of Keynesianism in France, with the national accounts at its heart (cf. Rosanvallon 1987, 40).

In Germany economic policy was more market oriented, under the inspiration of Ludwig Erhard (1943). The main task of economic policy

11. This is somewhat ironic, as it was just France that had been pushing for the EAEC (cf. Monnet 1976, 627).

was to create a secure and unobtrusive legal and financial framework within which markets could operate efficiently (cf. Lipschitz and Mayer 1988, 370). Following this *Ordnungspolitik* the main tasks of economic policy are: (a) monetary policy: ensure the stability of prices and the currency; a strong and independent central bank is appropriate; (b) fiscal policy: rather limited tasks for the government; and (c) structural policy: a more passive role; competition policy is emphasized. As concerning differences in national interests, one can remark that Germany was a more industrial country, while in France the agricultural sector was relatively more important.

From this background it is easier to understand the blueprint and the equilibria in the treaties. The creation of a common market was strongly favored by the Germans. In line with ordo-liberal thinking competition policy was an important feature of the common market. The common agricultural policy and the EAEC were due more to French inspiration.

A Blueprint for Monetary Union

Monetary union was not one of the original objectives of the European Economic Community. The chapters on macroeconomic policy in the Treaty of Rome were rather sketchy. Two factors can, to a large extent, explain this emphasis. First, the international monetary system, established at Bretton Woods, provided a stable monetary framework for the Community. Second, the creation of a customs union was already considered to be a far-reaching objective.

At the Hague Summit of December 1969 an ambitious program to stimulate European integration was adopted. Several factors contributed to the change in atmosphere that placed economic and monetary union at the center of attention:

- the successful completion of the customs union and, somewhat less satisfactorily, the common agricultural policy before the end of 1969. A new thrust forward seemed necessary to maintain the momentum and even to avoid retrogression.
- disenchantment with the central place of the American dollar in the Bretton Woods system. There was a sentiment, especially nourished by the French, that the EC needed its own "monetary individuality" (cf. Bloomfield 1973, 11).
- fear about the future of the fixed exchange rate system, also in

the European Community. The May 1968 events in France contributed to severe exchange crises, leading to a devaluation of the French franc and a revaluation of the German mark in 1969. The EC feared that further exchange rate instability could lead to the disintegration of the customs union and the demise of the common agricultural policy.

- the coming to power of new political leaders. In 1969 General de Gaulle resigned and Pompidou was elected president of France. He and his finance minister, Giscard d'Estaing, followed a more pro-European policy. The other major event was the formation of a new government in Germany by the Social Democrats and the Free Democrats with Willy Brandt as chancellor. The Brandt government supported the EMU project, one of the reasons being the need to counterbalance its *Ostpolitik* (recognition of the German Democratic Republic).

At the Hague Summit the heads of state and government requested the council to draw up a plan with a view to the creation of an economic and monetary union. A committee, chaired by the Luxembourg prime minister Pierre Werner, produced a report in October 1970 (Council-Commission of the European Communities 1970, hereafter referred to as the Werner Report). It contained a program for the establishment by stages of an economic and monetary union by 1980.

The Werner Report first presented a very general picture of economic and monetary union: "Economic and monetary union will make it possible to realize an area within which goods and services, people and capital will circulate freely and without competitive distortions, without thereby giving rise to structural or regional disequilibrium" (1970, 9). A monetary union is more closely defined as implying "total and irreversible convertibility of currencies, the elimination of margins of fluctuation in exchange rates, the irrevocable fixing of parity rates, and the complete liberation of movements of capital" (10). The establishment of a single currency for the EC is not considered necessary, even though it would stress the irreversible character of the monetary union. To assure the functioning of the economic and monetary union two elements are necessary: transfers of responsibility from the national to the EC level and a harmonization of the instruments of economic policy in various sectors. On the institutional plane, this implied the existence of two EC organs: a center of decision for economic policy and an EC system for the central banks. However, the report did not elaborate very much on these structures.

The Werner Report also underlined the fundamental political significance of the transfer of responsibilities to the EC level: "These transfers of responsibility and the creation of the corresponding Community institutions represent a process of fundamental political significance which entails the progressive development of political cooperation. The economic and monetary union thus appears as a leaven for the development of political union which in the long run it will be unable to do without" (26).

The Werner Report proposed three stages on the path to economic and monetary union. It did not lay down a precise timetable for the whole of the plan; rather it wanted to maintain a measure of flexibility, while concentrating on the first phase. Its main elements were: (a) a reinforcement of procedures for consultation and policy coordination; (b) a further liberalization of intra-EC capital movements and steps toward an integrated European capital market; and (c) a narrowing of exchange rate fluctuations between EC currencies. Of the second stage the report noted that it "will be characterized by the promotion on a number of fronts and on ever more restrictive lines of the action undertaken during the first stage" (28).

Of fundamental importance in the Werner Report is the concept of "parallel progress." This notion formed a compromise between the "monetarists" (favoring a narrowing of exchange rate fluctuations, mainly represented by France) and the "economists" (emphasizing the coordination of economic policies, and led by Germany). This notion enabled the Werner group to present a unanimous report (cf. Tsoukalis 1977, 101).

The Werner Report formed the basis for a first attempt at economic and monetary union in the early 1970s. However, it was not very successful, as noted in the Marjolin Report: "if there has been any movement it has been backward" (Commission of the European Communities 1975, 1). Two factors played an important role in the failure of the Werner Report: changes in the international environment and lack of political will.

The early 1970s saw the final collapse of the Bretton Woods system. Exchange rate instability increased dramatically, increasing also the tensions between the European countries. Pressures were further exacerbated by the oil price shock of October 1973. The lack of political will became very clearly apparent with the oil shock. Policymakers, thinking in terms of Phillips curves as a theoretical framework, concentrated on national objectives, while policy harmonization and coordination were put aside. It led to growing divergencies among the economies of the EC.

The 1970s and early 1980s can be seen as a period of stagnation. The main accomplishment was the creation of the European Monetary System (EMS) in March 1979. It was to a large degree a Franco-German initiative with the German chancellor (Helmut Schmidt) and the French president (Valérie Giscard d'Estaing) as the main architects.[12] The aim of the EMS was much more limited than the earlier attempt at monetary union. The objective was to create a zone of monetary stability; changes in exchange rates would still be possible, but subject to mutual consent.

On the whole, the EMS has functioned better than most experts had expected. The basic reason was a major change in the conception of economic policy at the end of the 1970s and the early 1980s: away from a policy of fine-tuning and toward a stability-oriented policy (cf. Baer and Padoa-Schioppa 1988, 58).

The Delors Decade

Before Jacques Delors became president of the European Commission at the beginning of 1985, he toured the member states, discussing ideas to relaunch European integration. A renewed campaign for a European internal market emerged as the most favored option, as it fit in with the general tendency toward deregulation, which had received a strong impetus with the Reagan presidency in the United States (cf. Colchester 1988, 6).

Delors sensed there was a favorable constellation of forces to push forward European integration. Lord Cockfield, the British commissioner for the Internal Market, prepared the famous "White Paper" (Commission of the European Communities, 1985), which identified existing barriers and presented a program of policy measures to remove them. A list of nearly three hundred directives was drawn up to eliminate these barriers and unify the European market. Moreover, a hectic timetable was laid out to have these directives adopted by the end of the next commission's reign, December 1992.

The 1992 program was adopted by the EC. It became a treaty obligation with the adoption of the Single European Act in 1986, the first major revi-

12. For a fascinating overview of the origins of the EMS, see Ludlow 1982.

sion of the founding treaties of the EC. The act extended greatly the scope of the EC and simplified the decision-making process. It constituted an early and crucial triumph for the 1992 project and further contributed to the renewed momentum of the EC. Moreover, the internal market program was also part of a more general economic policy strategy of the commission, aimed at improving the microeconomic foundations of the economy (cf. Mortensen 1990, 31). Other important elements of this strategy were wage moderation, budgetary consolidation, and increasing the flexibility of markets.

The European Community continued on this élan. At the summit meeting in Hanover in June 1988, economic and monetary union was brought back on the agenda. The heads of state or government decided to set up a committee with the task of studying and proposing concrete steps leading to economic and monetary union. This committee, mainly composed of central bank governors and chaired by Jacques Delors, produced its report in April 1989 (Committee for the Study of Economic and Monetary Union, hereafter referred to as the Delors Report). The Delors Report became crucial as a reference and anchor point in further discussions, just as the Werner Report had been nearly two decades earlier. The report basically revolved around two questions: What economic arrangements are necessary for a monetary union to be successful? What gradualist path should be designed to reach economic and monetary union? (cf. Padoa-Schioppa 1990, 22).

In defining the necessary conditions for a monetary union, the Delors Report referred back to the Werner Report. On the institutional level, the report proposed the creation of a European system of central banks. To attain economic and monetary union the committee proposed three stages; however, it underlined the indivisibility of the whole process: "the decision to enter upon the first stage should be a decision to embark on the entire process" (1970, 31). The committee's three phases, in contrast to the Werner Report's emphasis on the first stage, were all worked out in considerable detail. These stages imply, from an institutional and legal point of view: the preparation of a new treaty (first stage), the creation of a new monetary institution (European system of central banks, second stage), and the transfer of responsibilities to this new institution (third stage). From an economic and monetary point of view, these stages entailed an increased convergence and a closer coordination of economic policy.

The procedure to revise the treaties formally started in December 1990 with the opening of two intergovernmental conferences, one on economic and monetary union and one on political union. These conferences were concluded in December 1991, at the Maastricht Summit of the heads of state or government. The new treaty was, after long discussions, ratified by the member states in the second half of 1993.

The Treaty of Maastricht marks a step forward for the European Community on a par with the Treaty of Rome. It creates a so-called European Union, which is based on three pillars. The first is the old EC, but with greatly extended responsibilities. The main element is economic and monetary union. The treaty specifies the future monetary constitution of the EC, including the statute of the European Central Bank. To strengthen the economic and social cohesion of the union a cohesion fund will be set up. Also, the path to economic and monetary union is specified. Crucial is the fixing of a deadline, the first of January 1999 at the latest, for the third phase (the irrevocable fixing of the exchange rates or the introduction of the ecu). The second pillar is for foreign and security policy. The third concerns cooperation on such topics as immigration, asylum, and policing. These pillars will be intergovernmental bodies in which the commission, parliament, and court have a more restricted say.

Looking back one can notice a hectic and thoroughgoing integration process in the 1980s and the beginning of the 1990s. Two important factors contributed to this deepening process: the logic and momentum of the integration process, whereby integration in one area sets in motion forces that induce integration in other areas (e.g., from one market to one money); and the power of federalist forces, aiming at European integration. Essential was the strongly pro-European attitude of France and Germany, which together constituted a powerful axis. Important also was the increased role of the European Commission under the leadership of Jacques Delors.

5. Change and Continuity

Economic thought at the European Community institutions revolves, in essence, around the process of economic integration. It is closely related to economic policy, as one of the main aims is to develop an appropriate strategy to stimulate the integration process in the EC. This has some important implications:

- It is a highly "political economy" theory, as integration implies a transfer of sovereignty from the national to the European level.

The political economy dimension comes to the fore as different countries have different ideas on how to pursue European integration. These differences among countries are based on differences in both national interests and economic thought.

- the development of economic thought is largely a function of the actual situation, the quest for an appropriate strategy, and the need to support the integration process with well-documented studies. When the internal market program was elaborated, the commission produced a report, "The Economics of 1992" (Commission of the European Communities 1988), on the impact of completing the internal market. In 1990, just before the start of the intergovernmental conference on economic and monetary union, the commission published a report, "One Market, One Money" (1990), on the potential benefits and costs of an economic and monetary union.

In considering these past decades of development of economic thought at the European Community institutions one observes some important continuities, especially the tension between the logic of integration and the attachment to national sovereignty and the recurring debate between "monetarists" and "economists" about the appropriate strategy toward monetary union. The most important shift occurred at the end of the 1970s with the move from a more activist to a more structural and stability-oriented conceptual framework.

The Tension between the Logic of Integration
and the Attachment to National Sovereignty

Starting a process of integration sets in motion forces that push for a further deepening of integration. This was noted early in the theory of economic integration.[13] For example, the formation of a customs union will limit the scope of fiscal policy in a participating country, as taxes and subsidies affect trade flows. The quest for monetary integration in the EC was to a large extent motivated by the desire to consolidate and extend the achievements of the common market and the common agricultural policy (cf. Giavazzi and Giovannini 1989, 12). However, the attachment

13. Examples are Viner 1950, 136, and Meade 1953, 27; cf. Maes 1994.

to national sovereignty was a crucial element in the failure of several attempts at integration:

- the plans for the European Defense Community were rejected by the French parliament
- the European Atomic Energy Community was marginalized by de Gaulle as it was too close to France's nuclear force de frappe
- a crucial element in the failure of the Werner Report was the priority given to national policy objectives after the first oil shock
- the common market was eroded in the 1970s and first half of the 1980s as countries favored their own companies through subsidies and government contracts
- the ratification of the Maastricht Treaty was seriously delayed as some countries, especially Denmark and the United Kingdom, were reluctant to accept a new transfer of sovereignty

This tension between sovereignty and integration is also reflected in discussions on the concept of subsidiarity and its application.

The Strategy of Monetary Integration

In the discussions about how to proceed with monetary integration, it is customary to discern two basic approaches: the "monetarist" and the "economist." These terms have a very specific content in the monetary integration debate, which is very different from their use in other contexts.

According to the "monetarists," monetary integration will have a stimulating effect on the integration process. The stabilizing of exchange rates will induce a convergence of economic policies and performances. Monetary integration will stimulate economic and political integration. These views were mostly held in France, Italy, and at the European Commission.

It is noteworthy that in the European Commission monetary matters were to a large extent the responsibility of French and Italian officials. Also, the member of the commission responsible for monetary matters was often French: for example, R. Barre, F.-X. Ortoli, J. Delors, Y.-T. de Silgy. The director-general of DG II, Economic and Financial Affairs, was usually Italian: U. Mosca, T. Padoa-Schioppa, M. Russo, A. Costa, G. Ravasio; the director for Monetary Matters was usually French: F. Boyer de la Giroday, J.-P. Mingasson, J.-F. Pons, H. Carré.

There were also moments of close cooperation between the commission, France, and Italy on monetary integration, as during the discussions of the Delors committee on economic and monetary union. So Delors asked Ciampi and de Larosière, the governors of the Banca d'Italia and the Banque de France, to speak on his behalf during the meetings of the committee (cf. Grant 1994, 123).

Another important figure was Tommaso Padoa-Schioppa, who was director-general of DG II at the end of the 1970s and the early 1980s. At that period he got to know Delors, who was then chairman of the economic and monetary committee of the European Parliament. After his stay in Brussels, Padoa-Schioppa returned to the Banca d'Italia. When Delors became president of the commission, he requested a report by a study group, chaired by Padoa-Schioppa, on the implications of the internal market for the future of the EC (Padoa-Schioppa 1987). It contained a warning that the liberation of capital movements was inconsistent with the prevalent combination of exchange rate stability and national autonomy of monetary policy. According to Grant (1994, 199), Padoa-Schioppa was the man who convinced Delors that the time was ripe for a push for economic and monetary union.

Unlike the "monetarists," the "economists" emphasize the differences among countries in inflation, productivity, and government finances. They stress that a convergence of economic performances and economic policy is a necessary condition for monetary integration. Without sufficient convergence the fixing of the exchange rate could break down or lead to important regional problems. Monetary integration can only be the crowning act of a process of economic integration. These ideas were most prominent in Germany, especially at the Bundesbank (cf. Bundesbank 1994, 26).

Proposals for monetary integration in the EC were typically a compromise and synthesis of these two positions:

- Of fundamental importance in the Werner Report is the notion of "parallel progress" in the development of both monetary unification and the harmonization and unification of economic policies (Werner Report, 26). This notion enabled the Werner group to present a unanimous report (cf. Tsoukalis 1977, 101).
- The exchange rate mechanism of the EMS should form the basis of a system of fixed exchange rates, which portrays a monetarist signature. However, the fixity of exchange rates is diluted through

the existence of margins of fluctuation and the possibility of re-alignments.

- The Maastricht Treaty contains several deadlines; the most important is 1 January 1999 as the ultimate date for the third and final phase of monetary union (article 109J). This makes the transition to a monetary union as irreversible as possible. However, at the same time, the so-called convergence criteria concerning inflation, public finance, exchange rates, and long-term interest rates have to be satisfied (also article 109J).

The Shift from a More Activist to a More Stability-Oriented Economic Policy

At the end of the 1970s a shift occurred in Europe from a more activist policy to a strategy based on medium-term stability, market-oriented policies, and emphasis on measures enforcing the supply side of the economy. The shift was apparent in all major European countries. The clearest break was in the United Kingdom with the election victory of Margaret Thatcher in 1979. In Germany a more conservative government was formed in 1982 under Helmut Kohl. However, a major change in fiscal policy had occurred already in 1981 under his socialist predecessor, Helmut Schmidt. In France the change occurred somewhat later with the election victory of Mitterrand in 1981. After eighteen months of a rather disastrous experiment in "policy activism," the socialists reoriented their economic policy in a much less interventionist way.

An important element in this reformulation of economic policy strategy in the early 1980s was the failure of macroeconomic policy coordination at the end of the 1970s. At the G7 Bonn summit in May 1978 a coordinated macroeconomic strategy at a worldwide level, under the pressure of the American president Carter, was drawn up. The more expansionary budgetary policy in 1979 and 1980 coincided with an economic recovery, working pro-cyclically. This created a severe trauma, especially in Germany, which was confronted with a balance of payments deficit, and also in international institutions like the OECD and the European Commission, which were important advocates of policy coordination. It raised the issue of the efficiency of economic policy, especially at these international institutions. It made economists much more skeptical about possibilities for fine-tuning policy.

This shift toward a more stability-oriented stance of economic policy was also clearly reflected in the economic thought at the institutions of the European Community:

- In both the Delors Report and the Maastricht Treaty, price stability was emphasized as the overriding goal of monetary policy, which had to be carried out by an independent central bank. These ideas were not mentioned in the Werner Report when monetary policy was discussed (e.g., Werner Report, 13 and 21).
- Both the Delors Report and the Werner Report emphasize that monetary policy has to be centralized in the monetary union, under the responsibility of a European central bank. The Werner Report also proposed the creation of a "centre of decision for economic policy," which will exercise "a decisive influence over the general economic policy of the Community" (Werner Report, 12).
- A smaller budget for the EC was proposed. In a recent report of a study group an EC budget of 2 percent of EC GDP is considered capable of sustaining economic and monetary union (Commission of the European Communities [CEC], 1993, 6). This contrasts with the earlier MacDougall Report, which considered an EC budget of 5 to 7 percent of EC gross domestic product necessary for a monetary union (Commission of the European Communities 1977, 20). This shift reflects both a different politico-economic paradigm, with a more limited role for the government in economic life and a smaller role for the EC, given the attachment of nation-states to their sovereignty and the application of the subsidiarity principle.
- There was a new view on industrial policy, which had figured prominently on the policy agenda of the EC in the 1970s as a way to complement the internal market. Hereby special attention was given to sectors confronted with problems (cf. Commission of the European Communities 1973, 17; or 1977, 48). In the 1980s and 1990s, the emphasis is on a more "horizontal" industrial policy, where the creation of a favorable environment for firms is encouraged, as well as on competition policy (cf. Commission of the European Communities 1989, 62).

Even more important for the development of the EC was the way that a further push toward integration fit into this new conceptual framework. The completion of the internal market, with its elimination of the remaining barriers to a free flow of goods, services, persons, and capital, was compatible with the deregulation strategy being pursued in the various European countries. Macroeconomic policy in the countries of the EC became more stability oriented, as policymakers realized the illusory nature of the trade-off between inflation and unemployment. This orientation fit in with a policy of stable exchange rates and a move toward a monetary union (see appendix 3 for a chronology of integration).

6. The Internationalization Influence

It is not easy to assess the international or American influence in the thinking of the European Community, as many different elements play a role (cf. Coats 1992, 5). As the economic thought at the EC institutions is already a kind of international thought, it seems appropriate here to focus on the Americanization tendency and to contrast this with a "European economics."

One could argue that the American influence has been increasing during the last decades. This has been especially so for form and method (quantification and use of the English language), relatively less in matters of substance. Mathematization and quantification, which several observers consider typical for the American style of economics (cf. Portes 1987; Kolm 1988; Baumol 1995; Mayer 1995), have become more important in studies of the European Commission. Also, in practice, English is becoming more and more the dominant language in the EC institutions. The main reason is that English is the second language of most Europeans, apart from the British and the Irish (see table 4).

Several factors contribute to this growing Americanization:

- Academic economics in Europe is becoming more like academic economics in America (cf. Frey and Eichenberger 1993; Klamer 1995). So the intellectual environment, wherein economists at the EC institutions work, is becoming more Americanized. It implies also that economists who are newly recruited, both as administrators or as consultants, are nowadays thinking more along American lines.
- More young commission economists have studied abroad, especially at American universities (see table 2).

Table 4   Foreign Language Education in the European Community: Percentage of Pupils in General Secondary Education Learning English, French, or German as a Foreign Language, 1991–92

	English	French	German
Holland	96	65	53
Germany	93	23	-
Denmark	92	8	58
Spain	92	10	0.3
France	84	–	27
Belgium (Flemish)	68	98	22
Italy	61	33	3
Belgium (French)	58	1	6
Portugal	55	25	0.4
Britain	–	59	20
Ireland	–	69	24

Source. Eurostat, *The Economist*, 14 January 1995. p. 25.

- With the 1973 enlargement, the United Kingdom became a member of the EC. This has certainly contributed to a more Anglo-Saxon trait in the economic thinking at the EC institutions, as British economists are, in general, more in touch with American economics than are continental economists (cf. Backhouse 1996).
- The OECD has a very important role in the transatlantic transmission of economic ideas. It fulfills a "bridging role" between American and European officials, during both meetings and informal contacts.
- American economists also pay attention to the functioning of the European economy. Their analyses have, in differing degrees, an impact on the thinking of European economists and at the commission.
- There are also very direct influences, like the contribution of non-EC experts to studies undertaken by the EC (see appendix 4).

Summarizing, then, one could argue that the American influence is increasing, especially in respect of form and method (quantification, English language). However, economics at the EC institutions retains a somewhat different character. Important is its emphasis on certain conditions necessary for the functioning of a free-market economy, like competition policy and the need for wage moderation for a process of sustainable and balanced growth. These are mainly elements of (German) ordo-liberal thinking, coupled with a more activist (French) attitude toward economic policy. This rather differentiates economic thought at the EC institutions from a more noninterventionist (American) economics, notwithstanding many influences and interactions. These elements go to the core of economic thought at the EC institutions. The quest for monetary integration in Europe is something that meets with skepticism and criticism among American economists, who attach more importance to the exchange rate as an adjustment mechanism. In the economic thought at the EC institutions the role of the exchange rate as an adjustment mechanism is relativised (e.g., concern with the loss of effectiveness of the exchange rate instrument in very open economies, dangers of overshooting and misalignment). Moreover, the dangers of volatile exchange rates for the functioning of the internal market and the process of European integration are emphasized.[14]

Conclusion

Economic thought at the European Community institutions is, to a large extent, centered around the notion of economic integration. The "political economy" dimension is prominent, as integration implies a transfer of sovereignty from the national to the European level. This political economy dimension comes even more to the foreground as different countries have differing ideas on how to pursue European integration, based on both differences in national interests and in economic thought.

When analyzing the development of economic thought at the EC institutions one can discern some important continuities, especially the tension between the logic of integration and the attachment to national sovereignty, and the recurring debate between "monetarists" and "economists" about the appropriate strategy for monetary integration. The most important shift occurred at the end of the 1970s, with the move from a more activist to a more structural and stability-oriented conceptual framework.

Economic thought at the institutions of the EC has undergone important international (American) influences, both directly (e.g., studies of American economists on the European economy, participation of non-

14. An example is Feldstein's criticism of EMU in *The Economist* (1992), which provoked reactions in defense of EMU from numerous European economists, like De Grauwe, Giovannini, Gross, Steinherr, Thygesen, and others (see also Salmon 1995).

EC economists in important study groups) and indirectly (recruitment of American-trained economists, influences of American economics on academic economics in Europe). However, economic thought at the EC institutions also has some characteristics that differentiate it from American economics, such as a greater concern for conditions for the functioning of a free-market economy. Competition policy, price stability, moderate wage developments, and so on are important. Moreover, Europe's quest for exchange rate stability is met with more skepticism and criticism on the other side of the Atlantic.

References

Backhouse, Roger. 1996. United Kingdom. In *The Post-1945 Internationalization of Economics*. Edited by A. W. Coats. Durham, N.C.: Duke University Press. (Paper read in manuscript.)

Baer, Gunther, and Tommaso Padoa-Schioppa. 1988. [April 1989]. The Werner Report Revisited. In *Report on Economic and Monetary Union*. Edited by Committee for the Study of Economic and Monetary Union. Luxembourg. 53–60.

Balassa, Bela. 1961. Toward a Theory of Economic Integration. *Kyklos* 14:1–17.

Baumol, William. 1995. What's Different about European Economics? *Kyklos* 48.2: 187–91.

Bloomfield, Arthur. 1973. The Historical Setting. In *European Monetary Unification and its Meaning for the United States*. Edited by B. Krause and W. Salant. Washington, D.C.: Brookings. 1–30.

Bundesbank. 1994. Die Zweite Stufe der Europäischen Wirtschafts- und Währungsunion. *Monatsbericht* (January): 25–44.

Coats, A. W. 1981. Introduction. In *Economists in Government*. Edited by A. W. Coats. Durham, N.C.: Duke University Press. 3–26.

———. 1992. *The Post-1945 Global Internationalization (Americanization?) of Economics*. Duplicated.

———, ed. 1986. *Economists in International Agencies*. New York: Praeger.

Colchester, Nicholas. 1988. A Survey of Europe's Internal Market. *The Economist* (9 July).

Commission des Communautés Européennes. 1973. La Réalisation de l'Union Economique et Monétaire. *Bulletin des Communautés Européennes*. Supplément 5/73.

Commission of the European Communities. March 1975. *Report of the Study Group "Economic and Monetary Union 1980."* [Marjolin Report.] Brussels.

———. April 1977. *Report of the Study Group on the Role of Public Finance in European Integration*. Brussels.

———. 1985. *Completing the Internal Market*. White Paper from the Commission to the Council. Luxembourg.

————. 1988. The Economics of 1992. *European Economy* 35 (March): 222.

————. 1989. The Community Economy at the Turn of the Decade. *European Economy* 42 (November): 25–104.

————. 1990. One Market, One Money. *European Economy* 44 (October): 351.

————. 1993. Stable Money—Sound Finances. *European Economy* 53:123.

Committee for the Study of Economic and Monetary Union. 1989. *Report on Economic and Monetary Union in the European Community*. [Delors Report.] Luxembourg.

Council-Commission of the European Communities. October 1970. *Report to the Council and the Commission on the Realisation by Stages of Economic and Monetary Union in the Community*. [Werner Report.] Luxembourg.

Erhard, Ludwig. [1943] 1981. Wirtschaftspolitische Erfordernisse nach Beendigung des Krieges. In *Grundtexte zur Sozialen Marktwirtschaft*. Edited by W. Stützel et al. Stuttgart: Gustav Fischer Verlag. 15–18.

Feldstein, Martin. 1992. Europe's Monetary Union. *The Economist* 13 June: 19–22.

Frey, Bruno, and Rainer Eichenberger. 1993. American and European Economics and Economists. *Journal of Economic Perspectives* 7.4:185–93.

Giavazzi, Francesco and Alberto Giovannini. 1989. *Limiting Exchange Rate Flexibility: The European Monetary System*. Cambridge, Mass.: MIT Press.

Grant, Charles. 1994. *Delors: Inside the House That Jacques Built*. London: Nicholas Brealy.

Hay, Richard. 1989. *The European Commission and the Administration of the Community*. Brussels: European Documentation.

Klamer, Arjo. 1995. A Rhetorical Perspective on the Differences between European and American Economists. *Kyklos* 48.2:231–39.

Kolm, S-C. 1988. Economics in Europe and in the U.S. *European Economic Review* 32.1:207–12.

Lipschitz, Leslie and Thomas Mayer. 1988. Accepted Economic Paradigms Guide German Economic Policies. *IMF Survey* (28 November): 370–74.

Louis, Jean-Victor. 1990.*The Community Legal Order*. 2d ed. Brussels: Commission of the European Communities.

Ludlow, Peter. 1982. *The Making of the European Monetary System*. London: Butterworths.

Maes, Ivo. 1991. *The European Community in the 1990s: Deepening or Widening?* Global Forum Series. Occasional paper no. 92-2. Center for International Studies, Duke University.

————. 1994. State and Market in Postwar Integration Theory. In *National and European Markets in Economic Thought*. Edited by P. Roggi et al. Proceedings of the Eleventh International Economic History Congress. Milan. 83–94.

Marris, Stephen. 1986. The Role of Economists in the OECD. In *Economists in International Agencies*. Edited by A. W. Coats. New York: Praeger. 98–114.

Mayer, Thomas. 1995. Differences in Economics: Europe and the United States. *Kyklos* 48.2:241–49.

Meade, James. 1953. *Problems of Economic Union*. London: Allen and Unwin.

Monnet, Jean. 1976. *Mémoires*. Paris: Fayard.

Mortensen, Jurgen. 1990. *Federalism vs. Co-ordination: Macroeconomic Policy in the European Community*. Brussels: CEPS.

Noël, Emile. 1993. *Working Together: The Institutions of the European Community*. Brussels: European Documentation.

Padoa-Schioppa, Tommaso. 1987. *Efficiency, Stability, Equity*. Oxford: Oxford University Press.

————. 1990. *Financial and Monetary Integration in Europe: 1990, 1992 and Beyond*. Group of Thirty. Occasional paper no. 28. New York.

Pinder, John. 1991. *European Community*. Oxford: Oxford University Press.

Portes, Richard. 1987. Economics in Europe. *European Economic Review* 31.6: 1329–40.

Rosanvallon, Pierre. 1987. Histoire des Idées Keynesiennes en France. *Revue Française d'Economie* 4.2:22–56.

Ross, Georges. 1994. Inside the Delors Cabinet. *Journal of Common Market Studies* 32.4: 499–523.

Salmon, Pierre. 1995. Three Conditions for Some Distinctiveness in the Contribution of Europeans to Economics. *Kyklos* 48.2: 279–87.

Schor, A-D. 1993. *La Politique Economique et Sociale de la Ve République*. Paris: P.U.F.

Study Group on Economic and Monetary Union. 1973. *European Economic Integration and Monetary Unification*. Commission of the European Communities. Brussels.

Tinbergen, Jan. 1954. *International Economic Integration*. Amsterdam: Elsevier.

Tsoukalis, Loukas. 1977. *The Politics and Economics of European Monetary Integration*. London: Allen and Unwin.

Van Rompuy, Paul, Filip Abraham, and Dirk Heremans. 1991. Economic Federalism and the EMU. *European Economy*. Special ed., no. 1: 109–35.

Viner, Jacob. 1950. *The Customs Union Issue*. New York: Carnegie Endowment for International Peace.

Appendix 1

Structure of the Services of the European Commission, 1994

Cabinets
Secretariat-General
Forward-Looking Unit
Legal Service
Spokesman's Service
Consumer Policy Service
Task Force on Human Resources, Education, Training, and Youth
Translation Service
Joint Interpretation and Conference Service
Statistical Office

DG	I	Economic External Relations
DG	IA	Political External Relations
DG	II	Economic and Financial Affairs
DG	III	Industry
DG	IV	Competition
DG	V	Employment, Industrial Relationships, and Social Affairs
DG	VI	Agriculture
DG	VII	Transport
DG	VIII	Development
DG	IX	Personnel and Administration
DG	X	Audiovisual Affairs, Information, Communication, and Culture
DG	XI	Environment, Nuclear Safety, and Civil Protection
DG	XII	Science, Research, and Development
		Joint Research Center
DG	XIII	Telecommunications, Information Industries, and Innovation
DG	XIV	Fisheries
DG	XV	Internal Market and Financial Institutions
DG	XVI	Regional Policies
DG	XVII	Energy
DG	XVIII	Credit and Investments
DG	XIX	Budgets
DG	XX	Financial Control

DG   XXI   Customs Union and Indirect Taxation
DG   XXIII   Enterprises' Policy, Distributive Trades, Tourism, and
               Social Economy
Euratom Supply Agency
Security Office

Appendix 2

A Simplified Organigram of Directorate-General II (Economic and Financial Affairs) and Number of A Staff (December 1994)

Staff of the DG   18

Directorate A: National economies   17
1. Member states I: Denmark, Germany, and France
2. Member states II: Greece, Ireland, and United Kingdom
3. Member states III: Benelux and Portugal
4. Member states IV: Spain and Italy

Directorate B: Economic Service   18
1. Economic aspects of integration and evaluation of external policy
2. Evaluation of the structural funds and social and agricultural
   policies
3. Evaluation of competition and research and development policies; internal market and industrial affairs
4. Evaluation of transport, environment, and energy policies

Directorate C: Surveillance of the Community economy   22
1. Evaluation and surveillance of the Community economy
2. Surveillance of budgetary situations
3. Economic forecasts
4. Econometric models

Directorate D: Monetary matters   18
1. Monetary union: institutional, legal, and financial matters
2. ECU
3. EMS, national, and Community monetary policies
4. International aspects of monetary union

Directorate E: Financial instruments and capital movements   16
1. Coordination with the EIB and development of financial instruments
2. Analysis of financial circuits and instruments, including the EIB
3. Financial integration and capital movements

Directorate F: International economic and financial matters   21
1. Central and Eastern Europe, including the newly independent states
2. Other European countries and the international environment
3. International financial matters

Total   130

Appendix 3

A Succinct Chronology of European Integration

1950	May	Schuman Declaration
1952	July	Establishment of the European Coal and Steel Community (ECSC)
1954	August	France rejects the European Defence Community (EDC)
1958	January	Establishment of the European Economic Community (EEC) and the European Atomic Energy Community (EAEC)
1969	December	The Hague Summit. Monetary union becomes an objective of the European Community
1973	January	The United Kingdom, Ireland, and Denmark become members of the European Community
1979	March	Establishment of the European Monetary System (EMS)
1985	March	European Council agrees on an internal single market by December 1992
1987	January	Single European Act
1988	June	European Council relaunches monetary union project
1991	December	Agreement on the Maastricht Treaty
1993	November	Maastricht Treaty ratified
1994	January	Start of phase 2 of Economic and Monetary Union

Appendix 4

Participation of Non-EC Economists in Important Study Groups

Study Group on Economic and Monetary Union, October 1973	R. A. Mundell
Study Group on the Role of Public Finance in European Integration, April 1977	R. Mathews (Canberra) W. Oates (Princeton)
Efficiency, Stability, Equity, September 1987	P. Krugman (MIT)
One Market, One Money, October 1990	P. Kenen (Princeton) R. E. Baldwin (Geneva and NBER) R. Lyons (Columbia and NBER) R. Bryant R. Portes
Stable Money–Sound Finances, 1993	F. Schneider (Linz) C. Walsh (Adelaide) T. Courchene (Kingston, Ontario) H. Blöchliger (Basle) R. Frey (Basle)

Part 4

Economists in Political and Policy Elites in Latin America

Verónica Montecinos

The Economics Profession and Policy Reforms

Latin America has recently witnessed a massive ideological and strategic shift in the way developmental issues are addressed. While in some accounts the breadth of market reforms is said to amount to a "cultural revolution," others speak of a "technocratic revolution." In the struggle to reduce state interventionism, liberalize trade, and enter global competition, economists are now at the core of newly empowered technocratic elites. In what ways are the politics of economic reforms linked to the politics of the economics profession? I contend here that studying the professionalization of economics helps us understand how Latin American policy elites have (re)defined the challenges of economic and social change.

An unprecedented degree of consensus about the need to replace state-led development, the dominant paradigm since the 1930s, has followed decades of intense ideological controversies between the proponents of interventionism and the defenders of economic orthodoxy. From the political right to the political left, economists are now advocating the need to liberalize trade, maintain macroeconomic equilibria, and ensure higher levels of competitiveness and efficiency. In some countries, trade reforms to encourage export growth had been advised and partially implemented since the 1960s. However, the imminence of massive policy changes was not widely accepted until the debt crisis of the 1980s, when vast amounts of resources had to be transferred to foreign creditors and external funds stopped flowing to the region. Governments were forced to reduce their budget deficits and promote exports. Hyperinflationary processes added to a sense of crisis and disillusionment with the accumulated inefficiencies of state interventionism, the inadequacies of an industrialization process oriented to domestic and protected markets, and the inability of antiquated and overburdened state structures to respond to the challenges of a globalized economy (Muñoz 1994). The widespread adoption of market-oriented reforms has also been explained by the weakening of class and sectoral coalitions that in the past had supported expansionary, interventionist, and populist economic policies (Kaufman and Stallings 1991).

Gradually, and often reluctantly, aspects of the market-centered consensus that first emerged among economists have been incorporated into the agenda of political elites and other social actors. In several countries, the search for new economic models and new forms of political discourse has been heralded by professional economists. As members of an internationalized profession, economists are increasingly influential players. A growing number of individuals with professional credentials in economics have been placed at the forefront of ideological and institutional transformations, ascending to the highest positions of political responsibility, either through bureaucratic channels in the state apparatus, participation in political parties, or both. Latin American economists are now routinely recruited to ministerial positions in various policy areas, including education, health, public works, social insurance, and labor, which were the traditional terrain of politicians, lawyers, and other professionals. The economists' ascent to powerful positions in the legislature, in party leadership, and in the diplomatic corps parallels their increasingly influential role in government. In several countries in the region, economists have competed for and even held presidential office.[1]

The hybridization of economists and politicians is not limited to Latin America. Worldwide, professional economists have been playing an increasingly significant role in the recent "dual transitions" to market economies and democratic politics (Centeno 1993; Markoff and Montecinos 1993). Indeed, the political economy of reforms appears to be populated by a new social type, the "technopol" (Williamson 1994).

1. The impact of powerful technocratic elites has been most extreme in Mexico and Chile, but other instances of this trend can be found throughout the region (Montecinos and Markoff 1993; Centeno 1994; Montecinos, forthcoming).

Latin American technopols—most of them with degrees in economics—have been invested with the power to make decisions with profound political and social consequences, playing a very prominent role in the political economy of market reforms. However, little has been said about how this or the previous waves of economic and institutional change in Latin America might be related to the evolution, structure, and power of economics as a profession.[2]

More detailed studies on the evolution and characteristics of the economics profession in Latin America might help us explain national differences in the timing, speed, and depth of market reforms in Latin America. How much of the relative tardiness with which Latin Americans reacted to changes in the international economic environment is explained by ideological cleavages, institutional weakness, or other internal dynamics within the profession? In what ways are the conflicts (and agreements) within the economics profession reflected in ideological justifications of the reform process? How relevant is the number of available economists and the strength of their institutional networks in explaining the policy capability of reformist governments? To what extent has the internationalized education of economists enhanced their professional prestige, their ability to displace other professional groups, and their ascent in politics?

The Professionalization of Economics

This important research territory is waiting to be explored. Studies of the professionalization of economics in Latin America and other regions of the world are needed to better understand recent changes in the profession's cultural and political impact, its demographic patterns, and internal differentiation.[3] Economics has received surprisingly little attention in the sociology of professions. Perhaps this is because (unlike medicine, law, or accounting) economics lacks what sociologists have considered to be an important dimension of successful professionalization, namely, the legal monopoly over the performance of certain tasks. Like other groups

2. In general, studies of the politics of economic reform have neglected to consider the interests of actors located within the state apparatus (Geddes 1995).

3. Analyses of the economics profession have mostly referred to the United States, and cross-national comparisons tend not to go beyond the industrialized world (Frey and Eichenberger 1993). Moreover, most of the recent literature in the sociology of professions refers only to professions in advanced capitalist societies.

seeking to establish and enhance their professional status, economists have claimed the right to control certain social activities on the basis of their knowledge and expertise.[4] Although the making of economic policies is still routinely entrusted to noneconomists (many believe that the economy should *not* be managed by economists), and despite the lack of legal protection, the expansion of the economists' professional influence has been, so far, notably successful.

Another reason for the relative paucity of studies on the professionalization of economics is that "economists are inclined to resist the adoption of a sociological interpretation of their discipline" (Coats 1984, 223). In the last few years, however, economists have been looking intensely at their profession's internal structure, hierarchies, labor markets, intellectual traditions, rhetoric, and professional socialization (Colander 1989; Colander and Coats 1993; Colander and Brenner 1992; Coats 1993). Also, the crossing of interdisciplinary boundaries between economics and sociology has accelerated (Smelser and Swedberg 1994).

Studies in the sociology of professions (Abbott 1988; Hoffman 1989; Witz 1992) point to strategies commonly used in the professionalization of occupational groups. Members of a profession must convince relevant audiences—such as the state, powerful elites, and the public—that their knowledge, definitions, diagnoses, and solutions to problems are not only relevant but superior to the ideas and expertise of others. Strategies to legitimate and institutionalize professional claims include the connection of abstract knowledge with the solution of practical problems, the demarcation of a professional jurisdiction, the exclusion of rival groups, and the establishment of a dominant position within an area of work.

Professions emerge, develop (and decline) in the context of dynamic struggles of inter- and intraprofessional competition. All professions must ensure that their efforts to monopolize the provision of technical competence are perceived as necessary, beneficial, and therefore legitimate. To justify their claims, professions develop ideologies. Indeed, professions become cultures and subcultures of their own, constructing sets of symbols, beliefs, values, and norms that differentiate them from their environment and provide a source of self-identity and solidarity among their members (Trice 1993).

---

4. Since the boundaries of the economics profession are not protected by legislative privileges, increasingly "the Ph.D.s in economics stand guard over the subject" (Klamer 1990, 176).

Success in the achievement of professional status is also determined by the ability of professional groups to create organizational structures that advance their claims of superior knowledge and legitimate control of a market for their services. These organizational structures typically include the following forms: advanced schools to generate new knowledge and train new members; special credentials to rank members and limit entrance to professional practice; associations to exchange and diffuse information and develop professional networks and informal relations; professional journals to spread ideas and innovations; and the creation of specialized work organizations (Abbott 1991).

Professionalization is, then, a political process in which entire professions—or segments within professions—compete for the control of power and resources. Cultural and social forces combine to promote or constrain the viability of particular historical projects advanced by specific collectivities. For most professions, control is achieved at the national level (in particular, the obtention of a legal monopoly). By contrast, in the case of economics, the use of denationalized strategies seems important to legitimate professional projects.

It could be argued that economics as a profession cannot be but international in its scope, given the universalistic claims of its methodology and the market's tendency to defy administrative controls. But internationalization may be determined by the political dynamics of the profession itself. As other essays in this volume suggest, the economist's use of internationalization strategies is found in a variety of national settings. The internationalization of economists' training, of their career patterns, hierarchies, and networks may be especially important in societies that occupy a subordinate position in the international system.

Four phases in the evolution of the economics profession are delineated below. In the first phase only a handful of Latin American economists existed and the advice of foreign experts was common. In the second phase, a project centered on unorthodox economic ideas shaped the emergent profession and advanced to hegemonic domination. A third phase began as a reaction from mainstream economists and concluded with their own domination over the field. Finally, a broad convergence is achieved on the need to make strategic changes in the political economy of the region. The authority of the economics profession is widely legitimized as a source of technical competence and economists acquire a quasi-monopolistic control over economic and other policy decisions.

Internationalization as a Strategy of Professionalization

An integral part of the professionalization process has to do with the resolution of intraprofessional conflicts.[5] Economists, like other professionals, do not constitute a homogeneous group. In Latin America, decades of intense intraprofessional struggles among self-enclosed groups of economists preceded the current consensus.[6] In the postwar period, economics developed as a highly segmented profession, with competing groups advancing alternative forms of professional practice, inspired in different paradigms. On the one hand, groups trying to replace conventional economics with a "Latin American" economics called for state action to change the political economy of the region. On the other, groups closer to academic orthodoxy emphasized that market mechanisms would result in higher levels of prosperity. For both sides, strategies of internationalization were central.

Economists, more than any other professional group in Latin America, work in a highly denationalized environment. The international political economy of the region holds the roots of this phenomenon. In relatively poor export economies, elites tend to accommodate their economic practices to the ones used in the countries that control the investments, loans, and markets on which they so crucially depend.

The hiring of foreign advisers, the import of foreign economic doctrines, the assimilation of the latest economic techniques, and, more recently, the reliance on foreign economic education constitute strategies that not only enhance the prestige of the economic experts themselves but, more broadly, contribute to smooth exchanges with foreign powers, signal compliance with the rules and rituals preferred by foreign fi-

5. Hierarchies of power and prestige are based on rivalries between groups with distinct theoretical and methodological orientations. The use of different professional languages, values, metaphors, myths, and political beliefs results in the formation of professional subcultures and factionalism.

6. For evidence of the theoretical and ideological pluralism among Latin American economists, see, for example, the analysis of "populist" and "orthodox" policy cycles (Dornbusch and Edwards 1991). In the early 1970s, the conflict between Marxist and non-Marxist economists was such that the School of Economics at the University of Chile became physically divided into two schools. The left controlled the school located at the Northern Campus (Sede Norte), devoted to the teaching and research of political economy. At the Western Campus, controlled by the Christian Democrats, Keynesianism, structuralism, and neoclassical economics remained the main theoretical orientations. My interviews with economics professors involved in the dispute indicated that, when the library was divided, there were no conflicts over which books would go to each campus! (Montecinos 1988).

nanciers and investors, increase trust and creditworthiness, and facilitate the conduct of foreign relations. In sum, the cosmopolitan atmosphere in which economic analysts and policymakers operate is partly explained by the subordinated position that the region occupies in the international economic system.

Paul Drake (1994) has shown how, since the early nineteenth century, in successive cycles of debt crises, foreign "money doctors" have been called to Latin America to teach the natives how to reform their economies in accordance with the rules of international economic relations. The "science" of foreign experts has served not only as a vehicle to transfer the latest techniques of economic management, but also as a "political device." Money doctors have been mediators between Latin Americans and their foreign creditors, certifying that new loans could be granted and that troubled debtors could be allowed to reenter the financial game. The allegedly "apolitical," neutral advice of foreign experts has been used to defend and legitimize the claims of local elites against their rivals, to justify unpopular measures, expand the influence of wealthy nations, and instill trust among investors.

Following the steps of Edwin Kemmerer, Drake (1989) has traced the functional linkages between the economic and institutional reforms that modernized the Latin American states in the 1920s and the interests pursued by local and transnational elites. At the time, Kemmerer, a Princeton professor and an internationally renowned promoter of laissez-faire economic prescriptions, was one among many foreign experts working for the governments of the region.[7] His financial missions were most successful in casting a consensus around the adoption of sweeping reforms in the monetary, banking, and fiscal systems of several Latin American countries.

During the turn-of-the-century export prosperity, the doctrine of economic liberalism was accepted as a justification for Latin America's position in the international division of labor. Kemmerer's professional services and reputation were employed to signal the willingness of "Kem-

---

7. Drake (1989, 19–20) tells us that prior to World War II, Latin America was a leader in bringing in foreign experts and administrators (mostly, but not exclusively, from the United States). Although this reliance on foreign advisers met with resistance among nationalist groups, their widespread presence is an indicator of the local scarcity of professional economists. The first schools of economics in the region began to appear in the 1930s (many of them initially linked to other professions, such as accounting, law, and engineering). Before the 1950s, only a handful of Latin Americans had gone abroad (mainly to Europe) to pursue studies in economics.

mererized" countries to comply with the institutional standards and technical economic practices of the United States.[8] However, a period of "exhilarated creativity" was opened up after the Great Depression (Díaz-Alejandro 1984, 49). As Drake notes (1989, 29), the state institutions that Kemmerer had reformed in the 1920s began to be twisted far beyond Kemmerer's free-trade directives. For the next five decades, the Latin American "regionalization" of economic paradigms and policy experimentation was driven by statist, nationalistic, and protectionist principles.

Initially, the rationalization of economic isolationism was led by a group of mostly self-taught Latin American economists, technocratic managers (some were engineers- and lawyers-turned-economists) promoting the expansion of managerial states, claiming for themselves the autonomy, prestige, and prerogatives previously enjoyed by foreign experts. This new group of experts developed a professional project aimed at reducing foreign interference in economic management. "Economic nationalism" became the core of an expanding economics profession as well as the source of a new Latin American identity (Tancer 1976).

The Latin-Americanization of Economics:
A Professional Project

In the 1940s, as Latin American "economic nationalists" rejected the previous complacency with neoclassical economic doctrines and engaged in ambitious industrialization programs, the idea of development began to gain currency. The belief that a general economic theory was scientifically neutral and valid for all regions was replaced by the conviction that foreign ideas could not provide appropriate remedies for the problems of Latin America. The rules governing international trade ceased to be taken for granted, for it was the lack of control over external forces that had made the region vulnerable to major crises. Latin American analysts argued that the theory of comparative advantage in international trade was misleading, served ideological purposes, and justified international asymmetries. In the interest of Latin America, disillusioned economists called for a reformulation of the science of economics.

8. With the emerging hegemony of the United States, Latin America constituted a target for North American diplomats, bankers, and investors. However, for Latin Americans to benefit from the financial bonanza of the period, a technically valid certificate of economic fitness was necessary.

At the time, the most prominent Latin American economist was Raúl Prebisch.[9] An inspirational teacher and an effective organizer, known through his contributions in professional journals and as adviser to governments in the region, Prebisch's original insights contained the seeds of what would become, in the 1950s and 1960s, a distinctive school of economic thought.[10]

The "structuralist" school, considered a truly indigenous Latin American creation,[11] argued that the narrow focus of conventional economic analysis failed to identify the cultural, social, and historical ("structural") roots of underdevelopment. The concern with reforms[12] led many of these economists to social and political activism.[13] Hirschman comments that for Latin American thinkers, "the aim of development is . . . most importantly, [a] 'conquest for decision centers' that were previously in foreign hands, and a new ability to strike out on one's own, economically, politically and intellectually" (1961, 35).

For the establishment of an alternative professional project—a specifically Latin American economics—abstract critiques of "foreign" ideas had to be translated into practical advice. Prebisch and his followers argued that the policies derived from "conventional" economic doctrines were unrealistic and inapplicable to Latin America.[14] A niche for the

9. In the early 1930s, Prebisch had created the Argentine Central Bank, participated in trade renegotiations between Argentina and Great Britain, and attended meetings organized by the League of Nations and other international economic conferences. He was "one of the first to recognize the Keynesian revolution and make it known in Latin America"; his *Introducción a Keynes* was published in 1947 (Ferrer 1990, 27).

10. His thesis on the deterioration of the terms of trade challenged the assumptions used by conventional neoclassical economic analysis. The center-periphery theory served as a new paradigm for interpreting the gap between industrialized and nonindustrial countries.

11. In Fishlow's characterization, "structuralism was a Latin American theory of long-run development . . . [and] also a short-run macroeconomic theory that denied the effectiveness of orthodox monetary, fiscal and exchange rate policy in combating inflation" (1988, 91). Structuralists adhered to a "humanitarian and moral" concept of development (Larraín 1989, 114), and their ideas influenced a variety of nonorthodox theories (Cardoso 1977; Love 1980; Dosman and Pollock 1993; Dietz and Street 1987).

12. The structural obstacles to development included the imperfect operation of markets, the scarcity of capital and technology, the highly skewed distribution of income, and the traditional forms of policymaking.

13. Some of their studies appeared more sociological than economic. James H. Street (1987) has identified many commonalities between Latin American structuralism and institutionalist economics in the United States. Authors on both sides were basically unaware of the others' contribution. Most of the structuralists' work is not available in English.

14. Structuralists claimed to be inherently practical, as opposed to their competitors in mainstream economics, whose professional tools tended to be purely modelistic, abstract, and irrelevant. Latin American economists would, inductively, produce more rigorous empirical analyses,

legitimation of the new school of economics emerged with the demarcation of two new policy areas, namely planning and integration. Regional economic integration would generate the economies of scale necessary for the success of industrial programming and strengthen the region's collective bargaining with the rest of the world.

An important dimension in the professional project of structuralist economists was the establishment of work organizations controlled by members of this group.[15] The 1948 founding of the United Nations Economic Commission for Latin America (ECLA) was crucial for the structuralist project. Initially, the prospects for the new agency appeared bleak, since the number of available economists was very small. However, in only a few years an international staff was hired and ECLA became "the recognized spokesman for Latin America's economic development" (Hirschman 1961, 13).[16]

Imbued with a sense of mission, ECLA economists collected basic statistical information and organized advisory missions to several governments. The ECLA became a key reference within the emerging economics profession. It provided a coherent vision, a source of collective identity, and a tool kit of practical policy instruments to change antiquated, clientelistic, patronage-ridden bureaucracies through the rationalization of decision making. ECLA mobilized public opinion against economic orthodoxy, advised the creation of planning agencies, helped the coordination of common positions in international conferences, and shaped a new integrationist "conscience."[17] Among modernizing tech-

---

without the "stereotypes" often found among foreign advisers (Street 1987, 106).

15. In the postwar period, international organizations and multilateral lending agencies offered economists opportunities to advertise their practical value. Not only was development being measured in quantitative terms, but the region needed a lobbying mechanism to protest the lack of official resources (there was no Marshall Plan for Latin America).

16. Prebisch initially refused to head the new institution, doubting that an international organization would adopt a specifically Latin American economic perspective (Love 1980), but Prebisch's 1949 *Economic Development of Latin America and Its Principal Problems* (Prebisch 1962) became ECLA's institutional "manifesto." Prebisch directed ECLA until the early 1960s, when he was named the first secretary-general of the United Nations Conference on Trade and Development (UNCTAD), an organization he helped establish with the aim of creating a more egalitarian international economic order. Until his death in 1986, he exerted a continuing influence in the region. The first Premio Iberoamericano de Economía Raúl Prebisch was awarded in 1990 to Víctor Urquidi, a Mexican economist who had worked at ECLA under the direction of Prebisch and is considered a prominent representative of the structuralist school.

17. In the late 1950s, ECLA sponsored a series of meetings to discuss the creation of a free-trade area. In Central and South America integration treaties were signed in 1960. In the view of pro-integration economists, the Latin American Free Trade Association would serve as

nocratic elites, professional economists were already taking vanguard positions.

The consolidation of the ECLA school of economics was aided by the production and diffusion of innovative economic ideas, from the beginning recognized as an important institutional task.[18] ECLA's publications, including a scholarly journal, were distributed widely. Special attention and resources were devoted to the education of Latin American economists.[19] ECLA training program was initiated in 1953, when no texts on economic development existed.[20] For the next two decades, Santiago de Chile became a buoyant intellectual center that attracted social scientists and students from all over the region (many of them in exile).[21] Pinto and Sunkel, speaking of the phenomenon of "cultural alienation," praise the economic development courses taught at ECLA

---

an important forum for the expression of economic ideas (Camp 1977, 350). The creation of a powerful corps of "Latinocrats" (mostly economists) continued to be considered an important goal until the 1970s. The founding of SELA (Latin American Economic System) in Caracas was the last attempt to create the region's own "Brussels" (Herrera 1985, 126).

18. In 1951, after Celso Furtado, one of the first to join ECLA, visited academic economists in the United States (Leontief, Rostow, and Theodore Schultz, among others) he became convinced that "at ECLA we had advanced into uncharted lands and we were occupying vanguard positions" (Furtado 1988, 82).

19. With variations among countries, the number of graduates from economics programs was very low in the 1950s. In Mexico, the economics program remained a division of the Law School until 1935, and by 1946 only 161 individuals had graduated from the National School of Economics (Camp 1975). In Brazil, Haddad (1981, 321) indicates that although a degree in economics was created in 1931, its content was significantly different from currently accepted standards and the number of competently trained economists before 1945 was low. In Chile, by 1950, 163 graduates had degrees in "commercial engineering" (mostly business administration) from the two main universities (Montecinos 1988, chap. 6). Currie (1965, 9) says that in Colombia in 1950, "no faculties or economics courses existed and only two or three individuals held academic degrees in the field."

20. ECLA courses were taught mostly in Santiago, although teaching activities were also organized in several countries in the region. Course materials, elaborated by ECLA experts themselves, were sometimes published by Siglo XXI in Mexico. Osvaldo Sunkel (interviewed in Santiago, August 1994) noticed that although his book with Pedro Paz was in its twenty-fourth Spanish edition, it had never been translated into English. ECLA's professors collaborated in the teaching and production of studies on the economy of the region with the University of Chile's international graduate program in economics (ESCOLATINA), created in 1954. In 1961, the ECLA training program was transferred to the Institute for Economic and Social Planning (ILPES), created with the support of the Alliance for Progress and first directed by Prebisch. Between 1962 and 1992, ILPES organized 328 courses and seminars with a total of 12,272 participants (unpublished data, provided to the author by ILPES's director in 1994).

21. Prebisch's proposal to design a model school to study the economy of the region was debated at a Latin American conference of economics schools organized in Santiago in 1953. The idea did not succeed due to institutional rivalries (Valdés 1989, 161).

and other regional institutions. In contrast with the standard economics curriculum of North American universities, these training programs were oriented toward "indigenous needs" and designed to fill the gap between university and reality: abstract theory was adapted to the conditions of the region, "mathematical acrobatics" were avoided, and a commitment to social justice and economic independence was part of the professional training (Pinto and Sunkel 1966, 79; Valdés 1989, 164).

ECLA's intellectual dominance was especially high in the 1950s and early 1960s, when an "unusual consensus on method and development strategy" was achieved (Fishlow 1988).[22] Hundreds of economists trained at ECLA went to staff economic and planning ministries. Intellectual success, however, did not translate automatically into political influence. While plans began to be formally enacted and planning agencies created, the substance of many of ECLA's policy proposals was often perceived as a threat, ignored and resisted by political and bureaucratic elites.

In the 1960s, international attention and public funds for Latin America increased. The Kennedy administration supported the developmentalist goals of the Alliance for Progress. The theory of modernization gained acceptance among North American academics studying issues of development. With the growth of international lending, the ideas of planning and structural reform achieved further legitimation, since loans and technical assistance were conditioned on the governments' willingness to adopt economic planning. At least formal compliance with the techniques of rational economic management was necessary to satisfy external agencies. A web of development institutions nurtured the expansion of a new "expertocracy" (Wynia 1972, 44).[23] ECLA was no longer alone in fostering the development of the economics profession.[24]

22. Joseph Grunwald, an economics professor at Columbia University who taught at the University of Chile in the 1950s, has noted that, at that time, "all intelligent members of the economics profession in Latin America were structuralists" (Valdés 1989, 159).

23. Some of these agencies were offsprings of ECLA, for example SIECA (the Common Market Secretariat in Central America). Others were created by new hemispheric cooperation agreements, to evaluate the progress of planning (like CIAP, the Inter-American Committee of the Alliance for Progress) and channel public financing assistance.

24. After several unsuccessful efforts, the Inter-American Development Bank was founded in 1959. In 1949, the International Monetary Fund had opposed ECLA's request for a Latin American multilateral clearing mechanism. Later, the United States rejected several proposals for a regional financial entity expected to foster "monetary independence" and be more responsive to the needs of the region (Tancer 1976, 104). The IDB collaborated closely with ECLA. Technical and financial resources promoted planning and regional integration. In the

In the course of the 1960s, the development strategy that had been followed since the Great Depression was the subject of widespread frustration and ECLA became the focus of strong criticism. Critics on the right complained that import-substitution industrialization had fostered inefficient practices and attitudes inimical to competitive markets. Disillusioned structuralists and Marxist analysts argued that industrial expansion had not reduced social inequality but had increased external dependency (Cardoso 1977, 30).[25]

The belief that capitalist development in the periphery only intensified the problems of income inequality and international marginalization helped socialist models of development gain acceptance. Political struggles in the hemisphere intensified. In general, scholarship became more politicized and the economics profession grew increasingly polarized. Adversarialism within the profession was exacerbated by rivalries between academic centers and policy agencies. Groups of conservative economists and their critics became insulated, attacking each other in openly political terms as defenders of imperialist domination or as promoters of revolution.

The North-Americanization of Economics in Latin America

The campaign against the "bad economists" of the South and the ECLA approach in particular had been launched by mainstream economists in the 1950s.[26] A professional project built around conventional economic theory was aimed at debunking the dominance of the structuralist

---

words of IDB's first president, the bank would also serve as a "university for development" (Herrera 1985). The IDB-INTAL offered regular courses on integration and supported similar training programs in other institutions of the region (i.e., the Instituto de Estudios Superiores de Administración in Caracas and the Escuela Latinoamericana de Administración Pública in the Getulio Vargas Foundation) (Pietschmann 1981, 114).

25. Dependency writers incorporated historical and class analysis, criticizing modernization theory and denouncing that industrialization and growth had been, "so to speak, co-opted by an increasingly dependent and transnationalized sector" (Sunkel 1993, 29). Dependency theorists constructed their own internationalized networks and even in the United States many Latin Americanists began to work with concepts elaborated in Latin America (Portes 1988, 126). According to Packenham (1992), of all the approaches to development elaborated in the last three decades, none had a more pervasive influence than the dependency perspective, which in some scholarly areas became the new orthodoxy.

26. Facing "academic excommunication," structuralists felt that the more respectable (and arrogant) economists of industrialized nations relegated them to "an intellectual doghouse for being hopelessly wrongheaded if not professionally irresponsible" (Street 1987, 102).

approach. Many of the professionalization strategies used by the structuralists can be discerned within this rival group: the definition of a professional mission centered around the modernization of economic practices and institutions, the application of economic ideas to the solution of practical problems, the creation of work organizations, and the internationalization of professional training—North-Americanization, in this case.

Sponsorship for the development of a project to return the economics profession to the standards of the "North" came from the government of the United States, international agencies, foreign foundations, and academic institutions and groups within the local elites. This broad coalition joined in their criticisms of proponents of a Latin-Americanized version of economics for their parochialist, statist, and populist views, their lack of technical rigor, their contempt for efficiency and macroeconomic equilibria. Many development economists were accused of not even being economists in the modern sense. In general, the anti-ECLA campaign blamed unorthodox, leftist economists for contributing to the problems of the region and for "polluting economics" (Kay 1993, 693).

Conventional economists doubted that Latin American problems were so unique as to require a new system of ideas. In the words of Lincoln Gordon, a Harvard professor, "there should no more be a 'Latin American economics' than a Latin American physics or mathematics . . . there is no ground for systematic alignment of Latin Americans in one school of thought and North Americans in another" (1961, 68). The notion that a separate economic theory was appropriate was also discredited. The Brazilian Roberto Campos, in his analysis of the "monetarist-structuralist" controversy on inflation, calls the ECLA "stucturalist" theory "an exercise in 'unnecessary' originality," since inflation in Latin America seems to "conform pretty much to what might be expected in the light of old-fashioned theories" (1961, 71–72).

The newly defined mission of the economics profession was to challenge the hegemony of nationalist economic thinking and change the interventionist policies that rival economists had inspired. The application of scientific principles would legitimize economic liberalization, promote free enterprise and foreign capital, discourage interpretations that blamed the United States for the problems of Latin America, and stop communist infiltration in student organizations (Valdés 1989, 119).

The reform of higher education was an important component of the modernization policies sponsored by inter-American cooperation projects in the 1950s and 1960s. In particular, bringing economics education back to the mainstream of the profession would aid the emergence of new cosmopolitan elites. Existing training programs were thought to be defective, for Latin American economists tended to erroneous or purely ideological views and were being taught planning techniques instead of economic theory (Valdés 1989, 207; Currie 1965, 13). The curricula of reformed economics schools would be purged of the ideological biases of leftist economics to offer students only the most advanced techniques of modern economics. Graduate economics programs were created to prepare students for admission in major universities in the United States. Foreign foundations funded these programs and hundreds of scholarships to attend graduate programs abroad. It was expected that returning graduates would help transform the teaching of economics in their respective countries, follow conventional standards in the conduct of economic research, and adopt former professors as professional referents in their future careers. The University of Chicago played a significant role in the recruitment of Latin American students and in the establishment of alternative training programs for economists in the region.[27]

In just one decade, the number of economists and economics schools multiplied dramatically. By the end of the 1960s, the expansion of orthodox economics had once again transformed the demographic and ideological makeup of the profession. In the next decade, economists consolidated their control over various sources of professional power (influence over the state bureaucracy, material resources, cultural legitimation, international contacts), successfully excluding other occupational groups from the policymaking arena. Not only did the number and influence of economists increase but intraprofessional conflicts were reduced. The

27. Valdés gives a detailed interpretation of the context and results of the agreement signed in 1955 between the University of Chicago and the Catholic University of Chile designed to train a new elite of economists in the neoclassic tradition. In Valdés's account, once the School of Economics at the Catholic University was transformed into a subsidiary of the Chicago School, it served as a laboratory for the creation of professional networks that exported the Chicago approach to the rest of the region. In 1965, a graduate economics program for Latin American students was created at the Catholic University to compete with the already existing ESCOLATINA. The Ford Foundation supported this project, considering the economics program at the Catholic University to be the most competent in Latin America. Also in the mid-1960s, under the leadership of Prof. Arnold Harberger, the University of Chicago established a center for the graduate training of Latin American economists. A prerequisite of this program was the "delatinamericanization" of the students. By 1975, twenty-six Ph.D.s and seventy-four M.A.s had returned to Latin America (1989, 278–79).

"old guard" of economic planners was degraded as obsolete and incompetent. Forced into the status of outsiders, they became a subordinate group within the profession.

Although numerous orthodox stabilization programs had been implemented in Latin America since the 1950s (with the support of private foreign missions and the International Monetary Fund), it was not until the mid-1970s that state-led import-substitution industrialization was discontinued after military regimes took power in several countries. In the most radical neoliberal experiments (Chile, Uruguay, and Argentina), economists were allowed to exercise broad control over state institutions. Neoconservative economists offered technical justifications to attempt the foundation of a new social and political order. Economic liberalization and self-regulated markets would be the basis for political freedom, defined as the absence of government controls. Planning and regional integration were delegitimized. Professional schools that departed from North American standards were eliminated and, in some cases, the state sponsored the training of economists abroad. While under the military regimes many of their rival economists suffered repression, were expelled from universities, forced into exile, accused of ignorance and lack of professionalism, government economists presented their program of economic and political reforms as an ethical imperative, claiming that the superior rationality of the "true" science would redress the consequences of half a century of policy errors caused by excessive politicization and the tendency to replace the market by direct government intervention (Vergara 1985; Ramos 1986).

In Chile, the achievements of the "Chicago boys" were acclaimed in international circles as nothing short of an economic "miracle." Triumphantly, the neoliberal paradigm was presented through the media as a cultural revolution that would solve the problems of economic and political modernization. Generations of young economists were sent to the University of Chicago. Upon their return, they were employed in state agencies to implement neoliberal reforms not only in economic policies but also in labor legislation, health care, education, poverty reduction, and even in local government. After the crisis of the early 1980s, the extreme neoconservative dogmatism was replaced by a more pragmatic approach and economic indicators improved. The reforms have continued in the 1990s. Under democratic conditions, the government program has combined macroeconomic stability with growth and social equity. A new team, formed by Socialist and Christian Democratic economists, has followed many of the proposals contained in the emerging "neostructuralist" paradigm.[28] Chile, which had been the cradle of structuralism and dependency theory, is now paraded as *the* model of sucessful market reforms (Bosworth, Dornbusch, and Labán 1994). Indeed, Chile in the 1990s is an exemplary case of the new economic consensus.

Convergence within an Internationalized Profession

To a significant extent, the current consensus among Latin American economists is founded in the absence of competing professional projects. Reactions to the dominant neoliberal paradigm exist, but they do not involve fundamental challenges to the established mission of the profession nor do they attempt to create alternative professional hierarchies or subcultures. The differences regarding the liberalization of trade are seen mostly as a matter of degree, between gradualists and the proponents of abrupt change (Meller 1994). There is a search for a "synthesis" rather than a new "economics."

The various groups of unorthodox economists that were excluded from governments and universities during the period of authoritarian political rule responded to this exclusion with strategies to enhance their international status within the mainstream of the profession. Many received training in major universities in Europe and the United States. Think tanks were formed and professional contacts with international foundations and foreign academic institutions resulted in many collaborative publications. They too were incorporated into an internationalized community.

Dissident economists challenged the dogmatism with which neoliberal economists had idealized the market and opposed the regressive social consequences of their policies, but they critically examined their own previous assumptions, their naive conception of the state's ability to correct structural distortions, and their insufficient recognition of the importance of macroeconomic equilibria, their neglect of productive efficiency and of the need to provide incentives for capital formation (Ramos and Sunkel 1993, 7).

In country after country, preference is being given to the recruitment of

---

28. On the neostructuralist approach, see Sunkel 1993.

economists who have studied in universities abroad.[29] A doctorate degree in a foreign university has become not only a source of status within the profession but an avenue to international networks. "A Harvard degree may not be as important as belonging to the Harvard network" (Centeno 1994, 148). In a globalized economy, having contacts with professional peers in other countries is an important advantage in inter- as well as intraprofessional competition.

A new sense of pragmatism and their cosmopolitan outlook helped economists to play a major role in ideological redefinitions of the Latin American left. The trend toward convergence of economic paradigms was aided by these experiences as much as by the changes in the international economy or the structural reforms implemented by their neoconservative colleagues.

With the return of political democracy in the context of a lingering economic crisis in the 1980s, not only were multilateral agencies and foreign creditors pushing for the adoption of standard measures of economic adjustment, but Latin American economists themselves promoted convergence by accelerating informal contacts and by formalizing their own cycles of consultations.[30] They publicly credit each other with providing ideas in the design of programs for debt negotiation, deficit reduction, and stabilization.[31] The ability of technopols to communicate with peers across national and ideological boundaries has allowed them to expand their control over the bureaucratic state apparatus and acquire positions of power in political parties and legislatures and in the conduct of foreign relations.

29. ECLA courses no longer attempt to replace conventional professional training, but were redesigned to cover highly targeted issues and last only a few weeks. Students no longer come from planning ministries but from central banks and budget offices (interview material, Santiago, August 1994).

30. The first International Summit Meeting of Finance Ministers was held in Santiago in 1992.

31. It was at a cocktail party in 1990 that the then Finance Minister Alejandro Foxley learned of the initiation of NAFTA negotiations from his friend, Mexican Minister Aspe. Chile subsequently campaigned to sign in the trade agreement (interview with Alejandro Foxley, August 1994). The collaboration between Pedro Aspe (Mexico finance minister under President Salinas) and Domingo Cavallo (the Argentinian minister of economy under President Menem) is illustrated in a recent issue of the *Wall Street Journal*: "Dr. Cavallo stalked angrily out of a meeting with bankers, leaving Dr. Aspe behind to do the dealing . . . Dr. Aspe spent most of the night with the bankers thrashing out details of an Argentine agreement that Dr. Cavallo subsequently approved" (Moffett 1994). The two men had met while studying at MIT and Harvard in the 1970s.

References

Abbott, A. 1988. *The System of Professions. An Essay on the Division of Expert Labor.* Chicago: University of Chicago Press.

———. 1991. The Order of Professionalization: An Empirical Analysis. *Work and Occupations* 18.4: 355–84.

Bosworth, B., R. Dornbusch, and R. Labán, eds. 1994. *The Chilean Economy: Policy Lessons and Challenges.* Washington, D.C.: The Brookings Institution.

Camp, R. A. 1975. The National School of Economics and Public Life in Mexico. *Latin American Research Review* 10.3:137–51.

———. 1977. *The Role of Economists in Policy-Making: A Comparative Study of Mexico and the United States.* Tucson, Ariz.: University of Arizona Press.

Campos, R. 1961. Two Views on Inflation in Latin America. In *Latin American Issues: Essays and Comments.* Edited by A. O. Hirschman. New York: The Twentieth Century Fund. 69–79.

Cardoso, F. H. 1977. The Originality of a Copy: CEPAL and the Idea of Development. *CEPAL Review.* 7–40.

Centeno, M. A. 1993. The New Leviathan: The Dynamics and Limits of Technocracy. *Theory and Society* 22:307–35.

———. 1994. *Democracy Within Reason. Technocratic Revolution in Mexico.* University Park, Pa.: Pennsylvania State University Press.

Coats, A. W. 1984. The Sociology of Knowledge and the History of Economics. In *Research in the History of Economic Thought and Methodology.* Vol. 2. Edited by W. Samuels. Greenwich, Conn.: JAI Press. 211–34.

———. 1993. *The Sociology and Professionalization of Economics.* London: Routledge.

Colander, D. 1989. Research on the Economics Profession. *Journal of Economic Perspectives* 3.4:137–48.

Colander, D. and R. Brenner, eds. 1992. *Educating Economists.* Ann Arbor, Mich.: University of Michigan Press.

Colander, D., and A. W. Coats, eds. 1993. *The Spread of Economic Ideas.* New York: Cambridge University Press.

Currie, L. 1965. *La enseñanza de la economía en Colombia.* Bogotá: Ediciones Tercer Mundo.

Díaz-Alejandro, C. 1984. Latin America in the 1930s. In *Latin America in the 1930s: The Role of the Periphery in the World Crisis.* Edited by R. Thorp. New York: St. Martin's Press. 27–49.

Dietz, J. L., and J. H. Street, eds. 1987. *Latin America's Economic Development: Institutionalist and Structuralist Perspectives.* Boulder, Colo.: Lynne Rienner.

Dornbusch, R., and S. Edwards, eds. 1991. *The Macroeconomics of Populism in Latin America.* Chicago: University of Chicago Press.

Dosman E., and D. H. Pollock. 1993. Raúl Prebisch, 1901-1971: La búsqueda constante. In *El legado de Raúl Prebisch.* Edited by E. V. Iglesias. Washington, D.C. Inter-American Development Bank. 11–44.

Drake, P. 1989. *The Money Doctor in the Andes: The Kemmerer Missions, 1923–*

1933. Durham, N.C.: Duke University Press.

————. 1994. Introduction: The Political Economy of Foreign Advisors and Lenders in Latin America. In *Money Doctors, Foreign Debts, and Economic Reforms in Latin America from the 1890s to the Present*. Edited by P. Drake. Wilmington, Del.: A Scholarly Resources Inc. Imprint. xi–xxxiii.

Ferrer, A. 1990. The Early Teachings of Raúl Prebisch. *CEPAL Review* 42:27–33.

Fishlow, A. 1988. The State of Latin American Economics. In *Changing Perspectives in Latin American Studies: Insights from Six Disciplines*. Edited by C. Mitchell. Stanford, Calif.: Stanford University Press.

Frey, B. S., and R. Eichenberger. 1993. American and European Economics and Economists. *Journal of Economic Perspectives* 7.4:185–93.

Furtado, C. 1988. *La fantasia organizada*. Buenos Aires: Eudeba.

Geddes, B. 1995. The Politics of Economic Liberalization. *Latin American Research Review* 30.2:195–214.

Gordon, L. 1961. Abrazo vs. Coexistence: Further Comments. In *Latin American Issues: Essays and Comments*. Edited by A. O. Hirschman. New York: The Twentieth Century Fund. 63–68.

Haddad, P. R. 1981. Brazil: Economists in a Bureaucratic-Authoritarian System. In *Economists in Government: An International Comparative Perspective*. Edited by A. W. Coats. Durham, N.C.: Duke University Press. 318–42.

Herrera, F. 1985. *Visión de América Latina, 1974–1984*. Santiago: Pehuén Editores.

Hirschman, A. O. 1961. Ideologies of Economic Development in Latin America. In *Latin American Issues: Essays and Comments*. Edited by A. O. Hirschman. New York: The Twentieth Century Fund. 3–42.

Hoffman, L. M. 1989. *The Politics of Knowledge: Activist Movements in Medicine and Planning*. Albany, N.Y.: State University of New York Press.

Kaufman, R., and B. Stallings. 1991. The Political Economy of Latin American Populism. In *The Macroeconomics of Populism in Latin America*. Edited by R. Dornbusch and S. Edwards. Chicago: University of Chicago Press. 15–34.

Kay, C. 1993. For a Renewal of Development Studies: Latin American Theories and Neoliberalism in the Era of Structural Adjustment. *Third World Quarterly* 14.4: 691–702.

Klamer, A. 1990. A Case of Mistaken Identities. In *The Making of an Economist*. Edited by A. Klamer and D. Colander. Boulder, Colo.: Westview Press. 169–85.

Larraín, J. 1989. *Theories of Development: Capitalism, Colonialism and Dependency*. Cambridge, England: Polity Press.

Love, J. 1980. Raúl Prebisch and the Origins of the Doctrine of Unequal Exchange. *Latin American Research Review* 15.3:45–72.

Markoff, J., and V. Montecinos. 1993. The Ubiquitous Rise of Economists. *Journal of Public Policy* 13.1:37–68.

Meller, P. 1994. Latin American Adjustment and Economic Reforms: Issues and Recent Experience. In *Rebuilding Capitalism: Alternative Roads after Socialism and Dirigism*. Edited by A. Solimano, O. Sunkel, and M. Blejer. Ann Arbor, Mich.: University of Michigan Press. 241–78.

Moffett, M. 1994. Seeds of Reform: Key Finance Ministers in Latin America Are

Old Harvard-MIT Pals. *Wall Street Journal*. (August): 1.

Montecinos, V. 1988. Economics and Power: Chilean Economists in Government: 1958–1985. Ph.D. diss. University of Pittsburgh.

———. Forthcoming. Economists, Parties and the Modernization of Chilean Politics. In *Deepening Democracy in Latin America*. Edited by K. von Mettenheim and J. Malloy. Pittsburgh, Pa.: University of Pittsburgh Press.

Montecinos, V., and J. Markoff. 1993. Democrats and Technocrats: Professional Economists and Regime Transitions in Latin America. *Canadian Journal of Development Studies* 14.1:7–22.

Muñoz, O. 1994. Toward Trade Opening: Legacies and Current Strategies. In *Intricate Links: Democratization and Market Reforms in Latin America and Eastern Europe*. Edited by J. Nelson et al. New Brunswick: Transaction Publishers. 61–103.

Packenham, R. A. 1992. *The Dependency Movement: Scholarship and Politics in Development Studies*. Cambridge, Mass.: Harvard University Press.

Pietschmann, H. 1981. Integración y burocracia en América Latina desde el punto de vista histórico. In *Integración y cooperación en América Latina*. Edited by M. Mols. Mainz: Konrad Adenauer Stiftung. 57–117.

Pinto, A., and O. Sunkel. 1966. Latin American Economists in the United States. *Economic Development and Cultural Change* 15:79–86.

Portes, A. 1988. Latin American Sociology in the Mid-1980s: Learning from Hard Experience. In *Changing Perspectives in Latin American Studies: Insights from Six Disciplines*. Edited by C. Mitchell. Stanford, Calif.: Stanford University Press.

Prebisch, R. 1962. El desarollo económico de América Latina y algunos de sus principales problemas. *Boletín Económico de la América Latina* 7.1.

Ramos, J. 1986. *Neoconservative Economics in the Southern Cone of Latin America, 1973–1983*. Baltimore, Md.: Johns Hopkins University Press.

Ramos, J., and O. Sunkel. 1993. Toward a Neostructural Synthesis. In *Development from Within: Toward a Neostructuralist Approach for Latin America*. Edited by O. Sunkel. Boulder, Colo.: Lynne Rienner.

Smelser, N. J., and R. Swedberg, eds. 1994. *The Handbook of Economic Sociology*. Princeton, N.J.: Princeton University Press.

Street, J. H. 1987. The Latin American Structuralists and the Institutionalists: Convergence in Development Theory. In *Latin America's Economic Development: Institutionalist and Structuralist Perspectives*. Edited by J. L. Dietz and J. H. Street. Boulder, Colo.: Lynne Rienner.

Sunkel, O., ed. 1993. *Development from Within: Toward a Neostructuralist Approach for Latin America*. Boulder, Colo.: Lynne Rienner Publishers.

Tancer, S. 1976. *Economic Nationalism in Latin America: The Quest for Economic Independence*. New York: Praeger Publishers.

Trice, H. 1993. *Occupational Subcultures in the Workplace*. Ithaca, N.Y.: ILR Press.

Valdés, J. G. 1989. *La Escuela de Chicago: Operación Chile*. Buenos Aires: Grupo Editora Zeta S.A.

Vergara, P. 1985. *Auge y caída del neoliberalismo en Chile*. Santiago: FLACSO.

Williamson, J. 1994. In Search of a Manual for Technopols. In *The Political Econ-*

omy of Policy Reform. Edited by J. Williamson. Washington, D.C.: Institute for International Economics. 11–28.

Witz, A. 1992. *Professions and Patriarchy.* London: Routledge.

Wynia, G. 1972. *Politics and Planners: Economic Development Policy in Central America.* Madison, Wisc.: University of Wisconsin Press.

Good Economics Comes to
Latin America, 1955–95

Arnold C. Harberger

Introduction, with Some Reminiscences

To be asked to speak on this subject has a special meaning for me. It
takes me, willy-nilly, on a long trip down memory lane. It all started, for
me, with a trip to Chile in July 1955. On this trip a committee consisting
of Earl J. Hamilton, Simon Rottenberg, T. W. Schultz, and myself was
charged with assessing whether the Department of Economics of the
University of Chicago should enter a university-to-university arrangement with the Faculty of Economic Sciences at the Catholic University
of Chile.

In retrospect, one might wonder why we recommended favorably on
such an arrangement, for at the moment there was not a single full-time
professor on the Catholic University's economics faculty. Perhaps more
notably, full-time professors were hard to find on *any* Latin American
economics faculty. We take credit for making it a key component of the
agreement that the Catholic University would create a minimum of four
full-time positions for "alumni" of our Chicago-based training program.
They made that promise, and vastly overfulfilled it. By the time our
AID-sponsored agreement finally lapsed in 1964, there were thirteen
full-time economists on the Catholic University's Faculty of Economic
Sciences; today there are close to forty. In the interim members of that
faculty played a catalytic role not only in the transformation of economic
education in Latin America, but also in the wave of modernization and

liberalization of economic policy that has swept Latin America in recent decades.

The Catholic University of Chile was perhaps the focal point of the two revolutions (of economic training and economic policy), but it would be distinctly unfair not to mention, in addition, the University of Chile. Without the benefit of any formal agreement or contract, the University of Chile provided more than a third of the participants in the University of Chicago's AID-sponsored project and its economics faculty experienced a major resurgence, not unlike that of the Catholic University.

I certainly had no inkling during the first week in Chile that I was shaking hands and conversing with young men who would end up as major figures in Chile's economic transformation. Among them were Sergio De Castro, the unquestioned architect as minister, first of economics and then of finance, of the liberalization and policy reform undertaken in Chile in the middle and later 1970s; Carlos Massad, Central Bank president during the presidency of Eduardo Frei I (late 1960s) and currently minister of health in the presidency of Eduardo Frei II (1994–); and Ernesto Fontaine, who almost singlehandedly has given Chile what is probably the most thorough (and technically sound) system of project evaluation to be found in the world today.

I mention these people because they were literally present at the very outset of our project. Many others whose association with the project came later were also instrumental on both the educational and policy fronts. Our own project spawned more than a dozen key ministers, Central Bank presidents, and budget directors. Students of the reformed economics faculties of Chile provided still more. And other leading U.S. institutions provided powerful reinforcements to the Chicago-trained group. (In Chile, over the period 1955–80, more than half of the economists trained at leading foreign institutions studied at Chicago; for Latin America as a whole, the same fraction is more like a third.) Chicago's dominant role was determined more than anything else by the university admissions policies. At Chicago, for many years, Latinos made up a quarter to a third of each year's entering class of about sixty. At Chicago's competing institutions (Harvard, MIT, Stanford, etc.), the norm was more like 10 percent of an entering class of thirty or forty. But I think it is fair to say that the graduates of these other institutions sang a tune quite similar to that of the so-called Chicago boys, and they deserve their share of the credit for the transformations that took place.

Latin America in the 1950s

Latin America in the 1950s was very different from Latin America today, as far as economic policy is concerned. Interventionism, paternalism, nationalism, and socialism were watchwords. It was a world of multiple exchange rates; of interest rates that more often than not were negative in real terms; of bank credit that was tightly allocated—by fiat rather than the market; of chronic budgetary deficits patched over by inflationary finance; of widespread price controls covering scores and often hundreds of different goods and services; of public utility companies (typically public sector) suffering chronic losses and characterized by deteriorated services, by brownouts and blackouts; of import tariffs that were often in excess of 100 percent, with rates of effective protection reaching 400 percent, 500 percent, and even more; of public sectors that extended into heavy industries quite routinely, but often far beyond, and that had gaping shortfalls of funds. Inflations were common, particularly in South (as against Central) America, and no one seemed to know how to minimize their adverse impact on the economy. Tax systems were patchwork quilts of economic mistakes, burdened by excessive rates, blemished by literally hundreds of unwarranted concessions, exemptions, and "incentives," and devoid of logical coherency, even on a tax-by-tax basis and even more so for the tax systems as a whole.

Three Waves of Reform

As good economics came to Latin America all this gradually changed. A first important wave of reform started in Chile in 1964, with a conscious effort on the part of the government to learn to "live with inflation" while still combating its underlying causes. The first three years of the Frei administration saw the inflation rate drop from over 40 to less than 20 percent per year, while economic growth proceeded at some 5 percent per annum. One key to this success story was a policy of adjusting the exchange rate regularly, to keep the real exchange rate from being constantly whipsawed by ongoing inflation together with intermittent huge devaluations. Another key was a new policy of consciously keeping short-term interest rates above the rate of inflation. This supplemented an earlier reform, under President Alessandri, which set up a savings and loan system that received deposits and and made middle- to long-term loans, both indexed to the price level. Finally, the country's reliance on price controls was drastically reduced (though not eliminated).

These Chilean innovations were quite quickly followed by similar reforms in other countries, notably Colombia and Brazil.

A second wave of reforms, centered mainly in the 1970s, saw the proliferation through much of Latin America of modern value-added tax systems. At the same time the economies were dramatically opened to international trade. The kingpins here were (a) the drastic reduction of quantitative trade controls, in favor of the more "impersonal" mechanism of tariffs; (b) the sharp reduction of average rates of tariff; and (c) the great compression of tariff rates to a comparatively narrow band. This last was critical, for it was the key to an enormous reduction in the exaggerated rates of effective protection that had prevailed previously. Once again Chile took the lead in tariff reform, achieving a uniform rate of 10 percent (except for autos) in June of 1979. This uniformity essentially guaranteed a 10 percent rate of effective protection to all actual and potential import-substituting activities.

A third wave of reforms came mainly in the 1980s, though its seeds could be seen earlier and its fruition is still incomplete. The focus of this set of reforms was on slimming down the public sector and modernizing and greatly strengthening the financial system. Key elements in this set of reforms were (a) bringing rational "economic pricing" to public sector enterprises, especially to public utilities; (b) privatizing much of what had been in the public sector, starting with ordinary industrial, commercial, and service operations and ending, typically, with the major public utilities; (c) modernizing the regulations and control mechanisms under which the financial system operated; (d) greatly extending the degree of openness of Latin America to the world capital markets; and (e) a truly stunning set of social security reforms, in which the "public" social security systems have become effectively privatized, with each beneficiary being required to accumulate funds for his/her own retirement in one or more individually vested funds.

Not Everything Worked as Planned

As is the case in most real-life endeavors, the road to reform had its rocky places. One of the more tantalizing observations concerns Latin America's inflations. Back in the 1950s and early 1960s, that is, *before* the region "learned to live with inflation," most major inflationary episodes topped out at about 100 percent per year. By this point the country and its people seemed to have "had enough" and to be willing to make the sacrifices needed to bring down the inflation rate. This range of inflation rates often led to changes of government, even to military coups in a few cases. Later, in the 1970s and 1980s, after the mechanisms for "living with inflation" had been put in place, it seems that the choke point escalated upward, to perhaps 400 or 500 percent in the 1970s and to something like 30 percent a month or so (in Bolivia, Argentina, Peru, and Brazil) in the 1980s. This surely is not what the architects of "living with inflation" had in mind. Rather it is a commentary on human frailty, on our vulnerability to temptation, transposed to the political arena.

A second spate of stumbling occurred in the area of banking regulation and control. The international debt crisis of the early 1980s was magnified and exacerbated by the wholesale collapse of Latin American banking systems. It is hard to assign a single cause here, but it is clear that the systems of regulation that were in place were unequal to the task in Argentina, Chile, Mexico, Peru, and Uruguay, and in other countries as well. It remains now to be seen whether the modernizing reforms instituted in the wake of the collapse were sufficient to meet new serious challenges (such as those now facing Argentina and Mexico).

A third area in which modernizing reforms ran into trouble was in the volatility of capital flows. Some blame the "herd instinct" of the great private international banks, which crassly thrust petrodollars at Latin America in 1979–81, only to ask for quick repayment as the debt crisis struck. Colombia is notable among the larger Latin American countries for its apparent immunity to the debt crisis, but this was due to its having fended off most of the blandishments of the international banks in the initial phase. People often take doctrinaire positions in this matter and are reluctant to appear to sanction capital controls, but I do not think that any knowledgeable observer would deny that *if* the capital inflows of 1979–81 had "happened to be" spread over six years rather than three, the whole world, and Latin America in particular, would have been a lot better off. Indeed, such a scenario might have avoided the catastrophic debt crisis entirely.

Some Vignettes on Policy Change

In spite of yielding to temptation, in spite of the stumbling blocks along the way, in spite even of the cataclysmic debt crisis itself, there can be no doubt that Latin America has much, much better economic policies today than it did in the 1950s and early 1960s.

The extent of the change is illustrated by tariff policies in Central America. The first experiment with a Central American Common Market (CAMC) in the 1960s was based on pure, protectionist import substitution. It is not much of an exaggeration to say that the separate countries merged their tariff structures by "equalizing" on whichever was the highest of their separate tariffs for a particular item. Even as late as 1988–89, after the initial CACM had basically collapsed, various collaborators and I had a hard time even talking about a tariff range of 5 to 20 percent for any Central American country. Yet by 1992 that was the accepted range for the bulk of them.

In another episode, working in Mexico in the early 1990s a group of us was told that it was pure wishful thinking to contemplate electricity prices that would be linked to increments in the world market price of oil. Yet a couple of years later that too was enshrined as part of Mexico's electricity pricing policy.

Finally, it is interesting to note how the seeds of reform found their way to Latin America. The Chilean income tax reform of 1974 was largely based on the magnificent report of the Canadian Royal Commission on Taxation (the so-called Carter Commission), while the inspiration for Chile's innovative "privatized" retirement scheme came from none other than the Teachers Insurance and Annuity Association/College Retirement Equities Fund (TIAA/CREF), through which most U.S. academics have provided for their retirement for the past fifty years or more.

Issues of Doctrine

When "good economics" was just coming to Latin American in the late 1950s, the path was far from easy. In the way stood a bulwark of doctrinaire isolationism and protectionism: the "old" ECLA (UN Economic Commission for Latin America), which actively sponsored and fostered the interventionist, statist, illiberal policies of the era. That was an era of fierce debate between the so-called structuralist and monetarist schools, with the former counting ECLA as one of its principal bastions.

I find it hard, even from today's vantage point, to define precisely what structuralism was. It did not proceed via rigorous analysis from the ground up, as it were. Rather it referred vaguely to "inelasticities" of various types—of foreign demand for raw materials, of domestic supply of agricultural products, and so on—that somehow stood in the way of progress, made inflation almost inevitable (even, to some, desirable), and made widespread state intervention a sensible "solution" to Latin American problems.

A watershed in the debate between monetarism and structuralism was a major conference that took place in Rio de Janeiro in December 1961. It was attended by a cross section of the world economics profession, including people like Gottfried Haberler, Sir Roy Harrod, Ursula Hicks, Nicholas Kaldor, plus rising young stars like Robert Mundell and Mario Simonsen. The consensus that emerged from that conference was the following: If a substantial chronic fiscal deficit financed by monetary expansion was considered a structural phenomenon, then we were all (or nearly all) willing to be called structuralists; if, on the other hand, it was considered a monetary phenomenon, then we were all (or nearly all) willing to be called monetarists. On the fundamental cause of most of the great Latin American inflations, there simply was no doubt.

The Strengthening of Academic Institutions

I have already noted the initial weakness of centers of economic training in Latin America and their huge reliance on part-time faculty. One could also add, for many of them, a tendency to look at economics in philosophical or ideological rather than technical terms. Most of the ideology was left-wing (statist, structuralist, or neo-Marxist), but there were also isolated centers with a right-wing orientation. What they all had in common was the view that the "right" answers were more philosophical than technical.

I probably exaggerate when I say that this has vastly changed over the last four decades, because there are probably scores of institutions in Latin America that still fit the above description. The big point is that those scores of places contribute very little to the flow of young Latin American men and women to the great graduate schools of economics. Likewise they have not contributed at all to the coterie of ministers, central bankers, legislators, and heads of state who have effectuated the major economic reforms that we have described.

This coterie of reformers has come largely from a quite restricted set of schools; the two Chilean universities; the Getulio Vargas Foundation and the University of São Paulo in Brazil; the Universities of Córdoba and Tucumán and the Argentine Center for Macroeconomic Studies (CEMA) in Argentina; and in Mexico the Autonomous Technological Institute of Mexico (ITAM) and the Colegio de Mexico. These institutions might be called the core group that dedicated itself to the modern science of economics from quite early on. More recently, other institutions have joined the modernizing trend: the Catholic Universities of Buenos Aires, Lima, and Rio de Janeiro, the University of the Pacific in Lima, the National Universities of Costa Rica and Uruguay, the University of the Andes in Bogota, those of Nuevo Leon in Mexico and of La Plata in Argentina.

Let me apologize right away to those major modernizing institutions I may have left out; I did not attempt an exhaustive list. My point is that most of the modernizing entities can be listed in one paragraph. Those institutions where the old-time (ideological) religion still reigns are far more numerous, though happily much less influential. Ideology has today very little foothold in Argentina and Chile. It is still rife in the second and third tier of institutions in Brazil and Mexico and quite generally in Central America. This observation underscores how important is the task of generally improving the training of economists throughout Latin America.

The Econometric Society

It will come as a surprise to some economists to learn that the Econometric Society has played a major role in the establishment of modern economic science in Latin America. Most economists see that society as the ultimate center of rarified, abstruse theorizing and as the publisher of a journal that most economists cannot understand. The story of its role in Latin America takes on a special piquancy when viewed against this backdrop.

The facts are as follows. During 1978 and 1979, there was a move within the Econometric Society to broaden its membership in Latin America, which until then accounted for a bare handful of members. A committee of the society was set up, chaired by Marc Nerlove, to recommend a course of action. Thus were born the Latin American regional meetings of the Econometric Society, which take place annually except for the years in which a world congress of the society is held.

These Latin American meetings began in 1980 in Buenos Aires. They attracted modern, technically oriented young economists from throughout the region. The meetings featured papers of very high quality and discussion and debate at a level virtually unprecedented in Latin America. What was (and is) overwhelmingly notable is the absence of any ideological overtone, not to mention ideological conflict, at these meetings. I attribute this in part to the "brand name"—the label of the Econometric Society—which by itself probably serves as a repellent to most Latin American ideologues. But the founding committee took further steps to guarantee this result by recommending an ample representation of Fellows of the Econometric Society at each of its Latin American regional meetings. Such representation has become a genuine tradition. The presence of a dozen or so Fellows (who are almost by definition economists of world stature) helps to attract serious Latin American economists to the meeting. The fact that these Fellows serve as panelists, discussants, and commentators further helps to set a scientific tone for the entire proceedings.

The second most notable feature of the Latin American regional meetings of the Econometric Society is the fact that on the whole they do not share the abstruse, arid character of most of that society's other meetings (and its publications). This I attribute to the fact that economic problems are much more central issues in Latin American countries and societies than they are in the advanced industrial countries. So even highly technically trained Latin American economists want to focus on real-world problems and policies. This gives the Latin American regional meetings a liveliness and vitality that makes them "special events" for Econometric Society members from outside the region.

Latin American Economists in the World Profession

The preceding section leads quite naturally to the question, How do the Latin American economists of today stack up vis-à-vis their counterparts in the advanced countries? The answer is, Very well indeed. It is hard to believe, looking back from today, that in the early 1950s Latin Americans had virtually no representation as professors in, say, the top dozen or so economics departments in the U.S. Today, it is hard to find a top department without at least one or two representatives of Latin America in its faculty. If in the early days one could not find any, by the late 1960s and early 1970s there were a good handful or two, including Miguel Sidrauski, Carlos Diaz-Alejandro, Daniel Schydlowsky,

Carlos Rodriguez, Guillermo Calvo, and Marcelo Selowsky. Today the number is so great that it would be a major enterprise to put together a corresponding list.

The story is similar when it comes to the major international institutions. Not counting the InterAmerican Development Bank (for obvious reasons), one can easily list a dozen or so Latin Americans who have reached the very highest ranks in entities like the International Monetary Fund (Calvo, Mario Blejer, Claudio Loser, Mario Teijeiro) and the World Bank (Selowsky, Miguel Martinez, Sebastian Edwards, Vittorio Corbo), as well as scores who have played major roles such as IMF representatives and World Bank country economists.

The Policy Teams in Latin America

In my view, as one who looks for real-world contributions of the science and profession of economics, the true fruition of the development of modern economics in Latin American should be found in the policy reforms that have been implemented and in the benefits that have accrued to the peoples of the region. To me, it is notable how well economics has succeeded measured by this metric. Also notable is the degree to which teamwork has been involved in the process.

For the early (1964–67) Chilean policy success, I credit a team headed by Sergio Molina, Carlos Massad, and Edgardo Boenninger. Brazil's miracle years came under teams headed by Robert Campos and then by Antonio Delfim Neto.

Chile's military government had two sets of teams. Among the many leading figures in the first (1974–81) were Sergio De Castro, Jorge Cauas, Miguel Kast, Jose Piñera, Pablo Baraona, and Sergio de la Caudra. Among those in the second (1985–89) were Hernan Büchi, Martin Costabal, Jorge Selume, Juan Andrés Fontaine, Cristián Larroulet, and María Teresa Infante. Chile's magnificent transition to democratic government was managed by a team that included Alejandro Foxley, Jorge Marshall, Carlos Ominami, José Pablo Arrellano, and Rene Cortázar.

In Mexico, a particularly rich team of economists was active in the policy reform process. This was largely due to a brilliantly foresighted program of scholarships for education abroad (CONACYT), which was responsible for the education abroad of Presidents Carlos Salinas and Ernesto Zedillo; Ministers (Secretarios) Pedro Aspe, Jaime Serra, Guillermo Ortiz; key undersecretaries like Francisco Gil Diaz and Fernando Sanchez Ugarte; major reformers like Herminio Blanco and Arturo Fernandez Perez, and many more. I've often said that very likely CONACYT was a secret weapon without which Mexico's economic transformation would never have been accomplished.

A Postscript

I hope it is clear to readers how modern economic training has fed the process of liberalization, modernization, and policy reform in Latin America. The urgent need for the future is to continue this training process in the countries where reform is already well underway and to mount a comparable training enterprise in the numerous countries where it is sorely lacking.

Continuity is needed in the more advanced countries because the very success of their economies has led to a powerful drain of economic talent toward the private sector. Good salaries for policy economists are essential if the quality of the recent past is to be maintained. But more important, a continuing flow of fresh talent is needed, so that both the numbers and the quality of the policy teams can be preserved, even as a steady stream of very able people drifts off to other pursuits.

In the less fortunate countries, where economic training is still of low quality, enormous efforts are needed to effectuate what can fairly be called a rebirth of economics as a science and as a profession. Training abroad is essential to begin with, but this must be complemented by the creation of worthy centers of economic instruction in local universities or other institutions. This is not a task that can be accomplished by an occasional student going to Harvard, another to Stanford, another to Chicago, and so on. The situation demands a critical mass of talented young people willing and able to dedicate themselves to the tasks at hand. But it also demands that they be given the opportunity and the scope to accomplish that task. Somewhere on the local scene, the old guard has to be dislodged or else converted into an enthusiastic ally in this process.

The Evolution of Postwar Doctrines in Development Economics

William Ascher

Introduction

Development economics has gone through a peculiar evolution over the past fifty years, leaving the field curiously weak and ambivalent with respect to development doctrines and distributional issues. This paper traces some of the dynamics of this evolution, focusing essentially on the rise and dominance of a diluted neoclassicism in methodology and epistemology, and an antistatist doctrine that nonetheless is still pursued by and through state institutions. While this paper does not challenge the remarkably consensual views on which theorists and debates have been most notable in this evolution,[1] it does offer rather novel interpretations of the epistemological and professionalist roots of these debates and accounts for why neoclassical approaches have come to dominate even if neoclassical prescriptions are still highly arguable.

By "neoclassical" I mean the broad set of approaches to economic theory, research, and practice associated with the Walrasian commit-

---

1. Histories of the evolution of development economics can be found in two World Bank collective memoir volumes, *Pioneers in Development*, edited by Meier and Seers (1984), and *Pioneers in Development*, edited by Meier (1987); Hirschman's entertaining "The Rise and Decline of Development Economics" (1981); Lal 1985; Little 1982.

One striking characteristic of these histories is the overwhelming consensus on who were the leading (if not necessarily the most correct) figures in development economics. No one fails to mention Rosenstein-Rodan, Nurkse, Singer, Lewis, Leibenstein, Harry Johnson, Harrod and Domar, Prebisch, Hirschman, and Streeten. The same stories are being told around the campfires.

ment to mathematize economic theory and analysis, the Marshallian focus on marginalist analysis, and a strong egoist rationality assumption. Naturally, there are many other authorities associated with neoclassical economics besides these, and the "neoclassical movement" is still evolving—which is indeed a main conclusion of this essay. Perhaps the most parsimonious way to characterize the "neoclassical hard core" is to offer Remenyi's (1979, 56–59) list of hard-core propositions:

1. Consumers and producers can legitimately be assumed to be rational decision makers who know their wants.
2. Economic activity is motivated by individual self-interest.
3. More is better than less.
4. Given perfect knowledge and good government, economic welfare is maximized by free competition.
5. Although welfare and economic welfare are not synonymous, the latter is a good approximation for the former.
6. Stable Pareto-efficient equilibrium solutions can be defined for any and all markets relevant to economic research and analysis.
7. Everything has its opportunity cost.
8. Abstract, reduced-form models and simplifying assumptions are valid tools of economic analysis.

At least in the early post–World War II era, many leading development economists, and economic practice, often rejected some of these principles. The first two propositions concerning self-centered rationality were frequently challenged; the virtues of free competition were challenged even more strongly; and the wisdom of research and analysis relying on equilibrium analysis or abstract mathematized models was often questioned. Thus from the end of World War II through the 1970s development economics was an exciting, iconoclastic, contentious field, making profound if arguable diagnoses of why the economic structures in low-income countries inhibited economic growth. There were also monumental clashes over normative principles, ranging from the weight to be given to distributional objectives to the appropriate form of government involvement in the economy.

Yet today, leading development economists rarely proffer bold theories any more; their work seems to dissolve into technique. The most respected development economists generally embrace neoclassical rhetoric and methodologies, even though they reject first-order principles of neoclassical economics such as an efficient market price system. Their policy advice is split between doctrinaire exhortations that governments ought to eliminate policy distortions, and their practical work that takes these distortions as givens. Policy advice involving structural transformations is rare. Normative arguments seem to be practically nonexistent. The "end of ideology" predicted for so many fields seems to have struck quietly but effectively in development economics.

Furthermore, while much of development economics in the 1950s through the 1970s was devoted to the formulation and defense of *sectoral strategies*, broad development strategies based on the need to promote investment into particular sectors have largely disappeared among highly respected, technically admired economists. This disappearance of sectoral strategizing as a focus of development economics research *and* policy is both striking and serious. In theory, a sectoral "strategy," or at least a sectoral emphasis, emerges from the sum of micro, project decisions made in planning agencies, government budget offices, and elsewhere, through the process of selecting investment opportunities of the highest rates of return. Yet this process is often a sham. The rate of return is rather easily manipulated through the weighting of potential risks, how much indirect costs and benefits are captured by the analysis, and how noneconomic benefits and costs are monetized. Thus unstated sectoral strategies frequently guide the selection of projects by analysts who then rationalize them by assigning those projects high rates of return. In being left unstated, these sectoral strategies still operate, but without adequate analysis. In other words, the neoclassical substitution of project-by-project rate-of-return analysis for explicit sectoral doctrines has driven sectoral strategies underground, where they are under-examined and often undebated.

How do we explain these developments? This essay tries to link them to the evolution of development economics as well as to the actual twists and turns of developing economies. The argument is, first, that neoclassical economics has become the only professionally legitimate approach for development economists working in most government agencies (in developed and developing countries) and international organizations addressing economic development issues. Whereas Albert O. Hirschman (1981) argued fifteen years ago that neoclassical economics was competing with Marxism, neo-Marxism, and a distinctive development economics, today there is scant explicit competition.

Second, and ironically, in order for students of developing economies to adhere to neoclassical economics, the interpretation of neoclassical economics has been diluted in terms of its substantive and theoretical content. It has become an analytical framework for representing formerly heretical positions by invoking some maximization postulate. Yet these positions often do not conform to what had been considered as first principles of neoclassical economics. In terms of historiography, this means that the conventional interpretation of the evolution of development economics as a clash between so-called structuralist and neoclassical approaches, with the eventual victory of the neoclassicists, is profoundly misleading.

Third, much of the history of economic development doctrines has been a series of pleas to provide greater investment to particular sectors. But sectoral theories, qua theories, have no place in the neoclassical framework, which views investments only in terms of rates of return rather than the sectoral logic that dominated development economics debates in earlier periods. "Neoclassical" economists have sectoral preferences, but they are generally not expressed or defended in terms of neoclassical theory or methodology.

Fourth, the prescriptions of neoclassical economics, in a complicated and perhaps ironic way, actually support doctrines of greater progressivity of income distribution for the many developing countries with highly skewed income distributions. This is because of both the regressivity in the rigidities and rents that neoclassical perspectives condemn, and the more straightforward focus on poverty-prone sectors that neoclassical economists have targeted since the 1970s. However, neoclassical economics has retained an image of income regressivity, established early on by the infamous "trickle down" model and reinforced by both the theoretical silence of neoclassical economics on the equity issue and the apparent association of neoclassical restructuring with austerity programs.

Early "Structuralist" Tenets

When a sizable number of economists turned their attention to less-developed countries after World War II, the inadequacies of standard, so-called neoclassical economic theory of the day seemed palpable. The premise that markets would find the optimal balances of price, supply, and demand faced contradictions at every turn. Labor markets did not clear; unemployment and underemployment were endemic. Dualism in production technologies and labor pools was evident, but had no place in the early neoclassical models. Gunnar Myrdal (1956) pointed out that neoclassicists (such as Paul Samuelson) had shown that the neoclassical model implied equalization of incomes across countries, but that obviously was not occurring. This result may have been arguable as a significant falsifier of neoclassical theory, but it also undercut the normative basis of neoclassicism, since more rather than less inequality seemed to be emerging from a largely free-trade international regime.

Therefore development economics in the post–World War II period began by asking whether conditions distinctive to developing countries could account for their low levels of productivity. Underdeveloped economies may have structural rigidities that prevent market forces from generating economic growth. Such rigidities were seen as defying neoclassical premises (Myrdal 1956, 103-4). But what sorts of "structural" rigidities? Three classes of explanations were then available.

One class of explanations was *ontological*—the various types of economic actors may not fit the profit-, income-, and utility-maximizing mold of the classical model of the economic man: landowners content to leave their land underexploited despite profit opportunities, peasants unwilling to adopt more productive farming practices out of custom or habit, workers unwilling to move to better jobs, family firms emphasizing family solidarity at the expense of efficiency, consumers dazzled by the mere fact that particular goods were imported, and so on.

A second class of explanations was *macrostructural*: developing economies were marked by dualism of technology, productivity, and incomes; labor markets did not clear (Lewis 1954); economies of scale were lacking for private actors to undertake useful development of infrastructure and basic industries (Rosenstein-Rodan 1943); financial systems were too shallow to permit investment to go where it would be most productive (McKinnon 1973). Some of these macrostructural explanations invoked the position of developing countries vis-à-vis the richer countries in international trade: for example, that developing countries suffered from limited price elasticity of demand for their exports; that surplus labor enabled importing countries to enjoy consumer surpluses at the expense of domestic labor; that the terms of trade for raw materials would deteriorate (Prebisch 1949).

A third class of explanations was *parametric*: the very fact of being low-income, low-productivity countries meant that impressive rates of growth were impossible or unlikely without drastic action. For example, insofar as low incomes dictated low savings, poor countries could not depend on the market to mobilize high levels of investment; low incomes would also deter farmers and other actors from taking risks to try to achieve higher productivity; and low levels of technology made international trade difficult, even for goods and services for which the developing countries had comparative advantages. Some of these parametric explanations were antithetical to neoclassical assumptions; for example, the argument that demand for basic commodities such as food and shelter is primarily a function of income levels rather than prevailing prices.

However, *other parametric explanations were consistent with neoclassical assumptions*: even rational economic actors in well-functioning markets may not have enough capital or other endowments to propel economic growth. The concept of a "low-level equilibrium trap," used by Galenson and Leibenstein (1955) to denote the failure of potentially high-return investment opportunities to manifest their potential through market signals (i.e., a market failure), could just as easily denote an equilibrium of low endowments, low incomes, low savings, and low productivity-enhancing potentials in general that was consistent with neoclassical principles.

The two most important policy dilemmas emerging from these diagnoses revolved around the nature of sectoral strategies and the role of monetary and fiscal policy to promote investment. The connection between these dilemmas was the problem that if the economy on its own could not generate a sectoral balance conducive to high levels of economic growth, then higher growth might require monetary and fiscal policies that would enable the state to mobilize and direct investment across sectors.

The *sectoral strategy* issue concerns how investments ought to be allocated across the economy and has three direct facets:

- *who decides*: the loci of investment decisions
- *by what methods*: the analytics to be used by investors (public or private) to choose investment targets and amounts
- *to what result*: the distribution of investments across economic sectors, regions, and business-size categories

These three facets provide a rich set of doctrinal variation. The investment-locus issue separates the preferences for allocation by the government and the private sector, and, on a more specific level, entities within government or the private sector.

The *methodology* issue sets up the procedural doctrines of alternative economic frameworks, including the neoclassical approach. The alternatives include:

- *highest-return investment selection*: the neoclassical alternative, using market prices if the economy is not too distorted, shadow prices if it is; in either case determined econometrically. Where market prices are distorted, the state has the options of removing the distortions (the usual ideological stance of the neoclassicists), accepting the misallocation of investment due to the price distortions, or redirecting investment through subsidies or direct state financing.
- *input-output analysis*: identification of (a) missing or undersupplied inputs and (b) missed opportunities to use outputs productively, based on analysis of input-output matrices. The bottlenecks thus identified, if they cannot be overcome through importing or exporting, would warrant greater domestic investment, whether promoted by subsidization or direct state investment.
- *sectoral balancing*: based on holistic judgments of optimal sectoral sizes and relationships among sectors. This theoretical assessment of endowments yields predictions of which sectors and industries would be most productive, even if current empirical (i.e., econometric) indications of high returns and productivity are lacking. The concept of *potential* comparative advantage provides a rationale for "infant industry" subsidization or protection even if no measurable price signals are available.

The *outcomes*, in terms of sectoral (or even regional) balances, include:

- *heavy industry*: directing investment into the capital-intensive, basic industries (e.g., the so-called Mahalanobis model of India's Second Five-Year Plan)
- *import substitution industrialization*: directing investment into the production of imported manufactures, beginning with those industries (generally light or medium) most easily developed
- *basic needs strategy*: directing investment into the provision of minimal levels of goods and services for the lowest-income segments of the population
- *human resource development*: directing investment into education, nutrition, health, and other social sector expansions to increase the productivity of labor

- *decentralized development*: directing investment into less developed, less industrialized areas
- *frontier development*: directing investment into the least developed, generally natural-resource-rich areas; emphasizing whatever sectors (usually natural resource exploitation and processing) are most available in the frontier areas

The first wave of sectoral theories went under the broad rubric of "balanced growth." Balanced growth theorists asserted that sectoral (or regional) investment needed to be *rebalanced* because the economy would not do so of its own accord. In some of the earliest expositions (Rosenstein-Rodan 1943; Nurkse 1953, 1957; Scitovsky 1954), theorists argued that rebalancing of some sort was necessary, though its specific nature might vary from one country to another. Once this principle became enshrined, other theorists singled out specific sectors, as listed above, justified by theoretical arguments as to why their growth would be pivotal. An auxiliary argument was usually advanced to explain why a particular sector's investment opportunities had been ignored, typically a market failure argument.

A minority view was that input-output analysis could identify the bottlenecks and thus where sectoral investments ought to be directed, based on Leontief's methodology. If the overall configuration of the economy could be captured by assessing the existing and potential connections among and within its industries, then sectoral issues could be addressed explicitly and quantitatively. But in its applications, input-output analysis was less holistic and more inductive or econometric than the structuralist position, and yet decidedly nonclassical. The epistemology of the input-output approach was agnostic: the bottlenecks could be identified by comparing actual matrices of the country under examination with matrices of other, presumably more balanced economies, but the sources of bottlenecks could not be identified by the methodology. Intersectoral theory could not be expressed econometrically. Nor could this approach settle whether "getting the prices right" would solve the problem without state intervention.

One additional structuralist view that was clearly at odds with both "balanced growth" and the input-output philosophy was the *unbalanced* growth strategy popularized by Albert O. Hirschman (1958). The essential rationale was that low-growth equilibria could be jogged by investments in industries with potential "backward and forward linkages," but not the immediate linkages that an input-output matrix would address. The objection that neoclassical economists would make, namely that the demand at existing prices may not clear the supply that the new investment would generate, was seen as short-term and surmountable. In *Development Projects Observed* (1967), Hirschman went so far as to try to chronicle investment projects that produced decent results even though their original purposes proved to be impossible to pursue. While Hirschman was one of the few to make this approach specific, in fact it was implicitly accepted as a principle of various efforts at "forced development," wherein investments in a sector or area (e.g., a growth pole, a new city, an enterprise zone) not yet linked to relevant inputs and outputs (i.e., infrastructure and markets) would somehow stimulate the development of these backward and forward linkages. The unbalanced growth strategy was also strongly at odds with neoclassical premises, which questioned why the market would respond favorably in the absence of appropriate price signals.

The argument that economies needed to be moved to either greater balance or greater imbalance beyond what the price signals could accomplish led rather straightforwardly to the monetary and fiscal "structuralist" doctrines. This idea dovetailed nicely with the conviction that the sheer lack of savings and investable capital was also a crucial if not necessarily permanent problem for developing countries. Monetary and fiscal "structuralists," who often posited that deficit spending, easy money, and the resulting inflation were necessary evils, were convinced that the capital needed to finance sufficient expansion of key sectors would be provided neither by the private sector (which lacked either sufficient capital or the incentives to invest in the appropriate sectors) nor from tax revenues that could feasibly be extracted by governments (Felix 1961).

The Scientific Research Program of
Increasingly Neoclassicist Development Economics

In one sense, neoclassicists were conspicuously absent from the ranks of theorists producing the canon of development literature in the 1950–70s period. The few exceptions, such as Peter Bauer and Harry Johnson, seemed old-fashioned, as if they were clinging to an orthodoxy developed in Europe and the United States that simply did not hold in developing countries. The neoclassical theorists who entered into the balanced-growth debate typically addressed the balanced-growth hypotheses by asking whether being in the state of balance correlated with higher growth rates. Solow and Samuelson (1953) gave "balanced growth" a more or less neoclassical interpretation as the evenness in the expansion or contraction of commodity production across the economy, thus bringing it close to the concept of equalizing rates of return across the economy. This formulation defines balance with respect to whether industries are in equilibrium, but it does not address the question of what that equilibrium would be, how to identify it, or how to reach it. Chenery and Taylor (1968) defined balanced growth in terms of the proportionality of the primary, secondary, and tertiary sectors. Finally, Winegarden (1970) defined balance in a more explicitly neoclassical way as the similarity of rates of return across sectors. All of these approaches were amenable to econometric analysis. In contrast, the "structuralist" pioneer Ragnar Nurkse (1953) advocated investments in sectors with the greatest promise of domestic income elasticity of demand. This reflected the theoretical premises, rather than empirical or econometric findings, that latent domestic demand existed for various products, which could be stimulated by supply expansion even in the initial absence of price signals; and that international demand could not be a reliable basis for continued growth (the export pessimism later formulated more explicitly by Raul Prebisch). Scitovsky (1987, 55) points out that in its nationalistic mode, the income elasticity criterion runs counter to both comparative advantage theory and economies-of-scale theory.

These approaches were subjected to econometric testing in the 1960s and early 1970s (Swamy 1967; Chenery and Taylor 1968; Winegarden 1970; Yotopolous and Lau 1970, and 1975). The tests were generally cross-national and surprisingly crude. The cross-national testing approach did not distinguish the imbalanced countries that were moving toward greater balance from those that were in a steady state of imbalance, nor those balanced countries that were becoming less balanced from those that were not. Not surprisingly, the results were contradictory and inconclusive. The inconclusiveness of the results may well be responsible for killing the testing of balanced growth hypotheses as part of the "scientific research program"[2] of development economics.

By the 1970s, economists doing research on developing countries were similarly adapting or employing what appeared to be an increasingly

2. This Lakatosian concept has been applied to development economics by Remenyi (1979).

quantitative and marginalist methodology. In a remarkable article written in 1975, Hollis Chenery lauds twenty development economists as leading structuralists. Asserting that structuralist methodology "has evolved over the past twenty-five years from a set of rather intuitive hypotheses to models of increasing empirical validity and analytical rigor" (320), Chenery goes on to cite two-sector models, the development of techniques for estimating the shadow price of labor, and the simulation and optimization models used for input-output analysis as prime examples of structuralist accomplishments. Chenery also argues that the fundamental tenets of structuralist theory had been borne out, with the exception of the assumption of inelastic demand for exports—which he asserts needs to be "seriously qualified." Having established its premises, the scientific research program of structuralism, according to Chenery, then focused on "developing a second generation of models in the structuralist tradition that are designed for statistical application in individual countries, rather than for deriving broad generalizations." However, because "structuralist alternatives do not lead automatically to policy conclusions . . . they must also be embodied in an explicitly general equilibrium framework" (311–12).

Yet these are, by and large, efforts with which a neoclassicist would feel very comfortable. Indeed, many if not all of the economists mentioned by Chenery can be labeled neoclassicists as easily as structuralists. Gustav Ranis's claims to fame include his rejection of the usual structuralist assumption of fixed production coefficients in his study of Japanese capital use (Little 1982, 176). Chenery himself notes that John Fei, Gustav Ranis, Louis Lefeber, Allen Kelley, John Williamson, and R. J. Cheetham were developing *neoclassical* two-sector models (1975, 312). If the structuralist and neoclassic are different approaches, how can these gentlemen labor in the vineyards of structuralism?

Despite his initial differentiation among the three approaches, Chenery's account really deals with the *synthesis* of neoclassical methodology and structuralist theory. Whether these individuals identify themselves as structuralists or as neoclassicists may be important in terms of their impact on the discipline (as we shall explore later), but is not important in terms of our understanding of the synthesis.

Chenery argues essentially that despite the confirmation of structuralist tenets, neoclassical techniques were necessary to do rigorous economic analysis based on these theories. The other alternative, input-output analysis, was, according to Chenery, disappointing because of its lack of sensitivity to price responses.

Chenery's happy merger of neoclassicism and structuralism would seem to clash with Tony Killick's interpretation of structuralism as "antimarginalist." Killick (1978, 14–17) considers the structuralists' broadest attack on neoclassicism to be the rejection of marginalist methodology, including the validity of general equilibrium analysis. Some argued that whether or not price information could be trusted, it was of little relevance, because price changes simply did not elicit much response in supply and demand. If one accepts that supply and demand are sluggish in responding to price changes, then only very large price changes can shift supply and demand significantly, and the disruption of these very large price changes has to be taken into account in comparing the efficacy of manipulating prices (i.e., getting the "right" price for the desired levels of supply and demand) as opposed to manipulating supply more directly (Little 1982, 21). Theorists like Nurkse, Scitovsky, Hirschman, and Leibenstein worried that the basically static marginalist analysis would identify apparently optimal equilibria near existing levels of production that would be far inferior to more ambitious combinations of investment, production, and consumption. These scenarios would escape the attention of the marginalists, they argued, because marginal analysis does not take into account as-yet-unrealized gains from economies of scale, increased demand due to higher income levels, or increased profitability due to others' investments. The limitation of using econometrics is that the estimation depends on *prevailing* parameters and levels and that they have little value for estimating major departures (i.e., nonmarginal changes) from the existing structure.

But for Chenery (unlike Killick), structuralist tenets could be tested econometrically, and analysis based on assumptions other than those of neoclassical economics could be conducted through optimization and simulation modeling. With simulation models that can stipulate conditions far different from prevailing ones, the analyst can try to examine equilibria arising from nonincremental changes; how effectively is a matter of debate pitting the simulation devotees (such as Alan Manne) against the econometric purists and antimarginalists. If the development economist can model structural rigidities through the use of general equilibrium, then the *comprehensiveness* so important for the structuralist perspective can be brought into the analysis, and can be met with neoclassical tools. If the development economist can also model relationships holding under conditions very different from those currently prevailing, whether through the use of neoclassical methods or input-output methods, then the criterion of sensitivity to nonincremental changes is also met. *Thus these new neoclassical structuralists are methodological optimists.* Chenery does not recognize the structuralists' antipositivist skepticism on the feasibility of exact analysis. He says that the structuralists need—and can successfully use—a general equilibrium framework; Killick (1978, 16–17) points out that such a framework is antithetical to the epistemology of the methodological skeptics among the structuralists. Clearly, Chenery's definition of structuralism leaves behind these skeptics. In light of these considerations, it is fascinating that Paul Krugman (1994, 45–46) has recently claimed that the tenets of what he calls "high development theory" associated with Rosenstein-Rodan, Myrdal, Hirschman, and Nurkse—essentially equivalent to the so-called structuralist positions—could not be expressed rigorously with the methodological and theoretical tool kit available before the mid-1970s—but now they can.

Another, perhaps more subtle alteration of the neoclassical perspective masquerading as methodological improvement or expansion was the incorporation of expectations into the "optimization" framework. Poor information in developing countries could lead to large discrepancies between the actual state of the economy and what economic actors believed it to be. Why do rural workers continue to migrate to cities with high unemployment? The famous Harris-Todaro model explained the anomaly by invoking expected wages rather than the actual wages that the analyst might be able to calculate (Harris and Todaro 1970). By resorting to expectations, the model rejects the first-order neoclassical assumption of full information; without it, the labor market does not clear, but a rational-actor explanation can account for the migration. Put another way, the expanded methodological tool kit of neoclassical economics gave up the strongest version of (omniscient) rationality in order to be able to account for a market failure via somewhat milder rationality terms. It is significant, in light of the debate about whether development economics has lost its distinctiveness as a subfield of economics (Hirschman 1981; Lal 1985), that the need to represent discrepancies between perceived and actual income opportunities is much more compelling for information-poor developing economies.

Other initially distinctive approaches also converged in methods of or rationales to the neoclassical mainstream. Consider the *basic needs* approach, a sectoral strategy emphasizing health, nutrition, and education investments. Paul Streeten and others made eloquent pleas for these investments on the normative grounds that poverty alleviation was intrinsically important even if it cut into aggregate economic growth. To quote Streeten and Burki (1978, 413): "BN gives high priority (attaches considerable weight) to meeting specified needs of the poorest people, not primarily in order to raise productivity (though additional production is necessary), but as an end in itself."

However, research on returns on social sector investment (e.g., in education and health) seemed to show high private and societal rates of return; this prompted some basic needs adherents such as Streeten and Burki (1978) to shift their defense of the basic needs strategy to the more conventional rationale: targeted social spending has high economic payoff. This would seem a straightforward case of simply finding an additional reason on top of the still compelling normative rationale. Yet the resort to invoking rates of return proved to be problematic: private education returns may be due to credentialing rather than higher productivity; private health returns may exaggerate societal returns in that they do not take population effects into account (T. P. Schultz 1988; Behrman 1989). By putting the basic needs argument in terms of maximizing rates of return, its advocates have run the risk of having these investments rejected when the overall rates of return are not judged to be as high as those for investments in other sectors. Moreover, while basic needs theorists initially doubted that the true consumption benefits of proper nutrition, housing, health care, and education could be registered in market values, they ended up embracing the practicality of calculating rates of return based on econometric information.

Applications to Policy

During the 1960s, regardless of the fate of sectoral theories as subjects of economists' research programs, statist *policies* invoking balanced-growth sectoral strategies, and even occasionally imbalanced growth strategies, were implemented. They seemed to do well, at least if measured by the impressive aggregate economic growth of many developing economies. However, this growth was in no small measure due to factors apart from these policies, such as the influx of capital in the form of foreign investment and foreign assistance from bilateral and multilateral agencies.

Both the capital and the interventionism called for by these theories led to the establishment of national planning agencies; in Latin America they were required for nations to qualify for U.S. Alliance for Progress funds. Bilateral donors and the international development organizations (including the World Bank, the regional development banks, and the UN Development Program) expanded their activities in moving money into developing countries and correspondingly their own use of project evaluation. By and large, the financing of investment projects had to proceed through government agencies, which often monopolized the channels through which foreign assistance would flow.

Methodologies of Project Evaluation

Once these agencies were given the tasks of reviewing policies and selecting projects, they needed standardized methodologies. The methodologies that became respectable were developed by quantitatively oriented, price-sensitive methodologists such as Ian Little and James Mirrlees (1968; 1971) for the OECD; Dasgupta, Marglin, and Sen for the United Nations Industrial Development Organization (1972); and Lyn Squire and Herman van der Tak (1975) of the World Bank.

These methodologies were neoclassical in several respects. The approaches require specific price information, the calculation of shadow prices (generally based on border prices and other available data), and the projection of *proximate* economic effects; the marginalist logic prevails, and projects are examined essentially in isolation from one another. The analysis focused on the marginal impact of each specific project; it could not invoke long-term sectoral balancing unless the connections were quantifiable and easily defensible. In the culture of organizations such as the World Bank, invoking nonobvious indirect, secondary, or system-level consequences has long been professionally risky.[3]

However, behavioral studies of how these methods are actually used tell another story. The first deviation from the theoretical, optimal use of cost-benefit techniques is that the broad range of projects with the potential to have the highest rates of return can never be examined with any thoroughness. "Project identification" cannot proceed methodically; instead it proceeds through the choice of candidate projects selected

---

3. "Invoking secondary consequences is the refuge of the scoundrel" was an oft-cited aphorism.

on the basis of essentially implicit criteria. Nathaniel Leff (1985, 337) identifies these criteria as sectoral and structural balance:

> In reality, resources for economic development are often allocated on the basis of a procedure that is very different, even in conceptual terms, from the SBCA [social benefit cost analysis] approach. . . . A consideration of development plans and the reports of development agencies suggests that policy-makers usually determine the main lines of the investment budget on the basis of *sectoral* priorities. Examples of such sectoral priority determination are the familiar cases of agriculture vs. industry, heavy industry vs. light industry, export promotion vs. import substitution. Thus the de facto approach to investment choice usually involves a two-stage process: first designation of high-priority sectors, and then selection of projects within those sectors. The major allocation decisions, however, are taken on the basis of choices between sectors rather than between projects.

Leff cites Caiden and Wildavsky (1974), Hurni (1980), and Imboden (1978) to confirm this procedure as the operative mode of project selection. A more telling confirmation is the lament of Little and Mirrlees (1991), pioneers of technical project evaluation, that the calculations of rates of return and net present values are window dressing. Once projects are determined to be worthwhile, for a host of reasons ranging from political considerations to sectoral-balance theories, project evaluators can make the rate-of-return estimations as high as is necessary to obtain project approval. The fact that the identification process is implicit rescues the selectors from having to engage in any rigorous analysis to justify the selection of candidate projects. Once these projects are identified, the task is to determine whether they have, or can be said to have, rates of return or net present values that exceed some minimum standard.

Looking at development economics as an industry, albeit a small one, it becomes clear that the emphasis and methodologies of development economics must be consistent with the field's production and marketing processes. That is, economists have to be produced—dissertations must be written so that Ph.D.s can be awarded. Then these economists have to be placed, and have to survive, in positions in academe, development agencies, international organizations, and so on.

The archetypical empirical dissertation in development economics examines a rigidity, or first-order market failure, in order to account for it in terms of the returns to the firms, workers, lenders, or other actors involved. To be successful in the eyes of dissertation advisers, these studies will account for the apparent anomalies with respect to microeconomic premises by reevaluating the costs, benefits, and risks facing these actors. Why do higher wage sites sometimes fail to attract labor from lower wage sites, particularly the labor of the poorest people who would have the highest gain if they secured employment in the higher wage sites? Demonstrate that the expected utility of migrating, adjusting for the risks that the very poor face without savings, is actually lower than the expected utility of remaining in the lower wage site. Why is financing unavailable for promising investments? Demonstrate that transaction costs and risks of default are high enough to keep lenders away. Why do domestic industrial firms, small farmers, or informal sector micro-enterprises fail to adopt superior technologies that would appear to provide impressive productivity increases? Demonstrate that limitations in information make the adoption of new technologies too risky to have higher expected utilities. These answers reject the ontological exceptionalism of development economics: everyone is trying to maximize; economic actors are simply more aware of the risks and limitations they face than were the development economists of the previous decades. Theodore Schultz (1964) legitimized this position by declaring peasants to be rational and then interpreting low productivity by invoking government and market limitations.

And once doctorates in economics are awarded, their recipients must find and retain jobs. For development economists outside of academia, the best of these jobs—in finance ministries, national development banks, and international organizations—have gone to the technically, mathematically proficient. While a few celebrity development economists can get away with tilting against the mainstream neoclassical methodologies, the rank-and-file development economist must show proficiency in using these methods, at least formally.

Thus by the late 1970s and early 1980s, planning agencies, finance ministries, and other government agencies were formally employing the neoclassical project and policy evaluation methodologies. However, project and policy selection frequently remained political, or was otherwise decided on the basis of criteria other than the calculated rates of return. Clearly, many very poor projects were selected for government (and foreign assistance) financing. This led to the current doctrine of privatization, enshrined since the early 1980s as an article of faith among professional development economists. It is not that neoclassical theory has no place for government intervention or state enterprise: positive externalities still call for state action, even if the older rationale of mobilizing capital has become less important as capital has become more ample. The question was whether government actions to address market failures would result in *policy failures* that would make the economic distortions even worse. The neoclassical perspective was reinforced during the 1980s by a political economy theory that incorporated rational (if selfish) actions on the part of government officials to maximize their own benefits through poor economic policies. Whether cast as public choice perversities or as rent seeking, these models provided the theoretical rationale, consistent with neoclassical assumptions, of what had already become obvious from case diagnoses: governments cannot be depended on to do the "right thing."

Equally serious, the macroeconomic imbalances in many developing countries led to a widespread belief that investment strategies were of secondary importance without monetary, fiscal, and structural reforms to correct these imbalances. These diagnoses discredited state investment. And if the state cannot be a reliable vehicle for carrying out a sectoral strategy or providing appropriate incentives to the private sector, then there is little hope for a *planned* sectoral strategy. In contrast to their methodological optimism, the neoclassical critics had a profound political and administrative skepticism. Whether or not it was methodologically or theoretically feasible to determine the optimal sectoral strategy, the neoclassical proponents (Bauer 1981; Lal 1985) asked why the judgments of suspect governments should be placed above the signals of the market, even a distorted market. The irony, of course, was that neoclassical polemics were targeted against planning operations that were employing, at least on the formal level, neoclassical methods.

Implications for Doctrines of Income Distribution

During the 1980s, the neoclassical attack on macroeconomic imbalances through austerity packages as well as structural adjustment measures also reinforced the association between neoclassicism and income regressivity. The issue was not so much that structural adjustment was regressive; the dismantling of distortions offering special advantage to the wealthy and well connected could be defended as progressive (Mikesell 1983). Rather, the problem was that austerity programs reduced two very visible indicators of government efforts to address the poor: social spending and wage policy. Never mind that for many countries, both pertained not to the poorest segments of the population, but rather to the higher- (if not high-) income recipients of government benefits and of wages directly influenced by government policy—whose very vocal objections to austerity programs make such programs seem highly regressive.

Yet this association of neoclassical restructuring with allegedly regressive austerity programs only reinforced the preexisting reputation of neoclassical economics for hostility or at best indifference toward the equity issue. As the conventional historiography would have it, development economics "discovered" the equity issue only in the early 1970s, coincident with the appearance of empirical evidence of deteriorating income distributions in industrializing countries such as Brazil.[4] This interpretation is most intriguing. Simon Kuznets (1955) had demonstrated that the distribution of income deteriorated when the now industrialized countries went through the intermediate stages of development and industrialization. Lewis's (1954) two-sector model made the same prediction. It is therefore unclear why cases like Brazil would come as a shock. It is true that neoclassical models predicted some equalization of incomes when all factors of production were scarce, yet these models had difficulty incorporating surplus labor because labor markets were supposed to clear. Neoclassical theories later incorporated surplus labor and its wage-depressing effects by invoking the policy failure of artificially high regulated and negotiated wages.

The stance of neoclassical economics regarding income distribution was indeed much more complex. Neoclassical economics could have argued along classical Millian lines that distributional issues are best addressed through income transfers rather than investments in production. Income distribution was always recognized as an issue, but as one that required political decisions that could not be deduced from strictly economic considerations. Neoclassical economics also could have argued that its criticism of protectionist policies invoking either balanced growth or unbalanced growth amounted to a progressive stance, since these protectionist policies had exacerbated inequality and poverty by draining resources from the lowest income sector, namely agriculture.

One might think, therefore, that the neoclassicists could have taken the moral high ground. Instead, the "discovery" was conveyed with

---

4. Probably the most widely cited study was Fishlow 1972.

much hand-wringing and apologies.[5] Perhaps the theoretical neutrality of neoclassical economics with respect to the distributional issue put neo-classicists on the defensive. Perhaps the leftist, progressive rhetoric accompanying the state interventionist policies of the 1950s and 1960s was still persuasive. In any event, although the prescriptions of neo-classical economics would often be progressive in their impacts on in-come distribution (insofar as they entail dismantling income-regressive policies such as credit restrictions, exclusive licenses, protection and other subsidies for favored industries, and other monopolies), neoclassi-cal economists have failed to shed their regressive image.

The most remarkable thing about the "discovery" of equity by main-stream, nonstructuralist economists was that it implicitly staked out a sectoral strategy. The conclusion that poverty had reached crisis dimen-sions implied that a frontal assault on poverty was necessary; this, in turn, implied that investment must be directed to the sectors where poverty was most prevalent: agriculture and rural development. It was not that agricul-tural and rural development had immediately demonstrable high rates of return; the calculable profitability of agricultural and rural development projects was not particularly high. Poverty alleviation was the primary rationale. Most importantly, this frontal assault undercut the claims of the structuralists that their import-substitution industrialization strategy was a progressive policy. The most insidious aspect of the early structuralist preference for infant industries was that the industries typically targeted for assistance were urban centered, at least semi-skilled, and unionized (or soon to become so). In its emphasis on the presumed inequality of exchange between rich and poor countries, the structuralist models fo-cused largely on inequality among nations, paying little attention to the distributional implications of import substitution, all the while invoking broad rhetoric of income progressivity. Yet the new emphasis on agricul-ture and rural development in general raised by neoclassical, born-again equity advocates refocused on the issue of the *internal* distribution of income.

It is interesting to note that the agricultural/poverty alleviation strategy was manifested and implemented organizationally rather than method-ologically. That is, organizations such as the World Bank and USAID, because of top-level decisions (rather than technical analysis), expanded the offices and budgets for agricultural and rural development projects

5. See Adelman and Morris 1973.

and programs. The organizational capacity to identify, evaluate, and approve agricultural and rural development projects increased, and the grant or loan ceilings were raised for projects in these sectors. It was virtually inevitable that more investment would go into these sectors. Put another way, in the absence of a theoretical or methodological rationale for asserting that the greatest societal benefit would come from sectoral strategies targeted directly to the lowest income populations, the organizations' leaders incorporated judgmentally (or politically) derived sectoral strategies by organizational structures that could swamp the impact of cost-benefit analyses.

Out of this same concern over equity and poverty alleviation, there were several attempts to incorporate distributional concerns into project-evaluation methodologies. The so-called social rate of return methodology was developed essentially to increase or decrease the valuation of benefits going to families of various income levels, invoking the classic welfare economics insight that the utility of the same monetary benefit is greater for lower-income families. These methods have failed to be widely adopted, even in the institutions responsible for their development (Ascher 1983; Little and Mirrlees 1991). The rationales for dismissing these techniques included the difficulties of knowing how much greater utility to assign, the increased workload required by these methods, the political nature of deciding on the weightings, the danger to the professional integrity of the experts' role, and even the argument that such elaborate methods are unnecessary because the rate-of-return analysis does not really determine what projects will or will not be selected! Whatever the reasons, the result was that the equity concern was not incorporated into explicit methodology. Therefore this concern, like sectoral strategy in general, was captured apart from neoclassical approaches.

The most damning association for the neoclassicists' reputation was the apparent connection to the "trickle down" approach to mobilizing investment. The trickle-down logic is that higher-income individuals can afford to save larger proportions of their income; as long as these savings are devoted to domestic investment, the wealthy will contribute more to national growth. This seemed to fit with the neoclassical preoccupation with growth rather than distribution, but in fact the trickle-down approach was originally a creation of the structuralists. It was the archstructuralist Arthur Lewis (1954) who identified the top income-earning decile as the key to domestic investment; the more they earn, the more they invest. Yet the neoclassicists were saddled with the trickle-down label through the 1970s and early 1980s. One might speculate that the appropriation of trickle-down logic by conservative governments in industrial countries somehow contaminated the more general thinking about the relationship between neoclassical prescriptions and regressive income-distribution impacts. It was only with the clear failure of interventionist policies in the 1980s that the ridicule heaped on the presumably conservative trickle-down approach was displaced by disdain for heavy-handed government intervention.

Conclusions

The connections among economic theory, analytic approaches, and economic policy prescriptions have often been very loose. This has permitted the translations of neoclassical theory into applications and policy doctrines that have strayed rather far from original neoclassical tenets. This looseness has permitted the neoclassical *methodological* framework to swallow up alternative, so-called structuralist theoretical models. However, this neoclassical imperialism or consensus has limited the explicit consideration of development strategies, if not excluding the de facto selection of sectoral and distributional strategies. At the same time, the looseness has left neoclassical approaches vulnerable to suspect associations with regressive distributional doctrines, through equally loose or even unfair associations with austerity programs and "trickle-down economics."

Neoclassical analysis, the professionally safe approach, excludes the noncalculable. But what explicit methodology cannot accommodate may still be introduced without rigorous, systematic, or explicit analysis. We have seen that it may be introduced through sectoral preferences justified post hoc by quantitative project evaluation or by organizational emphases on particular sectors or income distribution strategies.

Neoclassical and alternative economic development doctrines differ, at heart, in the nature of their epistemological skepticism. The neoclassicists doubt that holistic theoretical assessments of economic structure can yield sound analysis and policy. Since the 1970s, this epistemological skepticism has been increasingly reinforced by skepticism regarding the willingness and abilities of governments to use their interventionist powers to address whatever structural problems such assessments may reveal. On the other side, the critics of neoclassical economics doubt that marginalist, econometrically based analysis can capture the holistic principles of structuralism, let alone capture the ontological deviations from the maximizing assumptions of neoclassicism.

The vacuum that several observers have noted concerning development economics as an intellectual enterprise is reflected not only in the generation of development doctrines, but also in academic research. The scientific research program of development economics has become largely an econometric exercise in accounting for what had been deviations from the narrower (or, perhaps, purer) neoclassical tenets by invoking parametric rather than ontological or macrostructural explanations.

Finally, the now dominant antistatist, market-oriented doctrine is more a reassertion of neoclassical premises than an outgrowth of neoclassical analysis. To be sure, in many cases state intervention has led to sectoral misallocations, rent seeking, and regressive distributive impacts that amply warrant cynicism toward the structuralist recipes. In essence, statism has been associated so strongly with blatant policy failures that it has been discredited quite apart from what professional economists may think. Yet it is striking that structuralist rigidities that first motivated or rationalized these statist policies have not been discredited, although the research program has reinterpreted their origins.

References

Adelman, Irma, and Cynthia Morris. 1973. *Economic Growth and Social Equity in Developing Countries*. Palo Alto, Calif.: Stanford University Press.

Ascher, William. 1983. New Development Approaches and the Adaptability of International Agencies: The Case of the World Bank. *International Organization* 37 (summer): 415–24.

Bauer, P. T. 1981. *Equality, the Third World, and Economic Delusion*. Cambridge, Mass.: Harvard University Press.

Behrman, Jere. 1989. Schooling and Other Human Capital Investments: Can the Effects be Identified? *Economics of Education Review* 6:301–5.

Caiden, Naomi, and Aaron Wildavsky. 1974. *Planning and Budgeting in Poor Countries*. New York: Wiley.

Chenery, Hollis. 1975. The Structuralist Approach to Development Policy. *American Economic Review* 62.2 (May): 310–16.

Chenery, Hollis, and Lance Taylor. 1968. Development Patterns: Among Countries and over Time. *The Review of Economics and Statistics* 50 (November): 391–416.

Dasgupta, P. , S. Marglin, and A. Sen. 1972. *Guidelines for Project Evaluation*. New York: United Nations Industrial Development Organization.

Felix, David. 1961. An Alternative View of the "Monetarist"-"Structuralist" Controversy. In *Latin American Issues*. Edited by Albert Hirschman. New York: Twentieth Century Fund.

Fishlow, Albert. 1972. "Brazilian Size Distribution of Income." *American Economic Review* 62 (May): 391–402.

Galenson, Walter, and Harry Leibenstein. 1955. Investment Criteria, Productivity and Economic Development. *Quarterly Journal of Economics* 69 (August): 343–70.

Harris, John, and Michael Todaro. 1970. Migration, Unemployment and Development: A Two-Sector Analysis. *American Economic Review* 60 (March): 126–42.

Hirschman, Albert O. 1958. *The Strategy of Development*. New Haven, Conn.: Yale University Press.

———. 1967. *Development Projects Observed*. Washington, D.C.: The Brookings Institution.

———. 1981. The Rise and Decline of Development Economics. In *Essays in Trespassing: Economics to Politics and Beyond*. Edited by Albert Hirschman. Cambridge: Cambridge University Press.

Hurni, Bettina. 1980. *The Lending Policy of the World Bank in the 1970s*. Boulder, Colo.: Westview.

Imboden, N. 1978. *A Management Approach to Project Appraisal and Evaluation*. Paris: Organization for Economic Cooperation and Development.

Killick, Tony. 1978. *Development Economics in Action*. New York: St. Martin's Press.

Krugman, Paul. 1994. The Fall and Rise of Development Economics. In *Rethinking Development Experience: Essays Provoked by the Work of Albert O. Hirschman*. Edited by Lloyd Rodwin and Donald Schon. Washington, D.C.: The Brookings Institution. 39–58.

Kuznets, Simon. 1955. Economic Growth and Income Inequality. *American Economic Review* 45 (March): 1–28.

Lal, Deepak. 1985. *The Poverty of Development Economics*. Cambridge, Mass.: Harvard University Press.

Leff, Nathaniel. 1985. The Use of Policy-Science Tools in Public-Sector Decision Making: Social Benefit-Cost Analysis in the World Bank. *Kyklos* 38:60–75.

Lewis, W. Arthur. 1954. Economic Development with Unlimited Supplies of Labour. *The Manchester School* 22 (May): 139–91.

Little, I. M. D. 1982. *Economic Development: Theory, Policy and International Relations*. New York: Basic Books.

Little, I. M. D., and J. A. Mirrlees. 1968. *Manual of Industrial Project Analysis in Developing Countries*. Paris: Organization for Economic Cooperation and Development.

———. 1971. *Project Appraisal and Planning for Developing Countries*. London: Heinemann.

———. 1991. Project Appraisal and Planning Twenty Years On. In *Proceedings of the World Bank Annual Conference on Development Economics 1990*. 351–91.

McKinnon, Ronald. 1973. *Money and Capital in Economic Development*. Washington, D.C.: The Brookings Institution.

Meier, Gerald. 1987. *Pioneers in Development*. Vol. 2. New York: Oxford University Press.

Meier, Gerald, and Dudley Seers, eds. 1984. *Pioneers in Development*. New York: Oxford University Press.

Mikesell, Raymond. 1983. Appraising IMF Conditionality: Too Loose, Too Tight, or Just Right? In *IMF Conditionality*. Edited by John Williamson. Cambridge, Mass.: MIT Press. 47–62.

Myrdal, Gunnar. 1956. *Development and Underdevelopment*. Cairo: National Bank of Egypt.

Nurkse, Ragnar. 1953. *Problems of Capital Formation in Underdeveloped Countries*. Oxford: Oxford University Press.

———. 1957. *Rich Lands and Poor*. New York: Harper.

Prebisch, Raul. 1949. *The Economic Development of Latin America and Its Principal Problems*. New York: United Nations.

Remenyi, Joseph. 1979. Core Semi-Core Interaction: Toward a General Theory of Disciplinary and Subdisciplinary Growth. *HOPE* 11.1: 31–63.

Rosenstein-Rodan, Paul. 1943. Problems of Industrialization of Eastern and Southeastern Europe. *Economic Journal* 53:202–11.

Schultz, T. Paul. 1988. Economic Demography and Development: New Directions in an Old Field. In *The State of Development Economics*. Edited by G. Ranis and T. P. Schultz. London: Basil Blackwell.

Schultz, Theodore. 1964. *Transforming Traditional Agriculture*. New Haven, Conn.: Yale University Press.

Scitovsky, Tibor. 1954. Two Concepts of External Economies. *Journal of Political Economy* 62 (April): 143–51.

———. 1987. Balanced Growth. In *the New Palgrave Economic Development*. New York: W. W. Norton. 55–58.

Solow, Robert, and Paul Samuelson. 1953. Balanced Growth under Constant Returns to Scale. *Econometrica* 12 (July): 412–23.

Squire, Lyn, and Herman van der Tak. 1975. *Economic Analysis of Projects*. Baltimore, Md.: Johns Hopkins University Press.

Streeten, Paul, and Shahid J. Burki. 1978. Basic Needs: Some Issues. *World Development* 6.3 (March): 411–21.

Swamy, D. S. 1967. Statistical Evidence of Balanced and Unbalanced Growth. *The Review of Economics and Statistics* 49 (August): 288–303.

Winegarden, C. R. 1970. "Balanced Growth" and the "Big Push": A Reappraisal. *Indian Economic Journal* 18.2 (October–December): 208–23.

Yotopoulos, Pan A., and Lawrence J. Lau. 1970. A Test for Balanced and Unbalanced Growth. *The Review of Economics and Statistics* 52:376–83.

———. 1975. The Balanced-Unbalanced Growth Controversy Revisited. *The Review of Economics and Statistics* 57:516–17.

The Internationalization of Economic Policy Reform: Some Recent Literature

A. W. Coats

Preamble

As the contributions to this volume demonstrate, the internationalization of economics is a vast, complex, and gradually evolving process. It encompasses the spread of economic ideas; the education, technical training, and professionalization of economists (the principal—but by no means the only—carriers of economic knowledge); and the multifarious activities of the individuals and groups engaged in the application of economic ideas and techniques to policy, whether in governments, central banks, international agencies, private research organizations, or serving as expert advisers and consultants. Economics is preeminently a policy science; it is therefore appropriate to include in this volume a review of some of the recent important studies of economic policy reform, a key aspect of the economist's work in the international arena.

Political Economy: The Current Confusion

Economic policy reform is increasingly referred to as political economy, the term by which the whole subject was generally known in the eighteenth- and nineteenth-century English-language literature. But, unfortunately, in the past two or three decades the meaning of political economy has become horrendously confused. Some of the recent international comparative studies of economic policy reform have referred to so-called "new" political economy without differentiating (or perhaps even knowing of) the variant species, such as the liberal, nationalist (or neomercantilist) and radical (or Marxist) forms.[1] In the mainstream version (i.e., liberal or neoclassical) some discussions of economic policy reform start out from and pay lip service to the public choice literature, which is often referred to as the "new political economy." But serious scholarly researchers usually dismiss that approach as too individualistic in its assumptions, too simplistic in its portrayal of crude rent-seeking political actors and crassly self-interested bureaucrats, and too negative in its conception of politics as "a spanner in the economic works" (Grindle 1991, 45).

As will be argued later, economics and politics interact in various ways in the making of economic policy, ways that the neoclassical and public choice approaches cannot comprehend owing to their treatment of politics either as given or as endogenized into economics, so that the same analytical apparatus can be applied to both. (This practice may economize on scarce intellectual resources, but it inhibits understanding of policy processes!) By contrast, recent economic policy research has been more particularistic, context dependent, empirically grounded, and historically sensitive. According to Robert Bates, a leading political scientist who favors "a form of political analysis that draws upon such orthodox concepts as rational choice and equilibrium analysis," much of the "new" political economy literature is "deeply flawed" (1991, 261). Its base is too narrow; he strongly urges the abandonment of the concept of a political market and the notion of government or the state as a maximizer. "The conventional techniques of political analysis employed by market-oriented economists . . . offer little help in understanding political behavior. Rather, analysts must employ an approach that views policy choice as the result of a political process that takes place within institutions other than markets" (272). Unfortunately, many economists lack either the inclination or the knowledge to undertake inquiries of this kind. As one critic has observed, perhaps with some exaggeration: "Because economists have traditionally focused on the individual consumer and entrepreneur, they have no history of concern over organizations as organizations—with an existence over and beyond the particular individuals who are within them. Instead, they have sought to reduce all issues of organization, including political organization, to the individual's

1. See appendix A for a brief review of the literature.

confrontation with alternatives" (Dearlove 1987, 8). Recently, however, there has been a reaction against this practice, for example in the "new institutional economics," which seeks to incorporate institutions into the structure of theoretical analysis. One of the leaders of this movement, Ronald Coase, has complained of the economists' common practice of undertaking blackboard exercises, "comparing what is actually done with what would happen in an ideal state." By contrast, he argues, in the real world "to influence policy we set up or abolish an agency, amend the law, change the personnel, and so on; we work through institutions. *The choice in economic policy is a choice of institutions.* And what matters is the effect that a modification of institutions will actually make in the real world" (Coase 1984, 230; emphasis added).

One of the gravest weaknesses of the "new" or neoclassical political economy in dealing with policy reform is its inability to explain change. It "offers no insight into the processes through which change occurred or into the ability of governments to select policies they believed would bring longer-term benefits to their societies" (Grindle 1991, 62). In the recent literature, much of which is focused on the experiences of the 1980s and early 1990s, serious efforts have been made "to assess how changes come about and, thus, how policy reforms can be introduced and sustained. A better understanding of process, for example, can provide insights into how problems become policy issues; what circumstances surround efforts to change policy; what role political elites, technocrats, advisers and others play in defining alternatives; how choices are determined; and what factors influence the implementation and sustainability of new policy initiatives" (57).

Historians of economics—presumably the principal but by no means the only audience for this volume—have much to learn from the economic policy reform literature. In understanding the policymaking process the interaction of ideas, interests, and institutions is fundamental, yet few historians of economics give adequate consideration to all three elements.

Ideas

An illuminating example of the more comprehensive approach required in tracing the impact of economic ideas on policy formation is Peter Hall's (1989) collection of essays on the dissemination of Keynesian ideas. In that volume he very properly criticized the two earlier studies

I edited—on the role of economists in national governments and in international agencies (Coats 1981, 1986)—as too economist-centered. As an alternative, Hall constructed a three-dimensional model encompassing (a) economic viability (the theoretical quality and problem-solving capacity of economic ideas); (b) administrative viability (how far ideas are compatible with administrative arrangements); and (c) political viability (the extent to which ideas are useful to politicians in winning support and building coalitions). Needless to say, the second and third of these dimensions are rarely considered seriously either by economists or historians of economics.

Hall concluded that there had been four significant determinants of the reception and implementation of Keynesian ideas in various countries: "the orientation of the governing party; the structure of the state, and state-society relations; the nature of political discourse; and the events associated with World War II." In practice, he maintained, the first of these had usually proved to be the most important (Hall 1989, 376; also 8).

Despite its limitations,[2] Hall's volume is a welcome contribution to our limited knowledge of the diffusion of economic ideas, for he is an enthusiastic advocate of the importance of ideas, ideology, rhetoric, and persuasion. An evocative set of ideas, he argues, "can alter the composition of other elements in the political sphere, like a catalyst or binding agent that allows ingredients to combine in new ways. . . . Politicians take up a new set of ideas to wield as a weapon in political conflict. But, like the magical weapons of wizards, new ideas have the capacity to change the very perceptions of those who wield them as well as the world itself in ways that their advocates often do not fully anticipate or desire" (1989, 367). Thus there is no direct causal connection between the ideas held by policymakers and the available array of policy choices.

Interests

In the policy reform literature interest groups play a much less straightforward and decisive role than conventional left-wing anticapitalist writ-

2. Hall's project focuses on a one-way propagation of a single, albeit major, body of doctrine. The classification of the determining influences is vague; and, by comparison with recent intensive studies of economic policy reform, it assigns too much weight to economic viability.

ings claim.[3] According to political scientists Judith Goldstein and Robert Keohane (1993), "Politics is an arena in which actors face continual uncertainties about their interests and how to maximize them" (11–12); consequently, "Policy outcomes can be explained only when interests and power are combined in a rich understanding of human beliefs" (13). Ideas shape agendas and can shape outcomes. They may serve as road maps, affect strategic interactions, or be embedded in institutions. In the political arena, ideas "serve to guide behavior by stipulating causal patterns or providing compelling ethical or moral motives for action" (16).

The difficulties encountered by particular groups seeking to calculate precisely where their interests lie have been elaborated by Robert Bates and Anne Krueger, editors and contributing authors of an eight-country study of economic reform:

> Even the economists who advocate changes in macroeconomic policies are unable to determine their precise impact on specific interests. They lack the models that would enable them to trace the microlevel impact of changes in the macroeconomic variables upon the fortunes of specific groups. . . . A result of this uncertainty is that people can be persuaded as to where their economic interests lie; wide scope is thus left for rhetoric and persuasion. In such situations, advocates of particular economic theories or ideological conceptions of how the economy works can acquire influence. . . . [Thus] rather than shaping events, notions of self-interest are instead themselves shaped and formed. In pursuing their economic interests, people act in response to ideology. (1993, 456, 455)

Institutions and Politics

During the past few years more than a score of detailed case studies of the experience of economic policy reform have been published, covering a wide variety of less developed and developing countries in Africa, Asia, Australasia, Latin America, and the European periphery. The successful performance of the newly industrializing Asian countries and the prob-

3. According to one student of economic policymaking in Latin America and the Third World, alternative explanations of policy outcomes have included: "economic interest group theories, relative autonomy of the state theories, theories on discourse and power, and rational choice/survival theories, all of which define 'interests' in different ways and place very little emphasis on the role of ideas" (Sikkink 1991, 6–7).

lems caused by the debt crisis in Latin America have been among the principal foci of interest. Also, the interactions of economics and politics in Eastern Europe and the former Soviet Union have added urgency to these investigations and provided additional incentives for generalizations.[4]

The most ambitious and systematic effort to generalize about the recent experience of economic policy reform has been undertaken by Stephan Haggard and John Williamson, who have analyzed the reform programs of thirteen countries between 1980 and 1990 in terms of thirteen hypotheses "about the circumstances under which policy reform is possible and the ways in which reform can be promoted" (Williamson 1994, 562; also 478). The hypotheses are:

1. the presence of an authoritarian regime
2. the presence of a rightist government
3. the existence of a crisis
4. the existence of a honeymoon period enjoyed by a new government
5. the solidity of the political base
6. the existence of a demoralized opposition
7. the existence of a social consensus in favor of reform
8. the presence of a visionary leader
9. the presence of a coherent economic team
10. whether the team is led by a technopol
11. whether the reformers practice "voodoo politics" (i.e., concealing their true intentions until they have won office)
12. whether there is a comprehensive reform program
13. whether the country receives substantial external aid

Most of these circumstances or factors influencing the success or failure of economic policy reform are self-explanatory, but the extent to which each is significant is, of course, a matter of historical judgment. Haggard and Williamson acknowledge that "there are no fully robust empirical generalizations; in every case there is at least one partial counterexample." Nevertheless, "the need for a strong political base, for visionary leadership, and for a coherent economic team" is firmly established. Also, the evidence suggests "the possibility of being able to exploit crises or honeymoons and the importance of a comprehensive program," while

4. The following paragraphs draw heavily on the following studies: Bates and Krueger 1993; Meier 1991; Nelson 1990; Przeworski 1991; Stallings and Kaufman 1989; and Williamson 1990, 1994.

"conditional external financial support" also contributes to success, a point to be noted by potential donors. Significant negative findings are that authoritarian regimes and right-wing governments are not needed either to launch or to sustain reforms. Indeed, "in some circumstances center left governments may have some advantages" in flexibility, for example, in relation to labor reactions to reform (1994, 589).

Although a bald summary of this kind significantly understates the variety and complexity of the policy reform experience of the past decade or so, it is neither necessary for the present purpose, nor indeed possible, to consider in detail all the variables involved. Success or failure in any case is heavily conditioned by the historical background (i.e., it is path dependent, to use the current jargon) and crucially dependent on the credibility of the government and on the timing and sequencing of reforms. According to a recent analysis of structural adjustment and liberalization programs: "Credibility requires the commitment of the government to sustaining the reform, but includes the political stability and strength of the regime, the design of the reform program and, hence, the responsiveness of agents. Sequencing reinforces credibility. If early reforms are achieved, a reputation for credibility can be established and the foundations for further reform can be made" (Greenaway and Morrissey 1993, 258; cf. Edwards 1990).

Economic Teams

Of special interest to historians of economics is the considerable weight recent students of economic policy reform assign to the contributions of coherent economic teams in the preparation and implementation of reforms. In his survey of the literature Williamson found "strong support" for this hypothesis "in every one of our cases of successful reform" (1994, 579; cf. 21–22, 479; also Ardito-Barletta 1991, 278–80); while Joan Nelson, discussing efforts to implement orthodox stabilization packages, argued that "The cases of clear failure all traced collapse in large part to divided economic teams" (1990, 347). These teams constitute an important component of the state's analytical, technical, and administrative capacity, and "A divided economic team is . . . liable to lead to indecisive action or to permit political leaders to choose the more optimistic interpretation. But divisions within the team, as distinct from its experience and skill, and the quality of information available to it, reflect political rather than technical and administrative factors; a split team is usually associated with weak leadership and/or deep divisions within the government" (Nelson 1990, 327; cf. Bates and Krueger 1993, 202–3). Strong governments can, of course, replace divided economic teams, and "Governments with limited capabilities, but nevertheless committed to reform, were able to use direct-hire expatriates and advisers seconded from external agencies plus technical analysis directly from external agency staff as partial substitutes for internal capacity" (Nelson 1990).

This is where the internationalization of economics comes into play, though obviously it is by no means confined to governments with limited capabilities. More generally, as Nelson observes:

> By the 1980's, in all developing countries some senior officials (and/or influential private economists) had spent some time as staff members of the IMF, the World Bank, or the regional development banks. At a minimum, that experience introduced a broader perspective, some familiarity with adjustment efforts in other countries, and an understanding of (if not agreement with) perspectives in international financial circles. Often, alumni of the international financial institutions played key roles in the dual political game of adjustment. They interpreted external pressures and attempted to persuade their colleagues in domestic decision-making circles, and they interpreted internal constraints and attempted to persuade their former associates in dialogue with external agencies. Both state capacity and interpretations of economic problems are influenced by these alumni of the international agencies. (1990, 331)

According to Miles Kahler, this internationalization process "has clearly increased the economic viability of orthodoxy by creating a cadre of economists who are attracted (in part) to its coherence" (1990, 59). However, orthodoxy's hegemony is by no means complete, as his lucid account of "Orthodoxy and Its Alternatives: Explaining Approaches to Stabilization and Adjustment" clearly demonstrates (see Asher, this volume).

Needless to say, even the most competent economic team will be rendered impotent if it lacks the support of the political leadership, and if the decision-making structure is inappropriate or ineffective. The team needs to be "insulated from legislative, interbureaucratic and interest group pressures . . . even in countries with potentially adequate institutions and procedures, the authority of central economic agencies may be sharply curbed by constitutional and legal allocations of power to operating ministries, semiautomatic public sector agencies, the legislature, or lower levels of government" (Nelson 1990, 21). Economic teams are not composed simply of economic advisers, that is, detached, neutral experts in economics who provide policymakers with a "menu of options." In the current literature they can comprise a mixture of specialists and generalists with a variety of professional backgrounds, and it is becoming customary to distinguish between economists, technocrats (for example, engineers) who may be given decision-making authority by politicians, and technopols, who have some political standing in their own right (Williamson 1994, 590–91). However, these categories overlap, and individuals may change their status, especially in the direction of increased political involvement.

The Emerging Consensus on Economic Reform Policy

Out of the so-called global stampede toward economic reform has come a remarkable measure of agreement about the principles and policy actions required to advance the cause. John Williamson, a leading international economist, has coined the term "Washington Consensus" to describe "the common core of wisdom embraced by all serious economists, whose implementation provides the minimum conditions that will give a country a chance to start down the road to the sort of prosperity enjoyed by OECD countries. It therefore provides a reference point for what one might expect technopols to aim at during the first stage of reform" (1994, 15).[5] Subsequently, in response to criticism, Williamson accepted that the expression "universal convergence" was preferable, on the grounds that while there is no exact consensus, broad agreement on the optimum

5. In this context "Washington" initially meant "both the political Washington of Congress and senior members of the administration and the technocratic Washington of the international financial institutions, the economic agencies of the U.S. government, the Federal Reserve Board, and the think tanks" (Williamson 1990, 7). According to the often provocative development economist Helen Hughes: "There is now no excuse for the governments of developing countries that do not approach the high long run GNP growth of the East Asian Countries" (cited in Meier 1991, 4).

Oddly enough, another member of our conference, Arnold Harberger, an economist with vast experience of Latin America and other developing areas, also compiled—a decade ago—a list of thirteen "lessons" representing the shared conclusions of most professional practitioners and students of economic policy (Harberger 1984, 428), while Bates and Krueger note that although "the essential prerequisites of a successful reform program are reasonably well understood . . . there is admittedly great uncertainty surrounding the quantitative orders of magnitude of the required adjustment" (1993, 459–60).

package of measures extends well beyond Washington. This consensus or convergence comprises a variety of topics that can only be listed here. They include fiscal discipline, public sector expenditure priorities, tax reform, financial liberalization, exchange rates, trade liberalization, foreign direct investment, privatization, deregulation, and property rights.[6] Williamson insists that this does not amount to a "neoconservative tract" and emphasizes that there is still "vast scope" for disagreement. To illustrate this he provides a catalogue of thirteen items on which there remain very substantial differences of expert opinion.[7] Nevertheless, despite the disagreements and reservations, there is an unmistakable whiff of self-satisfaction and economics imperialism in the consensus/convergence claim. According to Williamson, "There are few robust generalizations in political science," in contrast with "the reality that the stock of economic wisdom—empirically reliable generalizations about the nature of the economic policies that can be expected to yield good results in due course—is substantial, and larger than it used to be" (1994, 19). These generalizations are primarily inductive (Williamson was in fact rather surprised to hear them described as Baconian), and they are very largely based on historical experience. This does not mean that they are divorced from sophisticated modern economic theory in the formal sense of that term, but rather that they are not primarily the product of economic theorizing. Indeed, this would hardly be possible given the essential contributions of politicians, historians, sociologists, and others to the economic reform literature that is the central focus of the present paper.

6. From his "In Search of a Manual for Technopols" in Williamson 1994, 16–28, with criticisms by John Toye, 39–40. A full list is provided in appendix B. An earlier version appeared in Williamson 1990, 8–20, with criticisms by Richard Feinberg.

It is interesting to compare this catalogue with Harberger's "lessons," which focus on controlling budgets and monetary emissions; taking advantage of international trade; valuing neutrality in tax and tariff policy; avoiding excessive income tax rates and excessive tax incentives; steering clear of quotas, licences, wage and price controls; and stressing efficiency and profitability in public enterprises (cited in Meier 1991, 3–4).

7. These include the desirability of maintaining capital controls; the need to target the current account; how rapidly and far inflation should be reduced; the advisability of attempting to stabilize the business cycle; the usefulness of incomes policy and wage/price freezes (sometimes called heterodox shocks); the need to eliminate indexation; the propriety of attempting to correct market failures through such techniques as compensatory taxation; the proportion of GDP to be taken in taxation and spent by the public sector; whether and to what extent income should be deliberately redistributed in the interest of equity; whether there is a role for industrial policy; the model of the market economy to be sought (Anglo-Saxon, laissez-faire, the European social market economy or Japanese-style responsibility of the corporation to multiple stakeholders); and the priority to be given population-control and environmental preservation (17–18).

Postscript

An important new article on "Understanding Economic Policy Reform" by Dani Rodrik (*Journal of Economic Literature* 41 [March 1996] :9–41) appeared too late to be taken into account in my paper. It covers much of the same ground and reaches conclusions similar to my own, especially that more economists now realize that "good economic advice requires an understanding of the political economy of the situation. The result has been a remarkable degree of collaboration between economists and political scientists, as well as more work on political economy by younger economists" (38). However, unfortunately "the habit of attributing myopia or irrationality to political actors . . . persists" (38).

Appendix A

The Multiple Faces of Political Economy

As is well known, about a century ago the long-established term "political economy" began to give way to "economics," but since World War II the older designation has reappeared in many different guises. Generally speaking, "political economy" has been preferred by those dissatisfied with the narrower, apolitical and asocial, mathematico-quantitative, and technocratic conception of economics, which is self-consciously "positivistic" in its dissociation from "unscientific" normative statements and value judgments, and determined wherever possible to draw firm boundaries between economics and the other (lesser) social sciences.

By contrast, in the economic policy reform literature those who employ the term "political economy" nowadays favor a broader conception of economics that explicitly recognizes the interrelationships between the economy, the polity, and society. This can involve either the incorporation of an explicit political dimension into economics or the application of the methods of economics to political processes (as in public choice theory), or some combination of the two. This last, eclectic position may simply be woolly, as for example in Harry G. Johnson's characteristic admission: "I use the term political economy instead of the more recent 'economics' or the more technical 'economic theory' as an excuse for a broad discursive political-philosophical approach, and for a willingness to deal with difficult questions by sage circumlocution" (1960, 552, cited in Black 1983, 54).

Needless to say, Johnson is not alone in this: merely more honest than most. But his remark does not help with the business of sorting out the various meanings. The current terminological confusion is horrendous. "Modern," added to political economy, is perhaps unobjectionable, albeit unhelpful, but even less helpful is the concurrent usage of "political economy" and "political economics"; "international political economy" (or economics), the offspring of international relations rather than economics or political science;[8] and the emergence of a "new" international political economy (or economics) (Murphy and Tooze 1991). Often, though not invariably, political economics is preferred to political economy by those who wish to dissociate themselves from the radical or other heterodox critiques of neoclassical economics. Yet at the same time there are well-known authors such as Bruno Frey, James Alt, C. Alec Crystal, William D. Nordhaus, and Edward R. Tufte who have sought to develop nonideological (positive?) studies of such phenomena as the "political" business cycle, politico-economic models of inflation, or even politico-economic analyses of the Phillips curve (Barry 1985, 298–303; also cf. Alt and Crystal 1983; Alt and Shepsle 1990; Caporaso and Levine 1992). Works of this kind are legitimately placed under the capacious political economy umbrella.

Radical, Marxist, institutionalist,[9] and post-Keynesian uses of the term "political economy" are sometimes accompanied by the claim that a new paradigm is in the offing, destined to displace the neoclassical or Keynesian paradigms; but after some twenty years or so of this crystal ball gazing such an outcome seems unlikely. More relevant, perhaps, is the notion that all (and especially the first three) of these approaches seek to take account of power, which is ignored or at least underrated in more "orthodox" analysis. This is pertinent here because the economic policy reform literature cited above does indeed take more cognizance of power than is usual in the narrower mainstream approach.

Among the many present-day users of the term "political economy" it is customary to distinguish between the liberal, nationalist, and Marxist conceptions.[10] According to Marxists, politics, economics, and society

8. For example, see Gilpin 1987, and Stephen Gill and David Law 1988. While emphasizing the interdependence of domestic and international economics and politics, Gill and Law favor the term "global" political economy as encompassing issues transcending the international, such as the degradation of the environment and the militarization of space (preface and 14).

9. According to Gunnar Myrdal, "institutional economists generally are, at the same time, political economists" (*Political and Institutional Economics*, 1978, cited in Black 1983, 59).

10. For useful reviews of these variants see Gilpin 1987, chap. 2; Gill and Law 1988, chap. 3–

are seen as ultimately inseparable, with the economic substructure determining the social relations of production and the ability of one class to exert power over another. However, the relationship between sub- and superstructure varies according to different writers; Engels and Lenin, for instance, stressed the dominance of economic forces over politics, whereas Gramsci emphasized the crucial importance of politics and ideology in the development of capitalism. In neither case, however, did they follow the liberals in treating the market as relatively autonomous.

The nationalist (or neomercantilist or realist) conception of political economy treats political power as primary. The economy is assumed to be subservient to the state and its interests, which range from matters of domestic welfare to international security. International relations are assumed to be inherently conflictual, and the distribution of national power determines the pattern of relations between states in an interstate system. In the "realist" study of international relations the state is simply viewed as aggregating the sum of the interests of the members of civil society. But students of international political economy nowadays consider this "statist" view too narrow to be helpful in understanding the late-twentieth-century interdependent world economy.

Interpreted broadly, the nationalist perspective includes structuralism, the approach adopted in Latin America especially and closely associated with the Argentinian economist Raul Prebisch. Related to this, even more broadly, is dependency theory generalized to a "world systems" theory in the work of Andre Gunder Frank and Immanuel Wallerstein.[11]

However, more directly relevant to my paper is the liberal tradition, traceable at least back to Adam Smith, in which political economy, or later economics, became increasingly dissociated from politics. Writers in this stream of thought generally viewed politics as an obstacle to rational or efficient policies—what one recent author has termed it "a spanner in the economic works" (Grindle 1991, 45). However, the public choice approach stands out from the twentieth-century liberal stream of thought in seeking to integrate economics and politics, by viewing

---

5; and Tooze 1984, 1–22. According to Tooze (7), international political economy was consciously developed as a critique of economic orthodoxy designed to link empirical study much more explicitly with an analysis of basic assumptions and values. In this literature the term "perspectives" is sometimes treated as a loose equivalent to "paradigm."

11. For example, Frank 1969; Wallerstein 1969, 1974. For a penetrating review of the changing relations between orthodoxy and heterodoxy, including structuralism and dependency theory, see Kahler 1990, 33–61.

national policies largely as the results of supply and demand. The demand
for policies is the product of the self-interest of individuals and groups,
while on the supply side the main actors are governments, bureaucracies,
and politicians, all of whom are motivated by the need for electoral
support. Influenced by this objective they will "rationally seek to deliver
a set of policies which reflect the scale and intensity of some, though not
necessarily all, organized demands" (Gill and Law 1988, 49).

It is neither necessary nor desirable to expand on this bald description, for while some recent writers on economic policy reform refer to
the public choice "school" they soon introduce significant qualifications
and criticisms of that perspective. Following the liberal individualist pre-
suppositions of classical and neoclassical economics, this variant of the
"new" political economy focuses cynically on self-interest as the motive
for action and assumes that politics can be made endogenous to economics by applying the same economic analysis to both. Unfortunately,
this species of reductionism "makes it difficult to explain change and the
context of change or to envision a constructive role of politics" (Grindle
1991, 44, 63). In the new political economy's "society . . . centric explanation of public policy, economic agents use political markets for
economic ends; in the state-centric applications, political agents make
use of economic resources for political ends . . . but there is little support in either economics or politics for treating states as unitary actors
or assuming purposive behavior by the state as a collectivity" (51). In
the "new" political economy (or neoclassical political economy, as some
exponents term it) there is a serious lack of interest in, and consequent
failure to understand, political processes, that is, what occurs within the
state. Instead of self-interest and power maximization

> a model of political economy should provide a means of understand-
> ing what the preferences of policy elites are, how they are formed,
> and how interaction among policy elites and between them and other
> groups influences the choices made about the content of public pol-
> icy. A recent study of twelve reformist initiatives, for example, found
> that policy elites come into a decision-making situation with gen-
> eral policy preferences formed by ideological preconceptions, profes-
> sional expertise and training, memories of similar policy situations,
> position and power resources, political and institutional commitments,
> and personal attributes and goals. (63; referring to Grindle and Thomas
> 1989)

This thoughtful interpretation, reminiscent of the Bates-Krueger study cited in the main paper, is far removed from the cruder forms of liberal and public choice treatments of "political and economic interactions." There now seems to be a much more sensitive grasp of the issues involved in economic policy recommendations, decision making, implementation, and outcomes than was the case in the first three post–World War II decades.

Appendix B

The Washington Consensus[12]

Fiscal Discipline.   Budget deficits, properly measured to include provincial governments, state enterprises, and the central bank, should be small enough to be financed without recourse to the inflation tax. This typically implies a primary surplus (i.e., before adding debt service to expenditure) of several percent of GDP, and an operational deficit (i.e., the deficit disregarding that part of the interest bill that simply compensates for inflation) of no more than about 2 percent of GDP.

Public Expenditure Priorities.   Policy reform consists in redirecting expenditure from politically sensitive areas that typically receive more resources than their economic return can justify, such as administration, defense, indiscriminate subsidies, and white elephants, toward neglected fields with high economic returns and the potential to improve income distribution, such as primary health and education and infrastructure.

Tax Reform   involves broadening the tax base and cutting marginal tax rates. The aim is to sharpen incentives and improve horizontal equity without lowering realized progressivity. Improved tax administration (including subjecting interest income on assets held abroad—"flight capital"—to taxation) is an important aspect of broadening the base in the Latin context.

Financial Liberalization.   The ultimate objective is market-determined interest rates, but experience has shown that, under conditions of a chronic lack of confidence, market-determined rates can be so high as to threaten the financial solvency of productive enterprises and government. Under that circumstance a sensible interim objective is the abolition of

12. From "In Search of a Manual for Technopols" in Williamson 1994, 26–28.

preferential interest rates for privileged borrowers and achievement of a moderately positive real interest rate.

Exchange Rates.   Countries need a unified (at least for trade transactions) exchange rate set at a level sufficiently competitive to induce a rapid growth in nontraditional exports, and managed so as to assure exporters that this competitiveness will be maintained in the future.

Trade Liberalization.   Quantitative trade restrictions should be rapidly replaced by tariffs, and these should be progressively reduced until a uniform low tariff in the range of 10 percent (or at most around 20 percent) is achieved. There is, however, some disagreement about the speed with which tariffs should be reduced (with recommendations falling in a band between three and ten years), and about whether it is advisable to slow down the process of liberalization when macroeconomic conditions are adverse (recession and payments deficit).

Foreign Direct Investment.   Barriers impeding the entry of foreign firms should be abolished; foreign and domestic firms should be allowed to compete on equal terms.

Privatization.   State enterprises should be privatized.

Deregulation.   Governments should abolish regulations that impede the entry of new firms or restrict competition and ensure that all regulations are justified by such criteria as safety, environmental protection, or prudent supervision of financial institutions.

Property Rights.   The legal system should provide secure property rights without excessive costs and make these available to the informal sector.

References

Alt, James E., and K. Alec Crystal. 1983. *Political Economics*. Berkeley, Calif.: University of California Press.

Alt, James E., and Kenneth A. Shepsle. 1990. *Perspectives on Positive Political Economy*. Cambridge: Cambridge University Press.

Ardito-Barletta, Nicholás. 1991. Experiences of Policy Makers. In Meier 1991. 277–95.

Barry, Brian. 1985. Does Democracy Cause Inflation? Political Ideas of Some Economists. In Lindberg and Maier, 1985. 298–303.

Bates, Robert H. 1991. A Critique by Political Scientists. In Meier 1991.

Bates, Robert H., and Anne O. Krueger. 1993. *Political and Economic Interactions in Economic Policy Reform: Evidence from Eight Countries*. Oxford: Blackwell.

Black, R. D. Collison. 1983. The Present Position and Prospects of Political Economy. In Coats 1983.

Caporaso, James A., and David P. Levine. 1992. *Theories of Political Economy*. Cambridge: Cambridge University Press.

Coase, Ronald H. 1984. The New Institutional Economics. *Journal of Institutional and Theoretical Economics* 140.1:229–31; cited in Meier 1991. 304.

Coats, A. W., ed. 1981. *Economists in Government: An International Comparative Study*. Durham, N.C.: Duke University Press. (Also in *HOPE* 13.3 [fall 1981].)

———. 1983. *Methodological Controversy in Economics: Historical Essays in Honor of T. W. Hutchison*. Greenwich, Conn.: JAI Press.

———. 1986. *Economists in International Agencies: An Exploratory Study*. New York: Praeger International.

Dearlove, John. 1987. Economists and the State. *IDS Bulletin* 18:8.

Edwards, Sebastian. 1990. The Sequencing of Economic Reform: Analytical Issues and Lessons from Latin America. *The World Economy* 13:1–14.

Frank, Andre Gunder. 1969. *Capitalism and Underdevelopment in Latin America*. London: Reader Paperbacks.

Gill, Stephen, and David Law. 1988. *The Global Political Economy*. Baltimore, Md.: Johns Hopkins University Press.

Gilpin, Robert. 1987. *The Political Economy of International Relations*. Princeton, N.J.: Princeton University Press.

Goldstein, Judith, and Robert Keohane. 1993. *Ideas and Foreign Policy Beliefs: Institutions and Political Change*. Ithaca: Cornell University Press.

Greenaway, David, and Oliver Morrissey. 1993. Structural Adjustments and Liberalization in Developing Countries: What Lessons Have We Learned? *Kyklos* 44.2:241–61.

Grindle, Merilee S. 1991. The New Political Economy: Positive Economics and Negative Politics. In Meier 1991. 41–67.

Grindle, Merilee S., and John W. Thomas. 1989. Policy Makers, Policy Choices, and Policy Outcomes: The Political Economy of Reform in Developing Countries. *Policy Sciences* 22:213–48.

Haggard, Stephan, and John Williamson. 1994. The Political Conditions for Economic Reform. In Williamson 1994. 525–96.

Hall, Peter. 1989. *The Political Power of Economic Ideas: Keynsianism Across Nations*. Princeton, N.J.: Princeton University Press.

Harberger, Arnold. 1984. *World Economic Growth*. San Francisco: ICS Press.

Kahler, Miles. 1990. Orthodoxy and Its Alternatives: Explaining Approaches to Stabilization and Adjustment. In Nelson 1990. 33–61.

Lindberg, Leon N., and Charles S. Maier. 1985. *The Politics of Inflation and Economic Stagnation: Theoretical Approaches and International Case Studies*. Washington, D.C.: Brookings Institution.

Meier, Gerald M., ed. 1991. *Politics and Policy Making in Developing Countries:*

Perspectives on the New Political Economy. San Francisco: ICS Press.

Murphy, Craig N., and Roger Tooze. 1991. *The New International Political Economy.* Boulder, Colo.: Lynne Reiner.

Myrdal, Gunnar. 1978. *Political and Institutional Economics.* Dublin: The Economic and Social Research Institute.

Nelson, Joan M., ed. 1990. *Economic Crisis and Policy Choice: The Politics of Adjustment in the Third World.* Princeton, N.J.: Princeton University Press.

Przeworski, Adam. 1991. *Democracy and the Market: Political and Economic Reforms in Eastern Europe and Latin America.* Cambridge: Cambridge University Press.

Sikkink, Kathryn. 1991. *Ideas and Institutions: Developmentalism in Brazil and Argentina.* Ithaca, N.Y.: Cornell University Press.

Stallings, Barbara, and Robert Kaufman. 1989. *Debt and Democracy in Latin America.* Boulder, Colo.: Westview Press.

Strange, Susan, ed. 1984. *Paths to International Political Economy.* London: Allen and Unwin.

Tooze, Roger. 1984. Perspectives and Theory: A Consumer's Guide. In Strange 1984. 1–22.

Wallerstein, Immanuel. 1974. *The Modern World System: Capitalist Agriculture and the Origins of the European World Economy in the Sixteenth Century.* New York: Academic Press.

———. 1979. *The Capitalist World Economy.* Cambridge: Cambridge University Press.

Williamson, John, ed. 1990. *Latin American Adjustment: How Much Has Happened?* Washington, D.C.: Institute for International Economics.

———. 1994. *The Political Economy of Policy Reform.* Washington, D.C.: Institute for International Economics.

Part 5

Comments

Margaret Garritsen de Vries

This conference has centered on the internationalization of economics since 1945 in the sense that professional economists throughout the world have gradually come to use similar analytical techniques, methodology, language, and theories, perhaps most notably mathematical and econometric techniques. However, while the papers have explored developments toward this commonality, the discussions have ranged well beyond it, getting into such topics, for example, as the role of economists in governmental policymaking, the training of young economists, and even liberation theology.

A few conclusions emerge, both from the papers and the discussions.

I

Internationalization of economics predates 1945. Jacques Polak pointed out that the League of Nations in the 1930s studied questions relating to the international monetary system that were later taken up in the International Monetary Fund (IMF). I would also point out that even by the late nineteenth century economists had come to use a number of tools in common—comparative advantage, marginal analysis, purchasing power parity, laws of supply and demand, partial and general equilibrium, Pareto optimality—tools developed over time by British, French,

Austrian, Swedish, and Italian economists. American economists also participated in the development of a common economic framework. Alexander Hamilton was the first advocate of import substitution and Irving Fisher's quantity of money theory and index numbers were used across national boundaries. We have learned here, too, of an international conference in 1913 chaired by John Bates Clark.

In the same vein, by 1945 a "New Economics" had emerged—the Keynesian Revolution—and it, too, had become internationalized. The economists who gathered at Bretton Woods to create the IMF and the World Bank, the Europeans as well as the Americans, were all Keynesians and had a commitment to full-employment policies. Indeed, it was precisely because the major countries had the same economic objectives and agreed on the national policies needed for the post-1945 years that they were able to agree on establishing international economic institutions to help them achieve their objectives. It is paradoxical that today, notwithstanding the internationalization of economics that is the subject of this conference, the industrial countries are more nationalistic than they were fifty years ago and less inclined to cooperate in their economic policies.

II

Internationalization of economics has been heavily associated with the spread of topics, methods, books, teaching, professional journals, and the like originating in the United States. Evidence abounds. Professional journals and other publications are almost virtually all in English. English is the language used almost exclusively in international conferences. The great bulk of professional economists worldwide are educated in the graduate schools of the United States. An American education is virtually a prerequisite for a job as an economist "back home" in several countries. Academicians at all levels want to come, and do come, to the United States as visiting professors, as researchers at American think tanks, and in a number of other capacities.

At the same time, evidence has been presented here to the effect that internationalization of economics cannot be considered totally equivalent to Americanization. There has definitely been an international exchange of ideas: European and American economists and officials and economists and officials from developing countries learn from each other, and interchange exists through the international economic organizations.

The monetary approach to the balance of payments developed in the IMF in the 1950s, for instance, was partly an outgrowth of the IMF's staff contact with officials in the Bank of Mexico and work done earlier in the Netherlands. Internationalization of economics has gone beyond academia into officialdom, and financial officials and even heads of government have been meeting for the last thirty or more years in a wide variety of fora to consider economic problems, thereby learning from each other.

Furthermore, it is essential to take into account the cultural framework in which economics has become internationalized and/or Americanized. The spread of the use of the English language has been propagated through American television and movies, which are popular worldwide. The use of mathematics has become common in a number of disciplines in addition to economics, a use greatly enlarged by the increase in computers. Not only in economics but also in the natural sciences, theoretical innovation rather than laboratory experimentation has been paramount in the last several years, and theorists rather than practitioners have been in the driver's seat.

III

International economic institutions, including the various United Nations agencies and the GATT as well as the IMF and the World Bank, have had key roles in the spread of economic ideas and methods. What is unique about the post-1945 internationalization is that similar economic ideas and methodology now prevail in all industrialized countries, including Japan and most recently the countries of Eastern Europe and the former Soviet Union and in developing countries. The pre-1945 internationalization was more limited, covering only some European countries plus the United States and to the British English-speaking dominions, such as Canada, Australia, and New Zealand.

The role of international economic organizations in spreading ideas and methodology needs to be emphasized. From the beginning of these organizations, some developing countries that were already politically independent or were no longer protectorates of other countries—the Latin American countries, Egypt, Jordan, Syria, Lebanon, Iran, Iraq, Greece, Thailand—became members of the international community. Then, as the former colonies, such as in Asia and Africa, became independent in the 1950s, their first act was to join the IMF and the World Bank, as well as the United Nations. These countries sent their best and brightest officials from their ministries of finance and central banks to participate as executive directors and staff in the IMF and the World Bank, and they were immediately exposed to the kind of economic thinking and analysis going on in these institutions. They not only read the staff's analyses of the economic situations in various countries, including their own, and participated in consultations on their own countries, but they had to formulate and express their own views. They heard and gave speeches at the annual meetings of the boards of governors and had a host of informal contacts with each other and with the staffs. Because the IMF and the World Bank have, since their creation, been wrestling with a variety of new and continuously changing economic problems—Jacques Polak and Barend de Vries give several examples in their papers—people from developing countries as well as from the industrial countries were in on this groundbreaking work in different capacities.

In addition, the international organizations, in the interest of making statistical concepts and data more uniform and more comparable across country lines, developed and spread many new concepts and statistics: compilation of balance of payments statistics and fiscal accounts, techniques of model building, calculations and concepts of monetary reserves, measurements of debt and relevant ratios of debt to other economic variables, and even shadow pricing. The international organizations have provided enormous technical assistance to teach these concepts and to gather statistics.

When new problems have arisen, officials wanted discussion brought into international organizations. In the 1960s, for instance, when developing countries wanted to focus on trade rather than aid as a way to develop and began to change their import-substitution, inward-looking orientation to an export promotion, outward-looking orientation they set up UNCTAD. When they wanted to sharpen the focus on their own international monetary problems, they set up their own Group of Twenty-Four, and later when they wanted to sharpen the focus on development problems, the development committee. These were pressure groups, but they were learning groups as well.

IV

The last point, concerning what is "good" versus "bad" economics, has come up often in our discussions at this conference. The terms "good" and "bad" refer more to the policy implications of current economic thinking than to the accuracy of economic concepts. Clearly, what now prevails is universal advocacy of free markets, reliance on the price mechanism, privatization of enterprises, freedom from regulation or government intervention, trade liberalization, and emphasis on export expansion. These policies are now referred to as "the Washington Consensus."

There are several explanations for this resurgence of neoclassical economics. One is that for some years now Keynesian economics has been less popular than it had been (although some reversal is now in process), as concern about inflation persuaded many that Keynesian economics was better suited for curing unemployment than for preventing inflation. Hence, it has been increasingly supplanted by neoclassical economies. A second explanation for the renewed emphasis on neoclassical economics concerns the cost of the "welfare states." As social legislation programs encompassed more and more sectors of the population, a big expansion of the welfare state occurred, and as economic growth in industrial countries slowed, budget expenditures for the welfare state have become regarded as too costly. Many now argue also that since budget deficits necessitate government reliance on private sources of financing, private markets are more influential and demand deregulation and freedom from government interference. Still another explanation for the present emphasis on neoclassical policies, especially on freeing economics from government regulation and leaving market forces unfettered is the failure of the communist economies. Another is the failure in many developing countries of state-owned and operated enterprises to be efficient. Still another explanation is the fiscal and economic conservatism and antistatism ideology that has taken hold since Margaret Thatcher came into office in 1979 and Ronald Reagan in 1981. The international economic organizations have also had a role, as conditionality for use of their financial resources has emphasized all the current tenets of free markets, privatization, and the like, although it is worth noting that more recently the IMF and the World Bank have increasingly been stressing social concerns, safety nets, the environment, and helping the impoverished.

These are the causes for the present "good economics" that we are propagating. But let us look at some of the implications. One implication is that all the various special theories that were advanced for developing countries in the 1940s and 1950s, theories that insisted that the economics applicable to industrial countries was not applicable to developing countries, have been wiped out. The theories, for example, of underemployment and surplus labor of Sir Arthur Lewis, Raul Prebisch's theory of the periphery versus the center, the structuralist theories of Michel Kalecki and others at the United Nations, the balanced versus the unbalanced growth theories of Ragnar Nurkse and Albert Hirschman are now regarded as "old hat." And, of course, so are theories of the Marxists, the neo-Marxists, and the central planners.

Now economics for developing countries stresses that, just as for developed countries, it is imperative to get prices (including interest rates and exchange rates) right and that any governmental planning has to use the market as a determining instrument of policy. In effect, one size fits all.

In fact, we have heard concern from several economists around this table that the present economic analysis and methodology may not take adequately into account the different institutional frameworks of particular countries or may not even deal with the most pertinent local topics. Here may I suggest a country experience other than those of Latin America, which we have heard so much about at this conference—that is the experience of China. China is now growing more rapidly than any other country. It is sending economists to study abroad, especially to the United States, in enormous numbers and using economists trained in the United States at high levels. But, as I see it, these economists are returning to China and adapting what they have learned to Chinese circumstances and institutions and disregarding what is not useful to China's growth and development.

What is particularly worrisome, however, is not the resurgence of neoclassical economics or even the relevance of neoclassical economics to all countries. Rather it is the extreme form of antistatism that seems to be involved. I fear not neoclassical economics but the prospect of Frederick Hayek's "Road to Serfdom."

What I fear is that emphasis on increased market mechanisms, markets virtually free of government regulation, decreased budgetary expenditures for social programs, and the like may harm the poorest segments of society and divert efforts at fostering the big changes needed not only in developing countries but even in industrial countries, changes such as better nutrition and health, more education, population control, and empowerment of women. Our current economics, to be "good economics," needs to be supplemented by special policies for poverty alleviation or even eradication, for protecting the environment, and, in effect, for changing the basic conditions in an economy. I find hope in the fact that, though they endorse neoclassical economics, at the same time, lots of liberal economists (liberal in the political sense, not in the economic sense) are socially progressive, advocating restraints on, and supplements to, the forces of free markets.

Comments

John Williamson

Having been a student of Fritz Machlup, I find it natural to start by considering the meaning of three terms that have been at the center of our deliberations: internationalization, homogenization, and Americanization. I then propose to discuss whether they have happened to our profession since the end of the Second World War and, if so, why. I will conclude by offering my slightly idiosyncratic views on what I think they imply, and should imply, for the state of the profession.

Semantics

"Internationalization" seems naturally to mean the end of specifically national schools of thought, techniques, and practices.

"Homogenization" means that similar techniques, practices, and beliefs prevail throughout the world.

"Americanization" means that the common set of techniques, practices, and beliefs originated with U.S. economists. One then has to define what one means by "U.S." economists: Is it those born in the United States, those who were trained in the United States, or those who reside

Concluding comments at a conference on the Post-1945 Internationalization of Economics held at Duke University, April 9, 1995. Copyright Institute for international Economics: all rights reserved.

in the United States? Clearly Americanization implies homogenization and homogenization implies internationalization, but internationalization does not necessarily imply homogenization, and the latter does not necessarily imply Americanization.

Have They Happened and, If So, Why?

I think it would be difficult to deny that *internationalization* is a reality. It is difficult to think of anything resembling the national schools of former times (the Austrian School, the Swedish School, and so on) that survives today, and that is true even if one stretches the definition of a nation to encompass Latin America and its former intellectual heart, ECLA (CEPAL). I suppose the way one would test this proposition rigorously would be to estimate regression equations intended to explain the techniques that economists use and the beliefs that they embrace, and to introduce national origin/training/residence as one of the explanatory variables. The null hypothesis would be that an economist's nationality would not contribute significantly to explaining the techniques that he or she uses and the beliefs that he or she holds. I would not expect the null hypothesis to be rejected.

Why has economics been internationalized? We have had a number of pretty convincing explanations offered in the course of the conference: the decline in the cost of transport (see Backhouse), which has spawned ever more international conferences such as the one we are so enjoyably concluding; the decline in the cost of communications, witnessed most dramatically by the emergence of the Internet; the use of English as lingua franca (as expressed by Sandelin, without objections since there was no French economist present); and the growth of quantitative and mathematical analysis, which has assisted those for whom English is a second language to compete on more nearly equal terms with those of us enjoying the convenience of having been brought up in an English-speaking country.

I would argue that *homogenization* is also substantial, although far less complete than internationalization. We do still have economists who are happy to have themselves described as members of a school: post-Keynesians or new classicals or structuralists or whatever. Nevertheless, I have the impression that a broad majority are rather difficult to classify in this way: accepting too much in the way of broad mainstream economics to feel comfortable in any such school, but a bit too eclectic to fit the term "orthodox." I continue to feel that my "Washington Consensus," while invented for a rather different purpose, provides a useful indication of the extent to which views on policy questions have coalesced. It is of course true that other important policy stances have commanded a wide consensus at various prior points in the postwar period: Nurkse's views on exchange rates or the "neoclassical synthesis" in the early postwar period (see Polak); perhaps the Alliance for Progress policy consensus on the usefulness of planning and activist government (see Webb, although Bob de Vries told us the World Bank never shared that consensus, so it obviously was not a very wide one); or Harberger's thirteen lessons, which seem to me consistent with, though not going as far as, my Washington Consensus. And there has certainly been massive homogenization in terms of the techniques used, even across schools (see Ascher, this issue).

What explains this homogenization? I would submit it is because we actually are, in a very important sense, scientists. We do learn from experience, and we learn techniques that enable us to learn better from experience, and so over time the stock of widely accepted wisdom grows and so does the extent of agreement on how one should go about learning.

Has the profession been *Americanized*? Polak remarked early on that the United States has been a net exporter of ideas, although the size of its trade surplus surely depends on whether one interprets Americans as those born, resident, or trained in the United States (with a progressively increasing surplus as one proceeds through the three concepts).

What is it that the United States has been exporting? Professional graduate education, which we have heard about in just about every country paper. Specialization and specialized institutes (see Porta, this issue). Techniques, mathematical methods, and econometrics. Once upon a time, the neoclassical synthesis. The market paradigm—although the more extreme forms of this, which insist on the counterfactual assumption of ubiquitous perfect competition, have encountered resistance. (The change is most felicitously summarized in footnote 8 of Ambirajan's paper, where he remarks on how returning Cambridge-trained economists used to focus on the inadequacies of the Invisible Hand and now returning American-educated economists focus on the inadequacies of the Visible Hand.) Less happily, a redirection of emphasis away from non-U.S. applied economics, resulting from a refusal of "top journals" to publish applied papers about the problems of "foreign" economies (see Groenewegen, this issue). Another attempted export, the doctrine that income distribution is not the government's business, mercifully has not got far, at least as yet.

As noted, some of these putative exports have encountered market resistance. Backhouse has also told us that American domination of the European textbook market is a thing of the past. Most important, and contrary to what I said in an early session of the conference, I agree with Margaret de Vries that there is still an important reverse flow of ideas. Polak mentioned the revival of monetary policy, which originated from the Dutch monetary tradition. Loureiro pointed out the development of the theory of inertial inflation in Brazil. And if I may refer once again to the Washington Consensus, I think that three of its ten points would not have commanded a professional consensus twenty years ago: deregulation, which originated in the United States with the Carter administration; privatization, which was Mrs. Thatcher's gift to international economic policymaking; and property rights, which has two roots, the law and economics literature in the United States and Hernando de Soto's work in Peru. I conclude that Americanization, while present, is distinctly partial.

Why has Americanization occurred to the extent that it has? Because the United States is the largest and most competitive intellectual market in the world. Because of immigration. And because the United States has spent more on research.

Content of the Current Mainstream

Let me conclude by offering some comments on the state of the internationalized, substantially but incompletely homogenized, and partially Americanized economics profession.

Groenewegen quoted Marshall describing economics as an "engine for the discovery of concrete truth." That engine comprises the techniques against which we have heard so many complaints. I cannot challenge the consensus that has been expressed in this conference that mathematization seems to have been carried, not just to the region of diminishing returns, but actually to the point where returns are negative. (The closest to an explanation of this uneconomic behavior is Backhouse's reference to the "tyranny of the journals.") On the other hand, one must recognize that econometrics is still making important advances: to take the most conspicuous example, a decade ago we did not know anything about cointegration.

But is the "engine" all of economics? Or is the "truth" also a part of it? (Since concrete is permanent and solid, I have to say that I would not have chosen the same adjective as Marshall did.) I had not known it until Coats told me so today, but apparently I am "Baconian" because I certainly do believe that a crucial part of our job is identifying robust empirical generalizations.

Another attitude that I absorbed in graduate school, this one from William Baumol, is to think of economic theory as a toolbox from which one picks whatever may be the most useful theory or technique for the particular task at hand. A few of the tools in the box of economic theory seem to me to be dispensable: Marxism, dependency theory, and real business cycles, for example. But most of them have a time and place when they can be useful. I find it ridiculously narrow-minded to insist that what is probably the most useful single tool in the box, the neoclassical model, is the *only* legitimate tool.

What has been rightly resisted inside and outside the United States is the contention that real economics consists of a neoclassical model in which everyone engages in individual maximization and no one has any market power, and which holds that any analysis that departs from those assumptions is illegitimate. This is the approach that leads to its practitioners learning a free market catechism that they regurgitate on every occasion, very much like Richard Webb's liberation theologians wanted him to do. It ends up producing absurdities like real business cycle theory. But it is equally foolish to react against this by refusing to use a neoclassical model at all. My guess is that it is in large measure because economists outside the United States have been more successful resisting such nonsense than those inside that they have in recent years been making a more constructive contribution to the design of economic policy (see Coats, this issue).

Report of Discussions

A. W. Coats

The following account is based on an incomplete transcript of the conference discussions. It is perforce selective; and the organization is thematic
rather than chronological, for a session-by-session treatment would be
both excessively detailed and repetitious. References to individual speak-
ers have deliberately been kept to a minimum.

Internationalization or Americanization?

In its early stages the project was provisionally titled "The Post-1945
Internationalization (Americanization?) of Economics," but the term
"Americanization" was subsequently dropped for several reasons. It implied that the spread of economic ideas, education, and professional practices was essentially a one-way process, originating in a single source,
which is certainly not the case; and it also suggested that a species of
cultural imperialism was involved—a point that was not explored in the
discussions. Nevertheless, as the following account reveals, the dilemma
addressed in the original project title could not be entirely ignored.

Some participants viewed the terms "Internationalization" and "Americanization" as close, or even perfect, substitutes, while others considered the latter misleading, except as a characterization of the post-1945
trend toward the standardization of graduate training in economics up
to the Ph.D. level, in the United States and elsewhere (a matter considered below). American influence on economic ideas, education, and
policy was bound to be considerable given the number and quality of

American economists, the wealth of the country's resources, and the enthusiasm with which they were invested internationally by universities, government, and private bodies. Of course, doctrinal, ideological, and cultural resistances often impeded or shaped the propagation process. Thus British influences, which had been predominant up to World War II, continued to be so in the mother country, the Commonwealth, and India up to the 1960s; the introduction of American-style advanced economics was delayed in Latin America—until the later 1950s in Chile, the mid-1960s in Brazil, and elsewhere later still. In the case of Africa, a region that unfortunately could not be included in the conference program, there is currently a major effort, under international sponsorship, to develop economic education and facilitate the growth of an economics profession, for example, by providing funds to enable students to undertake advanced studies at home and abroad; by bringing in foreign economists as teachers, consultants, or policy advisers; and by providing additional research facilities and sabbaticals for academic and government economists, subsidizing the publication of journals and the holding of conferences, and more. This single example illustrates both the unavoidably restricted scope of this project, and the possibilities for future research.

With respect to international agencies, Jacques Polak, a Dutch national who has spent most of his distinguished career in the IMF, argued strongly that that agency's work could not be described as Americanization: it is much more a multilateral process. The IMF had contributed to the internationalization of economics in many ways, for example, by conducting international and bilateral negotiations, holding conferences, sponsoring publications, and through its training programs. In its early postwar years, when British and American personnel constituted the main sources of economic expertise, the organization made considerable efforts to recruit and assimilate staff from a wide range of countries. Some of the non-American economists served only for limited periods, returning home or taking up other employment, while many others, most of whom had undertaken their advanced economic education in the United States, remained in the country, marrying American citizens or becoming otherwise fully acculturated. Margaret de Vries, a longstanding staff member of the IMF, stressed the importance of officials from member countries all over the world serving on the executive board and learning a great deal from each other through the interchanges. These officials, often the best and brightest in their countries, not only read the staff's analyses of the economic situations in various countries, including their own, but also had to formulate and express their own views. Margaret de Vries also pointed out that the IMF developed new concepts and statistical methods—for example, balance of payments statistics, concepts of monetary reserves, and government fiscal statistics—and disseminated them throughout international organizations. Common definitions and standard procedures are essential for the purposes of international comparisons.

Much the same was true of the World Bank, according to Barend de Vries, and on an even larger scale. A smaller proportion of its staff than in the IMF were economists, but its innumerable multidisciplinary foreign missions involved initiating, formulating, implementing, and monitoring investment projects and programs in many countries. Its vast volume of publications on international economic affairs had had an impressive educational impact, and it also undertook extensive training activities. More often than not, the Bank's staff interacted with governments rather than simply with academics, and it was a major force in the dissemination of economic ideas, techniques, and policies.[1] Unlike the IMF, which had natural connections with central banks, the World Bank had no natural counterparts and had to create its own linkages.

One participant raised the interesting question of whether the IMF and World Bank would have evolved differently had they not been based in Washington, D.C. The matter was not taken up in the discussion, though it was pointed out that ECLA's location in Latin America kept it at a distance from the center of world economics.

What Was Being Internationalized?

The general question of what was being internationalized was raised by Verónica Montecinos, a sociologist specializing in Latin American affairs. She identified three dimensions:

1. the diffusion of economic ideas, doctrinal concepts, and techniques across international boundaries—the kinds of elements depending on the circumstances[2]

1. According to a recent commentator, the Bank's "role as a conveyor belt of ideas about development to the borrowing countries . . . is difficult to overemphasise." It is "the single most important external source of ideas and advice to developing-country policymakers" (Gavin and Rodrik 1995, 332).

2. For valuable studies of the international diffusion of economic ideas see Hall 1989.

2.   the training of disciples in a particular school of thought or techniques

3.   institution-building,[3] that is, the creation or reform of national or international organizations in which ideas are elaborated, research is undertaken, data are collected, economists are recruited and trained, and economic policy is formulated, advocated, and/or implemented

Internationalization serves various purposes. To Montecinos, it is a highly political process that strengthens the position of certain individuals or groups within the profession, assisting them in battles with other economists and with outsiders, such as politicians and environmentalists. Another function is to enhance the status and power of the more highly internationalized individuals or factions within the profession. Governments employing economists with transnational reputations are more favorably positioned to obtain loans from foreign governments, international agencies, and the private sector, or support from the great philanthropic foundations. This is partly a cultural phenomenon, since it appears that economic credentials carry considerably more weight in Latin America and, for example, Italy (according to Pier Luigi Porta), than in the United Kingdom (according to Roger Backhouse) and South Korea (according to Young Back Choi). Professional standards are not uniform, Montecinos observed, and the possession of a Ph.D. in economics is not necessarily correlated with knowledge or expertise, for some incompetent individuals seem able to acquire both high reputations and considerable influence! Richard Webb, speaking from personal experience in Peru, and elsewhere, strongly endorsed this point. Even so, those with internationally recognized credentials and connections usually find it easier to overcome what Montecinos termed "the stigma of localism" and to build up a network of valuable information and contacts with international organizations, foreign universities, and governments.

Viewing internationalization from a European standpoint, Ivo Maes argued that economists at the European Community institutions have been primarily concerned with problems of economic organization and the integration of the various member countries' economies and policies. This can be a delicate and controversial matter, for example, in dealing with tax harmonization. Bill Ascher suspected that in Europe, as was of-

3. The importance of institution building was especially emphasized by Harberger. See also Coats, this issue.

ten the case elsewhere, harmonization was simply a hidden agenda, even a Trojan horse, for the liberalization of economic policies; but Maes considered the situation more complex than this, owing to the marked differences between the various countries' objectives, for example, as between Britain, France, and Germany. These differences in objectives concerned not only the liberalization of economic policy but also other issues, especially the transfer of sovereignty from the member states to the Community, with subtle interrelationships between them. Polak commented that these national differences are much greater than, say, those between the various U.S. states, and this accounted for what he called "the disaster of Maastricht." Many of the governments involved did not realize what they were going in for, and only found out when it was too late, to which Maes responded that if true, this simply meant that they were inadequately prepared. The proposed European Monetary Union, for instance, is a highly complicated matter with serious economic and noneconomic features, and, like the question of German unification, the decision is essentially a political issue. Bob Coats asked whether the interdependence of economic and political considerations was such that economists in the EC were essentially functioning as technicians, trying to persuade people or countries to adopt policies that were set for them for political reasons. Maes demurred, arguing that EC economists were engaged in genuine economic analysis, but added that to identify oneself as an economist in the organization could entail a loss of political influence! The situation was very different from that in Latin America as depicted by Montecinos, Maria Rita Loureiro, and Al Harberger, where economists often enjoyed considerable prestige and power.[4] The EC's administrative structure and procedures were to a large extent modeled on the French bureaucracy and the standards of the renowned Ecole Nationale D'Administration. British influence was strong with respect to the economic input, which was mainly neoclassical economics. But the major issues of European integration, Maes asserted, were political. Central Bank and Ministry of Finance-type problems played a significant role, but they were not decisive. Most of the EC's proposals involved both economic advantages and disadvantages; the problem was how to evaluate them. A monetary union, for example, might have great possibilities; but how important was it, given the various member countries' ideas and

4. The influence of important individual economists was strongly emphasized in Harberger (1993, 343–50) and in John Williamson's study of Asian economics ("How East Asia Turned to Exporting," forthcoming).

interests? Questions of this kind called for careful and often protracted negotiations.

Polak remarked that if the European Commission is seen as the forerunner of a future government of the European Union, then the arrangement described in Maes's paper, whereby certain departments were always headed by people from the same country, is very odd indeed. It is as though the Department of Agriculture were to be always in the hands of Californians, and another department in the hands of another state, and so on.

The Reasons for Internationalization

One reason for the accelerated post-1945 internationalization of economics was the remarkable transformation and increased efficiency of communication. Of course, the internationalization of economics started well before World War II.[5] Polak, for example, noted that many of the questions taken up in the early days of the IMF were similar to those that had been studied in the 1930s by the League of Nations. Margaret de Vries added that for many years economists in various countries had been using tools like comparative advantage, purchasing power parity, marginal analysis, and Pareto optimality. The economists who gathered at Bretton Woods in 1944 to create the IMF, the Americans as well as the Europeans, were all Keynesians, with a commitment to full-employment policies. She also pointed out, incidentally, that despite years of further internationalization of economics, there is now much less agreement among the industrialized countries on their national objectives and policies. What is distinctive about post–World War II internationalization is the spread of economics to a wide range of developing countries. (Cf. Coats's paper, above, on the recent economic policy reform literature.)

The impact of internationalization on national "schools" of economics was one by-product considered at the conference with special reference to Sweden. According to a study edited by Bo Sandelin (1991), the so-called Stockholm School, which had had so many distinguished members

5. The conference participants were fascinated by Craufurd Goodwin's references to the activities of the Carnegie Endowment for International Peace in the internationlization of economics before and after World War I. The Rockefeller Foundation also contributed to this process during the interwar years. However, Williamson notes that most of the key individuals responsible for policy changes in East Asia were not economists.

in the 1930s and after, by the 1950s had been obliterated by American influences. Coats found this claim difficult to accept without qualification. Have there been no distinctive features of Swedish economics since then, for example in applied fields?[6]

To Polak, however, Sandelin's claim was no surprise. The "school" had died a "natural" death even before American influence was strong, and he cited the case of the Rotterdam School, which ceased to exist after Theil and Koopmans left for the United States. Jeff Biddle argued that the association of doctrinal schools with specific regions or nations was essentially arbitrary. Walras, for example, had settled in Lausanne largely because his career was blocked in France. There was nothing peculiarly Swiss, or indeed French, in Walrasian economics. Likewise, if Wicksell had decided to settle in Germany because he was for long persona non grata with the Swedish establishment, there might never have been a Stockholm School.[7] In practice it was easier for a national school to emerge and thrive in a small country, especially if it was led by an outstanding individual located in the leading university in the nation's capital. But on the other hand, small countries, for example Finland, were especially vulnerable to international influences. John Williamson pointed out that since 1945, apart from Keynesianism, no new doctrinal schools in economics had arisen outside the United States.[8] If so, this supports the contention that post-1945 internationalization and Americanization are not essentially different.

6. Sandelin accepted that this was so. And it is worth noting that in the natural sciences "pure" research is more easily disseminated internationally than applied research. Peter Groenewegen and John Williamson also pointed to the difficulty of getting leading international economics journals to publish important articles on "applied" subjects, which were too often dismissed as of only local or regional interest. The Americanization of major periodicals like the *Journal of Economic Literature* was evident in its book review policy, according to Groenewegen, for it gave very little attention to non-American and especially non-English-language publications.

7. At the time, and since, it has been argued that there never was such a phenomenon as the Stockholm School; and Sandelin and Weiderpass point out (see above) that, generally speaking, Swedish professors did not have disciples. If so, this is a fascinating institutional and cultural feature that certainly has no counterpart in many other countries, for example, in Europe and Japan.

8. This is debatable, for example, the "structuralist" school considered below and the French so-called regulation school. In postconference correspondence Williamson expressed a wish to withdraw his statement. Several conference participants, especially Pier Luigi Porta, argued that much of post-1945 Keynesianism was, in fact, an American rather than a British export. The Americanized version, deriving from Hicks's IS/LM model, was effectively disseminated in popularized American books.

The Forms of Internationalization

Internationalization takes a variety of forms, and, as Montecinos pointed out, improvements in communications facilitate the spread of heterodox as well as orthodox economic ideas. While the conference participants were primarily concerned with scientific or professional economics rather than popular movements, an unexpected topic of discussion was the role of the church in Latin America and the spread of liberation theology, with its focus on poverty and inequality in the distribution of income and wealth. Bob de Vries commented on the parallels between the spread of economics and religion; both had their international diffusion, prophets, a clear message, and supporting institutions. They even seem to have sacred scriptures. While liberation theology bore some resemblance to the "social economics" developed in nineteenth-century European Catholic countries, it evidently took a much more aggressive form in Peru, Central America, and some other parts of the continent. Richard Webb gave a vivid account of how, during his tenure as governor of the Bank of Peru, he had attended a two-day so-called "discussion" of economic affairs with supporters of liberation theology, including priests—an occasion he described variously as "a slugfest" and "an indoctrination session" propagating a species of "voodoo religion." He was astonished by the radical socialist doctrines he heard there, and also by the ignorance of elementary economics. The exponents of liberation theology were churchmen and social scientists rather than professional economists, and several conference participants doubted that this grassroots movement had had any perceptible influence on economic policy, though Ascher believed its effects could be traced in Chile, in the Christian Democratic Party prior to the election that brought Allende to power. Bob de Vries, a specialist on the World Bank's role in relation to the poverty problem, thought liberation theology had exerted an "enormous" influence in the United States, where its ideas were identifiable in the Catholic bishops' letter of 1986,[9] which had been favorably received by mainline Protestant denominations. A number of Jesuits who supported liberation theology were also professional economists. As in Latin America, this theological doctrine strongly supported economic development in the Third World, and full employment, and voiced profound concern about poverty. The letter had

9. S. Land Philips, S.J., *Catholic Social Teaching, As I Have Lived, Loved and Loathed It.* (Washington D.C.: Center of Concern, 1994).

been well received by some American economists, but was criticized by Milton Friedman because it initially ignored the price system. Subsequently a new version of the letter was issued, which rectified that omission.

Liberation theology strikingly illustrates the wide gap between professional or scientific economics and popular economic ideas. Webb considered that much of the discussion of economic policy in Latin America had little or nothing to do with economic "science," while Sandelin argued that in Sweden the two coexist on entirely different and unrelated intellectual planes. While the academic and professional economic literature is highly Americanized, the public discourse on economic affairs, focused largely on national or regional economic problems, is conducted vigorously in the newspapers and magazines and on radio and television. Even in the United States, Bob de Vries remarked, most of the well-known journalists and reporters demonstrated a notable lack of understanding of professional economics. One participant commented that in Latin America neoclassical, especially Chicago economics, is often said to be incompatible with Catholic teachings, but Harberger evidently considered that the dissemination of "good" economics involved an emancipation from the effects of ideological and philosophical influences. Whether so-called positive economics is purely technocratic, lacking in philosophical preconceptions and ideological implications, is debatable. By contrast, Porta claimed that although ideology is a negative aspect of internationalization, it can stimulate the dissemination of economic ideas. Bob de Vries objected that economics with a concern for poverty would not be regarded as professional; yet its professionalism was abundantly demonstrated in the World Bank's *World Development Reports* of 1980 and 1990. He also disagreed that "positive Chicago economics" and concern for poverty were compatible. Unbridled Chicago economics led to excessive competition, excessive unregulatory exploitation of labor, and deep pockets of poverty (Myrdal's backwash effect).

Harberger's presentation provided vivid examples of the dissemination of professional (*sic*) economics throughout Latin America during the past four decades. The process centered on the teaching and training of potential recruits by American faculty, their departure for advanced study in the United States, and subsequent repatriation, where they helped to raise the general quality of economic education in several countries. Opportunities for higher education in Latin America had risen to the point where students from poor countries like Guatemala and Costa Rica could go to Chile for their training. This, incidentally, is a reminder that internationalization need not be intercontinental.

Bob de Vries pointed out that Brazil and Colombia had gone their own way in making economics professional (e.g., Brazil's Getulio Vargas Foundation and Colombia's University de los Andes). They were quite independent from the University of Chicago. He also observed that in the countries Harberger cited increased professionalism in economics did not necessarily produce better policies. This became clear in the 1994–1995 Mexican crisis when both budget management and the exchange rate were grossly mishandled.

Turning to policy issues, although Williamson thought the terms "good" or "bad" economics seemed shocking at first sight, he staunchly defended the difference—as, indeed, is necessary for an advocate of the "Washington Consensus." When Coats voiced reservations about the meaning of success and failure in economic policy, Williamson tartly replied: "If you see a country that has improved structurally over the past decade, compared with any other country in Latin America, that constitutes a success." It was not simply a matter of the rate of growth; there was a variety of indexes of successful or unsuccessful economic performance.[10] However, Montecinos queried whether success could be credited to good economic policy, or was due to the economic conditions of the time or the ability of various groups in the country to agree or compromise on economic ideas and policy. Williamson conceded that the answer sometimes depended on what is meant by success or failure, but cited Chile as a case of success "by any criteria," even though major mistakes had been made in the first round of economic reforms under Pinochet. Bob de Vries was obviously unhappy with Williamson's judgment, remarking that the country had had to go through the agonies of Pinochet's brutal repression. Moreover, Chile had benefited from certain favorable circumstances unrelated to the policies adopted. No one seemed eager to discuss the relationship between economic success and the social and moral consequences of economic policy reforms. But in response to Williamson, Montecinos commented that the acute depression in Chile in the 1980s had shown that all the economists had failed. After that, they displayed greater humility—at least for a time!

Ascher thought the question of whether policies were good or bad

10. There is considerable recent literature on this matter, for example Nelson 1990; Stallings and Kaufman 1989; Williamson 1994.

could be treated either by adopting a neutral position, saying the issue could not be settled, or by adopting a clear-cut standard of correctness, as Harberger did. Policy conflict was usually a struggle for people's hearts and minds, in which the parties were arguing on different levels and talking past each other. Goodwin agreed. The concept of dependency, for example, might seem meaningless to many modern neoclassical economists, but he had been born and raised in Canada, where the notion of dependency "was in the air all the time." When Canadian economists talked to "the folks from Chicago" there was neither mutual understanding nor clear confrontation. Webb cited the example of Britain's and France's relations with their colonies, in which the dependency had been by no means all one way. He considered Montecinos's way of looking at things tremendously promising, for in discussing economic policy, government, and the economists' rise to power, we set aside any question of economics as a science. The upsurge of economists was in respect of a particular type of policy role. What did it mean from a functional, governmental, or societal viewpoint? If the demand for economists declines, what are we left with—economics as a science? Has economics advanced in the meantime? What does this activist policymaking, this participation of so-called scientists, mean for their scientific work? He doubted that Harberger would view rivalry among economists as an index of the resurgence of economics as a science. It was necessary to focus on questions of policy relevance and the relationships of economists to political actors—political leaders, parties, power structures, and outsiders. Do political leaders need economists as a legitimating device to a greater degree, say, in the Colombian parties? Also, do they need legitimacy externally as well as domestically?

Montecinos replied that in Chile, after the return of democracy, parties all across the political spectrum had economists as leaders. Economists were used as a legitimation mechanism to demonstrate that democracy works. For example, the Socialist Party wanted to be taken seriously, to show that they could be responsible members of a coalition and that they had learned from past mistakes. Coats suggested this entailed a species of *trahison des clercs* if economists were willing to be used by political leaders seeking legitimation. Webb drew attention to the economists' role in helping to create a climate of opinion—in radio discussions, newspaper columns, and so on—quite apart from their direct involvement with ministers and others in politics. This opinion-forming function had involved a mass breakthrough in Latin America some time in the 1980s, and in 1991 at an official level, preceded by considerable discussion in the press and elsewhere. Montecinos said that what happened depended on the period, especially the historical moment when the transition to democracy was being negotiated in the 1980s (cf. Stallings and Kaufman 1989). Though leading party politicians would not speak to each other, the economists in the different parties could talk, and did so. This was very important in creating a common ground.

The relationship between "good" and "bad" economics was also discussed with reference to doctrines as well as policy, especially structuralism versus neoclassical economics (cf. Kahler 1990). To its critics, structuralism is a woolly and misleading term; but as Margaret de Vries pointed out in her concluding commentary, neoclassical economics had been used in a confusing variety of ways during the conference. In fact, what was being spread, especially in the 1990s, was "free-market economics" that went well beyond "orthodox" concepts of neoclassical economics. Getting prices (including interest rates and exchange rates) "right" had become an overriding aim, even at the risk of harming the poorer groups in society. Yet "neoclassical" economics did not preclude progressive social policies. Ascher argued that in the economic development literature neoclassical economics had been watered down to a considerable degree. On the one hand it could be interpreted as a particular kind of tool kit, whereas on the other it was treated as coupled with a right-wing regressive outlook. In the debate with structuralism neoclassical economics had won, but rather as a label, a basis for analysis open to a wide range of interpretations. Structuralism, too, had changed substantially over time; indeed the debate with neoclassical economics was effectively over. In the 1950s, Werner Baer had been presenting the structuralist case in missions to modernize Latin American policies, to defend a region being exploited by the rest of the world. By the 1980s, however, a very different view of the debate had emerged, with the ECLA economists being more willing to concede deficiencies in their earlier position, to admit that some issues had been neglected and others overstated. Thus they displayed a willingness to proceed in a more consensual way.

An important question was whether the debate had been a healthy one—whether each side got a fair hearing and whether there were sufficient institutions and persons to represent the contending parties to policymakers. Jeff Biddle asked whether one side had steamrollered the other or resorted to illegitimate tactics or strategies. If the ECLA side made concessions, did the Chicagoans too? Montecinos thought the concessions came from the former rather than from Chicago, but considered that the discussion has now become more open, and in general it has enhanced the power of the specialists. Sometimes, of course, there were severe restrictions on freedom of expression. But there were also cases where economists enjoyed relative immunity from repression provided, Williamson added, that they expressed themselves in moderate terms.

Maria Rita Loureiro provided a fascinating example of how the study of inertial inflation developed in Brazil had become internationalized when it came to Williamson's attention, at the Institute for International Economics in Washington. Webb was convinced that the Brazilians' ability to present their ideas in a theoretical model—though not formalized mathematically—had played a major part in their ability to attract international interest and support. The fact that Williamson was present, and able to modify and supplement Loureiro's account, was a bonus for the conference participants.

Although Webb asserted that many of the economists' activities in popular discussion and high-level policy-making were not scientific, neither he nor any other participant was disposed to define "science" (doubtless a wise precaution). Similarly, while the term "professional" was frequently heard it remained undefined, possibly because its meaning was thought to be obvious and unambiguous. Harberger, for example, claimed that Latin American economists with advanced economic education at home and abroad had "joined the world economics profession," a species he evidently regarded as nonideological. Yet he put forward his own conception of professional ideology, which included an injunction to humility; recognition of the limits of professionalism, which he did not specify precisely; a distaste for highly abstract model building and mathematical flights of fancy; and a strong preference for a "down-to-earth," "real-world" orientation toward economic problems. Williamson essentially endorsed this view, saying truth is more important than precision, hence it is better to be approximately right than precisely wrong. The policy prescriptions in the Washington Consensus were provisional—neither complete nor written in stone.

Americanization

Much of the discussion of Americanization focused on the nature and spread of American graduate economics. In view of Bill Barber's regrettable absence this topic was introduced by Coats,[11] who emphasized the need to highlight those features of Barber's large subject most directly relevant to the conference's central theme.

In planning the project, Coats reported, an initial aim had been to compile comprehensive data on the inflows and outflows of foreign students who had studied in American universities; to identify those who remained in the United States working as professional economists or in other occupations; and to trace as far as possible those who had left the country after graduating, especially if they had gone into academic, government, or private employment as economists, whether in their home country, in international agencies, or elsewhere. Needless to say, that aim had proved to be hopelessly overambitious, for no such comprehensive and reliable statistics are available.[12] There are some valuable studies of the experiences of foreign students in the United States and after they left, but these do not specifically focus on economists.[13] Moreover, two further aspects of the international education process must be borne in mind. Not all students who studied economics abroad went to the United States; a smaller but nevertheless significant number went to Britain, to Germany, or to other countries.[14] Secondly, any serious investigation of the internationalization of economics must take account of the innumerable economists, American and other, who went abroad to teach, undertake research, or provide advisory or other services for academic institutions and government or private organizations. Unfortunately, here too no comprehensive and systematic data is avail-

11. It seemed inadvisable to open the conference with an unstructured question-and-answer session, even though Barber's paper had been circulated in advance. Also, the editor had a prior research interest in Barber's subject. See, for example, Coats 1992b, which was distributed at the initial session.

12. The available statistics do not usually identify economists. Moreover, some of those who went to the United States may have actually studied other subjects, and vice versa.

13. See, for example, Goodwin and Nacht 1984, and 1991. They deal with such topics as what students got from their education; what they took home with them; the longer-term psychological, cultural, and professional impact of their training, including pro- or anti-American attitudes; a sense of isolation from the center of world economics once they returned home; and eventually consciousness of increasing professional obsolescence, unless they were able to pay refresher visits to the United States.

The editor has a personal interest in these matters, having come to the United States on a one-year English Speaking Union Fellowship; stayed for two more years to complete the Ph.D.; and having spent the rest of his career shuttling back and forth across the Atlantic as a kind of semi-Americanized bipatriate.

14. Among the more exotic examples is the number of African students who obtained Ph.D.s in economics in Finland.

able,[15] although several of the conference papers cite examples of well-known economists who have moved frequently and influentially across national boundaries. And as noted earlier, the international economic agencies have played a major role in the creation of a global economics profession.

During the conference there were periodic references to the question of whether American graduate education has become more standardized, even homogenized, over the postwar period. Coats drew attention to the Bowen (1953) and Commission on Graduate Education in Economics (COGEE 1991) reports cited by Barber, but interpreted them somewhat differently (cf. Coats 1992b). Barber's comments on Bowen's "grand vision of an ideal graduate program" (see above) were justified; but he had not sufficiently emphasized the dramatic contrast between Bowen's conception and the narrowly professional focus adopted by COGEE. Bowen had been concerned with issues extending well beyond the graduate curriculum per se—such as the American economist's place in and responsibilities to society; the low reputation of the economics profession; and its contribution—or lack of it—to the public welfare. Anne Krueger, COGEE's chair, argued that these broader matters lay outside the commission's terms of reference. But whether or not COGEE had been bound by this constraint, the outcome was that a dozen of the nation's leading economists had missed a major, perhaps even a unique opportunity to reshape and reform graduate education in economics.

Few economists would dispute Bowen's observation that there was, in 1953, and indeed still is, "a substantial nucleus of subject-matter which should be common to all economists, regardless of their special interests" (quoted by Barber, above). More recently, however, this core has been whittled away by the actual or virtual exclusion of many matters Bowen considered essential. Barber noted, perhaps with some surprise, that "there are still some differences in the intellectual orientations of various departments," but Coats believed such differences are nowadays more rare than when Bowen wrote,[16] notwithstanding the deep doctri-

15. There is, however, an exemplary detailed study by Rosen (1985). During the conference it was suggested that a comparative study of the development projects undertaken by specific American universities, such as Stanford, Harvard, MIT, and others, would provide a fascinating insight into the doctrinal similarities and differences between their respective faculties. This could, of course, be extended to include similar projects undertaken by economists in other developed countries.

16. According to Anne Krueger, the main difference between the various quality tiers is that "the people in the top tier are doing the same things as those in the bottom tier, only doing them

nal, methodological, and policy disagreements within the profession. The COGEE investigation had revealed remarkable similarities in the content and objectives of economic instruction provided in the lowest (fifth) and highest (first) quality tiers of Ph.D. programs; this constitutes striking evidence of the standardization of present-day American graduate education in economics. Robert Solow had been fully justified when he expressed the fear, before the COGEE report was published, that it would be "predictably bland," suppressing the "strong" differences of opinion among the commission's members.[17]

Barber seemed remarkably unperturbed by the fall in the numbers of U.S. citizens taking Ph.D.s in economics, although the Kasper report submitted to COGEE by a group of heads of economics departments in liberal arts colleges had revealed the extent of students' disenchantment with the standard type of Ph.D. program in economics currently available. Moreover, a number of other as yet unpublished reports to COGEE on the state of various "applied" fields, and the dissatisfaction with recent cohorts of graduate economists expressed by employers, suggest that the current state of training in advanced economics in the United States is far from happy.[18]

Needless to say, Barber could not cover every facet of his huge subject in a conference paper of reasonable length, hence it seems appropriate to offer some supplementary comments. Reference to the growing percentage of foreign students taking graduate economics in the United States raises an interesting question about the increasing mathematical and technical sophistication of the courses. Could this be a conscious

---

a lot better" (based on a private conversation).

17. Solow, in Hansen 1990, 448, 450. Solow hoped that the commission would not "try too hard to achieve wide consensus, which tends to be vapid. This is the sort of thing on which difference of opinion is not merely healthy but inevitable. One or two strong recommendations might get our attention." In fact only two minor dissents by Robert Lucas were recorded, although the report acknowledged that "some members of COGEE have strong views that are not expressed in the document," which "sought to provide a coherent statement to which all could subscribe" (COGEE 1991, 1037).

18. The authors and titles of the unpublished reports are listed in Coats 1992b, 351–52. Washington employers reported that many ABDs (students with all but dissertation) "performed with distinction," and that "well trained master's degree holders in business and public policy often prove to be better equipped to carry out policy research than economics Ph.D.'s" (Hansen 1991, 36). According to Michael Darby, of the Department of Commerce, "If economics becomes less useful for getting into business or law school then we'll really be in trouble. . . . We're headed for the same route as classics" (cited in Bassi 1991, 8).

For more general discussion of the state of American graduate education in economics, see Klamer and Colander 1990.

response to the linguistic and cultural problems encountered by many but by no means all foreign students? What special provisions, if any, have been made to overcome these problems? For some years the AEA established foreign student screening panels in various countries, composed of economists who had studied in the United States and returned home after graduation; as they were familiar with the difficulties encountered by foreign students in the United States they could screen potential graduates to ensure that they had the requisite background and skills. This saved substantial resources and is a small but vivid example of the international network of economists.[19] Unlike Bowen, COGEE made no definite proposals for activities to be undertaken by the AEA on the profession's behalf; and Barber does not mention the association's varied activities in the international sphere. These have included organizing support for the rebuilding of foreign libraries in the early postwar years; maintaining a panel of foreign correspondents; support for the International Economic Association; sponsoring studies of postwar economic policy in various countries; occasional formal protests on behalf of economists suffering persecution abroad; and coorganizing a special series of U.S.-Soviet meetings of economists.

With respect to the complaint that American graduate schools tend to produce a standardized, even homogeneous type of recruit for the economics profession, Bill Ascher, a public policy economist with strong ties to political science, wondered whether the highly organized job market process at the annual AEA meetings encouraged job seekers to present themselves as possessing certain standardized skills, knowledge, and credentials. Goodwin, too, remarked that despite the wide range of academic and nonacademic employers present on such occasions, and the variety of schools from which the candidates came, they all seemed to be the same kind of economist. Ascher suggested that Neil de Marchi, as chairman of the Duke economics department, should undertake a self-study to explain why U.S. graduate education has become so mathematized. What were the pressures on him, as chairman, to emphasize the mathematical preparation and sophistication of his graduate students?

De Marchi replied that it was a mistake to assume that a chairman could actually direct his colleagues. He was desperately trying to hang on to the caboose of this runaway (mathematizing) train: it was a juggernaut—a

---

19. In more recent years the screening panels' work has been performed by the Economics Institute in Colorado, sponsored in part by the AEA.

vivid expression, compatible with the COGEE suggestion that the advance of technique was irresistible. De Marchi believed that there was a powerful internal momentum in the educational system that was difficult to stop "and still claim that you are playing by the rules of the main players." But, as Goodwin interjected, the key questions were how and why the process had started in the first place. Perhaps it was "physics envy," that is, the desire, especially in the early postwar decades, to present economics as a "hard" science. Bob de Vries said that, from his own experience as a foreign student, he had found it easier to study maths than some other subjects in the economics curriculum, and this may well be true for most students with a limited command of English. (Choi also observed that foreign students with a limited command of English have a comparative advantage in a mathematical and quantitative approach to economics.) Also, mathematical ability may be viewed by academic staff as a kind of IQ test, *a pons asinorum* (as the writer of this report can attest from personal experience!).[20] Moreover, as Barber pointed out (see above), making economics more quantitative and technical may have been a way of playing safe in the McCarthy period. Coats believed the above-mentioned similarity between the first and fifth quality Ph.D. programs was persuasive evidence of the power of interinstitutional rivalry in U.S. academia. Whether the same curriculum is appropriate as a preparation for nonacademic as well as academic employment as an economist is a major issue neither COGEE nor Barber had considered.

It is not clear whether the training of economists is as standardized in other countries as in the United States. Roger Backhouse gave a gloomy account of the pressures for conformity in British universities associated with the recent disturbing growth of central government influence on higher education: part of a calculated effort to promote "efficiency" by the introduction of "market" tests. The insistence on the number of economics articles published in so-called top journals as a basis for the allocation of research funding among universities was compatible with the already existing Americanizing tendency toward "publish or perish." It also constituted a serious threat to academic freedom. Yet despite a growing rapprochement between British and European universities, he still believed the former were closer to the transatlantic than to the

---

20. For those with the requisite ability it is easy to produce mathematical-type journal articles and so-called three-paper dissertations. Such publications are also favored by those seeking tenure, whereas serious empirical work is relatively slow and laborious. The triviality of much journal publication in economics is a common complaint.

cross-channel model. Choi likewise observed that competition in the job market for economists in South Korea—by means of a U.S. degree, especially from an elite university, and publication in leading journals—has led to a rapid Americanization of the profession. In some countries the postwar growth in the number of universities had encouraged diversity, by breaking down traditional academic practices, as was true of Brazil (as reported by Loureiro), Italy (Porta), and Canada (Goodwin). On the other hand, there was a movement toward a regional university network in Latin America as in Europe. Given the present state of our knowledge it is difficult to be confident about the general trends in this matter.

A related question is the extent to which the increased post-1945 production of Ph.D.s was concentrated in a relatively small number of universities. Barber's figures are striking, but they do not represent a major difference from the interwar period; and there is no clear correlation between the number of Ph.D.s produced and an institution's quality ranking.[21] It would be interesting to know whether this is also true of other countries.

Following the papers by Roger Backhouse and Peter Groenewegen there was a lively discussion of the consequences of the rapid post-1945 growth in the number of universities and students, both undergraduates and graduates. The Americans were the first to encounter and adapt to this expansion, which was already under way in the United States before World War II, especially in the state universities. The pedagogical and organizational solutions they adopted were frequently copied abroad, though often with modifications and after substantial time lags. Backhouse and Gronewegen cited examples of new universities in Britain and Australia in which energetic young economists, usually with American experience, consciously set out to emulate American methods, and Goodwin observed how, in Canada, the advent of new universities challenged the established academic elite.[22] In the new circumstances leading professors found it increasingly difficult to control their subject, resist

---

21. Admittedly the evidence is sketchy, but this relationship seems to have applied since the 1920s, with the conspicuous exception of Harvard. Generally speaking the number of doctorates awarded by a given institution has varied more than its ranking (cf. Coats 1992a, 413–14). Incidentally, Barber's data show that in 1990–91 over 48 percent of the doctorates in economics were awarded by institutions in the fourth and fifth quality tiers (see above).

22. Somewhat the same was true, *mutatis mutandis*, in the United Kingdom and Australia. Occasionally a given institution's status and quality changed dramatically in a relatively short period, for example, MIT in the early postwar decades and the Catholic University of Santiago in the 1950s and 1960s—needless to say, for somewhat different reasons.

innovation, and place their brighter students in suitable academic and governmental niches. The academic market was booming, and the newcomers, whether home produced or imported, were keen to experiment. This often meant copying American models, though often with variations reflecting established traditions.

As Bruce Caldwell pointed out, mass education called for significant changes in pedagogical methods—usually simplifications, in the interests of efficiency. The sheer weight of numbers made it impracticable to employ the Oxbridge-type tutorial system, which had been widely admired, albeit imperfectly implemented, in the British Commonwealth and India. The American practice whereby professors addressed large lecture audiences, with "sections" conducted by impecunious graduate students, proved an effective way of coping with increased undergraduate numbers and, at the same time, provided the means to maintain significant squads of postgraduates. There was also a concurrent growth in the number of faculty positions, making it possible to increase the specialization of teaching and research and provide a variety of instructional courses suitable for master's and Ph.D. degree candidates. With the rapid growth of knowledge in economics—including mathematization, quantification, and the proliferation of special fields, techniques, and subdisciplines—it became increasingly recognized that a good quality undergraduate degree plus a postgraduate thesis of some kind no longer constituted an adequate preparation for a career as a professional economist, whether in academia or outside. Those who had been able and fortunate enough to go to the United States for advanced training became active proponents of postgraduate coursework, sometimes involving a degree by examination without a dissertation or with a long essay. The introduction of such changes was usually slow and uneven, depending on local and/or national circumstances. In Britain, for example, the introduction of postgraduate coursework was much slower in economic history than in economics.

One feature of American higher education readily adopted in many countries was the practice of relying on textbooks rather than students' self-directed reading drawn from lengthy bibliographies. American textbooks in economics, especially for introductory courses, swelled alarmingly in size and became remarkably standardized, with accompanying workbooks designed for instructors, selections of readings, and other pedagogical aids. American publishers were extremely successful in tapping the student market at home and abroad, not only for elementary textbooks but right through to second-year graduate level work. Large numbers of volumes were distributed internationally, sometimes with government subsidies or foundation funds, either in the original or in translation, and often in a form adapted to non-American audiences, with appropriate updated statistics and descriptions of institutions and policy problems— such as the organization of banking and financial institutions; the nature of trade and tax policies; and the role of the state in economic life. For obvious reasons macroeconomics texts were usually less standardized, and more often home produced, than microeconomics texts, which were more concerned with general theory.[23]

In response to a question about language by Ascher, who said he had found it relatively easy to read a Ph.D. in Indonesian, because many of the same terms were used as in the United States, Sandelin replied that many Anglo-American economics terms had not been translated into Swedish. Polak wondered whether many of these economics terms had been translated into French. Bob de Vries thought very few had, judging from his experience in French West Africa. According to Loureiro, there had been considerable French influence on economics in Brazil. Bob de Vries recalled lengthy discussions with Japanese economists in MITI about problems of industrial policy in South and East Asia, in which he had been greatly impressed by the ease of communication both on the economic and the engineering side, because of similarities in the concepts and language used. He was shocked to learn that 90 percent of all Swedish dissertations are now written in English; but Polak added that much the same was true of the Netherlands, though the use of American terminology was probably more widespread than in Sweden. Sandelin reported that American influence in Sweden was so strong that Assar Lindbeck had suggested that postgraduate education in economics should be abandoned and the savings invested in sending Swedish students to the United States for advanced training.[24] Williamson thought Lindbeck's idea was unusual: the usual pattern involved import substitution when the country was capable of providing enough high-quality

23. Both the Netherlands and Sweden were too small to provide an adequate market for textbooks in the national language, although Sandelin remarked that some Swedish books were used "to provide the facts about the Swedish economy." Much the same was true of Japan, where undergraduate microeconomics books were used in conjunction with Japanese macroeconomics texts dealing with specifically Japanese problems.

24. It may be recalled that Harberger considered that while a number of Latin American universities could provide excellent training in economics up to master's level, it is still advisable for students from that continent to take a Ph.D. abroad. Needless to say, there are numerous other benefits to be derived from study abroad.

graduate education to reduce its dependence on America. According to Young Back Choi this is what had happened in Korea.

An aspect of internationalization (and, to a lesser extent Americanization) is the increasing use of English as the accepted medium of communication (together, of course, with mathematics). As economics seemed to be becoming more like a natural science in the early postwar decades, reliance on books—except for specific research purposes, and books containing collections of articles or readings—gave way to dependence on professional journals, both for the dissemination of theoretical ideas and research results, and as the major element in academic credentials on which appointments and promotions are based and careers built. The proliferation of new economics journals has been staggering, though not, of course, peculiar to economics. In many non-English-speaking countries new journals have been published in English, while other established periodicals have often been converted to the new lingua franca. Economists outside the United States have come to regard publication in English-language, and especially American, journals as the main route to professional recognition internationally. This is particularly important for economists in countries too small to support indigenous specialist journals. Some cynics contend that the emphasis on publication is such that science and scholarship have been swamped by careerism.

References

Amsden, Alice H. 1982. The Globalization of the Crisis in American Economic Education. *Journal of Economic Education* 23.1:353–61.

Bassi, L. J. 1989. Special Study to Interview Nonacademic Economists. Georgetown University. Unpublished.

Bowen, Howard R. 1953. Graduate Education in Economics. *American Economic Review*. Supplement, part 2, 43:1–223.

Coats, A. W. 1981. *Economists in Government: An International Comparative Study*. Edited by A. W. Coats. Durham, N.C.: Duke University Press. (Also in *History of Political Economy* 13.3 [Fall 1981].)

———. 1986. *Economists in International Agencies: An Exploratory Study*. New York: Praeger International.

———. 1992a. Economics in the United States, 1920–70. In *On the History of Economic Thought: British and American Economic Essays*. Edited by A. W. Coats. Vol. 1. London: Routledge. 407–55.

———. 1992b. Changing Perceptions of American Graduate Education in Economics, 1953–1991. *Journal of Economic Education* 23.1:341–52.

Gavin, Michael, and Dani Rodrik. 1995. The World Bank in Historical Perspective. *American Economic Review* 85.2:329–34.

Goodwin, Craufurd D., and Michael Nacht, eds. 1984. *Fondness and Frustration: The Impact of American Higher Education on Foreign Students with Special Reference to the Case of Brazil.* New York: Institute of International Education.

———. 1986. *Decline and Renewal: Causes and Cures of Decay among Foreign-Trained Intellectuals and Professionals in the Third World.* New York: Institute of International Education.

———. 1991. *Missing the Boat: The Failure to Internationalize American Higher Education.* Cambridge: Cambridge University Press.

Hall, Peter, ed. 1989. *The Political Power of Economic Ideas: Keynesianism across Nations.* Princeton, N.J.: Princeton University Press.

Hansen, W. Lee. 1990. Educating and Training New Ph.D.s: How Good a Job Are We Doing? *American Economic Review* 80.2:437–50.

———. 1991. Education and Training of Economics Doctorates: Major Findings of the American Economic Association's Commission on Graduate Education in Economics. University of Wisconsin. Duplicated.

Harberger, Arnold. 1993. Secrets of Success: A Handful of Heroes. *American Economic Review* 83.2:343–50.

Kahler, Miles. 1990. Orthodoxy and Its Alternatives: Explaining Approaches to Stabilization and Adjustment. In *Economic Crisis and Policy Choice.* Edited by Joan M. Nelson. Princeton, N.J.: Princeton University Press. 33–61.

Klamer, Arjo, and David Colander. 1990. *The Making of an Economist.* Boulder, Colo.: Westview Press.

Kruger, Anne O., et. al. 1991. Report of the Commission on Graduate Education in Economics (COGEE). *Journal of Economic Literature* 29.3:1088–109.

Nelson, Joan M., ed. 1990. *Economic Crisis and Policy Choice: The Politics of Adjustment in the Third World.* Princeton, N.J.: Princeton University Press.

Rosen, George. 1985. *Western Economists and Eastern Societies: Aspects of Change in South Asia 1950–1970.* Delhi: Oxford University Press.

Solow, Robert. 1990. *Educating and Training New Ph.Ds. American Economic Review* 80.2:437–50.

Stallings, Barbara, and Robert Kaufman. eds. 1989. *Debt and Democracy in Latin America.* Boulder, Colo.: Westview Press.

Williamson, John. Forthcoming. How East Asia Turned to Exporting.

———, ed. 1990. *Latin American Adjustments: How Much Has Happened?* Washington, D.C.: Institute for International Economics.

———, ed. 1994. *The Political Economy of Policy Reform.* Washington, D.C.: Institute for International Economics.

Part 6

Conclusion

A. W. Coats

As indicated in the preface, a central theme running through successive chapters in this volume is the relationship between the processes of internationalization and Americanization. Some of the implications of these two key terms, and the accompanying confusions, were considered in the conference discussions (see above) from which it is clear that neither term is entirely satisfactory nor entirely avoidable. Strictly speaking, Americanization implies an exclusive focus on the distinctive U.S. origins and characteristics of certain economic ideas, techniques, and professional practices; yet it is by no means easy to identify these origins and characteristics unambiguously. Moreover, as John Williamson noted in his concluding overview (see above), how do we define American economists: "is it those born in the United States, those who were trained in the United States, or those who reside in the United States?"

It would obviously be absurd to exclude any of the three categories, given the extraordinary mobility of professional personnel during the past few decades. Many native-born American economists live and work abroad; innumerable non-Americans have been trained in the United States and reside there, or live and work elsewhere, not necessarily in their native land. And the same is true, albeit on a smaller scale, of professional economists born outside the United States. All are relevant to the broader theme of internationalization. The sheer number of American economists, and the abundance of U.S. resources invested in economic affairs at home and abroad ensure that American influences inevitably loom large in our subject. But even here these differences are largely matters of degree rather than kind.

The term Americanization is perhaps most apt when applied to the content, organization, and spread of a certain type of graduate education in economics. But as indicated in the preceding chapters, this educational model often undergoes significant modifications when it is adopted outside the United States.

The concept of internationalization gives due weight to the non-American influences affecting the development and application of economics as an academic discipline and profession, including: the feedback effects on U.S. economists of foreign economic doctrines and techniques; the types of applied topics researched outside the United States; and the distinctive characteristics of policy problems and their solutions attempted in various countries. Although the selection of country studies in this volume was unavoidably limited, it was diverse enough to demonstrate that post-1945 developments in economic ideas and conditions have by no means obliterated all the differences between individual countries with respect to economists' beliefs, education and training, professional life, status and influence. The addition of further comparable studies would not undermine that generalization. Thus Williamson's suggestion that internationalization means "the end of specifically national schools of thought, techniques, and practices" (Williamson, this volume) is too exacting. The idea of a Washington consensus or universal convergence is intriguing but controversial; and it is, of course, essentially concerned with policy recommendations rather than the underlying body of economic doctrine or theory, and it tells us nothing about the variations in professional working conditions and practices in the converging countries or of the relationships between economists and other participants in the policy-making process. Here, as elsewhere in economics, it is important not to overlook the existence of a thriving alternative or heterodox tradition. The long-cherished belief that economics is, or can be, a universal science is still a chimera.

One of the most striking features of the history of economics over the past half century has been the remarkable increase in the supply of academically trained personnel, made possible by the unprecedented expansion of higher education in many countries (aspects and implications of this expansion are considered in chapters 1–9 of this volume).

The precise rate of growth of this qualified (or professional) labor force has, of course, varied over time and from country to country; but almost everywhere there has been not only a dramatic increase of academic employment but also a tremendous expansion in the number of economists working in local, regional, and national governments, in international agencies of many kinds, and in business, banking, and financial organizations. Indeed, the emergence of a global economy has in itself made economics a far more internationalized discipline than in earlier decades. The increased scale of academic institutions and the multiplication of nonacademic occupational opportunities have contributed to the growth of specialization; but there has not been a concomitant growth of professional organization and control. Nevertheless, economics would now be a much more heterogeneous discipline and profession had it not been for the extraordinary numbers of individuals who have received part (usually the most advanced part) of their training and professional initiation in the United States or in Europe—or who have been trained by economists who have themselves had such privileged experiences. Whether graduate education in economics has become too standardized, especially in the United States, so that the typical American economics Ph.D. is homogeneous, is a debatable point (see above). But the general effect of this training in raising professional standards seems undeniable.

What have been the principal factors—political, social, and cultural—facilitating or inhibiting the international dissemination and influence of late twentieth century Americanized economics? The present volume raises, but goes only a short way toward answering, this question, which goes well beyond the conventional boundaries of the history of economics. A more comprehensive and systematic effort to address it would require a much more ambitious investigation, within a much broader social science conceptual framework. Nevertheless, as noted in the preface (see above), despite the obvious geographical limitations of this volume, the heavy emphasis on Latin America is an advantage, for it has drawn attention to the significant role of economists as cultural leaders, as well as technocrats and policymakers, in that continent. Despite the difficulties of measuring such matters, it seems clear that in recent decades the status and influence of economists has risen markedly in less-developed countries at a time when it has been falling in Britain, Western Europe, and the United States. The generation of economists who contributed to the pioneering international agreements of the 1940s, staffed and led the new postwar international organizations, and participated in the rise of managed economies in the first world and economic planning exercises in the third, were optimists. They were confident of their ability to contribute to the making of a better world. More recently, however, especially since the end of the Keynesian era, there has been a loss of confidence among economists in developed countries that is in striking contrast with the professional environment in some of the developing countries.

Questions of this kind can, of course, be approached on a micro level by asking, more specifically, what has been spread internationally—is it theoretical ideas, quantitative techniques, empirical generalizations (laws?), policy recommendations—or some combination of these elements? Do abstract ideas or doctrinal systems travel more effectively than techniques, empirical results, or policy measures; and what transformation do they undergo in the process? Is it sufficient, for example, to think of the international spread of neoclassical economics when that ill-defined conceptual apparatus may be merely a cover for ideology, as Margaret de Vries suggests? As Bill Ascher demonstrates so effectively, in the development field neoclassical economics has changed considerably over the past few decades in response to intellectual and environmental challenges (see Ascher, this volume; also Kahler 1990, 19); and as Ben Ward has cogently argued, there are at least three leading contending economic ideologies: Conservative, Liberal, and Radical (Ward 1979). Which of these contenders has been most widely accepted, and why?

These broader considerations are pertinent when we recognize the internationalization of economic policy reform as one of the key manifestations of the internationalization of post-1945 economics (Coats, this volume). Irrespective of whether one is convinced by, or skeptical of, ideas of international consensus or convergence, learning and applying the lessons of historical experience in economic policy making may represent the economics profession's greatest opportunity to demonstrate its potential contribution to the global public welfare.

This is not to minimize the intellectual interest and practical significance of aspects of the internationalization process falling within the conventional domain of the historian of economics, such as the influence of economic doctrines (Keynesian, monetarism, Marxism, institutionalism, and latter-day species of anti- and post-Keynesianism). Are policy makers the slaves of defunct economists, as Keynes claimed; or are they deaf to these siren voices? International comparative studies of changing doctrinal fashions would be revealing (see Hall 1989). What, for example, has been the general relationship between economic "science" and popular economic ideas and economic ideologies? Under what circumstances, and in what ways, have the professional economists' postwar technical advances (for example, mathematical theory, more sophisticated quantitative methods, and econometrics) enhanced their understanding of economic processes and their capacity to shape the course of events? Given the widespread and authoritative protests about the narrowing scope and increasing technology of academic economics, answers to these broad questions could have a profound effect on the training of future generations of professionals.

The scope for future research on the internationalization of economics is enormous. It includes (a) additional country studies as in part 2, with special attention to the similarities and differences between advanced and developing nations; (b) the extension of part 4–type studies to other regions, for example, the former Communist countries, South-East Asia, Africa, and the European Union;[1] (c) looking beyond Americanization to the processes of internationalization initiated by other countries, for example, Britain, Western Europe, and the former Soviet Union; (d) the systematic collection and analysis of autobiographies of "international" economists, supplemented by interviews; (e) studies of economists' experiences of international education on the lines of Goodwin and Nacht's work (1984; 1986); (f) more detailed studies of the impact and effectiveness of American graduate education in economics in various countries; (g) research on the interaction of economics and politics in the policy reform process (see Rodrik 1996), and its relationship to the Washington consensus (or universal convergence).

If the present volume succeeds in further opening up significant parts of this vast intellectual terrain it will have achieved its purpose.

References

Goodwin, Craufurd D., and Michael Nacht, eds. 1984. *Fondness and Frustration: The Impact of American Higher Education on Foreign Students with Special Reference to the Case of Brazil.* New York: Institute of International Education.

1. The editor has initiated a comparative study of "The Post-1945 Development of Economics in Europe," with participants from thirteen countries, to begin late in 1996. Special attention will be paid to the changing character of economic education, the developing employment opportunities for economists, the supposed Americanization of European economics, and the role of economists in the process of European integration.

————. 1986. *Decline and Renewal. Causes and Cures of Decay in Foreign-Trained Intellectuals and Professionals in the Third World*. New York: Institute of International Education.

Hall, Peter, ed., 1989. *The Political Power of Economic Ideas: Keynesianism across Nations*. Princeton: Princeton University Press.

Kahler, Miles. 1990. Orthodoxy and Its Alternatives: Explaining Approaches to Stabilization and Adjustment. In *Economic Crisis and Policy Choice*. Edited by Joan M. Nelson. Princeton, N.J.: Princeton University Press.

Rodrik, Dani. 1996. Understanding Economic Policy Reform. *Journal of Economic Literature* 34 (March): 9–41.

List of Acronyms

ACT	Australian Capital Territory
AEA	American Economic Association
AID	See USAID
ANPEC	National Association for Graduates in Economics (Brazil)
ANZAAS	Australian and New Zealand Association for the Advancement of Science
ASEAN	Association of Southeast Asian Nations
BN	Basic Needs
BNDES	National Economic and Social Development Bank (Brazil)
CAMC	Central American Common Market
CAP	Common Agricultural Policy
CEPAL	See ECLA
CGIAR	Consultative Group for International Agriculture Research
CIAP	Inter-American Committee of the Alliance for Progress
COGEE	Commission on Graduate Education in Economics
CONACYT	Mexican Program of Scholarship for Education Abroad
DFC	Development Finance Companies
Dr.Habil	Doktor Habilitatus
D.Phil	Doctor of Philosophy
DSR	Debt Service Ratio

EC	European Community
ECE	Economic Commission for Europe
ECLA	Economic Commission for Latin America
EDI	European Development Institute (World Bank)
EMU	European Monetary Union
EPA	Economic Planning Agency (Japan)
EPGE	Getulio Vargas Foundation in Rio de Janeiro
ERR	Economic Rate of Return
ESCOLATINA	University of Chile, International Graduate Program
ESRC	Economic and Social Research Council (U.K.)
FAO	Food and Agriculture Organization
FEA/USP	Faculty of Economics, University of Sao Paulo
FGP/SP	Getulio Vargas Foundation in Sao Paulo
GARIOA	Government Relief in Occupied Areas (Japan)
GATT	General Agreement on Tariffs and Trade
GNP	Gross National Product
IBRD	International Bank for Reconstruction and Development (World Bank)
IDAP	Inter-American Development Bank
IDP-INTAL	Institute for the Integration of Latin America or the Inter-American Development Bank
ILO	International Labor Office
ILPES	Institute for Economic Planning
IMF	International Monetary Fund
IPE/USP	Institute of Ecomonic Research/University of Sao Paulo
ISO	International Organization for Standardization
ISTAO	Instituto Superiore di Studi Economici Adriano Olivetti (Italy)
JDP	Japan Development Bank
KAEA	Korean American Economic Association
KEA	Korean Economic Association
LDC	Less Developed Countries
LSE	London School of Economics
MAF	Ministry of Agriculture and Forestry
MITI	Ministry of International Trade and Industry (Japan)
MOF	Ministry of Finance (Japan)
M Phil	Master of Philosophy

M Soc Sci	Master of Social Science
NSF	National Science Foundation
OECD	Organization for Economic Cooperation and Development
OEEC	Organization for European Economic Cooperation
ONR	Office of Naval Research (USA)
PEP	Politics, Economics, Philosophy (Oxford Degree)
PMBD	Party of the Brazilian Democratic Movement
PUC	Catholic University of Rio de Janeiro
RAE	Research Assessment Exercise
SAL	Structural Adjustment Loan
SBCA	Social Benefit Cost Analysis
SDR	Special Drawing Rights
SIECA	Common Market Secretariat in Central America
SSRC	Social Science Research Council (USA)
UFRJ	Federal University of Rio de Janeiro
UNCTAD	United Nations Conference on Trade and Development
UNDP	United Nations Development Program
UNICAMP	State University of Sao Paulo, Campinos
UNIDO	United Nations Industrial Development Corporation
USAID	United States Agency for International Development
WHO	World Health Organization
WIDER	World Institute for Development Economics Research
WDR	World Development Report (World Bank)

Index

Contributors

S. Ambirajan is professor of economics at the Indian Institute of Technology, Madras, India. He is interested in the economic thought and economic cultures of non-Western societies, and is currently writing a small monograph on the evolution of India's economic policy since 1947.

William Asher is professor of public policy studies and political science at Duke University. He is director of the Terry Sanford Institute of Public Policy and director of the Center for International Development Research. He is currently directing research projects on the political economy of natural resource policy.

Roger E. Backhouse is professor of the history of economic thought at Birmingham University in the United Kingdom. He has recently completed a volume entitled *Interpreting Macroeconomics: Explorations in the History of Macroeconomic Thought* (1995) and is currently finishing a book on economic methodology to be entitled *Truth and Progress in Economic Knowledge*.

William J. Barber is the Andrews Professor of Economics Emeritus at Wesleyan University. His latest book is entitled *Designs within Disorder: Franklin D. Roosevelt, the Economists, and the Shaping of American Economic Policy, 1933–1945*.

Young Back Choi, Department of Economics and Finance, St. John's University,

Jamaica, NY is the author of *Paradigms and Conventions* (University of Michigan Press, 1993).

A. W. (Bob) Coats is emeritus professor of economic and social history at the University of Nottingham and formerly research professor of economics at Duke University. He is a founding author, member of the editorial board, and one-time associate editor of *HOPE*.

Barend A. de Vries worked for thirty-five years in the International Monetary Fund and the World Bank, where he was chief economist and director of Creditworthiness Studies. Since he left the Bank in 1984 he has been a guest scholar at the Brookings Institution, taught economics at Georgetown University, and written *Remaking the World Bank* (1987) and *Champions of the Poor: The Economics and Ethics of Fighting Poverty* (forthcoming).

Margaret Garritsen de Vries was a staff member of the International Monetary Fund from 1946 to 1987. She served in several capacities, including chief of the Far East Division and official historian.

Peter Groenewegen is professor of economics and director of the Centre for the Study of the History of Economic Thought at the University of Sydney, Australia.

Arnold C. Harberger is professor of economics at UCLA and also Gustavus F. and Ann M. Swift Distinguished Service Professor Emeritus at the University of Chicago, where he served for thirty-eight years. He has devoted a major portion of his professional career to the training of economists from Latin America. His former students include some twenty cabinet ministers, twelve Central Bank presidents, and eight university presidents (rectors).

Aiko Ikeo is professor of economics at Kokugakuin University, Tokyo. She is the author of *The Network of Economists in the Twentieth Century: The Development of Economic Studies as Viewed from Japan* (in Japanese).

Maria Rita Loureiro is a sociologist and works at Getulio Vargas Foundation in São Paulo and in the Department of Economics at the University of São Paulo. She is currently developing research in the areas of the institutional history of economics in Brazil and the participation of economists in the government.

Ivo Maes is an economist in the research department of the National Bank of Belgium and associate professor at Catholic University of Leuven. He was an administrator at the Commission of the European Communities (DG II, Economic and Financial Affairs) and a visiting professor at Texas Lutheran College and Duke University. His current research interests focus on Hicks and monetary theory in the 1930s, and economic thought and European integration.

Verónica Montecinos is assistant professor of sociology at the Pennsylvania State University, McKeesport Campus. Her research on the politics of economic policy-making in Chile has led her to examine the political and institutional dimensions of regional economic integration in Latin America.

Jacques J. Polak, a citizen of the Netherlands, holds a Ph.D. in economics from the University of Amsterdam. After working in the League of Nations (1937–43), the Netherlands Embassy in Washington (1943–44), and the United Nations Relief and Rehabilitation Organization (1944–46), he joined the staff of the International Monetary Fund in 1947. From 1958 he was the Fund's director of research and from 1966 also its economic counselor. After retiring from these positions he served from 1981 to 1986 as a member of the executive board of the IMF. He is currently the president of the Per Jacobsson Foundation in Washington.

Pier Luigi Porta is professor of economics at the University of Milan. He has worked extensively on the Cambridge school and edited in Italian a few volumes of Sraffa's *Ricardo*. He is currently working on the history of Italian economic thought and on the idea of "classical economics" in the history of economic analysis.

Bo Sandelin is professor of economics at the University of Göteborg, Sweden. His earlier research includes housing economics, the economics of crime, capital theory, and the history of economic thought.

Ann Veiderpass is assistant professor of economics at Göteborg University, Sweden. Her current research interest is production theory (nonparametric analyses of industry efficiency and productivity growth).

John Williamson is an economist who has been a senior fellow at the Institute for International Economics since 1981. He works mainly on international monetary issues and is currently engaged in a study of the performance of crawling bands in Chile, Colombia, and Israel.